Insurgencies and Revolutions

D0421650

Over the past six or more decades, John Friedmann has been an insurgent force in the field of urban and regional planning, transforming it from its traditional state-centered concern for establishing social and spatial order into a radical domain of collaborative action between state and civil society for creating 'the good society' in the present and future. By opening it up to theoretical engagement with a wide range of disciplines, Friedmann's contributions have revolutionised planning as a transdisciplinary space of critical thinking, social learning, and reflective practice.

Insurgencies and Revolutions brings together former students, close research associates, and colleagues of John Friedmann to reflect on his contributions to planning theory and practice. The volume is organized around five broad themes where Friedmann's contributions have risen to challenge established paradigms and generated the space for revolutionary thinking and action in urban and regional planning – theorising hope; economic development and regionalism; world cities and the Good City; social learning, empowered communities, and citizenship; and Chinese cities. The essays by the authors reflect their engagement with his ideas and the new directions in which they have taken these in their work in planning theory and practice.

Haripriya Rangan works for the Australia India Institute, and is Principal Fellow at the School of Geography, University of Melbourne, Australia. Trained as an architect, she studied planning with John Friedmann at UCLA, and has pursued a research and teaching career in geography in India, the USA, Australia, and South Africa.

Mee Kam Ng is Vice-Chairman of the Department of Geography and Resource Management and Director of the Urban Studies Programme at the Chinese University of Hong Kong. Her publications have earned her six Hong Kong Institute of Planners Awards and the AESOP Best Published Paper Award 2015.

Libby Porter is a scholar in planning and urban geography. Her work focuses on the role that planning and urban development play in dispossession and displacement. She is author of *Unlearning the Colonial Cultures of Planning* (2010) and *Planning for Coexistence?* (with Janice Barry, 2016).

Jacquelyn Chase is a Professor in the Geography and Planning Department at California State University, Chico. She has published articles on urbanization of agricultural regions, rural labour markets, gender, and fertility in Brazil and on county planning in California. She is the editor of the volume *Spaces of Neoliberalism*.

RTPI Library Series

Editors:
Robert Upton, *Infrastructure Planning Commission, United Kingdom*
Jill Grant, *Dalhousie University, Canada*
Stephen Ward, *Oxford Brookes University, United Kingdom*

Published by Routledge in conjunction with The Royal Town Planning Institute, this series of leading-edge texts looks at all aspects of spatial planning theory and practice from a comparative and international perspective.

Strategic Spatial Projects: Catalysts for Change
Edited by Stijn Oosterlynck, Jef Van den Broeck, Louis Albrechts, Frank Moulaert & Ann Verhetsel

Implementing Sustainability
Caroline Miller

Land and Limits, second edition
Richard Cowell & Susan Owens

Insurgencies: Essays in Planning Theory
John Friedmann

An Anatomy of Sprawl: Planning and Politics in Britain
Nicholas A. Phelps

English Regional Planning 2000–2010: Lessons for the Future
Corrine Swain, Tim Marshall & Tony Baden

Reviving Critical Planning Theory: Dealing with Pressure, Neo-liberalism, and Responsibility in Communicative Planning
Tore Sager

Planning for Growth: Urban and Regional Planning in China
Fulong Wu

Reconsidering Localism
Edited by Simin Davoudi & Ali Madanipour

Planning/Conflict: Critical Perspectives on Contentious Urban Developments
Edited by Enrico Gualini

Conflict, Improvisation, Governance: Lessons in Democratic Planning from the Netherlands
David Laws & John Forester

The Craft of Collaborative Planning: People Working Together to Shape Creative and Sustainable Places
Jeff Bishop

Future Directions for the European Shrinking City
Edited by Hans Schlappa & William J. V. Neill

Insurgencies and Revolutions

Reflections on John Friedmann's Contributions to Planning Theory and Practice

Edited by
Haripriya Rangan, Mee Kam Ng, Libby Porter and Jacquelyn Chase

NEW YORK AND LONDON

First published 2017
by Routledge
711 Third Avenue, New York, NY 10017

and by Routledge
2 Park Square, Milton Park, Abingdon, Oxon OX14 4RN

Routledge is an imprint of the Taylor & Francis Group, an informa business

© 2017 Taylor & Francis

The right of Haripriya Rangan, Mee Kam Ng, Libby Porter and Jacquelyn Chase to be identified as the authors of the editorial material, and of the authors for their individual chapters, has been asserted in accordance with sections 77 and 78 of the Copyright, Designs and Patents Act 1988.

All rights reserved. No part of this book may be reprinted or reproduced or utilised in any form or by any electronic, mechanical, or other means, now known or hereafter invented, including photocopying and recording, or in any information storage or retrieval system, without permission in writing from the publishers.

Trademark notice: Product or corporate names may be trademarks or registered trademarks, and are used only for identification and explanation without intent to infringe.

British Library Cataloguing in Publication Data
A catalogue record for this book is available from the British Library

Library of Congress Cataloging in Publication Data
A catalogue record has been requested for this book.

ISBN: 978-1-138-68264-1 (hbk)
ISBN: 978-1-138-68265-8 (pbk)
ISBN: 978-1-315-54501-1 (ebk)

Typeset in Goudy
by Taylor & Francis Books

Printed at CPI on sustainably sourced paper.

"John Friedmann is perhaps the greatest 20th/21st century mind to devote his scholarship to thinking about the concept and practice of planning. This book celebrates his wide-ranging contributions, which continue to inspire later generations of planning scholars, progressive activists and practitioners."

Patsy Healey, Professor Emeritus, Newcastle University, UK

"For over a half-century, John Friedmann has been one of the most restlessly creative critical theorists of contemporary urbanization, and one of the most forceful, rigorous advocates for an insurgent approach to planning as a mode of radical-democratic social empowerment. In this volume, several generations of his students and colleagues reflect on the wide-ranging contributions of Friedmann's work, and its enduring implications for planning theory, policy and practice. As such, it offers an accessible contemporary overview of Friedmann's massive oeuvre, as well as a powerful orientation for ongoing efforts to create more livable, democratic, ecological and socially just urban spaces."

Neil Brenner, Professor of Urban Theory, Graduate School of Design, Harvard University, USA

"Written by his former students and close associates, many who are prestigious scholars themselves, these fabulous and reflective essays provide vivid accounts of how John Friedmann transformed the discipline of planning. This volume presents a panoramic view of Friedmann's profound intellectual contributions to creating the 'good society' and details his revolutionary, worldwide impact on the planning field. The book is of both academic and historical values."

Fulong Wu, Bartlett Professor of Planning, UCL, UK

John Friedmann
Source: Manuela Friedmann

Contents

Illustrations

Figures

Tables

Box

Contributors

Yuko Aoyama (PhD, City and Regional Planning, University of California – Berkeley) is Professor of Economic Geography at Graduate School of Geography, Clark University, Massachusetts, USA. Her work addresses issues of globalization, technological innovation, industrial organization, and entrepreneurship involving various industries in Japan, the USA, Spain, and most recently, India. She served as the Editor-in-Chief of Economic Geography from 2007–2014 and has served on various editorial boards.

Robin Bloch is Technical Director, Urban Planning, ICF International, London. He received a PhD in Planning from UCLA in 1994 and has subsequently worked globally as a practitioner. He is Team Leader for Urbanisation Research Nigeria (URN), a four-year program implemented by a consortium of Nigerian and UK institutions.

Adolfo Cazorla is Full Professor at the Technical University of Madrid (UPM) where he leads the GESPLAN Research Group. He has been working in several positions for the Public Administration such as Regional Vice Minister of Economy of the Madrid Region. At the UPM he was appointed General Secretary in 2004 and Vice-rector of Economy. He has participated in several research projects at the international and European level and in rural planning and development activities. His publications include 21 books and more than 30 articles published in scientific journals.

Jacquelyn Chase is a Professor in the Geography and Planning Department at California State University, Chico. She has published articles on urbanization of agricultural regions, rural labor markets, gender, and fertility in Brazil and on county planning in California. She is the editor of the volume *Spaces of Neoliberalism* (2002).

Timothy Cheek is Professor and Louis Cha Chair in Chinese Research, Institute of Asian Research and Department of History, University of British Columbia. He studies Chinese intellectuals of the 20th century and the history of the Chinese Communist Party. His most recent book is *The Intellectual in Modern Chinese History* (2015).

Hemalata C. Dandekar (PhD) addresses issues of housing, urban–rural connections, rural and small-town planning, and women and development. She is Professor and Department Head of City and Regional Planning, California Polytechnic State University San Luis Obispo; Planning Commissioner, City of San Luis Obispo; and a licensed architect, California. John Friedmann chaired her doctoral committee.

Diane E. Davis is Charles Dyer Norton Professor of Regional Planning and Urbanism and Chair of Harvard's Department of Urban Planning and Design. She previously headed the International Development Group of MIT's planning program, later serving as Associate Dean. Her current research examines politics, planning, and socio-spatial dimensions of urban conflict.

Ignacio de los Ríos is Associate Professor at the Technical University of Madrid (UPM) where he is a member of the GESPLAN Research Group. During the last 17 years he cooperated with governments, universities and enterprises in the framework of engineering projects, planning and rural development in Europe and Latin America. He is the author of more than 100 books, book chapters, and articles in scientific journals such as *European Planning Studies* and the *Community Development Journal*.

José M. Díaz-Puente is Associate Professor at the Technical University of Madrid (UPM), where he is a member of the GESPLAN Research Group. His research activities on evaluation of public policies led him to be the recipient of the Europe Prize (2003) and a Fulbright Scholarship (2005–2007) to work at Stanford University. He has participated in several projects at the international and European level and has cooperated with governments, universities, and firms in the framework of the evaluation of public policies. His publications include more than 70 book chapters and articles published in scientific journals.

Mike Douglass is Professor at the Asia Research Institute and the Lee Kuan Yew School of Public Policy at the National University of Singapore. He is Emeritus Professor in Urban Planning at the University of Hawai'i at Manoa. He received a PhD in Urban Planning with John Friedmann as his advisor at UCLA.

Aftab Erfan (PhD) is a scholar-practitioner based in Vancouver, British Columbia. The areas of her teaching, research, and activism include community engagement and community development, facilitation and facilitative leadership, psychological approaches to planning dilemmas, cross-culturalism, and the conscious use of power.

John Friedmann is Honorary Professor of Planning in the School of Community and Regional Planning, University of British Columbia and Professor Emeritus in the School of Public Policy and Social Research, UCLA. His work over the past six decades has inspired urban and regional planners around the world and the contributors to this volume.

Michael Hibbard is Emeritus Professor at the University of Oregon's Department of Planning, Public Policy and Management. His research focuses on community and regional development, with special interest in the social impacts of economic change on small towns, Indigenous communities, and rural regions in the USA and other industrialized nations.

Claudia B. Isaac is an Associate Professor at the University of New Mexico who engages community economic development, community-based organization development, participatory evaluation, affordable housing, identity planning, and qualitative methodologies with community-based organizations in New Mexico committed to poverty alleviation, affordable housing, and advocacy for working people.

Roger Keil is York Research Chair in Global Sub/Urban Studies, Faculty of Environmental Studies, York University in Toronto. He researches global suburbanization, urban political ecology, and regional governance. He is the editor of *Suburban Constellations* (2013) and co-editor (with Pierre Hamel) of *Suburban Governance: A Global View* (2015).

Klaus R. Kunzmann is retired Professor of the School of Planning, TU Dortmund. He is an honorary professor at the Bartlett School of Planning at University College, London and visiting professor at Dong Nam University, Nanjing. He is married to a Chinese citizen and regularly teaches and works in China.

Michael Leaf is an Associate Professor in the School of Community and Regional Planning at the University of British Columbia. He works on planning and socio-economic change in rapidly urbanizing locales and has been involved in research and capacity-building projects in Indonesia, Vietnam, China and Sri Lanka.

Ute Lehrer (PhD, UCLA) is an Associate Professor at the Faculty of Environmental Studies, York University, Toronto. She has published on urban planning, public space, urban design, mega projects, urban form and economic restructuring, cities and globalization, and immigration to urban areas (together with John Friedmann).

Mee Kam Ng is Vice-Chairman of the Department of Geography and Resource Management and Director of the Urban Studies Program at the Chinese University of Hong Kong. Her publications have earned her six Hong Kong Institute of Planners Awards and the AESOP Best Published Paper Award, 2015.

Keith Pezzoli directs the Urban Studies and Planning Program and the Center for Sustainability Science, Planning and Design at the University of California, San Diego. He studied with John Friedmann at UCLA and received his PhD in Urban and Regional Planning in 1990. He is writing a book about new bioregionalism.

Libby Porter is a scholar in planning and urban geography. Her work focuses on the role that planning and urban development play in dispossession and displacement. She is the author of *Unlearning the Colonial Cultures of Planning* (2010) and *Planning for Coexistence?* (with Janice Barry, 2016).

Haripriya Rangan works for the Australia India Institute and is Principal Fellow at the School of Geography, University of Melbourne, Australia. Trained as an architect, she studied planning with John Friedmann at UCLA and has pursued a research and teaching career in geography in India the USA, Australia and South Africa.

Bishwapriya Sanyal is Ford International Professor of Urban Development and Planning at MIT. He is grateful for the way John Friedmann inspired and mentored him at UCLA.

Saskia Sassen is Robert S. Lynd Professor of Sociology, Columbia University (www.saskiasassen.com). Her recent books are *Expulsions: Brutality and Complexity in the Global Economy* (2014) and *Cities in a World Economy* (2012). Recent honors include the Prince of Asturias award 2013 Social Sciences Prize and Membership, Netherlands Royal Academy of Sciences.

Matti Siemiatycki is an associate professor of Geography and Planning at the University of Toronto. His teaching and research examines infrastructure planning, financing and project delivery. He studied with John Friedmann as a doctoral student at the University of British Columbia.

Shiv Someshwar is Director, Climate Policy at the Center on Sustainable Development, Earth Institute, Columbia University, New York, and teaches the graduate course Foundations of Sustainable Development Practice. Previously he was at the Rockefeller Foundation. He received his PhD in Urban Planning from UCLA and was Bell MacArthur fellow at Harvard University.

Tanja Winkler teaches in the School of Architecture, Planning and Geomatics at the University of Cape Town, South Africa. Her research interests include community-led planning interventions, exploring the nature and meaning of ethical values for planning actions, and planning education through engaged scholarship.

Chung-Tong Wu (Emeritus Professor, University of New South Wales and Emeritus Professor, University of Western Sydney) is the inaugural Chair of the Advisory Committee, Henry Halloran Trust, University of Sydney. His research interests include regional development, cross-border development, special economic zones, and shrinking cities.

Sheng Zhong is a lecturer at the Department of Urban Planning and Design in Xi'an Jiaotong-Liverpool University, Suzhou, China. She holds a PhD in Planning from the University of British Columbia. Her research interests include urban regeneration, industrial restructuring, creative city making, and China's urbanization in general.

Preface

As John Friedmann's life partner for the past 31 years, I was approached early in 2015 by two of John's former PhD students – Haripriya and Mee Kam, each now distinguished academics in their own right – wanting to do something to honour and celebrate John's approaching 90th birthday (April 2016). What they suggested was surprising John with a book of essays, possibly authored by a collection of his former doctoral students, some now academics, other practitioners of various hues. My immediate response was two-fold: John hates surprises (unless it's an actual magic show, which he adores), and he is uncomfortable with being celebrated.

That didn't mean it was a bad idea or a non-starter, just that perhaps I should run it by John. Which I did. John was simultaneously flattered, delighted, and dubious. A dialogue ensued, Friedmann style. And, astonishingly, 12 months later we have this wonderful collection for which I have been asked to write a preface and share some personal insights about John. Apparently there are quite a few things that his former grad students have wondered about in relation to John, starting with how he and I met and got together…

Our romance didn't begin when we overlapped in London for a year at the Centre for Environmental Studies in 1976 when I was a young Australian postdoctoral fellow and John was on sabbatical from UCLA. Nor did it begin six years later when he invited me out to dinner at a conference in Mexico City. Ironically, it did finally begin in 1984 when I wrote to ask about an unpublished paper of his on deindustrialization, and we got into a year-long correspondence about music and poetry. Yes, we fell in love by correspondence; got together for a trial weekend; followed that with a six-month sabbatical together; and then, with many emotional twists and turns and power struggles, began our 31 years and still counting of life together, first in Los Angeles, then in Melbourne, and now in Vancouver.

When John and I were both teaching at the Graduate School of Architecture and Urban Planning (GSAUP) at UCLA (1986–96) our teaching styles and ways of relating to graduate students, not to mention our writings – I was writing film scripts and dabbling in postmodern theory; John had recently published his encyclopedic *Planning in the Public Domain: From*

Knowledge to Action – were so different that, apparently, grad student sport was to speculate on what our pillow talk could possibly be about? Well…

I was not the least bit familiar with John's academic writings back then, insular Australian that I was, concerned only with Australian cities, so we didn't talk about his work at all. My first exposure, in fact, was reading various drafts of the manuscript of *Planning in the Public Domain*, and seeing John rage at its initial rejection by the University of California Press. As the royalty cheques continue to this day to trickle in from Princeton University Press, the eventual publisher, he likes to chuckle about the UC Press rejection, but he also acknowledges that the criticisms from their anonymous reviewers were right, and he went on to write a better book in response to them. Over the next few years I read a whole lot more of John's previous writing, as part of my task of teaching planning theory, and I came to appreciate what a wonderful, ever-curious, and reflective mind was at work.

I was, and still am, fascinated by John's capacity for self-criticism, his ability to reject past work and move on, to engage with and absorb the work of others (sometimes without acknowledgement: I have had to remind him, hang on, so-and-so said that already, or, I said that first!), forever forging new ways of thinking about a problem. It may (or may not) be some consolation to generations of doctoral students who have found John's teaching and supervising style somewhat brutal, that he is equally hard on his own work, and mine! It's all about the quality of the work, and if your ego gets bruised, too bad. Get used to criticism, develop a muscle for it, and after you're done raging about the injustice of it (the criticism), let it settle for a while then figure out what's worth responding to and how to respond.

John and I have discussed and argued – over breakfasts and dinners, while cooking and cleaning, on hikes in the mountains, on plane, train and ferry trips – about the purposes of planning theory, the meaning and value of postmodernism, the possibilities of radical planning, the relevance of grassroots activism versus transforming the state, the hopelessness of hope, whether pragmatism is the same thing as social learning, and why there is no such thing as the public interest. (Not an exhaustive list of our life-long conversations.) And yes, of course we discuss our students, passionately and endlessly, often in complete and permanent disagreement.

As this wonderful collection of essays by his former doctoral students, friends, and colleagues shows, John's inquiring mind has ranged over many more themes than most of us can contemplate in a lifetime (but then it has been a very long life). Thus his influence has been amazingly diverse, inspiring activists as well as theorists.

Indeed, when you've written 18 books, 180 book chapters and journal articles, and been translated into Chinese, Persian, Arabic, Italian, Spanish, Japanese, and more, all sorts of labels might be applied to you. John has been variously praised or condemned as a utopian, a Marxist, an anarchist and a pragmatist. And, among certain Europeans, ever since his Honorary

Doctorate 20 or so years ago from the University of Dortmund, he's admiringly referred to as the Pope of Planning.

In the Foreword to his most recent book, *Insurgencies: Essays in Planning Theory*, Patsy Healey describes John as 'perhaps the greatest planning scholar of the 20th century, and undeniably so in the field of planning theory'. I agree, and I am not biased. And here we are in the second decade of the 21st century, and John is still with us and still at it. For the past 15 years he has served as an Honorary Professor (that means distinguished but unpaid) in the School of Community and Regional Planning at the University of British Columbia, and has taught two courses each year, as well as advising up to five doctoral students at any one time.

At 89, John retired from classroom teaching, but continues to serve on doctoral students' committees and to write papers and give lectures 'on demand'. When there is no demand, John is liable to mild depression and extreme restlessness. Reading 12 hours a day, as he regularly does, is not enough. He needs someone/something to engage with! I used to be critical of what I saw as this 'inability to let go' of the university. Now I have nothing but admiration for John's desire to continue to make a difference in the realm of ideas. While others retire and sail boats, play golf, travel, become devoted grandparents, disengage from the world's troubles, or write memoirs, John continues to study the past and present of Chinese cities and politics, reads *The New York Times* every day, sends money to the Quakers for their good works in developing countries, and encourages the current generation of Masters students to get out of their comfort zone, whatever that is.

John has always sworn that he will never write a memoir. He has also been saying, ever since the publication of *Empowerment* in 1992, that that would be his last book. I always took that declaration with a grain of salt, and indeed, at least five more have followed. But I believe him about the memoir because, in spite of his public celebrity, John is very modest and does not think it's all about him. It's about the thinking.

Perhaps, given his age, we should be more interested in the secret of his longevity than in hearing more about his scholarship. But perhaps the one explains the other. In addition to being a life-long vegetarian, John has been a life-long scholar, devoted, I would argue, to planning as a moral inquiry and to planning practice as moral action in the public realm – a transformative activity focused on human flourishing. His singular devotion to the field is arguably what keeps him so alive, in addition to trying to keep up with his speedy wife!

Contrary to his public persona as a flinty Man of Reason, there are other dimensions of John's life world, the two most important of which are music and poetry. John has been a life-long avid amateur cellist, and has been known to weep at certain chamber music performances. It's always been a treat to listen in on his daily practising, especially as he gradually mastered the Bach cello suites. John's passion for poetry has been expressed both through his sublime translations of the poetry of Pablo Neruda, Federico García

Lorca, Paul Celan, Ingeborg Bachmann, and others, and through his/our hosting of poetry parties where friends and students bring their favourite poems and read them aloud. Over the years, we've heard poems in Mandarin, Arabic, Vietnamese, Swahili, French, Spanish, and more.

And now to things John would rather you not know about him: there's his fear of dogs (all shapes and sizes); his inability to navigate his way not only around a strange city but around Vancouver's downtown, where we have been living these past 15 years; and his tendency to refer to his second wife (me), to whom he has been married for the past 29 years, by the name of his first wife!

John Friedmann, the very agnostic Pope of Planning, has his moments of pessimism and despair, like the rest of us, but there are two things that keep him going: intellectual curiosity and a faith in the political and social project of human flourishing, through various forms of planning praxis.

What is so delightful and so gratifying about this collection of essays, as evident in John's response that closes the book, is that it showcases young, middle-aged and older scholars and practitioners all still engaging with his ideas. And likely it will inspire an emerging generation of planners, who are still knocking on John's door and sending email requests for help with their projects or advice on how to navigate a life in planning. What more could one ask for as a 90th birthday present?

Leonie Sandercock

Introduction to the volume

Haripriya Rangan

In his most recent book, *Insurgencies: Essays in Planning Theory*, published in 2011 as part of this Royal Town Planning Institute (RTPI) series, John Friedmann begins by describing his first overseas teaching assignment in Brazil in 1956. There he was, as a 30-year-old American academic, charged with the responsibility of instructing a group of Brazilian students on how to plan for regional development. In the first two decades following the end of World War II, 'planning' and 'development' were extremely popular words, used in all sorts of contexts and often conflated with each other. Nations everywhere needed development and development needed planning. John recounts a 'field trip' with his group of students in a boat up the Amazon River during which he felt compelled to address a question that puzzled everyone: "What is this new-fangled soft technology called planning?" (p.1)

Now, as John turns 90 years of age, one thing is certain. Planning is neither new-fangled nor a vague, all-purpose term. It has a clear identity as a vibrant field of study and profession in various parts of the world. And it is so, in large part, due to John's persistent efforts to answer this question through his work over the past 60 years. Planning, as his work has shown, is not simply a technique or technology, nor a narrowly defined profession defended by hefty experts, but a vocation that seeks to open up, navigate, and shape the collective purpose of human flourishing in place while being buffeted by the forces of change and uncertainty. Despite being criticised for whatever actions they undertake, planners prevail and thrive as they contend with new forms, constituencies, and contexts that challenge them in unforeseen ways. They can be in the private or public sector, radical practitioners, community activists or anarchists, but above all, they show that planning is a resilient practice that constantly questions and seeks new ways to ensure human flourishing in place to the fullest extent.

For many years, I could not understand John's enthusiastic adoption of the term 'insurgency' in relation to planning. It seemed bizarre because the word, in my mind, evoked images of armed militants rising up against the state, of constant disruption and danger in the everyday lives of people who would have to bear the consequences of the violent encounters between the insurgents and the government army. One can, of course, plan insurgencies against the state and execute them, but I didn't think that was what John was proposing in his use of the term. More recently, when I was reading *Insurgencies*, something caught my eye. It was from the preface to *The Good Society*. John responds to the question, "The Good Society then seeks to eliminate the state?" by answering,

> Neither to eliminate nor to replace it. The Good Society refuses hegemonic power, it does not wish to totalize itself. In attempting to do so, it would cease to be the Good Society and would transform itself according to the principle of hierarchy which is opposed to it.
>
> (Friedmann 2011, p.54)

And then, following a few expository exchanges, the comment, "A nonviolent struggle…", to which is the response:

> For a world that is made smaller, more comprehensible, in which we can reclaim our rights as autonomous, dyadic beings, in the relations of women and men, and in the worlds of work, education, and governance. In short, a struggle for a more dialogic world.
>
> (ibid.)

As I read this, all of a sudden, John's embrace of the term 'insurgency' made sense to me. To be the Good Society, to make the Good Society, required a practice of struggle "to extend itself in dialogue, creating conditions *within* the world of social planning that are conducive to a life in dialogue and to becoming human" (ibid., my emphasis). The struggle had to arise from within – surge up, *insurge* – the world of social planning to make it more dialogic, comprehensible, and meaningful for all, without resorting to the principle of hierarchy and power that forms the underlying logic of the state.

I'm pretty sure my epiphany was already thought through and debated ages ago by far more insightful planning theorists and scholars than myself, but I felt fairly chuffed about it. I could now see, with great clarity, why John's *Planning in the Public Domain* (1987) took the form it did in tracing the history of planning. It was – in the proper Darwinian and Kuhnian senses of the terms – an evolutionary and revolutionary history of planning as an activity seeking the Good Society. Not a simple, Hegelian teleology of progress towards enlightened Utopia, but the emergence of distinct traditions shaped by many insurgencies within the broader paradigm of the Good Society. I could see how critiques of state planning from both market and civil society reshaped its emergence in other forms; how comprehensive planning by state agencies is both required and inconceivable in its old forms; how urban and regional development has been revolutionised by globalisation.

Planning as 'Good Society paradigm' has evolved through adaptation to insurgent pressures, revolutionary shifts, and emergence of new spaces for extending dialogue about itself and its understanding of the Good Society. So when it came to putting this volume together and giving it a name, I felt that *Insurgencies and Revolutions* was a naturally fitting title to reflect on John's thinking, pedagogy, and practice of planning, and what we, his students and colleagues, have made of it.

On behalf of my fellow initiator of this book project, Mee Kam Ng, and co-editors Jacquelyn Chase and Libby Porter, I thank Robert Upton, editor of the RTPI Library Series, for his support for the volume, and the anonymous reviewers who provided excellent comments as well as the warning for us editors to watch out for any indulgence in hagiography. Having been his students, we didn't think this was likely to happen, but we did convey their views to our fellow contributors and followed their orders as best as possible. Our sincere thanks to Leonie for wisely quashing our idea of giving John the volume as a surprise birthday gift, to all our fellow contributors for sending their essay gifts in time, and to John for agreeing to go through all of them and write a response. We wanted him to have the last word. Thank you to Nicole Solano of Routledge for seeing the volume to publication. And finally, a heartfelt thanks to Sue Huang, my wonderful research assistant, for managing all the nitty-gritty details of putting together the volume, checking references and getting everything in order. We couldn't have produced this book without you.

Every generation sees itself at the verge of a new social era, one that it is about to create. John Friedmann has envisioned and led the vanguard in creating several of these eras in planning, and has enjoyed the good fortune of a long life to see his students and colleagues forge new eras of their own. This volume is not simply a celebration of John's contributions to planning but a celebration of the discipline itself, and for the many insurgencies and revolutions that will shape its future.

References

Friedmann, J 1987, *Planning in the Public Domain*, Princeton, Princeton University Press.

Friedmann, J 2011, *Insurgencies: Essays in Planning Theory*, London, Routledge.

Part 1

Practising hope

Libby Porter

It is not an overstatement to say that John Friedmann is one of the most important voices in planning theory today. His contribution to planning theory is both rich and diverse, ranging from urban systems to the good society, to alternative development, to social learning and more. Friedmann is not a theorist motivated to contribute through a single theoretical or conceptual lens, and this quality makes his contribution both unique and interesting. Nor are his theoretical contributions prone to abstraction or loftiness. Instead, they are grounded in real-world observations and reflective of the real situations that his work both attempts to understand and calls the field to grapple with.

In this section, we take the grounded nature of Friedmann's theorizations of and for planning to heart. In doing so, this section offers four essays that deal not so much with his contribution to theory per se, but with the way his contribution is framed as a practical, yet utopian, politics of hope. There is a consistent theme across Friedmann's work that has proved over the years to be a rich source of inspiration and insight. This theme is the hope for, and in, the possibility of a good society imagined through utopian thinking. Instead, then, of framing this section as engaging with "Friedmann's contribution to planning theory" we want to call attention to the way John's diverse theoretical contributions are each hopeful: carefully attentive to and critical of the conditions that produce injustice, inequality, poverty and alienation, and insightfully imaginative about how the world could be different.

My essay takes a broad sweep across Friedmann's writings looking for his contribution to hopeful theorizing and what it still teaches us today for theorizing planning. I argue that hopefulness is intrinsic to John's work yet not in a naïve or simplistic way. The essay presents how Friedmann's stance of radical, openly possible hope is not only a basically good quality of planning theory, but one we must nurture in the face of global challenges.

Bish Sanyal takes up the theme in relation to territoriality. His essay weaves together a critical account of the contested concept of territoriality with his own personal encounter with Friedmann's thinking. Sanyal shows how the phenomenon of "being territorial," both its inclusive possibilities and its darker tyrannies, remains an important one for planning to think about the relations between people and their places and how those relations are governed.

Diane Davis takes us deeper into a particularly contested site, that of Jerusalem, and interrogates Friedmann's seminal essay on utopian thinking, "The Good City." The essay examines the dilemmas and difficulties of actually putting utopian thinking into practice through an examination of a participatory design project to achieve a more just and tolerant Jerusalem. Davis argues that the value of utopian thinking lies as much in the conflict it gives rise to as the possible outcomes it might produce. Her essay offers a deepening of Friedmann's contribution of the value of utopian thinking and the dilemmas of practising hope for planning theory in situations of deep conflict.

Shiv Someshwar discusses the new UN Sustainable Development Goals for 2030. He argues that without concerted attention to the kind of social transformation, the "unity of opposites" that Friedmann has advanced, these goals are likely to succumb to the same problems as previous attempts such as Agenda 21. This requires communities to engage with state and market but also be critical of, and challenge, their powerful tendencies and delusions. For Someshwar, planners are best equipped to engage in hopeful practice by transcending sectoral and disciplinary boundaries to achieve these goals of social transformation.

Finally, Adolfo Cazorla, Ignacio de los Ríos and José M. Díaz-Puente present a practical pedagogy of project planning for rural development informed by Friedmann's theories of social learning and empowerment. They show how the changes to planning education in the European Higher Education Area due to the implementation of the Bologna Agreement enabled their pedagogical practice of "social learning" and transactive engagement in project planning to become a successful way of preparing graduate students to work in an international context.

1 "Resistance is never wasted"

Reflections on Friedmann and hope

Libby Porter

Reading across the body of work John Friedmann has produced, I have always been struck by the hopefulness intrinsic to his thinking. This is more than merely optimism, and certainly not empty of critical analysis or considered strategic action. Instead, John offers, through the multiple dimensions of his work, an honest, constructive, radically open hope that is at once inspiring and politically engaging. "Resistance is never wasted," as he says in *Planning in the Public Domain* (1987, p.390). This dimension of his work is, to my mind, a rich and important one for planning theory, practice, education and research.

I first met John in Melbourne, just as I embarked on my graduate research journey. I had of course met him "intellectually" during my undergraduate planning studies and so I already had a perspective of him in that fascinated, awe-inspired way that perhaps most students feel about the "names" they enjoy reading. John ran the PhD colloquia and it was there that I gained insight into the politically grounded and hopeful dimensions of his work, aspects I had not, up to that point, fully appreciated.

And so, in this brief essay, I offer a reading of hope across a selection of Friedmann's work, with the aim of providing an account of this important contribution to the field of planning and urban studies, particularly his linking of hope with resistance and struggle. Along the way, I also provide some brief personal reflections and some thoughts about the enduring legacy of his guiding principles for our field in the future.

First, then, to the dimension of hope in Friedmann's work. John has argued that there are three central tasks of planning theory: tasks of philosophy, adaptation and translation. The philosophical task might also be read as a normative one: to provide a human-centred, or humanist, philosophy for planning action based on guiding values. To my reading, this central philosophical task is the spark that lights a fire across Friedmann's body of work, for it ignites a drive that is inherently hopeful: hope for what else might be possible and the different alternatives that might be imagined, and hope as a commitment to pursuing those alternative, transformative possibilities in the face of painful, unjust realities. Others have called this a "curse" (Flyvbjerg 2001), but Friedmann casts it quite differently. As he writes in *The Good*

Society, planning is intrinsically engaged with a future that "rises up in our mind as a transcendent possibility, a challenge, and a hope" (1979a, p.xi).

Neither these challenges, nor hope, arise, however, from abstract theorizing or generalist norms. Across his work, John both urges and practices a politically aware and critical engagement with the world, with actual realities and events. There is evidence across his writing that he is profoundly moved by desolation and destruction, by poverty and injustice, by the "horror of placelessness" (Friedmann 2010, p.152)—moved to write and to think, to suggest actions and alternatives, and to find solutions through a hopeful engagement with those very horrors. Perhaps this arises from his early decision, as he recalls it in a biographical essay (Friedmann 2014), to refuse to see planning as a narrow, technical endeavor and instead to situate it as a practice, action and aspiration about possibility. Or, in John's more eloquent words, as "always engaged *with* and *in* the world" (ibid., original italics). It is perhaps also shaped by the influence of Chinese philosophy on his thinking, where dialectic is not a confrontation but always a productive tension, enabling the transformative possibility to be always near-at-hand. Consequently, his work displays a tireless motivation to provide the basis for fundamental and transformative change, always looking "beyond the visible horizon" (Friedmann 1998, p.16), to ask: "what shall we hold out as a vision, so that political practice (and planning) do not merely chase after problems, making small improvements here and there as opportunities arise, but move coherently towards an agenda of a truly human development?" (ibid., p.16).

It is instructive, then, to look at how he achieves this across his work. One important dimension might be that he always situates his writing in response to key world events and conditions. The writing of *Retracking America* (1973) was an attempt to not only find appropriate theories for explaining the major social and political upheavals of the late 1960s and early 1970s, but also to provide normative "guiding beacons" to orient those upheavals to socially just practices. Or in other words, giving hope (see Friedmann 2011, Introduction). *Empowerment* (1992) was written to present a vision of alternative development that was explicitly anti-poverty, turning upside-down the standard categories used in development theory. He has written in response to the 9/11 terrorist attacks in the US (Friedmann 2002) and as a critique of what he saw as the emergence of a violently regressive economic order (Friedmann 1979b).

The site for such hopeful thinking and action in Friedmann's work has always been the city. Long convinced of the centrality of cities and urban life to the articulation of a just society, John's work seeks to connect broader and more fundamental socio-economic injustices and problems with the daily work of planning: place-making and city-building. As his focus came to rest in the "small spaces of the city" (Friedmann 2010) where everyday life is practised, I believe we can find ever clearer evocations in his work of the pursuit of certain hopeful values: cherishing, centrality, civility, identity, emplacement.

I would like to call this a "hopeful engagement with the world," and it offers planning scholarship, practice and urban activism a deep source of inspiration and know-how. For behind all of John's writing, from his early work on regional development, to general planning and urban theory, to urbanization in Asia, is evidence of this hopeful engagement with the world. His work on urban development in China is at least in part motivated by the results of a naked economic drive at the heart of the emerging Chinese boom economy, with the potential to destroy anything in its way. His early regional development work was a response to the injustices produced by leaving the allocation of resources and goods to markets. The lesson we can draw from this is the importance of writing against trends that create unjust and regressive outcomes, and persistently articulating alternatives for socially progressive and just transformation.

Even in the early influences on his thinking, hope appears to have been not just present but a central drive. Friedmann was influenced by the "bias of hope" in the work of thinkers like Hirschman (1971; see also Friedmann 2014). Perhaps his most significant contribution to the field has been his express refutation of the positivistic method, and his commitment to articulating the link between social knowledge and social action. Entwining hopefulness with knowledge in this way involves neither moral zealotry nor naïve optimism, but "processes of mutual learning that are closely integrated with an organized capacity and willingness to act" (Friedmann 1973, p.247). His Arendtian view of action, being to take an initiative or to "set something into the world" (Friedmann 2000), demands hopeful, utopian thinking to strive towards action (ibid., p.471).

He articulates this most forcefully and clearly, as we all know, in *Planning in the Public Domain* (1987), where the need for knowledge (but not of a positivistic elitist form) is fundamental to social transformation: "only an epistemology of social learning based on the unity of practice of transformative theory within the context of a continuing process of action and inquiry can give us grounds for hope" (p.416). But I find that it was in his semi-poetic book *The Good Society* (1979a) where he best articulates the intrinsic and central connection between planning and hope. One reason why this book is a personal favourite is the way the form contains the message as much as the content. Rather than offer a treatise or a conventional analysis, he uses a much freer and creative style to provide structured reflections and invocations that both express and perform hopefulness as a practice necessary for the world.

A further important expression of hopefulness in John's work is in his own scholarly practice. Just as in the way that *The Good Society* performs its central message through its very structure and form, I find the way that John *practices* hopeful scholarship very instructive. In 1979, he published a hard-hitting review in *Development and Change* of the increasingly regressive penchant emerging among mainstream economists and development experts for socially regressive economic theories that essentially amounted, as he incisively argued, to violent wage suppression in the service of profit and greed. He was specifically writing against an economic and development policy regime that he saw as socially regressive and politically repugnant, and his review was published along with very critical commentaries from well-known development economists who really didn't like what he said. In practising a scholarship that is engaged in crucial, world-changing debates in order to show alternatives, exposing socially regressive agenda, and making critical alternative interventions, John's work not only offers, but performs, a politics of hope.

This hopefulness is also performed in a commitment to precise definition and accurate conceptualization. This is not to infer that all of John's conceptualizations are uncontested, or to state that they do not contain misrecognitions or occlusions: any definition or conception is at some level an abstraction and might always be seen differently. What I find instructive, and an articulation of hopeful scholarship, is the careful way he defines his terms. As a reader of his work, you are quite clear on the grounds about which he writes, and he offers this not only for obvious purposes of clarity, but I sense also as an invitation to critically engage with his thinking. In defending "utopian thinking" (Friedmann 2000), he articulates a hopeful scholarly practice of yearning and daring, of being committed to creating, debating and articulating a common good for the city. For it is in the trying and the debating where we find a hopeful practice. Also intrinsic to a hopeful practice of scholarship is his commitment to exposing obfuscation as a political power game and a claim for territory, both in academic and in practice domains (see also Friedmann 2010).

The articulation and practice of a hopeful, engaged scholarship is one of the major but perhaps less acknowledged contributions John Friedmann has made to the field. His absolute conviction that planning is an empty gesture unless it is political in its orientation, explicitly linking normatively defined knowledge to philosophically guided action, remains a core principle for all those, including myself, committed to critical perspectives. His explicit refutation of the positivistic perspectives continues to push our thinking because it requires us to view planning ideas or decisions as immediate interventions in the world: interventions that, for good or ill, are both hopeful and require us to be accountable.

The choices John makes about his interventions occur in the field of scholarship, research and writing. This is not a criticism, but to mark an edge or limit to his work, one that I find deeply instructive for clarifying the choices we each make every day as planning academics, theorists or practitioners, or indeed perhaps as activists. That is not to say that John's scholarly work does not *speak to* social practice, activism and struggle. One of his major contributions to planning theory has been to de-couple his own (Friedmann 2011) and the field's insistence that it is only through the state that transformation is possible. Instead, he has located radical practice for and of planning, in the work of social movements, bottom-up grounded struggles and mobilizations, and the recovery of active political community (Friedmann 1987).

This, then, imagines hope as a *politics*, essentially linked with resistance and struggle. For me, the most influential aspect of John's work is his conviction and demonstration, made both through careful empirical analysis and theoretical argument, that planning is inherently conflictual and must involve struggle. He argues forcefully that "only large-scale political mobilization can hope to constrain the single-valued logic of the market" (ibid., p.29).

While this interest in social mobilization and the location of radical practice in everyday life clearly had roots much earlier in his career, it was in *The Good Society* that he found a unique and semi-poetic voice to express the important agency in social movements. Writing in an era when social movements seemed to be gaining in strength and sophistication, and by then no longer quite so enthralled by the possibilities of state-based planning (Friedmann 2011, Introduction), *The Good Society* and then *Empowerment* both locate hope for a better world in social movements. As he later described, social movements are "often the principal sources of positive change and perhaps our one best hope for a *better* society?" (Friedmann 2014).

Empowerment (1992) is a clear statement of his theorization of the importance of politically active and organized struggle and voice against injustice. It contains chapters addressing political claim-making and practice which remain insightful for current social trends (the book has been translated into many languages, including most recently, Arabic in 2010). It is also here that he explicitly locates the source of empowerment not within the state but in everyday life and the livelihoods of households (Friedmann 1996). Considering the concept of power from a different angle, Friedmann defines it as a "capacity" rather than as a "power to." And once again taking aim at the normalizing categories through which neoclassical economics insisted on defining dimensions of the economy, Friedmann placed households at the centre of the production of livelihoods, rather than as simply sites of consumption. Through such radical work of careful redefinition, a whole raft of possibilities and transformative alternatives then open up. Citizens have much more radical claims to make upon states, such as the "right to a livelihood" rather than the much less politically active agency of "choice" over, say, housing options. Moreover, placing households at the centre of a model of empowerment creates an intrinsically collective, social and relational political process. Households cannot do things on their own, and so it is through networks, claim-making, political organization and grassroots mobilization that empowerment takes life.

In turn, however, those organizations and their social mobilizations must mount political claims and seek to turn those claims into rights through engagement with both states and markets. This particular expression of hope, however, is a less convincing aspect of his work, in my view. *Planning in the Public Domain* posits that when state-based planning attempts to constrain and regulate the operation of markets, that constraint can only be successful with accompanying grassroots social and political mobilization (Friedmann 1987, p.29). Today, the extent to which the state is willing to intervene for a public interest such as environmental regulation with market operations is ever-decreasing. The lesson that Friedmann draws about the importance of large-scale political mobilization accompanying even the most basic aspects of planning is even more prescient for our current age. The practice of this radical planning would be undertaken through the art of mutual learning and, building on his earlier ideas of the power of transactive, dialogical approaches, by linking knowledge to action for the purpose of progressive change.

Friedmann is firm that such transformative social change cannot be achieved through mediation, consensus-building and deliberation. All, he acknowledges, are important dimensions of a political practice, but none suffice. Indeed, he cogently argues that on their own, such approaches tend to be too stripped of political context, power and normative values to be of much use in the business of radical social change. Planners who act merely as "facilitators" to achieve consensus among participants sitting at the table are in danger of drifting with the prevailing neoliberal agenda without fully appreciating the contradictory outcomes of such action. Moreover, he argues that consensus-building in situations where the power differentials are enormous is not only ineffective but inappropriate. Instead, there must be active political struggle.

These critiques of the tendency in some planning approaches to reduce conflict to a problem that can be mediated away are necessary and insightful. Yet his conception of the behaviour and role of the state and state-based planning remains a little opaque. While he acknowledges that the state will only ever act (against capital) to the extent that political interests allow, he does not invest the state with its own drive. This is a view of the state as a monolithic and somewhat disinterested party, without an agenda of its own. And this sometimes gives rise to a faith that planning that is not in the service of the urban elite, or the system of naked economic drive and political power, might be possible and worth pursuing. A different analysis (a less hopeful one) would argue, as many have, that state-based planning is by definition in the service of these ends. It cannot be anything else, given its provenance and the source of its authority.

This is perhaps best demonstrated in a paper Friedmann published in response to the 9/11 terror attacks on American cities, where he argues that the work of creating just societies and the "open city" has to be done from below by non-state, insurgent actors (Friedmann 2002). His recommendations for the focus of that insurgent practice turns out to sound a little bit state-enthralled. In the essay, he calls for local citizenship charters that institutionalize recognition of both basic human needs and the right to participate fully in civic life at the local level. I am not convinced such measures of recognition adequately anticipate the actual relationship between insurgent activists and states. City councils and local levels of government are now some of the more neoliberal forms of governance worldwide, though admittedly also the location where alternatives can find genuine space to thrive. To rely on a politics of hope that locates the focus of insurgency as recognition from the state seems to be at odds with other dimensions of Friedmann's work that carefully unpacks the workings and structures of power.

It is also an especially Western perspective on a possible politics of hope that he offers in this regard. De-privileging such a perspective might lead us to ask about situations where power relations are so complex and interwoven that good people acting with good intentions can produce terrible results with enormous costs. There is, as always with theories of transformative change, a danger of hope becoming a naïve allocation of "good" and "bad" agency, in situations where the specter of co-optation, hegemonic practice and dominance in social relations is eternally present. The hopeful politics that Friedmann articulates offers an extremely important perspective, but there is more work to be done articulating these dilemmas.

While I am not entirely convinced by his argument articulating the open city (Friedmann 2002), it concludes in what I have to come to value as typically Friedmann style: he makes crystal clear that each of us has political choices to make in how we will respond to the particular forms of injustice we each encounter, and we are each powerful in the sense that our diverse capacities can be usefully employed in socially progressive ways. Hope lies in the fact that there is always a choice. Whether we are scholars, researchers, activists, residents, practitioners, or decision-makers, Friedmann invites each of us to look critically at any given situation and ask ourselves what interventions are possible that might shift the balance toward justice and equity, rather than allowing the forces that produce privation, greed, poverty and ecological collapse to operate untrammelled. His work, to my reading, insists that such interventions are not just possible but necessary, and that we can all be active participants.

I learned this particular lesson about John's work and influence the hard way, albeit a very instructive way. In 1999, he published a paper in *disP* in which he critiqued a government report that I had been central in writing in my then role as a senior researcher with the Victorian Government's planning department. At the time, I was simultaneously fascinated and horrified by his paper because it so clearly, and apparently easily, exposed a terrible discomfort that I had felt while writing the report but did not then have the language to articulate. The critique concerned the way the document I had helped to write occluded and obfuscated the "city of everyday life" and in so doing perpetuated conditions of repression and exclusion. Friedmann was writing, in the wider paper, about the small spaces of the city as the places where we create our lives every day, the actual substance of life, its rhythms and dreams and desires and failings.

Through his typically clear and careful analysis, he showed that the kind of report I had been instrumental in producing deliberately obfuscated that city, presenting instead a mega-structure of spatial typologies, of trends and population statistics, as if everyday life and its quality could be measured and understood by these things. Yet the care taken in his critique gave me hope because it enabled different kinds of questions to be asked. For me, it was instructive about how to be more attuned to how and when stories and knowledge will serve power (Friedmann 1999) and when they will challenge existing power relations. His articulation of "counter-planning" inspired in my own practice a willingness to go and find those ways of producing knowledge and acting on it in my own small corner of the world.

At the same time I was just embarking on a PhD and John had assumed responsibility for the PhD colloquia first at RMIT University, and then later at the University of Melbourne. We had a conversation during that time that has stuck with me to this day. It was about the *value* of thinking in general and of *utopian* thinking specifically. This conversation was instructive because at the time I was operating under the assumption that academic life (which at the time I was definitely *not* pursuing, even though I was doing a PhD) was for people who were disinterested in intervening in the world. Academics just write stuff, so I thought—stuff that nobody reads except students, and they were really only doing so under sufferance. In that conversation he challenged this view that I had, of the mythical division between those that "do" (aka practitioners) and those that "think" (aka scholars or writers). I later discovered that Friedmann famously challenged Castells on precisely the same point (Friedmann 2000), beautifully arguing that all practice, including scholarly practice (teaching, research, writing, thinking), is action and will have some kind of effect in the world.

Still to this day I interpret this argument as an invitation toward the scholarly responsibility of offering hope: that in part, the role of scholarship is to articulate alternative, grounded, real visions of the world that are based in careful critique of the current order. For any critique is at the same time, by definition, an articulation of a set of values. You can't see something is wrong if you are not judging the wrong thing against a set of values. These are the two interconnected moments of utopian thinking (Friedmann 2000, p.463) central to Friedmann's hopeful practice of scholarship. I value them personally and am struck by how they continue to structure my own thinking. More importantly, they should rank among his most important contributions to our field.

Together, this critique of my work and a brief conversation that I'm sure only I now recall set me on a completely different path, one that has attempted to pursue, albeit in different ways, the same critical, utopian politics of hope. I remain grateful to John personally. But I am also grateful for the legacy of his work on the field, particularly his insistence that it is only by striving to look beyond the current field of vision that we will find real alternatives and transformative possibilities to build the good society. However we choose to do it, we have John Friedmann to thank for continually daring us toward a politics of hope.

References

Flyvbjerg, B 2001, "Beyond the limits of planning theory: response to my critics", *International Planning Studies*, 6(3): 285–292.

Friedmann, J 1973, *Retracking America: A Theory of Transactive Planning*, Anchor Press, New York.

Friedmann, J 1979a, *The Good Society*, MIT Press, Cambridge, M.A.

Friedmann, J 1979b, "The crisis of transition: a critique of strategies of crisis management", *Development and Change*, 10(1): 125–153.

Friedmann, J 1987, *Planning in the Public Domain: From Knowledge to Action*, Princeton University Press, Princeton, N.J.

Friedmann, J 1992, *Empowerment: The Politics of Alternative Development*, Blackwell, Cambridge, M.A.

Friedmann, J 1996, "Rethinking poverty: empowerment and citizen rights", *International Social Science Journal*, 48(148): 161–172.

Friedmann, J 1998, "The common good: assessing the performance of cities" in *City, Space and Globalization: An International Perspective*, ed. HC Dandekar, Conference Proceedings, University of Michigan: College of Architecture and Urban Planning, M.I., pp. 15–22.

Friedmann, J 1999, "The city of everyday life: knowledge/power and the problem of representation", *disP: The Planning Review*, 35(136–7): 4–11.

Friedmann, J 2000, "The Good City: in defense of utopian thinking", *International Journal of Urban and Regional Research*, 24(2): 460–472.

Friedmann, J 2002, "City of fear or open city?", *Journal of the American Planning Association*, 68(3): 237–243.

Friedmann, J 2010, "Place and place-making in cities: a global perspective", *Planning Theory and Practice*, 11(2): 149–165.

Friedmann, J 2011, *Insurgencies: Essays in Planning Theory*, Routledge, Abingdon.

Friedmann, J 2014, "Towards an intellectual autobiography". Unpublished essay available from: <http://www.scarp.ubc.ca/sites/scarp.ubc.ca/files/users/%5Buser%5D/profile/Towards%20an%20Intellectual%20Autobiography.doc> [20 November 2015].

Hirschman, AO 1971, *A Bias for Hope: Essays on Development and Latin America*, Yale University Press, New Haven.

2 Territoriality

Which way now?

Bishwapriya Sanyal

I was introduced to the notion of *territory* as a basis for regional planning in a course that professors John Friedmann and Clyde Weaver co-taught at the University of California, Los Angeles (UCLA) while they were writing *Territory and Function: The Evolution of Regional Planning* (1979). At the time, their description of the tension between planning that draws its priorities from within the territory, and planning that integrates spatial entities on the basis of external functional priorities, such as national economic growth, struck a chord in me both personally and professionally. As a South Asian student of Indian origin living in southern California, I was acutely aware of the emotions evoked when thinking about my native Bengal—its landscape, language, music, art, cuisine, and, of course, politics[1]—and I understood intuitively that territorial allegiance and regional identity were not mere academic ideas.

Before joining the planning program at UCLA, I had completed my undergraduate education and two years of professional practice as an architect in India and had developed a particular liking for built environments that incorporated locally available building materials, were sensitive to the natural particularities of the region, such as monsoons, and respected local cultural practices. When looking at buildings, I always searched for architectural motifs that were specific to the region—certain types of entrances, internal courtyards, windows, decorative elements, and so on. Through both the cultural identity I inherited at birth as a Bengali and my chosen identity as a student of architecture, I was immensely drawn to Friedmann's and Weaver's formulation of planning based on territoriality. Planning from within a region seemed to me a more authentic and meaningful way of making decisions than the conventional style of regional planning, which allocated resources for sectoral activities primarily based on enhancing national economic growth.

From the very beginning of my interest in the idea of territoriality, I was cognizant that the concept was contested from both sides of the ideological spectrum. The new-neoclassical economists treated regions as mere subnational administrative entities whose primary function was to serve the nation-state (Richardson 1979). In contrast, the neo-Marxist geographers viewed territories according to the spatial distribution of conditions under which capitalism unfolded, unevenly, as dictated by the power of local as well as global actors (Massey 2005; Soja 1980). Friedmann had emerged out of the ranks of the new-neoclassical regional economists but was now more critical of their ideological assumptions (Friedmann & Alonso 1975; Perloff 1968). In 1974, while I was a student at UCLA, he offered a new year-long course: the fall semester was titled "National Approaches to Regional Development"; the spring semester presented an alternative, "A Regional Approach to National Development." Friedmann's intellectual sympathy for the alternative approach was vivid. It was built on a serious critique of conventional theories of economic growth, which led to his advocacy for the recovery of territorial life (1978a), the importance of local autonomy in decision-making (1983), and the development of communal wealth (1992). Friedmann had decided that progressive planning required a basis in social movements and resistance from below, and clearly saw this movement from below as resulting in a better form of planning than the conventional, technocratic way bureaucratic hierarchies produced comprehensive plans (1978b).

By then, Friedmann had also developed the notion of *transactive planning*, in which he called for dialogic deliberations among small groups of citizens as an alternative to the way public concerns were incorporated in traditional planning (1973). He described the need for transactive planning processes and territorially based governance in "good societies," which should be self-reliant and provide for the basic needs of all, particularly the poor who lacked "access to the social bases of power" (Friedmann 1979b). In proposing such a new approach, he referred to the problem of urbanization and lack of rural development in newly industrializing countries; but his prescriptions had relevance for the U.S., which he saw as connected in more than one way with "theaters of actions" around the world. Though somewhat similar to the neo-Marxists in his reliance on the core-periphery model, Friedmann varied widely from them in his suggestions for action. While the neo-Marxists advocated class struggle, Friedmann proposed that external cultural and economic domination be opposed by territorial units committed more to sustaining local life forces than to acting as small cogs in the gigantic wheel of global economic flows. Yet Friedmann was neither a romantic communitarian nor a naïve traditionalist. He never argued for a total victory of small communities and territorial regions in their fight against national governments and/or external capital.

Friedmann urged us to think critically about the relationship between territories and external forces imposed, for example, by the global movement of capital or the national government. He preferred that relationships between territories and external forces be negotiated, not dictated, and hoped that such negotiations would lead to more equitable outcomes (Friedmann 1985). If not, he was willing to go one step further and propose that under certain circumstances some territories might "selectively delink" themselves from the larger set of globally linked social forces. Unlike the Marxists, who called for the workers of the world to unite against structural exploitation via global linkages, Friedmann, building on the sentiments of Karl Mannheim—and later, the Frankfurt School—proposed decentralized opposition from below sustained by the reciprocities of human relationships which could only be nurtured in small territorial communities.

Though my cultural upbringing as a Bengali and my education in architecture had drawn me to the notion of territoriality, in neither of these contexts had I been concerned much about social inclusion—or the lack of it. As a doctoral student at UCLA, however, I was exposed to the concept of social inclusion in multiple ways—by Friedmann, Soja (1980), Marris (1996), Hayden (1981) and others,[2] who explained, each in their own way, why certain groups of citizens were consistently excluded from receiving their share of the economic pie that they had helped to create. There was very little doubt among the UCLA planning faculty that the outcomes of the dominant economic and social processes were unfair and that the unfair status quo was not to be accepted. The consensus was that grassroots-based social opposition from below had more potential to rectify the situation than traditional, top-down public planning (Sanyal 2008). There was uniform opposition to the negative consequences of global flows of capital, labor, commodities, and the dominant ideology of modernization and economic growth. This overarching critique of the status quo and of traditional planning, led by Friedmann—in which he was joined by his colleagues—created a unique intellectual climate at UCLA to deliberate, freely, about alternative ideas of development and planning with great concern for gender, race, and income inequalities. As Friedmann proposed (1979a), the time had come to rethink the role of planning not simply as an allocative mechanism, but as a catalyst to create new types of innovative institutions, small in scale, but more accountable to the people in territorial communities that would serve as the democratic cells of the larger social formation.

The truth about my territorial allegiance

As a doctoral student at UCLA, I absorbed, like a dry sponge, every new idea which pervaded scholarly planning discussions in the early 1970s. Like other graduate students, I too worried about the ill effects of globalization, underdevelopment, and neo-colonialism, which led us to critically re-examine the notions of progress and of economic and social modernization. Paradoxically, as I was becoming increasingly familiar with all the "ideas in good currency" at UCLA, my own territorial attachments were in flux: even though I was new to the U.S. and even newer to the Los Angeles area, I began to feel connected increasingly to my friends, colleagues and faculty (including Friedmann, who invited me to regular poetry readings at his residence) at UCLA. Moreover, I had met Diane E. Davis, my wife, in Friedmann's two-semester course on regional development. As enrollees in this course, we had ample time to get to know each other and had developed a good friendship and a loving relationship by the end of the term. The UCLA campus, the beautiful setting of the Perloff Hall, and the vibrant neighborhoods of Western Los Angeles, Santa Monica, Venice, and Culver City provided the backdrop for our romance. Gradually, I came to appreciate those places, not simply as the temporary setting for my foreign studies, but as deeply shaping my emotions: the theater where we first saw a Woody Allen movie; the hole-in-the-wall jazz club in Venice; the Santa Monica beach where our French friends went skinny dipping; and then the sunsets we observed so many times as we drove home to Culver City from Los Angeles on I-405. My territorial attachment was expanding beyond Kolkata, thanks to the warm hospitality and the vibrant intellectual culture I enjoyed at UCLA.

As Friedmann's advisee, professional opportunities opened up for me. On the recommendation of one of his ex-students, Susana Mendaro, I was hired by the World Bank, even before I had started working on my dissertation, to lead a team conducting a major evaluation of housing in Lusaka, Zambia. By then I had begun to look at the world through the core-periphery model, as was customary at UCLA at the time (Sanyal 2008); and yet, I was beginning to enjoy the benefits of belonging to a global network of professionals educated at a planning program which, paradoxically, was intensely critical of globalization. And, all along, my territorial allegiance was evolving as my social life and political familiarity with Los Angeles and southern California grew. I began to better understand and become attached to the geographic setting I had been living in, on and off, for six years. This did not reduce my territorial affinity for either Bengal or India, however. Quite the opposite: I came to appreciate their particularities by noticing contrasts with my current surroundings and grew, intellectually, by explaining such contrasts to myself. I also began to see similarities among what on the surface looked to be very different settings (Sanyal 2010). Occasionally, I did wonder whether I was becoming too Americanized, whether my old self was dissolving in the proverbial American melting pot! Overall, the trespassing between two very dissimilar territories was life-giving and liberating for me; it never felt as if I had to opt for one over the other, that any territorial allegiance had to be redirected. It was not a zero-sum game—thanks to the sensibilities I had developed at UCLA.

Territoriality: the dark side

For each positive outcome of territorial trespassing, as in my case, there are many stories of territorial resistance, rejection, bigotry, and even violence against outsiders. As Lefaivre and Tzonis (1996) describe in their historical overview, territorial resistance against outsiders can be traced as far back as the Renaissance. It is equally true, though, that territorial communities without external influences have a long record of flourishing from within, as is often highlighted by writers in the anarchist tradition (Turner 1972). The social structure and functions of territorial communities have evolved with the emergence of nation-states, a succession of wars, and the steady penetration and expansion of market relationships (Hirschman 1997). In particular, the relative autonomy of local communities from both the state and the market has changed, significantly altering what was earlier called "a territorial life." Yet the uniqueness of specific territories remains pronounced, and there is much evidence for the strength of territorial identities (Schama 1995). It is in that spirit that Heidegger (1971) defended the notion of territoriality in reference to German identity, and evoked the importance of "blood" and "land" as two critical components of what constitutes a territory. In short, the notion of territory has a long history, and much of that history ascribes the notion of culture to the expression of territorial identity. To stretch the argument further, as I did in editing the multi-author volume *Comparative Planning Cultures* (Sanyal 2005a), one could propose that there is a causal link between territorial identity, its culture, and the way a territory plans to allocate resources, protect its environment, provide livelihood for its members, and, of course, defend itself against external threats and domination.

The twist to this story of how the culture of any place shapes its territorial identity became clearer to me as I compiled detailed case studies of planning cultures in twelve nations around the world. A major cross-cutting theme emerged: in all twelve nations, externally induced ideas, flows of people, and all kinds of cross-border influences had ultimately changed the homogeneity of the "original culture," which in itself might have been the product of a long history of prior changes (Sanyal 2005b).

As we ponder the notion of territoriality and planning, it is important to acknowledge that territorial identity is not a fixed thing: it changes and evolves, but not always in a progressive way. There has always been tension and anxiety within territorial formations as a result of such changes, may that be new flows of migrants, as in 1890s North America, or changes in the political power of previously oppressed groups, as in North America after the Civil War.

In India, territoriality has been defined and redefined multiple times. Two painful examples in modern history are its 1947 partition along religious lines into two separate nations—Pakistan and India—and the creation of Bangladesh in 1971, when affinity for the Bengali language triumphed over religious affinity (for Islam). Even though such different cultural affinities do not need to clash all the time, when primordial affinities—for religion, language, etc.—are juxtaposed with territorial attachments, the opposition to outsiders can be very strong. Salman Rushdie's novel *Midnight's Children* (1995) captures the violence of such resistance quite vividly and should serve as a reminder to all that territorial identity can be misused to undermine human solidarity. We need not look back at history to make the point: what is happening daily to the refugees from Iraq, Afghanistan, and Syria should remind us of the relevance of the idea for our time. Who will plan, and how will they plan, to stop the current resistance of some territories to the displaced adults and children knocking on their door? What kind of planning, if any, can be relied upon to communicate the urgency and moral gravity of the moment?

Territories of inclusion

This is not a normative concept: it is not theoretical hope in the face of cruel reality. There has been intermingling of cultures through flows of people, trade, technology, and ideas for more than five hundred years, if not more. Not all such influx and hybridization has led to parochialism or communitarianism. Until recently in India, for example, there have been multiple flows of people who look different, practise different religions, and speak different languages. True, there have been communal riots and mass killings too, as during the partition of the nation; but there have been equally powerful social acts of tolerance, acceptance, and even celebration of differences. Such acts of human solidarity are not one-time historical exceptions: look at the recent acceptance of new refugees in Berlin and Dortmund in Germany and in Toronto, Canada. Such acts, not by isolated individuals but by social groups, sometimes as large as nations, need to be understood better if we are to refine the concept of territorial identity so as to make it more inclusive.

In this regard, it may be worthwhile to rethink what role, if any, the state should play in structuring the territorial imagination of citizens. In the planning literature, territoriality is usually associated with small communities, almost against the incursion of the state (Etzioni 1994; Walzer 1995). Anarchists and communitarians usually support the notion of territoriality because they dislike state power, which they argue has a homogenizing effect and is ultimately driven not by the specific interests of any cultural territory, but by national development priorities. Friedmann used his two-semester course at UCLA to juxtapose national approaches to regional development against an alternative regional approach to national development.

Amidst the current flow of political refugees across the globe, the instances of embrace of the other being led by national governments are intriguing. Even in Germany, a nation whose sentiments were well expressed by Heidegger, it is the *national* planning council under the leadership of Angela Merkel, the chancellor, which has taken the lead to be more inclusive. In Canada, too, it is the new prime minister, Justin Trudeau, who opened his arms, literally, to embrace immigrants from the Middle East. These kinds of gestures at the national level should make us rethink the meaning and significance of territoriality. How to reconcile the dual demands of territoriality and inclusion is still not evident. What is clear is that John Friedmann raised a very important issue for planners nearly fifty years ago, and the time has come to revisit the question he raised, but with a new understanding of our times.

Notes

1 The formation of Bangladesh in 1971 started as a regional movement against the national government of Pakistan. Bangladesh's national anthem is about the special landscape and identity of Bengal.
2 Such as Grabow and Heskin (1973); Cullen and Levitt (1999).

References

Cullen, JB & Levitt, SD 1999, "Crime, urban flight, and the consequences for cities", *Review of Economics and Statistics*, 81(2): 159–169.

Etzioni, A 1994, *The Spirit of Community: The Reinvention of American Society*, 1st Touchstone edn, Simon & Schuster, New York.

Friedmann, J 1973, *Retracking America: A Theory of Transactive Planning*, Anchor Press, New York.

Friedmann, J 1978a, *The Active Community: Towards a Political-Territorial Framework for Rural Development in Asia*, School of Architecture and Urban Planning, University of California, Los Angeles.

Friedmann, J 1978b, "The epistemology of social practice", *Theory and Society*, 6(1): 75–92.

Friedmann, J 1979a, "The crisis of transition: a critique of strategies of crisis management", *Development and Change*, 10(1): 125–153.

Friedmann, J 1979b, *The Good Society*, MIT Press, Cambridge, M.A.

Friedmann, J 1983, "Life space and economic space: contradictions in regional development" in *The Crises of the European Regions*, eds D Seers & K Öström, Palgrave Macmillan, UK, pp. 148–162.

Friedmann, J 1985, "Political and technical moments in development: agropolitan development revisited", *Environment and Planning. D. Society and Space*, 3(2): 155.

Friedmann, J 1992, *Empowerment: The Politics of Alternative Development*, Blackwell, Cambridge, M.A.

Friedmann, J & Alonso, W (eds) 1975, *Regional Policy: Readings in Theory and Applications*, MIT Press, Cambridge, M.A.

Friedmann, J & Weaver, C 1979, *Territory and Function: The Evolution of Regional Planning*, University of California Press, Berkeley.

Grabow, S & Heskin, A 1973, "Foundations for a radical concept of planning", *Journal of the American Institute of Planners*, 39(2): 106–114.

Hayden, D 1981, *The Grand Domestic Revolution: A History of Feminist Designs for American Homes, Neighborhoods, and Cities*, MIT Press, Cambridge, M.A.

Heidegger, M 1971, "Building dwelling thinking" in *Poetry, Language, Thought, M Heidegger*, Harper & Row, New York, pp. 141–161.

Hirschman, AO 1997, *The Passions and the Interests: Political Arguments for Capitalism before its Triumph*, 20th anniversary edn, Princeton University Press, Princeton, N.J.

Lefaivre, L & Tzonis, A 1996, "Critical regionalism" in *The Critical Landscape*, ed. AH Graafland, 010 Publishers, Rotterdam, pp. 126–148.

Marris, P 1996, *The Politics of Uncertainty: Attachment in Private and Public Life*, Routledge, London and New York.

Massey, DB 2005, *For Space*, SAGE, London and Thousand Oaks, C.A.

Perloff, HS 1968, *RFF Urban and Regional Economics Set: Issues in Urban Economics*, Taylor and Francis, Baltimore, M.D.

Richardson, HW 1979, *Regional and Urban Economics*, Pitman, London.
Rushdie, S 1995, *Midnight's Children*, A.A. Knopf, New York.
Sanyal, B 2005a, *Comparative Planning Cultures*, Routledge, New York.
Sanyal, B 2005b, "Hybrid planning cultures: the search for the global cultural commons" in *Comparative Planning Cultures*, ed. B Sanyal, Routledge, New York, pp. 3–25.
Sanyal, B 2008, "Critical about criticality", *Critical Planning*, 15: 143–160.
Sanyal, B 2010, "Similarity or differences? What to emphasize now for effective planning practice" in *Crossing Borders: International Exchange and Planning Practices*, eds P Healey & R Upton, Routledge, Oxon, pp. 329–350.
Schama, S 1995, *Landscape and Memory*, 1st edn, A.A. Knopf, New York.
Soja, EW 1980, "The socio-spatial dialectic", *Annals of the Association of American Geographers*, 70(2): 207–225.
Turner, JFC 1972, *Freedom to Build: Dweller Control of the Housing Process*, Macmillan, New York.
Walzer, M 1995, *Toward a Global Civil Society*, Berghahn Books, Providence.

3 The difficulties of employing utopian thinking in planning practice

Lessons from the Just Jerusalem Project

Diane E. Davis

Utopian thinking with relevance: easier said than done

In "The Good City: in defense of utopian thinking", John Friedmann (2000) critiqued Manuel Castells for what he interpreted as a departure from prior activist ideals and an embrace of empirically based social science as the most appropriate foundation for planning education and practice. As he articulated a set of uncompromising principles for guiding planning action, John called for the embrace of utopian thinking as a method for re-affirming the profession's longstanding idealism and radically transformative aims. Utopian thinking, he argued, encourages much-needed criticism of "what is" while also justifying the search for alternatives, a process through which that which is to be constructed must be envisioned first on the basis of emancipatory ideals (Friedmann 2000, p.462). By situating his appreciation of utopian thinking in the history of the profession (with references to Fourier and others) and in the context of activism around social justice and the city (as theorized and advocated by scholars such as David Harvey [2000] and Susan Fainstein [2010]), John argued that the planning profession must continue to foster an appreciation of utopian thinking among future generations of planners.

It is hard to disagree with John's intentions or ambitions. Many of us have joined the discipline of planning because we are committed to ethical outcomes that require a forceful critique of the *status quo*. But it is one thing to embrace the dream that a better world is possible, or to motivate future planners to fight the good fight in the service of equity, toleration, and other ideals, and quite another to construct planning practice around utopian thought. Friedmann does acknowledge this when he argues that "constructive visioning," which he sees as central to utopian thinking, is always political and that its implementation is bound to be fraught with obstacles (2000, p.463). But the problem is not merely disagreement over grand visions or the ideals they articulate. There is also the issue of process.

As Susan Fainstein and others have argued, grand visions are often seen as elitist, top-down, moralistic, or created from a vantage point that removes one from the messy realities of actually making things different. For precisely this reason open, participatory, or negotiated processes rarely produce utopian visions. The normative promise of utopian thinking may run up against some of the most significant and widely held tenets in the planning profession, which include participation, thus explaining why the embrace of small-scale, modest, and more pragmatic action has tended to characterize the profession. Yet this is not to suggest that one should discard utopian thinking altogether. Quite the opposite. The problems inherent in advancing utopian thought and constructive visioning need to be reckoned with. They require that we as planners become less cavalier and more sanguine about whether, how, and why to embrace such loftier ideals.

Rather than relegating them to the normative high-ground of personal belief and commitment, we must critically interrogate the array of problems and barriers associated with introducing utopian thought into planning practice. To do so, we need a more self-reflective understanding of the dilemmas that emerge when attempting to transform utopian thought into constructive action. Doing so will not only advance the larger aims of creating "good cities" (Friedmann 2000), it also allows us to call into question the imagined split between empirical social science and utopian thought that motivated Friedmann's critique of Castells in the first place.

In the service of breaking down this divide, I analyze the obstacles confronted while designing an experimental project squarely informed by utopian ideals. Called Jerusalem 2050: Visions for a Place of Peace, this initiative was undertaken by faculty at MIT's Department of Urban Studies and Planning in 2004, in conjunction with the Center for International Studies.[1] Three years later, in 2007, it came to fruition with the launching of The Just Jerusalem Competition. The project relied on a visioning methodology to solicit nonconventional ideas for improving conditions in that quintessential world city. Taking the form of an international "ideas" competition that called on citizens rather than state actors to offer future visions, the aim was to solicit constructive ideas that might lead to a more just, peaceful, and sustainable Jerusalem by the year 2050.[2] As such, this initiative embraced the kind of utopian ideals expressed in Friedmann's essay, albeit focused specifically on Jerusalem.

As we undertook this challenge a series of dilemmas and disagreements plagued progress from the get-go. Many revolved around tensions over the utopian versus pragmatic aims of the competition. Others owed to conditions specific to Jerusalem: how best to frame a call for utopian visions without undermining the initiative's material aims of soliciting ideas and projects capable of producing an alternative future that would make life better for all Jerusalemites, regardless of religious attachment. Overall, our efforts to advance this initiative were far from easy, and not only because of its self-evident utopian aims or the intractability of the Israeli–Palestinian conflict. This is why it took us three years to move from the drawing board to the launch of the competition.

Using the lenses of participant observation as well as a comparative-historical understanding of the specificities of Jerusalem, I recount the dilemmas and how they impacted the project's final contours. My objective is to produce a much more nuanced understanding of the limitations as well as the possibilities associated with deployment of utopian aims informed by a real-world project that aspired to produce a Friedmann-inspired "good city."

When lofty ideals confront institutional realities

This MIT-based project originated with a visit from a team of Israeli and Palestinian civil society activists with prior connections to the university who sought advice from its Center for International Studies and the Department of Urban Studies and Planning about how to advance peace and reconciliation in the face of a renewal of violence in 2003 following the failure of the peace talks and the advent of the so-called 3rd Intifada. In the course of frank discussions with planners and political scientists about the ways in which the city was becoming less livable in the context of recent developments, the visitors speculated that one way to find peace and better the daily lives of residents would be to move the capital city. They reasoned that with both Palestinians and Israelis claiming Jerusalem as a capital of respective but competing nation-states, the city was no longer "just" a city. Planners and urbanists responded by saying that there were few successful examples of physically relocating capital cities, Brasilia notwithstanding. Moreover, citing the example of East Berlin, they argued that there was little academic evidence to suggest that such a politically complicated set of moves would fundamentally alter the nationalist conflicts between Israelis and Palestinians. It would most likely be impossible, given the political intensity with which both sides sought to claim Jerusalem as their capital.

Despite such objections, the idea of making Jerusalem a more peaceful, tolerant, and less ethno-nationalistically divided locale persisted as a motivating vision for the project. Yet rather than having the MIT team propose a specific plan or set of policies that might achieve such aims for the city, the group elected to hold an ideas competition in which the public would be invited to offer constructive visions for a future Jerusalem in which bettering the conditions for all the city's residents would be the principal point of departure, not the sovereignty or territorial autonomy aspirations of two competing nation-states. In this sense, the Just Jerusalem Competition had a double meaning: it was intended to solicit visions for Jerusalem as "just" a city (not an epicenter of nationalism), as well as visions that would make it a more socially just city.

The Steering Committee charged with mounting the competition comprised planners, urban designers, political scientists, sociologists, historians, and others. Some were personally familiar with Jerusalem and others were approaching the project out of more principled scholarly and activist concerns with equity and social justice. The group began meeting weekly in the context of a semester-long academic colloquium titled "Cities Against Nationalism," in which we invited scholars from multiple disciplines to share their research on the conditions under which the fate of cities and their citizens had been overly dominated by a national state or nationalist sentiments in ways that produced conflict, inequality, or injustice. Speakers focused on contested sites as distinct as Bosnia and Herzegovina, Belfast, and Berlin while also examining questions of conflict from the scale of the individual to the city and nation. The idea was to establish general principles for further reflection and action without diving directly into a discussion of Jerusalem.

The group was far from naïve; all involved were aware that conditions in this city were considered the "third rail" of global politics, having been contested historically for centuries, even before the renewal of heated conflict that motivated support for the project in the first place. All knew that differences of opinion and interpretation were extremely wide with respect to Jerusalem, not just in the diplomatic and political world, but also with respect to assessments about the degrees of justice and injustice in Jerusalem, about the root causes of conflict, and about who was most at fault for the situation. Even so, all were committed to moving forward constructively.

Dilemma #1: Balancing imaginative visioning with practicality

Despite agreeing to work together, the move from academic discussion in a scholarly seminar to the designing of a tangible project that would address, acknowledge, or advance the utopian aims of delinking Jerusalem from its embeddedness in nationalist conflicts was not easy. Ironically, the very first stumbling block was whether vision was to be preferred *over*—as opposed to *alongside* or even *secondary* to—practical action in the framing of the project. While some members of the Steering Committee were happy to solicit utopian visions for a better future, others strongly believed that any professional efforts emanating from a university like MIT should lead to some tangible or implementable ideas. Some in the Steering Committee felt that the problems of violence and injustice in Jerusalem were so pressing that it would be unconscionable to keep the conversation at the level of romantic aspiration; yet for others, the intractability of the conflict was precisely something that required out-of-the-box thinking. Complicating matters, still others thought that by focusing on visioning and bypassing needed practical action, the project would be accepting the *status quo* of injustice. Furthermore, many of those who came from the region had a different view of all these dilemmas, if only because even policy proposals that at one time were considered to be pragmatic and implementable in Jerusalem had failed to bring desired outcomes.

One explanation for skepticism about the value of practical action was the fact that prior diplomatic negotiation and inter-group dialogue among stakeholders had failed to achieve peace. The Steering Committee was cognizant that the city's history, with its unequal distribution of decision-making power, and the protracted nature of the conflict, set serious limits on open dialogue or negotiation between opposing parties. Constructive visioning thus came to be seen as one of the few alternatives. The group argued that imaginative visioning might be particularly effective in locations where patterns of extreme social exclusion and urban injustice prevailed. In such settings, city residents often feel constrained by the grounded social realities and the power structures of the present. Animosity, antagonism, and mistrust often limit faith in the capacity of authorities or fellow neighbors to build a city that can be embraced by all. That is, traditional and pragmatic consensus-oriented planning techniques may be least useful in such cities because they fail to acknowledge the deep divides and tensions that lurk beneath the surface of formal planning exercises.

All this is not to say that a concern with tangible outcomes fell off the table, but rather, that it would be important to order the stages of constructive visioning and action to begin imaginatively and then move to the practical. It became a matter of trade-offs and strategic calculation about what should come first. Many felt that undertaking actionable change might be easier after the array of possibilities was widened by a visioning exercise. The logic was that once alternative visions or scenarios were placed on the table, they could be used as a basis for creating new conversations or even consensus, which in turn could be parlayed into a basis for practical action in the future. But in order to ensure that constructive visioning would itself be oriented towards "actionable" ideas, some guidance would be necessary. Likewise, there was a concern that because the methodology of a competition is more known to architects and designers than planners and policy-makers, the call for constructive visioning would be interpreted as a call for master planning or other largely physical interventions that might have little impact on issues of social justice, equity, or tolerance.

With these concerns in mind, and to resist too much abstraction, the Steering Committee decided to call for ideas in four specific sub-areas: the economy, infrastructure, institutions, and arts. This was done to discourage people from offering large comprehensive plans for the city, and to encourage them to focus on the tangible activities that make the city function. We hoped that while all entries would speak to the larger issue of Jerusalem as a city, that they would articulate their ideas by focusing on urban spaces, infrastructures, and institutions central to the city's practical operations, thus avoiding philosophically abstract narratives that often masquerade as utopian ideals.

Dilemma #2: Who should vision?

The second problem that materialized concerned who should be asked to vision—or in the lexicon of our project, from whom would alternative ideas for the city be solicited, and why? This was not merely a question about discipline (should we ask planners, designers, politicians, citizens, and so on). It also had a territorial component. Should only residents be asked their views for the future, or should the competition be open to all? In traditional planning practice where social justice is an overriding aim, local residents are directly privileged because they are seen as the most democratic antidote to the intrusive views that are often generated through top-down planning exercises or the imposition of master plans from authorities whose allegiances often lie elsewhere. But one of the big issues of socio-political contention in Jerusalem concerns who exactly is recognized as a resident. What about refugees and others who claim the right of return? What about persons outside the city who see it as a religious capital and part of their identity? What about persons in other parts of Israel and Palestine who claim it as their capital, despite not living there? And then there was the almost deal-breaking question of what exactly were the territorial boundaries of the city (pre-1948; pre-1967; post-settlement construction; etc.).

In short, precisely because the inter-related questions of what territorially constitutes the city and who is a resident were both so fraught (and a source of the intractable conflicts we were hoping to address), we decided that the best way to solicit utopian visions was to open the competition to all persons without restriction on the basis of discipline, location, nationality, religion, or any other status. We devised an entry system where all visions were identified by numbers (rather than names and addresses). To make clear that we were open to the idea of different perspectives on the territoriality and composition of the city, we asked all entrants to "define" their Jerusalem as part of the competition specification package.

To be sure, there were drawbacks associated with opening the competition to global civil society. Not only would the project's visibility be greater among universities, established organizations, and NGOs, but there was also the possibility that people who knew very little about Jerusalem would propose a vision. This was a worry because we wanted people who lived in Jerusalem to generate ideas and knowledge that would hold actionable intent rather than mere utopian dreaming. Even so, we agreed that a degree of physical distance from the conflict might be as likely as familiarity to produce innovative or thought-provoking ideas and alternative visions that could potentially break through the existing political deadlock over the city.

Dilemma # 3: Temporalities of constructive visioning

One final issue that preoccupied the Steering Committee involved the temporal correlates of this constructive visioning exercise. As a concept, visioning is by definition a practice that produces ideas about what could be. But the question was how far in the future should entrants be projecting their visionary ideas if the goal remained peace, toleration, and justice: the immediate future, the distant future, or somewhere in between? Faced with these questions, we again pondered the tensions between utopianism and pragmatism. Given the political issues at stake at local, national, and global levels and the protracted state of the conflict, we recognized the practical impossibilities of making deep and substantive changes in Jerusalem in the absolute present. The years 2020 and 2050 were proposed as reference points for a better future, as was 2048 (to mark the centenary of the founding of Israel). Yet some in the Steering Committee thought that focusing too far in the future might appear overly cavalier and not sufficiently responsive to the dire conditions and injustices of the present.

To address these criticisms, we kept our sights on the future, maintaining the nomenclature of "Jerusalem 2050: Visions for a Place of Peace," understanding that the year 2050 was intended as a metaphor for an alternative future that might conceivably be realized within a single generation. We knew that any change would be a long-term endeavor; even so, we did not want entrants to become so fixated on a utopian future for the city that they forgot the present. Neither did we want imaginations curtailed, which might have occurred had participants focused only on rectifying current conditions or the existent institutions and power structures responsible for them. The whole idea of constructive visioning is about laying out new futures, but in our case we wanted to make sure such thought exercises would serve as useful guides for directing current actions. All this led to our collective efforts to bridge the conceptual gap between practical action and utopian visioning by making the competition all about linking the future to the present, rather than about focusing on one *or* the other.

To highlight this ambition, we gave the competition a new name, the Just Jerusalem Competition, so as to focus attention less on temporalities and more on outcomes and even process. By focusing on justice and by highlighting the importance of re-visioning the city *qua* city as the object of thought, we not only sought to alert potential entrants that temporality was less important than the types of visions we were seeking, but we also were able to partially bridge the divide among the utopians and the pragmatists because both shared the concern with thinking about the city and its functioning, independent of the nationalist aspirations that inserted themselves into the urban terrain.

Despite the consensus within the Steering Committee after all these modifications, controversy did not end. The project received its share of criticism, hate mail, and ridicule for its articulated ideals, some of which required upper-level administrators to invoke the principles of academic freedom. It also faced obstacles with respect to funding, some of which derived from the implications that there was a justice deficit in Jerusalem. Several detractors thought universities should not be involved in real-world political controversies. But against these odds, the project was successfully launched. We received hundreds of entries from around the world, producing an array of both conventional planning strategies as well as out-of-the-box visions that became part of the public record,[3] some of which have inspired new peace projects in the region or new careers for their proponents.[4] It goes without saying that peace in Jerusalem—or any fundamental transformative change, utopian or otherwise—remains elusive.

Conclusion

Under the auspices of the Just Jerusalem Competition, constructive visioning was meant to unlock collective imagination to produce inventive proposals for reducing conflict and advancing justice and equity in a highly contested city. Far from a naïve celebration of utopian thinking, the basic premise of the competition was that by providing opportunities to envision a different and better future for Jerusalem, new ideas would be generated both for urban planning action and for action-theoretical policy research that could lead to the construction of alternative social, political, and spatial arrangements.

This experiment was very much in congruence with John Friedmann's (2000) call for utopian thinking. Planners often criticize the deployment of such measures as naïve, foolhardy, or irrelevant. But such exercises can also produce knowledge and, under certain conditions, can stoke the fires of change independent of any immediate outcomes in the short term. In an assessment of the visions generated through the Just Jerusalem Competition, we found that the call for utopian thinking served as a methodological tool that exposed uncensored views about the city and the source of its problems, including unequal power balances and the nature of the conflict (Davis & Hatuka 2011). At their best, constructive visioning exercises can produce a critical understanding of real-world institutional and political–economic constraints, while at the same time nurturing the hope that the future can be different. At their worst, they reveal the misperceptions, intransigence, and biases of observers or stakeholders, although these views must also be recognized as key elements in the planning process because of their role in reducing consensus and setting limits on action.

Notwithstanding these potential gains, mounting a project that promotes utopian thinking in the context of an actually existing city is a complex endeavor, worthy of further scholarly analysis and reflection. This is clear from the discussion of dilemmas that we as designers of the Just Jerusalem Competition faced in launching an ideas competition built around the principle of constructive visioning. While the highly contested nature of Jerusalem explains some of the barriers we encountered, others had to do with the general difficulties of thinking utopically in settings where practical action and immediate change are urgent, and with laying out the most appropriate conceptual, territorial, and temporal frameworks for pursuing such ideals in the face of palpable problems. These lessons have relevance beyond Jerusalem, and can be summarized in the form of four basic questions that can serve as guides for others considering whether and how to introduce utopian thought into planning practice.

First, *under what conditions* should advocates of emancipatory ideals prioritize planning efforts around visioning rather than practical action? There may not be a one-size-fits-all approach to thinking about creating equitable, tolerant, and just cities. In the case of Jerusalem, the many pragmatic actions that would produce such outcomes were severely limited by the power imbalances and lack of equal access to decision-making structures at the scale of the city. While the assumption of many is that practical action and the commitment to concrete (even if small-scale) change should motivate planning efforts, sometimes practical action may forestall justice or impede the realization of larger visionary goals.

Second, is there a *preferred ordering* to thinking about the relationship between visioning and pragmatic action; and will the ordering be different in certain settings or under certain conditions? This question is related to the first, to the extent that under certain conditions, visioning may be the only way to challenge the *status quo*, whereas in other contexts achieving consensus on practical action may be the best way to enable progress on emancipatory ideals. In some ways, this all comes down to strategy and tactics, and the potential uses of pragmatism to achieve larger visionary goals. Although the ideal may be a simultaneity of purpose in which pragmatists and visionaries work together, this itself may be impossible to achieve. At that point, a strategic decision must be made about the gains and the losses associated with taking a pragmatic versus strategic approach.

Third, what is an appropriate *time frame for projecting a better future*, and how might further attention to this help distinguish the benefits of constructive visioning vis-à-vis pragmatic action? In any given planning project there will be a given temporality of realization. A single building can be designed and implemented in months, but it can take years to redevelop a neighborhood or rehabilitate a downtown, and decades to construct a new city. Utopian thinking by its very definition conceives of alternative social, spatial, and political relationships as ambition or perhaps even archetype, some of which may be brought to life in one of the built environmental interventions noted above. The time needed to simultaneously achieve both social-political and physical change must be accommodated into the constructive visioning process in some way, if only because a vision's location in conceptual time (i.e., near or distant future, current or future generations) may have some bearing on content. By its very definition, utopia is a place that does not exist on earth; it is imagined. It is placeless and timeless. So imposing a time frame on utopian thinking allows its protagonists to bring lofty ideals into a concrete history and geography.

The final question is, *who should be involved in visioning processes?* This is less a question about discipline and expertise, and more a concern with the scale at which visioning could or should be deployed. In the field of advocacy planning, the scale tends to be quite local, and it often involves local organizations speaking on behalf of resident constituencies, many of them collectively defined. When one is projecting change at a scale larger than a neighborhood, perhaps for the city as a whole, it may be necessary to think differently about who should have the "right to vision." Indeed, what makes or constrains justice often transcends a single spatial location, suggesting that one must consider whether visioning processes should be widened to include a larger variety of voices who are willing to pay attention to the multiplicity of scales simultaneously. This not only means individuals *qua* individuals with potentially liberating ideas for producing something different both in neighborhoods and the city as a whole. It also includes mediators, like universities or other institutions without any particular territorial allegiance, who are committed to ensuring that the visioning processes remain open to ideas and interventions that are not overly tethered to conventional stakeholder constituencies.

This final claim reveals perhaps the greatest tension between pragmatic and utopian approaches to planning the so-called "Good City" (Friedmann 2000). Indeed, to suggest that grounded stakeholders should not necessarily be privileged is to call into question the holy grail of much planning theory and practice. But when dealing with cities marked by intractable conflicts where equity and justice are clearly at stake, and where power balances and residential dynamics call into question capacities for effective citizen participation strategies, new approaches will be needed.

As I look out on the world today, I see many cities around the globe that are suffering through violence and ethno-national conflict in ways that traditional planning practice will be hard-pressed to accommodate. These are the settings where utopian thought and constructive visioning may have a large role to play. These are the settings in which we must be more reflective in addressing questions about the scales, temporalities, and the participants in such visioning processes. Being committed to utopian thinking about good cities is the easy part. Figuring out how to establish the epistemological and programmatic contours that will give constructive visioning a shot at making a real difference in the future of these cities is the hard part. That is what should preoccupy us now.

Notes

1 Professor Leila Farsakh and I took the responsibility for co-directing this project, joined by a Steering Committee that included Larry Vale, Bish Sanyal, John de Monchaux, Richard Samuels, John Tirman, Yosef Jabereen, Tali Hatuka, Everett Mendelsohn, and Naomi Chazan (with research assistance from Ariel Bierbaum and Hania Maraqa). All discussions and interpretations of what transpired during the course of this project presented in this essay are completely my own. For a more scholarly analysis of the outcomes of the project, including a quantitative and qualitative analysis of the entries to the competition, see Davis and Hatuka (2011; 2014).

2 For detailed information on all aspects of the project, including funders, competition specifications, jury, and results, visit web.mit.edu/CIS/jerusalem2050/index.html.

3 In fact, most submissions were extremely practical suggestions drawing on conventional planning ideas that were far from utopian. Less than a third could be considered utopian visions, with another third falling somewhere in between in a category we labeled as "visionary." For further discussion of competition entries, analytical justification of the categorical breakdown, including the distinction between utopian and visionary, and overall implications for planning theory and practice, see Davis and Hatuka (2011).

4 For example, among the five winning teams several participants have gone on to do doctoral work in planning, into international advocacy, and to teaching careers focused on Palestinian–Israeli peacemaking. Other competition entrants have established planning and design firms that work on issues of peace and co-existence in Jerusalem. As of yet, no serious evaluation has been undertaken to assess the longer-term trajectories of those participating in the Just Jerusalem Competition.

References

Davis, D & Hatuka, T 2011, "The right to vision: a new planning praxis for conflict cities", *Journal of Planning Education and Research*, 20(10): 1–17.

Davis, D & Hatuka, T 2014, "Imagination: a method for generating knowledge of possible urban futures" in *The Routledge Handbook of Planning Research Methods*, eds EA Silva, P Healey, N Harris, & P Van den Broeck, Royal Town Planning Institute/Routledge Press, London.

Fainstein, S 2010, *The Just City*, Cornell University Press, Ithaca, N.Y.

Friedmann, J 2000, "The Good City: in defense of utopian thinking", *International Journal of Urban and Regional Research*, 24(2): 460–472.

Harvey, D 2000, *Spaces of Hope*, University of California Press, Berkeley.

4 Realizing sustainable development goals

The prescience of John Friedmann

Shiv Someshwar

In September 2015 at the United Nations Sustainable Development Summit, 193 countries unanimously adopted the *2030 Agenda for Sustainable Development*, a framework for shared action "for people, planet and prosperity." The agenda includes 17 sustainable development goals (SDGs) to be achieved by 2030.[1] The SDGs promise economic growth that is simultaneously equitable and environmentally sustainable. Promise, however, is far removed from realization. A potential danger is that the SDGs end up as a foil to counter-attacks on the dominant mode of development rooted in capital accumulation and guided by the mantra of market efficiency. The example of a previous attempt from the 1990s, the global Agenda 21 for sustainable development, is a grim reminder of our collective failure to advance a transformative development agenda. In this brief essay, I argue that realizing the SDGs requires planning in the tradition of John Friedmann: as a skilful weaving of the "unity of opposites" (1987), and morally driven while not succumbing to dogmas.

The process of arriving at the SDGs

Sustainable development is an idea with universal appeal. In all societies, a combination of economic development, social inclusion and environmental sustainability is considered worth striving for. The balance amongst the three and the urgency of actions required, however, varies, and does so widely. Some societies seemingly tolerate social exclusion (purportedly for the sake of a higher rate of economic growth or due to "cultural" factors), while the natural environment is forsaken more easily in others. And that's where sustainable development goals become important, representing a framework reflective of the common consent over environmental, social and economic goals. Arriving at the 17 goals was a long and demanding process involving 193 countries and taking more than three years.

In January of 2012, the United Nations (UN) Secretary-General Ban Ki-moon's High-Level Global Sustainability Panel issued a report recommending that the world adopt a set of sustainable development goals (UN 2012).[2] A key outcome of the UN Conference on Sustainable Development, held in Rio de Janeiro later that year, was an agreement to develop a set of

SDGs. The Sustainable Development Solutions Network (SDSN) was launched in 2012 at the request of the UN Secretary General to mobilize global scientific and technological knowledge on the challenges of sustainable development.[3] To enable global consultations across 193 countries, an Open Working Group (OWG) with 30 member states was formed by the UN General Assembly in early 2013 to prepare a report on SDGs. Following a series of meetings around the world, the OWG released its proposal for a post-2015 development agenda for consideration and appropriate action by the UN General Assembly.[4] Following another year of deliberation, the UN member states adopted *Transforming Our World: The 2030 Agenda for Sustainable Development* (UN 2015) with 17 goals and 169 targets.[5] The SDGs are voluntary and are not legally binding. Societies are expected to use them as scaffolding, to devise plans and programs appropriate to their circumstances for a path towards sustainable development over the coming years (see Fig. 4.1).

SDGs have special and unique characteristics. They are truly universal – applying to all people and communities everywhere. Striving for equity, to leave no one behind, is at the heart of the goals. They are indivisible in that they cannot be broken into separate lines of action to be pursued independently, and conditions for success require simultaneous actions on a geographic scale. They are multi-stakeholder driven and signal a transformative agenda for humanity. For all of these reasons, advancing SDGs in all countries is a challenge that planners must seize. No other profession is better placed. The efforts of economists, engineers, ecologists, sociologists, agronomists and public health specialists should be inter-linked, reinforcing and integral to a plan that advances the SDGs.

Figure 4.1 The UN sustainable development goals
Source: Available at http://www.globalgoals.org/resource-centre/. Full terms at http://www.globalgoals.org/asset-licence

Challenges to achieving the SDGs

Sustainable development requires transforming the state, in form and function, with large-scale changes to the role and remit of market and civil society institutions. The dominant economic structures that have resulted in accelerating economic inequities and environmental destruction need to be understood, challenged and resolved. It requires us to consider the mechanisms of "bringing knowledge to action" with several attendant questions (whose knowledge, what action, when and how), and to do so simultaneously across three tenets – social inclusion, economic growth and environmental sustainability, at the local, national and international level.

SDGs are goals to guide development of all societies, rich and poor. While the modalities would vary, achieving sustainability in the social, economic and environmental dimensions is a challenge for all countries. No country has achieved sustainable development. Unlike the UN Millennium Development Goals (which were pursued from 2000 to 2015), the SDGs are not about development in the low-income countries alone. The choices vary on a number of factors, including the state of environmental risk, income gap between classes and within geographies and drivers of social and political stability. Each country will need to work out its unique pathway to achieving sustainable development. The acceptable balance between, say, environmental conservation and industrial job creation, for example, would be fundamentally different in Chile, Sweden and Timor Leste. So also the question of how to go about achieving this – internal versus external resourcing, level of technology and human capacity deployment – would help determine the specificity of the pathways.

Another challenge is the role of market mechanisms and their appropriate weight in policies and programs on market mechanisms. This would vary not only across but within countries. Given the current skepticism towards both the state and the market, societies need to plan for appropriate incentives and regulations for the production and delivery of goods and services, as well as for local private entrepreneurs and civil society groups. While all countries have committed to social inclusion, issues of fairness and equity have nuances that are locally determined. They require state action, in the global North and South, to counter discrimination on the basis of religion, race, gender, ethnicity, language, age and sexual preference. Organizing action and determining the mix of judicial, administrative and societal instruments to advance inclusive outcomes in health, education, livelihoods, employment and environmental quality are to be locally accommodated through dialogue, reflection and learning. They are not issues to be surrendered to economic ideologies.

Advancing sustainable development requires "sound" governance. What constitutes sound governance is relative to what exists and the aspirations of people. While issues of accountability, transparency, subsidiarity and participation are universally agreed to be desirable, the manner of how they come about, the mix of formal and non-formal institutions in their delivery, their control and the pace of change are to be nationally determined in the pursuit of SDGs.

Our understanding of the three sectors critical for development – state, market and civil society – has undergone several dramatic shifts in the last few decades. The state is no longer the "neutral arbiter" of natural rights nor is it an entity to be automatically retrenched. The private sector, and especially multinational companies, bring advanced technologies and high management capacity to execute complex solutions to a global audience. They ruthlessly lobby against policies seen as inimical to their profit-maximizing interests. Civil society groups, and especially the large non-profits, are an important element of the development landscape, in promoting and advancing a variety of rights and development efforts. Increasingly they too are recognized as being captive to their own institutional interests, which may be distinct from or even at odds with their social mission. Planning the practice of sustainable development requires finding the right balance to involve all three, rather than making a Hobson's choice.

Practice of sustainable development

Leaders from around the world came together to affirm the common basis for human aspirations everywhere and the responsibilities of all nations to advance sustainable development. That was the easy part. The challenging part is the practical delivery of the agenda. It is instructive to examine the fate of a similar global call for universal sustainable development – that of Agenda 21, launched some decades ago.

Adopted by 178 member states at the United Nations Conference on Environment and Development (UNCED) in 1992 in Rio de Janeiro, Agenda 21 articulated a "blueprint for action" from the global to the local level on sustainable development (UN 1992). It was designed to be comprehensive and undertaken globally, nationally and locally by all stakeholders in every area in which humanity impacts on the environment. A decade later, in 2002, all countries reaffirmed its implementation in Johannesburg at the World Summit on Sustainable Development (WSSD). Agenda 21 was an ambitious undertaking with three lofty goals: to improve the living standards of those in need, better management and protection of ecosystems and bringing about a more prosperous future for all. Covering major social, economic and environmental issues, the sprawling agenda was detailed in over 40 chapters. On the social and economic dimensions it included international cooperation and combating poverty, promoting healthy cities and changing consumption patterns. On the environment the extensive portfolio of action included protection of the atmosphere, of land, of fresh water and of marine resources, and the sound management of biotechnology, solid waste and radioactive materials. The agenda considered at length the role of a galaxy of stakeholders including women and children, indigenous people, workers and trade unions, businesses, industry and the epistemic community of scientists and technologists. It laid out as well the requirements for the means of implementation of the Agenda in terms of financial mechanisms, technology transfer, capacity building and training, as well as national and international institutional arrangements and legal instruments.

The promise of Agenda 21, however, was never realized. Despite its near universal appeal, it did not result in fundamental changes to the way governments approached development. Economic growth continued as the *summum bonum* of development. The language of social, economic and environmental transformation was confined mainly to the "Forewords" of national development plans. While Agenda 21 was "adopted" by over 6,000 local authorities around the world, their adoption strategy and outcomes remain unknown. A formal review of the agenda undertaken for the UN in 2011–12 confirmed that implementation was poor and progress negligible (UN 2012).[6] All in all, given the scale of ambition and the potential for transformative good, Agenda 21 did not leave a legacy of positive structures, processes and development outcomes to advance sustainable development at national or international levels.

Significance of the ideas of John Friedmann

The SDGs are important to help communities and societies achieve economic growth that is environmentally sustainable and socially inclusive; not as utopian ideals, but to be realized through practical application. In President Kennedy's famous appraisal on the importance of goals for public action, "So let us persevere. …By defining our goal more clearly – by making it seem more manageable and less remote – we can help all people to see it, to draw hope from it and to move irresistibly towards it."[7] Feasible pathways to long-term sustainability are highly complex, subject to technological uncertainty and require substantial financial resources. Sound policy-making in *each* society requires long-term planning that integrates strategies vis-à-vis many challenges: food and nutritional security, social service delivery, energy policy, water resource management, urbanization, infrastructure, human rights, biodiversity, adaption to climate change, mitigating greenhouse gases (GHGs), sustainable business, good governance and much more.

Achieving SDGs is estimated to require an incremental US$2–3 trillion of investments in infrastructure, energy, agriculture, health and education from 2016–2030 (Sachs and Schmidt-Traub 2014). The level of investment is well beyond the capacity of governments in the global South and North to fund on their own. A significant portion of this investment needs to be from private sources, including institutional investors such as pension funds, sovereign wealth funds and insurance firms (World Bank 2013; OECD 2015). Civil society organizations are very much needed to facilitate and help advance priorities of the community groups they serve. Private businesses and civil society stakeholders all need to be held accountable (Manji and O'Coill

2002; Banks et al. 2015). Governments are required to frame regulations to govern their own behavior as much as that of other stakeholders. Institutions of the state, the market and civil society will play significant parts, in consonance, to help realize the SDGs. Understanding their limits and managing the challenges should be a major preoccupation of planning.

Sustainable development requires transforming the economic systems with respect to society and the environment. Let us consider for a moment the challenges of meeting a single SDG, "Take urgent action to combat climate change and its impacts" (SDG 13). It demands keeping global average temperature change to less than two degrees centigrade, and requires all countries transition on a technological pathway to a low-carbon economy.[8] The world would need to cut global net emissions of GHG to approach zero between 2050 and 2075, consistent with the 2014 Intergovernmental Panel on Climate Change (IPCC) findings. Such a pathway demands the profound transformation of energy systems through steeply reducing carbon intensity in all sectors of the economy. Scholars and activists in the Deep Decarbonization Pathways Project (DDPP) have highlighted the transformational nature of demands confronting policy-makers for successful outcomes over the coming 30 to 50 years (DDPP 2015).[9] Governments, in partnership with the private sector, would need to devise practical ways to advance energy-carbon decoupling, while having to contend with the fossil fuel industry and their well-funded lobby groups. The growing energy needs of poorer communities and regions need to be recognized and respected in the new energy architecture. Perturbations from the changes in the energy systems of countries in advancing SDG 13 would profoundly impact every other development sector, just as changes wrought by advancing the other SDGs would in turn ripple and cascade across communities and societies, creating new winners and losers, with profound implications to their polity.

I turn to the writings of John Friedmann on planning as the dialectical means of engaging the current/now with future/vision to advance social transformation. Social transformation is the *bon motif* of sustainable development. Friedmann's ideas are needed now more than ever, for their content as well as for the methods they champion. As Patsy Healey notes in her Foreword to *Insurgencies*,

> the planning endeavour [for Friedmann] should focus on transformative development… It is about 'system change'. Friedmann warns against ideologically driven revolutionary change or change agendas driven by dogma or narrow doctrine, since it is ordinary people and especially the poorest who may well suffer most in such experiences.
>
> (Friedmann 2011, p.xiii)

To advance sustainable development on the social, economic and environmental dimensions, Friedmann (1987) argues that planners need to skilfully weave a "*unity of opposites*," not succumbing to despair over hegemony of the elites (recourse being instantaneous revolutions everywhere?) nor falling prey to the seductiveness of the subaltern (condemned forever to insurgencies?). Planners need to use state power while not being delusional ("above politics") or amoral ("means justify the end").

The greatest responsibility to advance the SDGs falls on the state. Profit maximizing drive of the private sector needs to be channeled, and the profit time horizon made commensurate with social purpose. Civil society organizations are needed to advance just causes, amplifying the voices of communities and of marginal populations, and to be checked from becoming uncritical partners of businesses. The state needs to be fairer and held to a higher standard of accountability. Planners have a role in all this. Friedmann's "unity of opposites" is a metaphor for the manner of engagement required to envision and design sustainable development (op. cit., p.405). Delivering *techne* is not the only role of planners. While required, more important perhaps is helping communities and nations to envision and plan for a future that is more socially inclusive and environmentally sustainable in cities, villages, hinterlands and rural areas; to help leverage the market and the state; to unite global scientific advances and local knowledge; and to balance the risks and opportunities of trade with distant markets, for that purpose. It requires understanding, reflecting and forcing rules of engagement to help transform behavior of powerful businesses in diverse fields of food and agriculture, finance, health care and energy. Passionate calls to reduce the power of businesses are not useful in the absence of constructive alternatives or are made solely on the basis of ideology, whether religious or secular. The state, as a bulwark for promoting the interests of the poor and vulnerable, is needed to regulate the interests of powerful entities, private and public, that too long have spoken for the poor while remaining unaccountable to them.

Very few governments have shown and are likely to have the enthusiasm to initiate on their own the deep transformations required of sustainable development. The experience of Agenda 21 should serve as an alarm signal. Implementing the SDGs requires more than "transdisciplinary efforts," "multi-ministerial coordination," "up-scaling successes," "strategic repurposing of institutions" and "innovative public–private partnerships" – the customary reactions of the development community, from multi-lateral banks to think-tanks and global consultancies. In response to the SDGs, Colombia, for example, has created a coordinating body for sustainable development within the office of the president. With power residing in mainline ministries and captive to powerful interests, such an effort is unlikely to lead to transformative changes. Other countries are dusting off older institutional efforts such as in the Philippines (from 1992) and the Czech Republic (from 2003), with Germany maintaining that no major changes are required since sustainable development has always been taken seriously. Steps that governments take on their own will be modest and potentially insufficient. Political mobilization from below and reflection from within, while critically needed, are increasingly uncommon in the practice of governance.

Social inclusion, along with economic growth and environmental sustainability, is a key pillar of the SDGs. In the run up to the adoption of the SDGs, social exclusion was singled out for attention. The UN Secretary General's report juxtaposes the impressive progress of humankind with the social and economic inequities that exist in the world, that "[O]ur globalized world is marked by extraordinary progress alongside unacceptable – and unsustainable – levels of want, fear, discrimination, exploitation, injustice and environmental folly at all levels" (UN 2014, p.4). Social exclusion is a reality in both North and South, of industrialized and less-industrialized societies. Home to the fourth largest numbers of dollar billionaires in the world after the US, China and Germany, India has a third of the world's poor and hungry. The rise in incarceration in the US has been dramatic and different between races. In 2010, 37% of young black males and high school dropouts were in prison, compared to less than 13% for white and 8% for Latino high school dropouts respectively. Comparative figures from 30 years ago were 12% for blacks, and less than a third of that for whites and Latinos (Western & Pettit 2010). However, the focus on social inclusion in the framing of the SDGs is not borne out by the level of attention that scholars and governments are giving it. A review of the scholarly outpouring following the adoption of the SDGs reveals a curious lacuna of efforts on how to advance social inclusion in practice (Castellino & Bradshaw 2015).[10] There is a lot of writing on the necessary conditions – comprehensive data base, sophisticated monitoring and evaluation system, transparent functioning of the rule of law, scaling up investments – and on innovative forms of partnership between the state and private sectors, but very little consideration of practical aspects of advancing social inclusion.

A real fear is that instead of advancing the transformational promise, the pursuit of sustainable development may end up reinforcing inequality. Economically dominant societies and the elites in others may ensure environmental safeguards or undertake deep changes in the economic system to accommodate "planetary boundary" considerations, as a matter of survival. The SD goals of social inclusion and putting the poor first may remain only in rhetoric. It is critical, hence, to have a clear understanding of the nature of transformation required for a socially inclusive and environmentally sustainable development.

Friedmann's (1987) conceptualization of the household access to the bases of social power in "What radical planners do" is a simple and powerful way to further our understanding. The manner in which households are linked, draw upon and exercise control over key asset classes (financial, knowledge and skill, space, time, informal networks, social organization, information and tools of production) provides an understanding of the connections between society, polity and the economy, and the nature of linkages to the environmental subsystem. Collective mapping of the dominant typologies (within a city, state or country) resolved to a higher scale enables investigation of linkages to the overlay architecture of institutions of market and the state. Mapping the development landscape in this manner allows for a contextually relevant understanding of the environment, of the drivers of policy and of the challenges and opportunities for contestation. It enables a more nuanced approach to stakeholders, sources of power and manner of its deployment, while identifying likely champions for policy change.

Undertaking simultaneous efforts to advance social, economic and environmental gains is an enormous policy challenge with very few past examples of success. Doing this at local and national levels, while also ensuring that flows of capital, technology and information remain available for similar changes to take place simultaneously in other countries as well, is not something that comes naturally within globally connected but competitively divided economies. A deeper understanding of the "local" governance landscape, as sketched out above, would enable prioritization of the transformation effort vis-à-vis technological and financial necessities, and deployment of political capital. Planners, who can conceptualize in spatial terms rather than being constrained by sectoral or disciplinary boundaries, are better placed to pragmatically lead this charge.

Sustainable development of cities and regions is the principal challenge for humankind now. Friedmann's reasons for the pursuit of planning admirably fit this great challenge: "of obtaining results in the 'real world'"; recognizing the "dynamic balances between the part and the whole, the technical and the normative, the empirical and the theoretical, the pragmatic and the utopian, the near present and the distant future"; an "emphasis on values …of social justice, ecological sustainability, …and human flourishing"; a result of "'transdisciplinary' expertise …made operational at multiple scales"; and engaging in "continuous social learning (Friedmann 2011, p.11)" to remain cognizant of challenges as they merge. Ultimately, what has drawn me back to Friedmann's conception of planning is its moral directedness and unswerving emphasis on practical action. At the cusp of humanity's greatest challenge, to realize humane and sustainable societies everywhere, the ideas of John Friedmann are more needed than ever.

Notes

1 <http://www.un.org/sustainabledevelopment/sustainable-development-goals> [25 February 2016].
2 <http://sustainabledevelopment.un.org> [25 February 2016].
3 <http://unsdsn.org> [25 February 2016].
4 <https://sustainabledevelopment.un.org/index.php?page=view&type=400&nr=1579&menu=1300> [25 February 2016].
5 <https://sustainabledevelopment.un.org/post2015/transformingourworld> [25 February 2016].
6 Reviewers of Agenda 21 considered it successful at a conceptual level rather than delivering on social, economic or environmental outcomes. They argued that it

made sustainable development the core of development, displacing more instrumental understandings such as "rapid industrialization," influenced subsequent international agreements and generated a strong notion of participation in decision making, especially the role of non-governmental actors (UNDESA 2012).

7 J.F. Kennedy, "American University Speech'. Washington DC: June 10, 1963. Indebted to Jeffrey Sachs for the quote.

8 See Carbon Brief for a useful timeline of research and advocacy over limiting globally averaged temperature to a maximum of two degrees. <http://www.carbonbrief.org/two-degrees-the-history-of-climate-changes-speed-limit> [25 February 2016].

9 Research groups from 15 major greenhouse gases-emitting countries came together to investigate how individual countries can transition on a technological pathway to a low-carbon economy consistent with the internationally agreed goal of limiting anthropogenic warming to less than two degrees Celsius (2°C). See Deep Decarbonization Pathways Project (2015).

10 An exception is a section of the human rights community that has engaged in finding practical ways to promote socially inclusive aspects of the SDGs. See Castellino and Bradshaw (2015).

References

Banks, N, Hulme, D & Edwards, M 2015, "NGOs, states, and donors revisited: still too close for comfort?", *World Development*, 66: 707–718.

Castellino, J & Bradshaw, S 2015, "Sustainable development and social inclusion: why a changed approach is central to combating vulnerability", *Washington International Law Journal*, 24(3, June): 459–494.

Deep Decarbonization Pathways Project 2015, *Pathways to Deep Decarbonization 2015 Report*, SDSN – IDDRI, New York and Paris.

Friedmann, J 1987, *Planning in the Public Domain: From Knowledge to Action*, Princeton University Press, Princeton, N.J.

Friedmann, J 2011, *Insurgencies: Essays in Planning Theory*, Routledge, Abingdon, UK.

Manji, F & O'Coill, C 2002, "The missionary position: NGOs and development in Africa", *International Affairs*, 78(3): 567–583.

Organisation for Economic Co-operation and Development (OECD) 2015, "Investment for sustainable development", *OECD and Post-2015 Reflections*, Element 11, Paper 3, OECD, Paris.

Sachs, JD & Schmidt-Traub, G 2014, "Financing sustainable development: implementing the SDGs through effective investment strategies and partnerships", UN SDSN, New York.

United Nations 1992, "Agenda 21", *The Earth Summit – UN Conference on Environment and Development*, Rio de Janeiro.

United Nations 2012, "Resilient people, resilient planet: a future worth choosing", UN, New York.

United Nations 2014, *The Road to Dignity by 2030: Ending Poverty, Transforming all Lives and Protecting the Planet: Synthesis Report of the Secretary-General on the Post-2015 Sustainable Development Agenda*, UN, New York. Available from: <http://www.un.org/ga/search/view_doc.asp?symbol=A/69/700&Lang=E> [3 August 2016].

United Nations 2015, *Transforming our World: The 2030 Agenda for Sustainable Development*, Resolution Adopted by the UN General Assembly, New York, 25 September.

United Nations Department of Economic and Social Affairs (UNDESA) 2012, *Review of Implementation of Agenda 21: Detailed Review*, UN, New York. Available from: <https://sustainabledevelopment.un.org/index.php?menu=1362> [19 December 2015].

Western, B & Pettit, B 2010, "Incarceration and social inequality", *Daedalus*, 139(3): 8–19.

World Bank 2013, *Financing for Development: Post-2015*, World Bank Group, Washington D.C.

5 How to prepare planners in the Bologna European education context

Adapting Friedmann's planning theories to practical pedagogy

Adolfo Cazorla, Ignacio de los Ríos and José M. Díaz-Puente

Introduction

It is impossible to talk about planning as a scientific meta-discipline without mentioning one of the most influential worldwide figures in the second half of the 20th century: John Friedmann. His contributions to planning theory and practice have yielded a rich harvest both in the context of regional development and planning education (Friedmann 1973; Friedmann & Alonso 1975; Friedmann 2001). They have not only strengthened the theoretical foundations of regional planning but extended knowledge from policy analysis and evaluation of practical planning experiences in a variety of national settings. Since the beginning of the Urban Planning Program at UCLA in the 1960s, Professor Friedmann has launched an entirely new way of thinking about planning pedagogy which culminated in a new distinctive epistemology for planning.

A similar revolutionary approach to planning education was taken up in Spain under the intellectual drive of Angel Ramos and Ignacio Trueba. They were pioneers in the field of project planning in engineering. They saw project planning as a transformational tool that required a different approach from what prevailed during the 1970s in planning across both public and private domains. They also called for structuring knowledge and action in a different way, both in academic institutions where their disciples helped to bring about change, and with direct action through projects (Cazorla & De Nicolás 2015).

Professors Ramos and Trueba initiated the Project and Rural Planning Department at Technical University of Madrid (UPM—Universidad Politécnica de Madrid) in 1985. From the very beginning they contributed to the creation of the Engineering Projects Spanish Association (AEIPRO—Asociación Española de Ingeniería de Proyectos) and promoted the international conference with regard to professional standards and core requirements for project planning. Below we show the intellectual connection between these three visionary professors (Friedmann, Ramos and Trueba) and how their knowledge and ideas have been integrated at the UPM to prepare planners in the Bologna European education context.

The European dimension of planning for rural development is relevant for at least three reasons: the need for the rural planner to be aware of the different systems of territorial planning that operate across the EU; the increasing cross-border planning policies and other transnational project planning for rural development; and the European level in the hierarchy of planning levels (Kunzmann & Yuan 2014).

Bridging education and practice: project-based learning in planning

Planning and project concepts are deeply linked in both public and private domains. They come together in what could be called "operability" and are intertwined academically because they share teaching and research topics. The relationship between plans, programs and projects is traditionally included in the curricula of technical universities.

The aptitude and abilities that society demands of its future professionals are fundamental when considering the design of any educational strategy. The concept of competency is the essential foundation in the professional world and is a key element of any educational model. Competence is an amplification of the concept of ability and qualification resulting from a rapid technical evolution in the organization of work and planning activities. Most enterprises today demand competent professionals.

Within this general framework, numerous studies around the world (Gijselaers 1996; Johnson 1999; Padmanabhan & Katti 2002; Chinnowsky et al. 2006) have proposed project-based learning (PBL) as the most suitable means of achieving effective competence-based education (Mulcahy 2000; Parsons et al. 2005; Kelly 2007) that integrates knowledge, skills and values. The models integrating PBL have their scientific basis in generating learning processes (Chinnowsky et al. 2006). They are grounded in the belief that humans construct new knowledge over a base of what they already know (Gijselaers 1996) and of what they have experienced. This information is shared through active participation and interaction with others.

Currently, we are involved in a wide-reaching process of reflection and change oriented toward promoting a qualitative leap in the educational model of the universities of the European Union. This approach stems from different agreements reached in the EU to construct the European Higher Education Area (EHEA) to be the basis of a new knowledge-based economy that responds to the challenges of globalization.

EHEA stresses that one of the measures necessary for achieving employability is developing transversal skills and competencies, including competency in communication and languages; the ability to handle information; the ability to solve problems and to work in teams; and the ability to lead social processes (European Commission 2001).

However, the starting point of our strategy was to maintain a clear idea of the end goal and of the functions of the university. Whatever model we adopted, we believed that one thing should remain unaltered in the university institution: "the incessant search for truth in which the teacher teaches what he discovers day to day, subjecting his own knowledge to permanent criticism, with a marked vocation for service to the society in which he is immersed" (De los Ríos et al. 2010, p.1368).

In the following sections we present the fundaments of a methodology of cooperative education that is designed to prepare planners within the European Higher Education context.

Conceptual framework of the new methodology

In 1987, a new educational methodology was first applied with fifth-year students of the Agricultural Engineering School at UPM. This emerged out of an agreement between the Project and Rural Planning Department at UPM and the Regional Government of the Community of Madrid. This agreement and the subsequent projects implemented in the course of 20 years have been the foundation for consolidating the PBL approach that has permitted adapting methodological aspects in teaching to real problems. The students employed a novel activity called pre-professional experience which was based on the idea of learning by doing, learning from reality and learning from their relevant disciplinary knowledge.

During these early years, the methodological educational framework was based on the concept of planning as the professional practice that specifically seeks to link knowledge to action. This definition, as Friedmann (1987) observed, clearly indicates that planning is different from an activity like engineering where means are efficiently related to ends and projects determine the course of action. The relationship between knowledge and action is interactive—a continual process of social learning. It is not about articulating a theory and then applying it to a situation. Friedmann noted that it was an altogether different way of thinking about planning, "the art of linking knowledge to action in a recursive process of social learning" (Friedmann 2011, pp.3–4).

Until this program was launched, Friedmann's theories of planning pedagogy and social learning were merely referred to, but had never been applied to the European context of project planning for rural development. This was our main contribution at the time. We emphasized that the knowledge we use and develop is not just the systematized knowledge of scientists, professors and technical experts. The experiential knowledge in the course of the action (Friedmann 2011) is equally important to the planning process.

The program introduced students to this new vision of planning and encouraged them to gain external knowledge from direct contact with diverse people. These professional relationships and complementary information enrich the students' base knowledge and lead them to develop new knowledge. This was one of the main elements of the strategy: participation in projects and programs which respond to real needs, giving students the opportunity to leave the classroom to solve problems directly with external agents.

Real concepts of action, namely projects, result in the development of new styles of planning that affect the interaction of people with nature and other people, leading us to say that what is not fair by nature cannot be, at the same time, optimum and functional (Spaemann 1986). In other words, even though some strategies may be technically possible, it is not appropriate to implement them (Ramos 1993).

The project-planning education process has a dynamic element in which students "learn to learn" about the reality of the rural world and how public administration—the project client—works. In the coordination of the project-based learning activities a method of logic is applied in which learning experiences respond to structuring the methodologies of project planning and evaluation. The active method of "learning by doing" (Bartkus 2001; Hackett et al. 1998; Johnson 1999) has special relevance in the projects and planning education and provides enormous potential for originality, creativity and common sense.

New professional standards and international competences in the pan-European education context

In 1999, in order to improve student mobility in Europe, the member states of the European Union agreed to create a pan-European structure of higher education. The internationalization of higher education and rise in international student mobility was accompanied by much reflection on the extent to which universities were equipping their students to be future world citizens or "world professionals" (Sykes et al. 2015). The new focus of higher education in the EHEA required that universities begin methodological changes with approaches oriented toward new competences. In this context, the concept of "life-long learning" was described as any learning activity carried out throughout life with the aim of improving knowledge, competences, and aptitudes under a personal, civic, social or job-related perspective (European Commission 2001).

The Bologna Agreement had many positive impacts on planning education (Kunzmann 2004), opening up new opportunities that were well linked to the international framework. One of these was the Erasmus Mundus Programme, which enabled students to combine degrees of different disciplines to develop planning competences.

In many Master of rural planning programs, territory and social dimension includes both a broad academic research and a professional field. It is similar to Friedmann's description of urban planning:

> As a professional field, urban planning is an institutionally embedded practice. It is also a practice that is inevitably interwoven with politics

> and with on-going conflicts over the allocation and use of public and private resources. Thus politics is institutionally embedded as well. It follows that the activity of planning is understood and practiced differently in different institutional settings that vary significantly across countries and even cities. Moreover, within any given setting, planning must continuously reinvent itself as circumstances change.
>
> (Friedmann 2005, p.29)

We used the EHEA experience to advocate a methodological change in which learning and evaluation were oriented toward international competences of Project–Program Management. UN-Habitat argued for the adoption of a "one-world" approach to planning education which equips students to work in different "world contexts" (UN-Habitat 2009). The most suitable way to implement the change was to adopt a professional point of reference that would represent the needs of society. Thus, the standard of the International Project Management Association (IPMA) was adopted. The IPMA is an organization of more than 20 national professional associations from around the world. Adoption of this international standard enabled initiation of the university stage of specialized training for future professionals, providing them with more opportunities to work in different "world contexts."

As planning education varies so much over the world, reflecting each country's specific planning practices, any statement on the "core curriculum" of European planning education must pay respect to these variances and, therefore, cannot and should not be explained in too much detail. Nevertheless, since 1995, Association of European Schools of Planning (152 member schools) adopted the core requirements as guidelines—common principles and values shared by the community suitable for a high quality planning education all over Europe (AESOP 2008).

Project planning for rural development: an educational strategy

As mentioned in the earlier section, the GESPLAN Research Group[1] at UPM conducts applied research that complements planning teaching and broadens the scope of graduate studies. The methodology is the result of 25 years of experience in sustainable rural development project planning by GESPLAN in several European contexts and emerging countries.

An international context for sustainable rural development

Teaching and research are integrated in a scheme that provides escalated training from basic to advanced levels of competence. Their knowledge increases and their attitudes are shaped as they journey over this educational "road." They are given opportunities to acquire certain basic experience in advance. The graduate level includes an Erasmus Mundus Master (International Master of Sustainable Development), in cooperation with six universities in the EU and another nine universities outside the EU, and a doctoral program adapted to the Bologna Agreement. The general objective of this program is based around validating the competence of individuals with respect to their knowledge, experience and attitudes in relation to project planning for sustainable rural development.

The Master's Program of the UPM is officially recognized by the European Union and is fully integrated in the European Space for Higher Education. Characteristics of the program are thus enriched with the criteria emanating from the Erasmus Mundus programmes: cooperation and mobility within higher education in order to achieve the objectives of improving European higher education and promoting intercultural understanding through cooperation with non-member countries. The Master's Program offers direct access to the PhD Program of the UPM and complements the experience with the participation of noted professionals from other universities, including Stanford (USA) or Berkeley (USA). The Master's Program has reinforced its international dimension (with an internationalization rate of 87%) through the international Alliance for Sustainable Rural Development.

Study program from three professors: planning, projects and sustainable management

Experience shows that even within Europe, schools of planning do not agree on which competences professional planners should have. Planning is still understood quite differently from country to country and from dominating discipline to dominating discipline, even though planning education aims to teach students how to plan "for people" (Kunzmann 2015). In our case, adapting Friedmann's planning theories to practical pedagogy, this real approach is not only understood as working for others, but as working "with others" (Cazorla et al. 2013). From this social dimension and perspective, the Master's Program has a mission to provide participants with a specialization in subjects and content that is directly related to professional activity in the field of three bodies of knowledge: planning, projects and sustainable management of the environment. These three main bodies of knowledge have a close relationship with the perspective of Professors Friedmann, Trueba and Ramos.

The *planning* models and the planning concept as the professional practice that specifically seeks to link ways of knowledge with ways of acting reflect the perspective of Professor Friedmann.

Professor Ramos' scientific research contributions and his colossal sensitivity and respect for nature have focused on *sustainable management* and environmental awareness in the management of projects and the value of the environment as a resource for planners and public managers.

Regarding *engineering projects and social integration in the project cycle*, the experience and knowledge of Professor Trueba, including his contributions in the design of new methodologies for projects planning, were integrated into the knowledge of the Master's Program. This allowed us to establish a close link between engineering teaching—until then merely technical—and the management of the big initiatives of international organizations, as well as the link between the mission of technique and engineering and their role in the solution of the great problems of humanity—the fight against hunger and poverty in the case of rural areas.

From the previous body of knowledge, the program of studies and the students' workload are in a close relationship with the following modules:

(I) *Planning, evaluation and project management of rural development:* rural planning with ecological base and development models; evaluation design, methods and tools; project management for rural–local development projects; competence in project management; planning in the public field; participative and collaborative evaluation for entrepreneurship.
(II) *Quantitative techniques for sustainable development*: technologies for territory study; remote sensing and GIS; complex support systems for decision-making in rural development.
(III) *Sustainable management of a territory and its biodiversity*: techniques and models for sustainable management and biodiversity conservation; sustainable management of soil and water; socioeconomic sustainability assessment; evaluation of the state of nature conservation.
(IV) *Human development*
(V) *Final Master's Thesis*: scientific articles.

Learning and teaching strategy

The European Credit Transfer and Accumulation System (ECTS) enables measurement of each student's ability to acquire knowledge and the abilities and skills necessary to understand the different subjects in the study plan (De los Ríos et al. 2015). Thus, it is about a new educational approach based on "learning" under the interaction of the students with real case studies and real projects. This environment provides the opportunity for both action and reflection, showing that learning is both an active and reflective process, and also the opportunity to include research in the field of project planning and related fields.

Our learning and teaching strategy for planning education aims to teach students how to plan "with others" and "with people," combining academic rigour and high-quality researchers with practical relevance; creating an intellectual and international environment; and thinking and acting together to solve the problems of society. As Siemiatycki says: "over the past fifty years, a recurring theme in planning scholarship has been to comprehend and categorize the roles, epistemologies, and dilemmas commonly faced by the planning practitioner in society" (2012, p.147). With these goals in mind, our learning and teaching strategies are focused on PBL as the most suitable means of achieving effective competence-based education, fostering holistic thinking/acting, and encouraging teamwork and leadership (De los Ríos et al. 2010).

Our PBL educational model is understood as the pre-professional team practice that seeks to connect learning/knowledge to action by common projects, which, in addition to the technical competences, incorporates capacity building and the value of the people who are involved and participate within the context of the PBL (Cazorla et al. 2013). Planning requires continuous communication while working with politicians, stakeholders, target groups and people. The PBL educational model gives emphasis to small "action groups" and inter-personal dialogue among multi-stakeholders, capable of providing a moral foundation for planning, similar to what Friedmann suggested in *The Good Society* (1979).

Agreements to provide our students the opportunity to work on real projects with local organizational structures, such as the local action groups of the European Initiative LEADER (EU 1990), enabled educational tools and a new experimental approach to planning as social learning in a rural development context. Friedmann's planning theories have been applied in several instances to practical pedagogy of the PBL model in rural development (Cazorla et al. 2005, 2015; Cazorla & De los Ríos 2012). Planning students wishing to work in planning practice in their country have to learn how to communicate with people and stakeholders, with politicians and real estate managers.

Local and contextual conditions differ from international conditions, even in times of growing globalization (Kunzmann 2014). Expert knowledge, experiential knowledge and interactive knowledge (Dewey & Bentley 1946; Lindblom 1990; Friedmann 2011) have been intertwined throughout the PBL model using case studies and planning experiences in Latin America and Europe (Díaz-Puente et al. 2009). Following the PBL approach, the students conduct a pre-professional experience connecting technical and contextual competences in the sphere of rural development projects planning while dealing with the needs of the productive sector and real problems.

This PBL model combines Project–Program Management competences organized in three dimensions of competences—technical, behavioural, and contextual (ISO 21500 2012)—and covers four fields of the social-relations system—politics, public administration, private entrepreneurship and civil society (Alexander 1994)—as a synthesis of societal models. Friedmann's book on *Empowerment* (1992) rethinks development strategies for the alleviation of poverty, providing a model of access to the "bases of social power" which has the household economy at its centre, and including knowledge and skills, defensible life space, social networks, social organizations, appropriate information, instruments of work and livelihood and financial resources. Our PBL model has been applied in several real experiences adapting Friedmann's ideas and empowerment theory to practical pedagogy in rural development.

Our planning program attracts a large number of international students (87%), and hence one of the challenges to our learning and teaching strategy is the cultural and contextual implications in "crossing borders" (Friedmann 2010) in both/either consolidated knowledge or way of knowledge within the framework of the epistemology of planning, projects and sustainable rural development. As Kunzmann and Yuan (2014, p.69) note, "Teaching foreign students requires experience, sensibility, and an understanding of cultural differences. It also requires time and patience." In order to prepare planners for practice across the EU, planning education needs to be modified to take these differences into account. Debates are promoted from the different students' backgrounds and their cultural differences. The discussion and debates are made through Friedmann's (1987) four major traditions of planning—social reform, social learning, policy analysis and social mobilization—and through the contributions of the students from our PBL model. We consider it important to keep debates completely open to improve understanding among various perspectives, planning traditions and cultures. The aim is to value, not to eradicate, differences (Allmendinger 2002).

Other general principles that support this approach in our Master's Program are as follows: a) greater involvement and autonomy of the student; b) use of active methodologies (PBL, practical case studies, teamwork, debates, tutoring sessions, conferences-discussions, seminars, study visits, specialized conferences, multimedia technology, research study); c) flexibility and participation to facilitate the interchange of experiences and knowledge between the classroom and professional life; d) role of the teaching staff as designers of environments of learning and joint reflection; e) for ongoing assessment of students, each Master's student must have a tutor-professor to act as a guide while the student is preparing a final Master's thesis.

With this approach, all activities that are undertaken reinforce the globalization of knowledge in the sense that different disciplines are integrated—economics, sociology, agrarian policy, environmental sciences, territorial planning, engineering projects—consistent with the needs that arise as contextual competences of project/program management. In this way, teaching modules are not treated in isolation, but present a relationship among the three dimensions of competence: technical, behavioural and contextual.

Conclusions

John Friedmann's work has inspired and informed our engagement with the Bologna Process throughout our experience with the PBL approach to prepare planners in the European Higher Education context. The transactive planning and PBL approaches involved processes of integrating mutual learning with a commitment to action, both of which are essential to effective competence-based education. We have learned about communication and dialogue from Friedmann's work. These concepts are also an essential part of our PBL model, grounded in the belief that humans construct new knowledge over a base of what they already know and have experienced.

Based on our experience, we can see that planning as social learning from PBL is the most adequate educational methodology for developing competences to prepare planners in the Bologna European education context. This learning strategy is based on linking teaching planning models with the professional sphere. It is based on cooperation, active participation and interaction, offering multiple possibilities for developing technical, contextual and behavioural competences promoted by Bologna.

Throughout their experience, students are immersed in active pre-professional learning thanks to the links between university, entrepreneurs, civic groups and public administration. Expert knowledge, experiential knowledge and interactive knowledge have been intertwined throughout the PBL processes, combining academic rigour and research activities and using real case studies and planning experiences.

The methodology fosters a research spirit and innovation, creativity for the generation of new knowledge, productive thought and motivation to learn and solve problems. The cooperative learning model allows the confluence of action through real experiences with reflection on the activities to create new knowledge. The necessary competences approach advocated by EHEA has been used as an opportunity to establish a new connection with the professional world and adopt the professional standard recognized internationally as our point of reference. This connection also permits linking university education with a system of professional certification, which opens up better future opportunities for UPM's planning graduates.

Note

1 See http://www.ruraldevelopment.es/index.php/en.

References

AESOP 2008, "Core requirements for a high quality European Planning Education" in *Towards a European Recognition for the Planning Profession*, eds A Geppert & R Verhage, Proceedings of the second meeting of AESOP Heads of Schools held at the Arenberg Castle, Leuven, Belgium on 14 April 2007, AESOP Planning Education N°1, pp.23–25.

Alexander, ER 1994, "The non-Euclidean mode of planning: what is it to be?", *Journal of the American Planning Association*, 60(3): 372–376.

Allmendinger, P 2002, *Planning Theory*, Palgrave, New York.

Bartkus, KR 2001, "Skills and cooperative education: a conceptual framework", *Journal of Cooperative Education*, 36(1): 17–24.

Cazorla, A & De Nicolás, L 2015, "Planning and projects: three visionaries—Friedmann, J., Trueba, I. and Ramos, A." in *Project Management and Engineering Research*, eds JL Ayuso-Muñoz, JL Yagüe-Blanco & S Capuz-Rizo, Springer, New York. DOI: 10.1007/978-3-319-26459-2_20.

Cazorla, A & De los Ríos, I 2012, *Rural Development as "Working with People": A Proposal for Policy Management in Public Domain*. Available from: <http://oa.upm.es/10260/1/WorkingWithPeople_2012.pdf> [17 May 2016].

Cazorla, A, De los Ríos, I & Díaz-Puente, J 2005, "The LEADER community initiative as rural development model: application in the capital region of Spain", *Scientific Journal Agrociencia*, 39(6): 697–708.

Cazorla, A, De los Ríos, I & Salvo, M 2013, "Working With People (WWP) in rural development projects: a proposal from social learning", *Cuadernos de Desarrollo Rural*, 10(70): 131–157.

Chinnowsky, P, Brown, H, Szajnman, A & Realph, A 2006, "Developing knowledge landscapes through project-based learning", *Journal of Professional Issues in Engineering Education and Practice*, 132(2): 118–125.

De los Ríos, I, López, FR & Pérez García, C 2015, "Promoting professional project management skills in engineering higher education: project-based learning (PBL) strategy", *International Journal of Engineering Education*, 31(1–B): 1–15.

De los Ríos, I, Cazorla, A, Díaz-Puente, JM & Yagüe, JL 2010, "Project-based learning in engineering higher education: two decades of teaching competences in real environments", *Procedia–Social and Behavioral Sciences*, 2(2): 1368–1378.

Dewey, J & Bentley, F 1946, *Knowing and the Known*, Beacon Press, Boston.

Díaz-Puente, JM, Cazorla, A & De los Ríos, I 2009, "Empowering communities through evaluation: some lessons from rural Spain", *Community Development Journal*, 44(1): 53–67.

EU 1990, *The Community Initiative for Rural Development: LEADER*, Information Memo, 25 July 1990, EU Commission, Brussels.

European Commission 2001, *Making a European Area of Lifelong Learning Reality*, Communication COM (2001) 678 final, European Commission, Brussels.

Friedmann, J 1973, *Retracking America: A Theory of Transactive Planning*, Anchor Press, New York.

Friedmann, J 1979, *The Good Society*, MIT Press, Cambridge, M.A.

Friedmann, J 1987, *Planning in the Public Domain: From Knowledge to Action*, Princeton University Press, Princeton, N.J.

Friedmann, J 1992, *Empowerment: The Politics of Alternative Development*, Blackwell, Cambridge, M.A.

Friedmann, J 2001, "Regional development and planning: the story of a collaboration", *International Regional Science Review*, 24(3): 386–395.

Friedmann, J 2005, "Planning cultures in transition" in *Comparative Planning Cultures*, ed. B Sanyal, Routledge, New York and London, pp. 29–44.

Friedmann, J 2010, "Crossing borders: do planning ideas travel?" in *Crossing Borders: International Exchange and Planning Practices*, eds P Healey & R Upton, Routledge, London, pp. 313–327.

Friedmann, J 2011, *Insurgencies: Essays in Planning Theory*, Routledge, London and New York.

Friedmann, J & Alonso, W (eds) 1975, *Regional Policy: Readings in Theory and Applications*, MIT Press, Cambridge, M.A.

Gijselaers, WH 1996, "Connecting problem-based learning with educational theory" in *Bringing Problem-Based Learning to Higher Education: Theory and Practice*, eds L Wilkerson & WH Gijselaers, Jossey-Bass, San Francisco, C.A., pp. 3–21.

Hackett, RK, Martin, GR & Rosselli, DP 1998, "Factors related to performance ratings of engineering students in cooperative education placements", *Journal of Engineering Education*, 87(4): 445–458.

ISO 21500 2012, *Guidance on Project Management*, Project Committee ISO/PC 236, Project Management, ISO International Organization for Standardization.

Johnson, PA 1999, "Project-based, cooperative learning in the engineering classroom", *Journal of Professional Issues in Engineering Education and Practice*, 125(1): 8–11.

Kelly, W 2007, "Certification and accreditation in civil engineering", *Journal of Professional Issues in Engineering Education and Practice*, 133(3): 181–187.
Kunzmann, KR 2004, "Culture, creativity and spatial planning", *Town Planning Review*, 75(4): 383–404.
Kunzmann, KR 2014, "Smart Cities: a new paradigm of urban development", *Crios*, 1/2014: 9–20. DOI: 10.7373/77140.
Kunzmann, KR 2015, "Challenges of planning education in times of globalization" in *Excellence in Planning Education: Local, European & Global Perspective*, ed. I Mironowicz, AESOP Planning Education N° 3, pp. 58–73.
Kunzmann, KR & Yuan, L 2014, "Educating planners from China in Europe", *The Planning Review*, 50(4): 66–70.
Lindblom, CE 1990, *Inquiry and Change: The Troubled Attempt to Understand and Shape Society*, Yale University Press, New Haven.
Mulcahy, D 2000, "Turning the contradictions of competence: competence-based training and the beyond", *Journal of Vocational Education and Training*, 52(2): 259–280.
Padmanabhan, G & Katti, D 2002, "Using community-based projects in civil engineering capstone courses", *Journal of Professional Issues in Engineering Education and Practice*, 125(1): 12–18.
Parsons, C, Caylor, E & Simmons, H 2005, "Cooperative education work assignments: the role of organizational and individual factors in enhancing ABET competencies and co-op workplace well-being", *Journal of Engineering Education*, 94(3): 309–316.
Ramos, A 1993, *¿Por qué la conservación de la naturaleza?* Speech at the reception ceremony at the Royal Academy of Exact, Physical and Natural Sciences, Madrid.
Siemiatycki, M 2012, "The role of the planning scholar: research, conflict, and social change", *Journal of Planning Education and Research*, 32(2): 147–159.
Spaemann, R 1986, "Ende der Modernität?" in *Moderne oder Posmoderne?*, eds P Koslowski, R Spaemann & R Low, Acta Humaniora VCH, Weinheim, pp. 19–40.
Sykes, O, Thakur, UJ & Potter, K 2015, "What's love got to do with it? Some reflections on the internationalisation of planning education" in *Excellence in Planning Education: Local, European & Global Perspective*, ed. I Mironowicz, AESOP Planning Education N° 3, pp. 82–91.
UN-Habitat 2009, *Global Report on Human Settlements 2009: Planning Sustainable Cities*, United Nations Human Settlements Programme (UN-Habitat), Earthscan, London.

Part 2

Economic development and regionalism

Haripriya Rangan

John Friedmann started his career in regional development in the 1950s, a decade after the end of the Second World War. Development, at the time, was primarily focused on something called 'the economy', which Timothy Mitchell (2002) describes as emerging in its currently understood form during the 1930s and 1940s. Mitchell notes that there were two processes that interacted to make the economy the dominant concern for governments at the time. On the one hand, there was the expansion of mathematical modelling and statistical techniques within the discipline of economics that generated new branches of study such as national income accounting, econometrics and macroeconomics. On the other hand there were a number of global political and financial crises, such as the Great Depression and the collapse of European imperial structures before and after the Second World War. Out of this context emerged a new way of thinking about 'the economy' as "the totality of monetarised exchanges within a defined space" (p.4). The national space of economy was, in effect, an abstract mathematical and statistical geometry that was supposed to correspond with the spatial geography of a country (p.83). This concept of economy gained authority in the 1950s because it could be modelled and compared with other national economies, and because governments could use this analysis to decide how to invest their fiscal resources for further economic development.

John's work during the 1950s and 1960s was extremely influential for showing the importance of urbanisation and city-regions in driving economic transformation and also highlighting the flaws in economic theories that rendered them ineffective for regional development. He reconceptualised the spatial dimensions of national economies by focusing on the core–periphery relationships between urban areas and hinterlands as the context for regional development (Friedmann 2013). As political and economic crises consumed many parts of the world during the 1970s and 1980s and neoliberal economic theories replaced Keynesian, state-led economic development, Friedmann's critiques drew attention to the urban neighbourhood and household economies that were critical for the survival of communities and regions.

The essays in this section engage with different aspects of John's work on economic development and regionalism. Robin Bloch shows how John's early concept of the 'urban field' has informed and inspired contemporary research on urbanisation and spatial expansion in Nigeria. Chung Tong-Wu shows the contradictory situation arising when cross-border development occurs in the adjoining peripheries of two nations. Keith Pezzoli shows how bioregional theory and sustainability science can be combined to build rooted communities and transformative city-region development. My essay critically explores the rise of social innovation and enterprise in relation to John Friedmann's ideas of economic activity and radical planning challenges to neoliberal development. And Yuko Aoyama explores how social enterprises have reconfigured the economic and governance sphere into a hybrid domain that links communities, civil society organisations, corporations and government agencies in new partnerships for economic development.

References

Friedmann, J 2013, 'Planning for sustainable regional development', RDD: Regional Development Dialogue, 34(2): 1–10.

Mitchell, T 2002, Rule of Experts: Egypt, Technopolitics, Modernity, UC Press, Berkeley and Los Angeles.

6 City-regions, urban fields and urban frontiers

Friedmann's legacy

Robin Bloch

Introduction

More than a half a century on, John Friedmann's early writings on urbanization and regional development resonate with policy-makers, planners and political actors, notably in the rapidly urbanizing countries, regions and cities of the "global South." This influence can also be felt in the work of researchers, which often provides the "evidence base" for urban and regional policy and practice. The impact is felt most strongly in contemporary Asia and Africa, which are, not coincidentally, at the leading edge of global urbanization and global urbanism.

According to United Nations estimates, Africa had the highest rate of urban demographic growth over the last 20 years, at 3.5 percent per year. Some 40 percent of Africa's population of 1.2 billion now lives in urban areas; this is estimated to rise to 56 percent by 2050. Africa and Asia will add 90 percent of the expected 2.5 billion addition in urban population by 2050, with India contributing 404 million, China 292 million and Nigeria 212 million (United Nations 2014).

I begin this essay by attempting to understand why these writings inform contemporary urban and regional planning and specifically, "influence the decisions of politicians and administrators," to use Friedmann's words in describing his interlocutors and clients at the time (1966, p.255).

I then use Friedmann and Miller's ground-breaking paper "The Urban Field" (1965) to discuss how its identification of a new "scale of urban living" (p.313) informed the initial research into the massively scaled and conjoined urbanization and urban–suburban–regional spatial expansion process in contemporary Nigeria (Bloch et al. 2015).

I conclude by identifying a number of productive tensions in Friedmann's work. Building from these, I propose directions forward, for both planning research and planning practice.

A game of two halves

In his retrospective account "A Life in Planning" (2002b), Friedmann presents his career as a game of two halves, to use the saying beloved of football commentators. The first half, from the mid-1950s, saw him practicing as a planner and researcher, and writing articles and books that established regional planning as a practical discipline and which defined urbanization as a topic of study.

The urban field paper and the book *Regional Development Policy: A Case Study of Venezuela* (1966) are the best-known examples of a wider body. This work, and that of allied researchers and planners, stimulated regional policy and planning intervention and experimentation all over the world.

Regional planning practice was founded on the precepts that Friedmann identified and synthesized—and initially applied to the case of Venezuela. A case was made for infusing national development planning with the then missing spatial dimension, arguing that alleviating regional inequalities required national policy. An overarching core/periphery framework was elaborated to explain the causal factors for and impacts of these inequalities. Techniques to identify and categorize the types of regions in a national territory and the policy implications for each were developed. Finally, the goal of national spatial integration through the incorporation of the periphery into the national economy was promoted through growth poles, as a set of complementary economic attractors to the core, brought into life by investments in plant and infrastructure, and connected by growth corridors (Friedmann 1966; 2002b, p.130).

By the late 1960s, though, while practising in Chile, Friedmann's "thoughts about planning were...undergoing a dramatic change" (p.133):

> I was moving away from a classical decision model of planning, which, I was certain, had come to a dead end. What I proposed in its place was a form of action planning in which planners would no longer serve as handmaidens to power but become personally engaged, as individuals, in bringing about progressive social change.
>
> (2002b, pp.133–34)

In Friedmann's new formulation, planning became "the art *of linking knowledge to action in a recursive process of social learning*" (2011, p.4). The rupture became decisive—and permanent. The publication (with Clyde Weaver) of *Territory and Function: The Evolution of Regional Planning* (1979), saw a wholesale shift in paradigm from functional (broadly, statist and economic) to territorial (cultural and political) conceptions of planning. The authors declared that "growth center doctrine is quite useless as a tool of regional development" (p.175).

The years which followed at UCLA saw Friedmann producing unique and innovative work which was broadly directed at establishing the dimensions, underlying values and practical means of the transformative, progressive and radical urban and regional planning approach and agenda he had identified. He simultaneously (and relatedly) conducted research into the urbanization process and the politics and economics of territorial spaces, with a focus on the role of city-regions in economic growth (2002b, p.145).

A new era for regional and spatial planning

As a large and exhaustive literature on the topic demonstrates, the original era of regional planning had its heyday in the 1970s (Gore 1985). Much rethinking by its theorists and implementers followed. Despite the disavowal by its progenitors, the "growth center doctrine"—as a shorthand for the first wave of regional planning (or, as Ed Soja (2015) called it, the old regionalism)—never disappeared. Nor did social and economic inequalities, to use that anodyne term to indicate the devastating disparities—within, and between, regions and urban areas—in living conditions, incomes and opportunities, and the frequently growing levels of poverty, both urban and rural, that characterize the space economies of the urbanizing "global South."

Regional (typically now termed spatial) policy and planning have in fact made something of a recent comeback and Friedmann's insights and judgements from the "first half" of his career continue to inform and inspire research, policy and plan-making in many parts of the world. Spatial policy and planning at both the regional and city-region scales have become prevalent in the last decade in Asia and Africa. Their drafting is often mandated by new legislation for incorporation within national development planning, programs and related investments.

At national and sub-national levels, the World Bank's 2009 *World Development Report* (WDR), *Reshaping Economic Geography*, and its subsequent refinements, have been influential as have the national spatial policies and plans made by European Union member countries. The WDR distinguishes between (1) serving people (in place—i.e. where they live), through social, community and welfare policies and programs ranging from health and education through to pensions, and (2) targeting specific places, through investments in physical and social infrastructures and institutions. A main strategic concern remains spatial integration: policies, initiatives, investments and instruments to link and ease movement between leading areas (which exhibit economic growth and dynamism) and lagging areas (which can be growing slowly, or are in decline).

In sub-Saharan Africa, to cite examples, the governments of Ethiopia and Ghana have recently developed a *National Urban Development Spatial Plan* and *National Spatial Development Framework* respectively; Sierra Leone has produced a spatial strategy; the previous and current Nigerian governments are deeply involved with spatial policy-making and planning for the country's northern region and its city-regional complexes in the wake of the violent and destructive Boko Haram movement; and Botswana has begun a revision of its regional and urban policies and planning system.

Such policies and plans continue to use the syntax (e.g. the core-periphery spatial structure, regional typologies, development corridors), goals (reduction of regional disparities, spatial integration, regional convergence) and instruments/tools (growth poles, growth centers) for regional (and city-regional) development that characterized the first wave of regional planning.

This syntax is combined with the conceptual advances made in recent years in the understanding of the benefits of both urban and economic agglomeration. To implement, instruments that support the positive effects of economic concentration (such as cluster and value chain initiatives and catalytic investments) and connectivity (transportation and communications infrastructure) are prioritized. Strengthening the management of urbanization and urban development is not neglected, through such means as land management, urban and land use planning, better resourced municipal administration and finance, and improved infrastructure services; neither is the boosting of agricultural productivity with such tools as extension services and improved rural education and health care.

Today's spatial policies and plans also show concern with environmental sustainability and resilience to climate change. They tend to be developed in collaborative and participative processes. These can involve political actors, officials of government ministries and departments at different levels, representatives of the community and private sectors, and staff members from the academic departments, research institutes and consultancies which provide technical support and services. Their different political interests require consideration—and, where necessary, careful accommodation.

In my view, there are a number of reasons why the concepts and approaches charted by Friedmann and other regional planners in the 1960s are still relevant for practitioners and politicians.

To begin, and it is not a minor point, theoretical and technical concepts were explicated and communicated clearly, confidently and without superfluous jargon. Administrators and planners understood Friedmann. His prose, even when allusive or speculative, is to-the-point, stimulating and pleasurable to read. This permitted wide dissemination of his work and its assimilation into and prominence within what became, in time, the commonly held narrative of regional planning theory and practice.

A second reason is that Friedmann consistently asserted the necessity and, indeed, importance of planning as an active practice in the public domain—in what he often called the "real world," as "a world in movement, apparently capricious, elusive and understood only in fragments" (1966, p.256). Nonetheless, planners had a responsibility to "be concerned with effecting desirable changes on the ground and, therefore, with strategies, politics and relations of power" (Friedmann 2002b, p.120). A practical and incremental but progressive approach was encouraged, as was experimentation and tolerance for failure:

> I live now, and I am willing to deal with questions piecemeal rather than holistically, embrace the dialectics of both/and, and accept pragmatic solutions based on negotiation and compromise.
>
> (Friedmann 2002a, pp.xxi–xxii)

Practitioners have found this approach and standpoint inspiring.

Finally, as implied above, Friedmann conceived of planning as intrinsically political, embedded (a word he liked to use) "in the inherently conflictual, painful nature of politics" (p.xviii). For him, "Planning thought is also political thought, and the practice of planning is a political practice" (p.153). This acknowledgement chimes with the lived experience of planners—and politicians.

Urban fields, city-regions and urban frontiers: United States 1965, Nigeria 2015

I now move to a specific example of influence. In "The Urban Field," Friedmann and Miller set out to portray "the expanding scale of urban life" built on "the constantly widening patterns of interaction in an urbanizing world" evident by the early 1960s in the United States. The urban field, as the "basic element of the emerging spatial order," (1965, p.313) was constituted as an interdependent amalgam of existing metropolitan cores and their inter-metropolitan peripheries.

> [It was] an enlargement of the space for urban living that extends far beyond the boundaries of existing metropolitan areas—defined primarily in terms of commuting to a central city of metropolitan size—into the open space of the periphery.
>
> (ibid.)

The naming—and imaging—of the urban field was one of several attempts to find a fresh conceptual vocabulary for the urban spatial expansion of the time; other terms devised were megalopolis, spread-city, and the non-place urban realm. It opened a line of inquiry into the nature and functions of the various urban settlement forms which comprised the urban field, as well as its overall spatial, economic and political structures. Friedmann's own sustained work on the city-region, most notably its world city variant, exemplifies this effort.

Friedmann and Miller identified some 70 urban fields in the US centered on core metropolitan areas of 300,000 people and stretching out 100 miles (as a vehicular commuting limit). In the spirit of the time, they took an optimistic perspective on a spatial construct that would, on their reckoning, soon house up to 90 percent of the US population.

Urban fields were therefore another new frontier, with "great opportunities" for wider life spaces, environments and political communities of interest. "The expansionary forces that suggest the possibility of urban fields are irreversible; what we make of them is our choice," they asserted (Friedmann and Miller 1965, p.319).

But potential gains would outweigh losses only if the prospects for planning for housing, infrastructure, services and recreation on the scale of urban fields were grasped and backed by the assembly of the requisite information for plan-making. State governments, in particular, would initially take the key responsibility for the development of urban fields, in collaboration with other levels of government and with what are now termed "stakeholders": "The formulation of a regional development plan in joint consultation with all the relevant parties will be necessary to provide the common framework for decisions" (ibid.).

The urban field concept prefigured a more recent discussion in the last 15 years or so on what Ed Soja describes as "regional urbanization"—a process within metropolitan areas which "is erasing the once fairly easily identifiable boundary between urban and suburban and…between urban and rural, city and countryside" (2015, p.374).

At the wider spatial scale that exists beyond the (now polycentric) city-region, the regional model takes the form of "extended regional urbanization"—categorized in such terms as the extended or expansive urban region, megaregions, and regional corridors, amongst others (Soja 2015, p.376). In both these distinct urban-regional configurations, Soja argues, "Never before has the necessity for effective regional governance and planning been so great" (p.379).

I turn now from mid-1960s America to contemporary Nigeria.[1] Some 47 to 48 percent of the country's estimated population of 180 million lives in urban areas. It is broadly agreed that the urban population has increased rapidly over the past 50 years—at an estimated rate of at least 4.5 percent in the last five years—and will continue to grow rapidly in the coming decades, likely doubling within the next 30 years, and perhaps even sooner.

The preliminary research I have done with colleagues under the Urbanisation Research Nigeria (URN) program indicates that the underlying cause of rapid urban population growth—and the urban expansion which accompanies it—is demographic growth based on declining mortality and persistently high fertility. Natural increase plays a significant (and possibly dominant) role in producing urban population growth.

This is an important finding. Rural–urban migration certainly contributes to urban growth and plays an important role in the urbanization of the country (as the urban proportion of total population). But its role has likely been overstated in Nigeria, and indeed in sub-Saharan Africa more generally. The significance of both urban natural increase and of reclassification due to rural densification have not been properly acknowledged by policy-makers.

In recent years, there has been an increase in settlements reclassified from "rural" to "urban" using different population size definitions, both above 10,000 and above 20,000 inhabitants. These "emerging" towns and cities have lower building and population densities than older, established urban settlements, and contribute to urban expansion alongside the ongoing enlargement of existing urban boundaries. Both these kinds of expansions have coalesced into new urban settlement forms.

At the national scale, urban spatial expansion has been concentrated around four massive urban agglomerations:

- A northern agglomeration centered on Kano, which has a north–south axis running from Katsina to Zaria and beyond to Kaduna, and an east–west axis running roughly from Funtua in southwestern Katsina State to Hadejia in eastern Jigawa State.
- A southwestern agglomeration stretching from Lagos northwards to Ilorin, the capital of Kwara State, and eastwards to Akure, the capital of Ondo State.
- A southeastern agglomeration within a roughly square zone encompassing Benin City, Port Harcourt, Calabar and Enugu.
- An emergent central agglomeration running from Abuja in the southwest to Jos in the northeast.

These agglomerations do not always represent continuously built-up areas, but rather networks of cities, towns and rural settlements of varying sizes linked by roads, which include national highway corridors. The northern agglomeration around Kano ranks among the top five most rapidly expanding urbanized regions in Africa and is forecast to experience the most rapid urban expansion in coming decades (Seto et al. 2012).

As our team considered how to name and visualize these agglomerations, we looked at the range of commonly used terms mentioned above before settling on Friedmann and Miller's overarching concept of the urban field. The term also effectively captured the trend Professor Akin Mabogunje described in his path-breaking book *Urbanization in Nigeria* (1968), which foreshadowed the current process of extended regional urbanization in the country:

> the prospect of future urbanization in Nigeria is likely to be the emergence of a few centres of spectacular agglomeration of population comprising the merging together of a number of relatively contiguous cities, towns and villages. It is possible to surmise three axial belts where such development can be expected...between Lagos and Ibadan in the west, between Aba and Port Harcourt in the east and between Kano and Kaduna in the north.
>
> (Mabogunje 1968, p.322)

The term "conurbation" is also helpful: an urbanized region made up of metropolitan areas, secondary cities, large towns, and other urban areas, often anchored by a predominant metropolitan center (like Lagos or Kano). Through urban population growth and urban spatial expansion, these settlements join together to form an extended urban field.

The figure below draws on a combination of satellite imagery and population density data to map these spatial formations. It illustrates population density in 2014 according to the WorldPop database, which offers the most fine-grained detail and incorporates de facto built-up area estimates from satellite data and population data from the 2006 Nigerian census (see Figure 6.1).

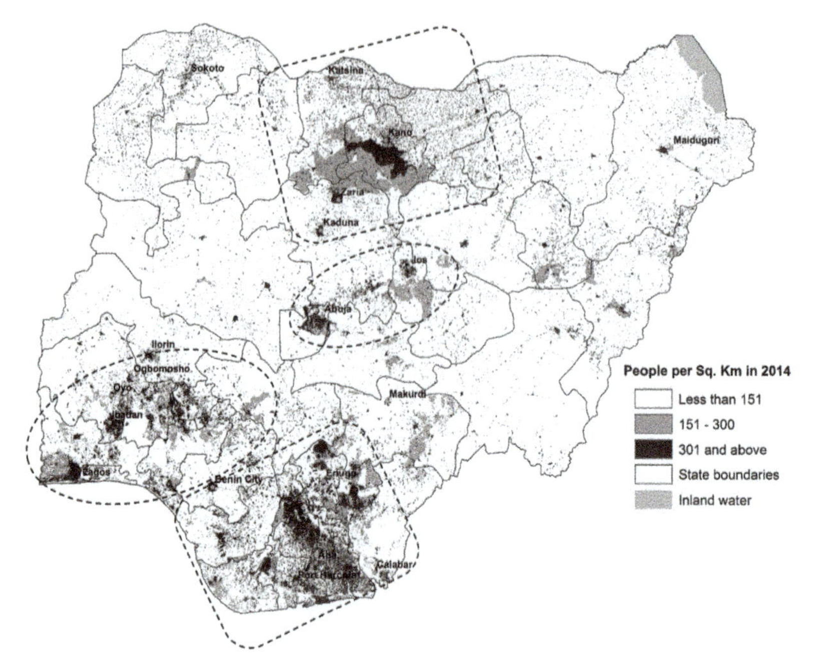

Figure 6.1 Nigeria: people per square kilometer in 2014
Bloch et al. 2015, p.15

While this is the most rigorous geospatial dataset currently available, there is some suggestion that it underestimates urban population densities and overestimates rural population densities (Rose & Bright 2014). Even so, it confirms the general pattern of four zones of concentrated urban expansion.

At the narrower city-regional scale, we identified multi-faceted, highly dynamic spatial entities. Cities such as Lagos, Ibadan, Kano, Port Harcourt and Kaduna are assemblages which now combine the traditional core city and its residential, commercial and industrial zones with new peripheral suburban and periurban areas. The new periphery contains a wide range of new economic functions and social activities such as space-extensive manufacturing, warehousing, and transportation facilities, as well as large-scale planned communities and stand-alone apartment and single-family housing complexes for Nigeria's growing urban middle class.

The dispersal of both population and economic activity within such increasingly low-density metropolitan areas is also resulting in the emergence of new centers of activity which hold commanding functions for adjacent residential areas—as well as for the city and its region. A formerly residential suburb like Jabi in Abuja and the suburbs of Lagos's Lekki Peninsula now feature business services (offices), retail (shopping malls) and accommodation (hotels and guesthouses) that serve the immediate area and, progressively, the wider city. This process is transforming the spatial organization of socio-economic activity: with the appearance of these new functions, the urban form is evolving in a polycentric fashion.

The remaking of urban functions and boundaries at the city-region level and the emergence of new, unprecedented scales of urbanization in the form of complex urban fields have major implications for urban politics, governance and planning.

Urban expansion concentrates on the periphery and the urban edge is constantly redefined (Bloch 2015; Mabin et al. 2013). As urban frontiers push relentlessly ahead in a number of directions, something like moving weather fronts, the better planning and management of urban growth and expansion becomes more urgent. In "The Urban Field," Friedmann and Miller wrote of the need for "an adequate framework of information" (1965, p.318) that would be required for public policy-making. The URN program is now investigating the urban expansion process critically and in greater depth to inform and influence such policy-making for Nigeria's urban fields where it is feasible—for, as Friedmann usefully reminds us, "painstaking empirical research is not necessarily a high road to policy innovations, which, in the end, are political, not scientific matters" (2002a, p.167).

Such policy then needs to guide and encourage *action* through planning processes that are, of their nature, political: to develop the plans and the investment programs to provide and to improve housing, infrastructure, municipal services, transportation and economic opportunities for a burgeoning and largely poor urban population in city-regions and expanding urban fields.

Our research to date indicates that a key issue for better policy and planning is a fuller understanding of the increasing mismatch between the land which is occupied as urban frontiers move forward, and the existing political and administrative boundaries of the 774 Nigerian local government areas (LGAs). Urban expansion is not constrained within local government limits but overlaps or spills over between LGAs—or even across the boundaries of the 36 federal states.

In Nigeria's federal system, local governments and their elected councils are created by state legislation and endorsed by the national assembly. There is no distinction between urban and rural councils; no city-level authorities exist as such. Local governments are subordinate to state government ministries—and, further, are often the creatures of influential state governors and their energetic, patronage-dispensing political machines. As urban frontiers advance and already vast urban fields widen and thicken, state governments and governors emerge as key actors in the strategic and highly politicized policy and planning activities that potentially offer "great opportunities" to counter the cruel inequalities that mark Nigeria's urbanization and urban expansion.

Conclusion: two requirements for action

My example of the moving urban frontier shows how useful Friedmann's concept of the urban field has been for us in identifying and then further developing analytical constructs to investigate the spatial dimensions, structure and workings of the enlarged settlement forms that characterize rapid urbanization in today's Nigeria.

Our ongoing research addresses a number of topics: the political and administrative structures that characterize expanding city-regions and "cross-border" urban fields; the politics of city-building on the new peripheries; and state and local government responsibilities for municipal finance, housing and providing services such as water, sanitation, solid waste, green space, schools, hospitals and clinics.

This research will support urban and regional policy, plan making and institutional reform, and also encourage the allocation of funds targeted at improving what are, for most residents, very poor conditions.

There are two critical issues arising from Friedmann's early work that are relevant to such contemporary planning practice.

The first concerns learning the lessons from planning processes—or, for that matter, research initiatives. Friedmann, to my knowledge, did not much discuss his practical experience in formulating or implementing plans—and what could be derived from them to assist planners to improve their ways of acting.

Nonetheless, in *Regional Development Policy* (1966), Friedmann posed the right question: "The rules under which one may pursue philosophical or scientific truth are well established; but what are the requirements for action?" (p.255). His answer came in the form of seven suggestive "rules for successful problem-solving" (ibid.). These are quoted below—for emphasis, in the text box format characteristic of planning reports (see Box 6.1)—and are a reminder for further thinking on a topic that remains too little explored: analysis of how and why practical planning (or implementation) experiences work (or do not work) is indispensable for improving planning practice—and theory.

Box 6.1 A practical planner's wisdom

1. Learn to live with an imperfect world that is perfectible in the part only, never in the whole.
2. Learn to appreciate that some improvement is better than none at all.
3. Do not try for symmetry in the design of solutions: tailor solutions to local circumstances and needs.
4. Do not attempt to solve all problems at once; do not even try to understand them all; you will find yourself plumbing a bottomless pit. Concentrate on the truly important things first. Some problems may vanish if you leave them alone.
5. Proceed stepwise, incrementally, along the path of least resistance: among the important things to do, turn first to those that are easy to solve.

6. Do not be overly concerned with overlapping functions, fuzzy boundaries, conflicting jurisdictions. Some redundancy may be worthwhile, uncertainty makes one proceed with caution, competition is also a problem-solving device.
7. Step back occasionally to regard your handiwork: assess the total situation with a keen, objective eye, divine the changes in values that have occurred, if necessary redefine your problem, clarify your objectives, critically review your strategy and tactics.

(Friedmann 1966, pp.255–56)

The second issue is to address what is perhaps the largest inconsistency in Friedmann's work, namely the role of the state in planning. In the second half of his career, he appeared to move decisively away from planning by, with or through the state (and the national state in particular) by counter posing it to what were seen as the more innovative planning modalities that arose from civil society and its institutions. He referred often to a shift away from "state-centric planning" to a more desirable process conducted by "citizen-planners" (Friedmann 2011, p.xii). At the same time, though, and specifically while discussing city regions, Friedmann also argued that the state, particularly its local variant, needed to ensure that a democratic consensus on sustainable territorial development be reached by its citizens (Friedmann 2002a, p.31).

As seen above, Friedmann, as a pragmatist, encouraged an embrace of the dialectics of what he called both/and. He rejected either/or choices, and acknowledged the necessity for planners to "live with contradictions" (2002b, p.148). When it comes, however, to prescribing the state's role in planning, he fluctuates between either/or and both/and—with the stronger positioning on the either/or side.

In day-to-day planning practice, though, this inconsistency cannot stand, and requires continual resolution if any of Friedmann's requirements for action are actually to be met. If planning is intrinsically political (and it is!), then an understanding of and reckoning with the state's place, powers, interests and, indeed, internal contradictions, within the contexts of any planning initiative or process—which will always involve a variety of conflicting interests—is a necessity, rather than an option.

Planning practice, then, is a *both* (the state)/*and* (civil society) (or vice versa), rather than an *either/or* proposition. Moreover, an effective, properly resourced state is essential—not least at the local or city-regional level—to address the challenges that global urbanization and its changing spatial forms bring to planning practice. Friedmann's ambiguous conceptualization of the state needs fundamental reconsideration so that it better reflects current political realities for practitioners who will certainly need to work within (and alongside) state authorities and agencies both to plan and to resource better today and tomorrow's city-regions and urban fields—in Nigeria, as elsewhere.

That I am now able to make this assertion, in 2016, is further testimony to John Friedmann's wide-ranging and enduring influence on how we think about and how we conduct planning practice.

Note

1 This account of recent urban growth and urban expansion is drawn from Bloch et al. 2015. For more information on the URN program and its reports, see the website http://urn.icfwebservices.com/.

References

Bloch, R 2015, "Africa's new suburbs" in *Suburban Governance: A Global View*, eds P Hamel & R Keil, University of Toronto Press, Toronto, pp. 253–277.

Bloch, R, Fox, S, Monroy, J & Ojo, A 2015, *Urbanisation and Urban Expansion in Nigeria*, Urbanisation Research Nigeria Program. Unpublished report available from <http://urn.icfwebservices.com/> [28 December 2015].

Friedmann, J 1966, *Regional Development Policy: A Case Study of Venezuela*, MIT Press, Cambridge, M.A.

Friedmann, J 2002a, *The Prospect of Cities*, University of Minnesota Press, Minneapolis.

Friedmann, J 2002b, "A life in planning", in *The Prospect of Cities*, University of Minnesota Press, Minneapolis, pp. 119–158.

Friedmann, J 2011, *Insurgencies: Essays in Planning Theory*, Routledge, London.

Friedmann, J & Miller, J 1965, "The urban field", *Journal of the American Institute of Planners*, 31(4): 312–320.

Friedmann, J & Weaver, C 1979, *Territory and Function: The Evolution of Regional Planning*, University of California Press, Berkeley.

Gore, C 1985, *Regions in Question: Space, Development Theory and Regional Policy*, Methuen, London.

Mabin, A, Butcher, S & Bloch, R 2013, "Peripheries, suburbanisms and change in sub-Saharan African cities", *Social Dynamics*, 39(2): 167–190.

Mabogunje, AL 1968, *Urbanization in Nigeria*, University of London Press, London.

Rose, A & Bright, E 2014, *The Landscan Global Population Distribution Project: Current State of the Art and Prospective Innovation*, Population Association of America 2014 Annual General Meeting. Available from <http://paa2014.princeton.edu/abstracts/143242> [28 December 2015].

Seto, KC, Güneralp, B & Hutyra, LR 2012, "Global forecasts of urban expansion to 2030 and direct impacts on biodiversity and carbon pools", *Proceedings of the National Academy of Sciences*, 109(40): 16083–16088.

Soja, E 2015, "Accentuate the regional", *International Journal of Urban and Regional Research*, 39(2): 372–381.

United Nations, Department of Economic and Social Affairs, Population Division 2014, *World Urbanization Prospects: The 2014 Revision, Highlights* (ST/ESA/SER.A/352).

World Bank 2009, *World Development Report 2009: Reshaping Economic Geography*, The World Bank, Washington, D.C.

7 Periphery, borders and regional development

Chung-Tong Wu

Introduction

In one of his major contributions to the regional development literature, *Regional Development Policy: A Case Study of Venezuela*, John Friedmann developed his core-periphery model (Friedmann 1966) which was subsequently elaborated in other publications including his book on urbanization and national development (Friedmann 1973). In the 1970s and 1980s, the concepts underlying the core-periphery model and the implied regional development strategies were adapted to the idea of growth poles/growth centres for regional development. Scholars and politicians alike embraced both the strategy of regional development and the terminology of growth poles. These concepts were successively adapted to development strategies based on export process zones or the now popular terminology of special economic zones. More recently, the centre-periphery concept was extended to the notion of 'peripherality' by researchers studying European regional and cross-border development (Copus 2001; Crone 2012). Several decades later, Friedmann, reflecting on development planning, commented that too many policy-makers thought just designating a region for growth was sufficient for development to take place. For Friedmann, development planning is a learning process, and *who* learns *what* is one of the crucial aspects of development planning (Friedmann 2009).

Friedmann's core-periphery model was conceived largely in a national context. The term periphery was used in the sense of backward regions, or ones that are dependent on other regions. The periphery also refers to the region's geographic location relative to the rest of the country. The more challenging cases are those that are dependent, underdeveloped and remote from the economic and population centres of the country. In this essay, the term periphery refers to regions geographically remote, economically dependent and lacking political autonomy. With few exceptions, the geographic periphery of one nation usually borders one or more neighbours. In such cases, the development of one nation's periphery can have implications on the periphery of another by design or by circumstances. With few exceptions, these neighbouring regions are also dependent peripheries. Formulating development policies for what might be called double-periphery is that much more demanding. This essay utilizes examples of cross-border regions to explore the complexities of double-periphery and the main elements that need to be considered for their development.

The periphery is often imagined only as a recipient of development projects and as a location of new public and private investments. Seldom are they involved as participants in formulating the projects. Friedmann (1973) noted the core regions tend to control decisions affecting the periphery (p.74). In countries as diverse as Myanmar, Russia and China, the development problems of the periphery are no less critical today than the period when Friedmann conducted his research in Venezuela (United Nations Development Programme Russia 2007; European Commission 2010). In many countries, regional inequalities have not diminished and nowhere is this more obvious than in China. After four decades of phenomenal economic growth, China is recognizing the deep divide between the economically advanced eastern region and parts of the central region, with the rest of the country. Since the 2000s, China has implemented 'opening the West' and 'renewing the Northeast old Industrial Zones' strategies to develop its periphery. China's border economic cooperation zones (BECZ) are part of these development strategies. This essay compares the relevant characteristics of the periphery with the program's premises to highlight the need for in-depth understanding of the periphery.

China's BECZ

The economic success of China began with decisive steps to establish four 'special economic zones' (SEZs) in late 1977 (Yeung et al. 2009). While the coastal economic development of China, spearheaded first by the SEZs and quickly followed by the 14 'coastal open cities', attracts the lion's share of attention, scant notice has been paid to the 16 nationally designated border development zones. These are the 'border economic development zones' (BECZs) or 'cross-border economic cooperation zones' located in the provinces of Nei Mongol, Heilongjiang, Jilin, Liaoning, Guangxi, Yunnan and Xinjiang at border crossings with six of China's neighbours (Table 7.1). The majority of these zones were first designated by the State Council in early or mid-1992. In spite of a flurry of media reports in 2010 and early 2011 on the progress of these zones and new zones designated in 2013, there is very limited information on their state of development.

There are important reasons for paying attention to the development of these zones. First, for several decades now, the BECZs represent an important element of China's regional development policies and, more recently, an integral part of its investments abroad strategy (Luo 2012). In August 2010 the Chinese government, in renewing its 'Greater West' development strategy, committed to fast tracking the development of border regions (State Council People's Republic of China 2010; Wei 2010). In line with the above

Table 7.1 China's border economic cooperation zones: locations and neighbouring countries

Province	*BECZ*	*Neighbouring country*
Nei Mongolia	Erlianhaote Manzhouli	Mongolia Mongolia
Heilongjiang	Heihe Suifenhe	Russia (Blagoveshchensk) Russia
Jilin	Hunchun	Russia & N Korea
Liaoning	Dandong	N Korea
Guangxi	Dong Xing Pingxiang	Vietnam Vietnam
Yunnan	Hekou Wanding Ruili Lincang (2013)	Vietnam Vietnam Myanmar (Muse) Myanmar
Xinjiang	Yining/Khorgos Bole Tacheng Kashgar (2011)	Kazakhstan Kazakhstan Kazakhstan Kazakhstan/Tajikistan

strategies, China announced policies to uplift its economically backward regions, and all of the BECZs are located in such regions. New BECZs announced in 2011 and 2013 signal the national government's renewed interest in these zones and their potential. Second, most of these zones are in geopolitically sensitive locations that are crucial to energy and resource supplies and for access to major transcontinental routes. China's recent promotion of the 'new Silk Road' (One Belt One Road) is an outcome of this deepening awareness (Tiezzi 2014). Third, China and the neighbours next to the BECZs are all in varying stages of transition. Understanding the development process of these border zones has potential lessons for similar zones being developed elsewhere. Fourth, multilateral organizations such as the Asian Development Bank promote development through 'economic corridors' that span the borders of Southeast Asian nations (Asian Development Bank 2010). Cross-border development of peripheral regions is therefore a current strategy deserving close scrutiny.

Previous studies have noted that even with limited available data, it is obvious the BECZs have not lived up to expectations (Wu 2011). First, BECZs have not performed nearly as well as the SEZs at similar stages of implementation. Second, their lacklustre performance is chiefly due to unclear goals and objectives, multiple and potentially conflicting programs and inherent locational constraints. Third, the BECZ program failed to consider neighbouring countries' complex cultural, historical, political and economic concerns.

The 16 BECZs are located at or near ports of entry with neighbouring countries on trade routes, such as the historic Silk Road. Other locations are where convenient crossings can be established in hilly terrains and where strong cultural and ethnic ties mean frequent crossings are part of daily life (Buursink 2001). Consequently, history, geography, cultural ties, national sovereignty and geopolitics exert influences on the economic development of the border regions. These locations are also far from the core economic regions of China but none of these factors seems to have mattered when the BECZs were assigned into three development types: industrial zones (Hunchun, Heihe, Ruili, Hekou, Pingxiang, Dongxing and Dandong), industrial and trade zones (Suifenhe, Yining, Tacheng and Bole) and trade zone (Erlinhaote) (China Academy of Urban Planning and Design 1994).

Three premises underpinning this top-down approach can be deduced. First, cooperation from the relevant regional government and from the neighbouring country's relevant regional authorities will be forthcoming. Second, like the SEZs, the foundation of the program is industrialization, specifically export-oriented industrialization. Trade is considered useful but secondary to industrialization. Third, the BECZs are expected to be beachheads for China's development initiatives such as securing energy supplies and investments abroad.

Two illustrative cases

To contrast the diversity and complexity of the periphery, I will discuss one case each from the far north and southwest Chinese border regions. The first is the case of Heihe (Heilongjiang Province) and Blagoveshchensk (Amur Oblast, Russia), and the second is Ruili (Yunnan Province) and Muse (Shan State, Myanmar).

Situated 880 metres across the Heilongjiang (Amur River), Heihe and Blagoveshchensk have mooted the construction of a road and rail bridge to link together the two cities since 1988 (Urbansky 2012). These discussions started soon after the 1984 visit of the then General Secretary of the Chinese Communist Party, Hu Yaobang, who declared that Heihe would become the 'Shenzhen of the north' (Poole 1994). On numerous occasions, the Heihe government unveiled plans and announcements about the bridge but to no avail. Implementation of visa-free entry for Russians from July 1999, however, sparked a constant flood of Russian shuttle traders crossing the border to obtain goods for resale in other parts of Russia. Border trade between the two cities has continued to blossom. Prior to the devaluation of the Russian rouble in 2014, an average of over 2,000 Russians visited Heihe daily to shop and enjoy themselves. Chinese have also invested in small businesses in Blagoveshchensk and in larger agriculture and resource projects in the region beyond. Neither the Russian nor the Amur government reciprocated these initiatives. For example, it was not until early 2014 that Russia and China agreed to synchronize the opening hours of the border custom offices at the Heihe–Blagoveshchensk border.

Ruili and Muse are located across a narrow river marking the border between China and Myanmar. Muse is the border town at the main trade route to China leading to the business and trade centre of Mandalay, the second largest city in Myanmar. Trade between China and Myanmar prospered during the decades of military rule in Myanmar partly due to sanctions imposed by the West. Since the start of reforms of 2012 in Myanmar, trade has flourished and investments in Muse have responded accordingly. Since cross-border trade is regarded as a positive contribution to the economic well-being of both sides, China and Myanmar have instituted a border identity card system to facilitate the daily movement of their citizens across the border.

Several characteristics of the two case studies challenge the three premises of the BECZ program. The premise of assumed cooperation of the peripheral region and its cross border counterpart is tested by dissonance between the regions and the national governments and the obstacles posed by ethnic and cultural groups. The program design, based on industrialization, is challenged by the lack of infrastructure and preconditions for industrialization as well as the lack of local capacity for development. The expected benefits of economic interactions are confronted by the suspicions engendered by vast economic disparities across the border and the divergent expectations of cross-border interactions.

Policy conflicts between regional/local governments and the central government

Regional governments in peripheral locations often have regional interests that are inconsistent with those of the national government. Entrenched regional interests have the ability to upset the implementation of national policies. At the same time, what regional interests may desire could be frustrated by central government inaction.

The failure to build the bridge between Heihe and Blagoveshchensk, after over 30 years of intermittent discussions, is a prime example and symbolic of the mismatch of interest between the Russian government and the Amur Oblast government. The lack of funding from Moscow to support the Russian portion of the bridge is frustrating for the Amur government and a constant reminder of its dependent relationship with Moscow.

On the other hand, the Amur regional government managed to delay the implementation of central government policies allowing foreign ownership of agriculture land and the signing of economic cooperation agreements by citing border security concerns (Jack 2002; Wishnick 2009).

Ethnic diversity and local autonomy

Peripheral regions are often the home of ethnic groups with long historic and cultural ties that span the borders. In the Myanmar–China border regions, Myanmar ethnic groups feel their needs and aspirations are ignored by the government, compounding a sense of dependency and resentment sometimes expressed in armed conflicts.

Yunnan Province, which borders Myanmar and Vietnam, is the location of four BECZs. The province has eight autonomous Prefectures where many ethnic minorities reside. The mountainous regions between Yunnan, China and Myanmar is home to a number of ethnic groups who have a shared culture and who reside in the border regions and cross the border as part of their daily lives (Schoenberger & Turner 2008). Some 20 armed ethnic groups are active in the peripheral regions of Myanmar since independence from British colonial rule in 1948. Ethnic groups in Myanmar demand control over the resources located in their regions and recognition for their culture and languages. In the ethnic-dominated peripheral regions of Myanmar, the government's attempt to extend state control through appeasement of regional armed groups has developed what is called 'ceasefire capitalism', criticized for enriching only the powerful and entrenching corruption (Woods 2011). Since much of the resources are exported to China, ethnic armed group interests, state control and cross-border trade are often conflated.

Inappropriate program design

The BECZs were chiefly modelled on the SEZs. This premise is symptomatic of a central planning approach that lacks understanding of the particular peripheral region and fails to consult with the regional governments. The BECZs ignored the lack of infrastructure and skilled labour required for industrialization. The current approach is still based on industrialization through the establishment of industrial zones but they are lacklustre compared to the booming trade and tourism sectors. The drive for industrialization, however, persists. In 2013, the Heihe government announced another industrial zone, a Russia–China High Tech Zone, but it is unclear what industries would be located there. Heihe imports electricity from Amur to support its industries, which could have the potential for further cooperation but instead has created further conflicts about supply and pricing.

Heihe's infrastructure was unprepared for any major economic development. Rail service to Heihe was resumed in 1989 but its airport was incapable of taking jets such as the Boeing 737 until 2003. Its national highway link is now complete but the regional roads linking to the highway are extremely poor. In 2000, Japanese aid funding was allocated to make the roads safe for all weather conditions (Japan International Cooperation Agency 2001). Failure to build the bridge means that in the summer months passenger traffic is served by hydrofoils. In winter, when the river is frozen, a temporary bridge over the ice allows traffic to pass. None of the above solve the fundamental transport problem hampering closer economic ties.

Local capacity for development

Cross-border trade has become a means of incubating local entrepreneurship and a means for local small businesses to take advantage of nascent development opportunities. More recent policies for the new BECZs recognize the role of trade as part of the development strategy.

In spite of the lack of convenient cross-river transportation, trade and tourism have flourished in Heihe chiefly based on the fact that to the Russians, Chinese goods are of better quality and much cheaper, and the services they get are superior. Consequently, many Chinese entrepreneurs in Heihe (chiefly immigrants from other parts of the province or elsewhere in China) have established small businesses and hotels to cater to the needs of the Russian traders and tourists. Over the years, facilitated by the establishment of a free-trade zone in the city core, the economies of Heihe and Blagoveshchensk have developed close consumption linkages, initially through shuttle trade but more recently expanded to Heihe becoming a tourist destination for Russians in the Far East (Mikhailova & Wu 2015).

For both Russia and Myanmar, access to inexpensive consumer goods from China is a key attraction. Both countries and their respective border regions rely on this supply to satisfy local demands as well as helping to keep the cost of living down. In the case of Blagoveshchensk, the thriving cross-border trade and the intransigence of the Russian government with regard to regulations of foreign enterprises and investments have encouraged the existence of a thriving grey market (Holzlehner 2007; Ryzhova 2008). The grey market and the ecosystem that grew alongside benefits some officials and their collaborators but it has become an obstacle to economic development based on legitimate foreign investments from responsible businesses.

For Myanmar, the flow of trade via Muse and other border towns is a significant part of the national and regional economy reaching well beyond the border region. To facilitate border trade, the Chinese government has extended the rail network to Ruili across the border from Muse, Myanmar. Indeed the cross-border trade through Ruili–Muse constitutes 60% of Myanmar's national cross-border trade in value. Since Muse is in a relatively remote location, its road link to the central Myanmar city of Mandalay helps to reinforce the latter's role as the premier trade centre and the location of much Chinese investment.

Divergent expectations of economic interactions

Heihe officials make no bones about their aim to export to Russia and beyond. For China, the Russian Far East is merely the start of a Europe land bridge. One of the premises of the BECZ is providing a platform for China's policies of investing abroad and reclaiming its historic role as a dominant trade and investment nation in its region. This is illustrated by Heihe's announced intention of establishing a car parts industrial zone aimed at exporting to Western Russia and Europe. Heihe also encourages Chinese investors to exploit the resources of the Russian Far East for Chinese industries. There has never been any emphasis on co-development, of jointly establishing industries or development projects that lead to the expansion and deepening of both regional economies – as the name 'economic cooperation zone' may imply. On the contrary, the Russians (both national and regional governments) expect Chinese investments to expand local employment and development of its regional economy. Since the Chinese developments require energy supply from Russia, the latter has been slow to cooperate with industrial development located only in Heihe. At the same time, the officials in Blagoveshchensk have been overwhelmed by the deluge of proposals from Heihe which they feel will only benefit Heihe. They would rather develop more projects of their own choosing to benefit Blagoveshchensk (Mikhailova & Wu 2015).

Disparities in economic power

China's economic ascendancy has elicited increasingly wary responses from its neighbours. Whereas in the 1990s its neighbours may have regarded the BECZ initiatives positively, they are presently much more cautious and concerned about domination by the Chinese. There are fundamental differences in the economic relations between the two sets of cross-border regions. For Russia, Heihe is a low-cost location and a source of inexpensive consumer goods and low-cost labour. Chinese investors tend to regard Russian labour as expensive and unreliable, so they press for more generous labour import permits. Vast disparity of economic development and population density are sometimes exploited by the Amur officials as excuses to limit the import of Chinese labour, enforce complicated business registration regulations, impose strict regulations on Chinese traders and be uncooperative with land leases.

In contrast, for Chinese investors, Myanmar is the passageway to the Indian Ocean and beyond, a source of low-cost labour and a low-cost location for investment and much needed energy and mineral resources. A Chinese built and operated oil and gas pipeline, starting at the Myanmar port of Sittwe on the Indian Ocean, traverses the country into Yunnan, but it provides no benefit to any of the regions that it passes. The Myanmar government, until very recently entirely reliant on China and its investors, had been compliant about resource exploitation and investment in large schemes such as mining and hydroelectricity generation. But this situation has changed since 2012 as the Myanmar government and NGOs seek to review agreements to build hydroelectricity and mining projects such as the Myitsone Dam which is part of a seven-dam cascade in Kachin State and temporarily halted the Latpadaung copper mine in Saigang Region.

Conclusion

The BECZ program ignored the special circumstances of the periphery regions and was unprepared for the complexities of the double-periphery. It represented a top-down development approach understandable in the context of 1990s China, but no longer appropriate to the contemporary dynamics of border regions. The limited success that has been eked out after several decades of implementation is confined to trade and tourism, though recent implementations have started to incorporate logistics and border trade as central features.

Friedmann's earlier work on the core-periphery model remains a valuable tool to understand relationships of spatial dependence and the causes of regional inequalities within nation-states. It provides a framework to investigate what is required for equitable and sustainable development in the periphery. But this model becomes complicated when it has to take into account adjoining peripheries of two or more nation-states. Such situations are increasingly prevalent in cross-border developments as the global economy becomes more intertwined and nations regard economic connections as preferable to isolation.

The case studies in this essay illustrate some of the multi-dimensional issues that can be found at the double-periphery of China and its neighbouring countries. They highlight the particularly contested and fraught circumstances of remote and dependent regions at the borders of nations undergoing mismatched phases of social, economic and political transition. One of the few successful examples of double-periphery development between Finland and Russia is based on local knowledge, cross-border dialogue and cultural interactions (Eskelinen et al. 2013). These dimensions need to be the focus of substantial in-depth research and action for the development of double-peripheries between China and its neighbouring countries.

As Friedmann noted, 'more than a knowledge of purely economic relations is required to understand the process of regional development' (1966, p.37). The case studies presented here reinforce his observation that development planning is not just about designating a location or even designing a program for development. It is about learning the local needs, expectations, capacities and circumstances in order to jointly design programs that promote local entrepreneurship, creativity and networks to support inclusive, equitable and sustainable development.

References

Asian Development Bank 2010, *Strategy and Action Plan for the Greater Mekong Subregion East-West Economic Corridor*, ADB, Manila.

Buursink, J 2001, 'The binational reality of border-crossing cities', *GeoJournal*, 54(1): 7–19.

China Academy of Urban Planning and Design 1994, *Zhongguo Ludi Bianjing Diqu Chengzhan Kaifa e Guihua Yanjiu* (Research on the Development and Planning of Cities and Towns in the Land Border Regions of China). (In Chinese). Academy of Urban Planning and Design, Beijing, China.

Copus, AK 2001, 'From core-periphery to polycentric development: concepts of spatial and aspatial peripherality', *European Planning Studies*, 9(4): 539–552.

Crone, M 2012, 'Re-thinking "peripherality" in a knowledge-intensive service-dominated economy', in *Regional Development in Northern Europe: Peripherality, Marginality and Border Issues*, eds M Danson & P De Souza, Routledge, London, pp. 49–64.

Eskelinen, H, Liikanen, I & Scott, JW (eds) 2013, *The EU-Russia Borderland: New Contexts for Regional Cooperation*, Routledge, London.

European Commission 2010, *Investing in Europe's Future: Fifth Report on Economic, Social and Territorial Cohesion*, European Union, Brussels.

Friedmann, J 1966, *Regional Development Policy: A Case Study of Venezuela*, MIT Press, Cambridge, M.A.

Friedmann, J 1973, *Urbanization, Planning, and National Development*, Sage, Beverly Hills.

Friedmann, J 2009, 'Encounters with development planning', *International Development Planning Review*, 31(2): 117–126.

Holzlehner, T 2007, 'The harder the rain, the tighter the roof: evolution of organized crime networks in the Russian Far East', *Sibirica*, 6(2): 51–86.

Jack, A 2002, 'Russia's wary Far East begins to open up to outsiders', *Financial Times (UK)*, 13 August.

Japan International Cooperation Agency 2001, *ODA Loan Report 2001*, JICA, Tokyo.

Luo, SY 2012, 'Yunnan cross border economic cooperation zone development research', *International Economic Cooperation*, (6): 81–87.

Mikhailova, E & Wu, CT 2015, *Ersatz Twin-City Formation? The Case of Blagoveshchensk and Heihe*. Unpublished paper.

Poole, T 1994, 'Chinese set out stall for Russia: the city of Heihe', *The Independent*, 17 March.

Ryzhova, N 2008, 'Informal economy of translocations: the case of the twin city of Blagoveshensk-Heihe', *Inner Asia*, 10(2): 323–351.

Schoenberger, L & Turner, S 2008, 'Negotiating remote borderland access: small-scale trade on the Vietnam-China border', *Development and Change*, 39(4): 667–696.

State Council People's Republic of China 2010, *On Deepening the Implementation of Western Region Development Strategy*, State Council, Beijing.

Tiezzi, S 2014, 'China's "New Silk Road" vision revealed', *The Diplomat*, 4 July.

United Nations Development Programme Russia 2007, 'Russia's regions: goals, challenges, achievements', *National Human Development Report*, UNDP, Russia.

Urbansky, S 2012, 'Gaps in the fence: negotiating grassroots relations in the Sino-Soviet borderlands (1983–1993)' in *Eurasia Twenty Years After*, eds A Sengupta, S Chatterjee & S Bhattacharya, Shipra Publications, New Delhi, pp. 445–463.

Wei, HK 2010, 'Our Nation's new round of Western region development policies'. 7 September 2010. *Wei Houkai: Blog*. Available from <http://weihoukai.blog.163.com/blog/static/12223219520108751325422/> [10 February 2011].

Wishnick, E 2009, 'The securitization of Chinese migration to the Russian Far East: rhetoric and reality', in *Security and Migration in Asia: The Dynamics of Securitisation*, eds M Curley & SL Wong, Routledge, London, pp. 83–99.

Woods, K 2011, 'Ceasefire capitalism: military-private partnerships, resource concessions and military-state building in the Burma-China borderlands', *The Journal of Peasant Studies*, 38(4): 747–770.

Wu, CT 2011, 'The edges of China: dreams of cross-border development', *Cross-border Issues in the Pearl River Delta*, Zhongshan University, Guangzhou, China.

Yeung, YM, Lee, J & Kee, G 2009, 'China's special economic zones at 30', *Eurasian Geography and Economics*, 50(2): 222–240.

8 The bioregionalization of survival

Sustainability science and rooted community

Keith Pezzoli

Introduction

Much of John Friedmann's scholarly work has long grappled with value-based philosophical challenges underpinning diverse conceptions and struggles for the "Good Society." One of his early books on this subject spells out three conditions that must be met by those trying to sketch a theory of the Good Society: "a foundation in specific values must be made explicit; in the light of these values, a critical theory of reality must be devised; and a consistent set of action principles to bring about a changed reality has to be stated" (Friedmann 1979, p.xv). John has significantly advanced this line of thinking in a series of major works, including his magnum opus, *Planning in the Public Domain: From Knowledge to Action* (1987).

Friedmann (1987) fleshes out four major traditions of planning theory: social reform, policy analysis, social mobilization and social learning. His passion lies with the latter two traditions which include radical planning and practice. The central task of radical planning in complex times, Friedmann argues, is "the mediation of theory and practice in social transformation" (1987, p.391). John's advocacy for linking theory and practice, knowledge and action has had a lasting impact on my academic work. In his Foreword to my book *Human Settlements and Planning for Ecological Sustainability* (Pezzoli 2000), John writes: "[T]here are two interconnected human struggles going on in the world today that, despite their local particularities, are fundamentally the same. I refer to the struggle for a subsistence livelihood and the struggle for the life space of land and housing" (p.ix). Friedmann inspired his students to do immersive field research at the front lines of social struggle—especially where grassroots organizations are mobilized as countervailing forces for transformative development.

I've kept in touch with John ever since first linking up with him as my graduate studies advisor over three decades ago. Most recently I've interacted with John about urban agriculture in poor neighborhoods of Southeastern San Diego where I work with other researchers, land owners, nonprofit organizations and local residents in building community gardens and urban food forests on vacant land. John shares my enthusiasm for neighborhood-based work of this sort, but he is less optimistic about the potential of bioregionalism or sustainability science. I appreciate his perspective; he is not alone. Many scholars with an interest in regionalism argue that the term "bioregion" is a fuzzy concept, hard to define, too large and remote from the exigencies of daily life in neighborhoods and unknowable as an object of study. As for sustainability science, many find it to have a de-politicized technocentric emphasis, notwithstanding its call for building knowledge–action collaboration at a regional scale for sustainable development.

During his early career Friedmann identified himself as regional planner—including work at the famous Tennessee Valley Authority (TVA)—and since then has published serious contributions to the field of regional planning (Friedmann & Bloch 1990; Friedmann 2001). But as time goes on many cities of the world are expanding into sprawling megalopolitan messes, and the prospects for meaningful civic engagement in comprehensive regional planning are declining. Friedmann's (2015) most recent work thus concentrates on challenges posed by "recovering our cities, neighborhood by neighborhood" (p.9); this approach, he argues, is the most expeditious way to make our cities socially more sustainable. I agree. But at the same time a new bioregional narrative for the 21st century can bolster neighborhood struggles by embedding them in a transformative theory that speaks more broadly about socio-ecological change in the context of progressive and transformative development.

I'll argue the case here for the utility of bioregional theory and sustainability science using a handy metric that Friedmann (2008) provides in his article on the "Uses of Planning Theory." John identifies three ways that planning theory can contribute to the field of planning, including practice and education: (1) articulate a deeply considered humanist philosophy for planning attuned to practice; (2) adapt planning practices to their real-world constraints with regard to scale, complexity, and time; and (3) translate knowledge and ideas generated in other fields into the domain of planning (p.247).

Bioregional theory, justice and imagination

Two of the earliest proponents of bioregionalism in the US define the term "bioregion" as follows: "The term refers both to geographical terrain and a terrain of consciousness—to a place and the ideas that have developed about how to live in that place" (Berg & Dasmann 1977). A bioregion's boundary is not fixed. It takes into account factors including climate, topography, flora, fauna, soil and water together with the territory's sociocultural characteristics, economy and human settlement patterns. Bioregional theory has roots in utopian and anarchist ideas from the late 18th and early 19th century and in the call for ecological regionalism first articulated in the late 19th and early 20th century.

Thayer (2003), a widely noted bioregional activist-scholar, argues that "the bioregion is emerging as the most logical locus and scale for a sustainable, regenerative community to take root and to *take place*" (p.3). That a bioregion is a fruitful place-based organizing concept stems from the premise that "a mutually sustainable future for humans, other life-forms, and earthly systems can best be achieved by means of a spatial framework in which people live as rooted, active, participating members of a reasonably scaled, naturally bounded, ecologically defined territory, or *life-place*" (p.6). The operative terms here are "rootedness" and "attachment."

The most basic tenet of bioregional theory is that we human beings are social animals; if we are to survive as a species we need healthy relationships and secure, "rooted" attachments with one another and with the land, waters, habitat, plants and animals upon which we depend. Bioregional theory offers one way to imagine rootedness:

> By imagination we recognize with sympathy the fellow members, human and nonhuman, with whom we share our place....As imagination enables sympathy, sympathy enables affection. And it is in affection that we find the possibility of a neighborly, kind, and conserving economy.
> (Berry 2012)

People are not likely to experience affection for land or fellow human beings when they face chronic situations of displacement. People who get displaced experience what Fullilove (2004) describes as root shock: "Root shock is the traumatic stress reaction to the loss of some or all of one's emotional ecosystem. Root shock can follow natural disaster, development-induced displacement, war, and changes that play out slowly such as those that accompany gentrification" (p.11). The significance of rootedness—defined here as secure attachments to one's life place and the people associated with sustaining it—is a crucial component of bioregional theory and needs much more attention. This is especially so given the degree to which our society has become hypermobile and unrooted as the norm (the case of large-scale migratory flows of people fleeing large swaths of the earth surface that are war-torn and disaster ravaged is extreme).

Bioregional theory critiques the following four features of global urbanization as especially problematic and needing course correction: (1) global urbanization is dependent on unsustainable, resource-intensive growth that degrades the planet and fuels hyper-mobile competition among the world's burgeoning city-regions; (2) it exhibits an urban-centric bias that largely disregards (undervalues) the rural, wildland and hinterland realities upon which the urban is inextricably dependent; (3) it institutionalizes a culture of disconnect that divides nature from the city; and (4) it generates land use patterns, infrastructure grids and built environments that wholly transform biological and physical landscapes and waterscapes much to the detriment of the people, animals and ecosystems living there.

Countervailing measures, inspired in some places by forward-looking bioregional imagination, are emerging in response to these highly problematic trajectories. Examples of countervailing measures include: (1) community-oriented initiatives that favor localism in economic relations, job creation and resource use; (2) placement of greater value on healthy rural development and wildlands in relation to the urban and metro; (3) innovative design that couples nature and the city physically and aesthetically such that life and livelihood are meaningfully reconnected to a place's landscapes, watersheds and ecosystems literally and imaginatively; and (4) creating new participatory approaches to sustainable, resilient and just place-making that grapples with ecosystem degradation, climate change and other risks associated with human activities on a planetary scale. Countervailing measures of this sort are likely to gain strength over time.

To varying degrees, and in diverse ways, many cities, towns and regions around the world are beginning to experience what I have conceptualized as "Bioregionalization of Survival." Bioregionalization of Survival is a localization dynamic. It is fueled by a convergence of megatrends (a perfect storm) that is beginning to force changes in how we build and operate our cities, towns, and infrastructure and working landscapes/waterscapes. Bioregionalization of Survival has two main defining features: (1) a shift to increasingly endogenous (localized) strategies and means of economic development as compared to the contemporary mainstream exogenous (export-led industrialization) emphasis in economic development; and (2) an intensification in the ways local bioregional sources of natural capital (e.g., soil, water, ecosystems) and natural sinks for wastes are intentionally designed into economic systems as well as built environments for purposes of realizing sustainable and resilient development. The notion here is that society as a collective survival enterprise will necessarily become more tightly tethered to place (i.e., less wind in the sails of hypermobile capital flows circulating the earth). In the US, for instance, the concept of homeland security may take on a whole new meaning. Rather than being almost entirely preoccupied with the risks of exogenous attacks of a military or terrorist sort or domestic attacks from inside the country, more attention will likely focus on food–water–energy security risks at a bioregional scale and other complex and interlocking riskscapes tied to land and ecosystems. I am using the term "riskscape" as shorthand for the kind of emergent analytical perspective Ulrich Beck describes in the rise of what he calls the "risk society" (Beck 1992). In the risk society of the late-20th century and now 21st century, Beck observes how:

> The gain in power from techno-economic "progress" is being increasingly overshowed by the production of risks. In an early stage, these can be legitimated as "latent side effects." As they become globalized, and subject to public criticism and scientific investigation, they come, so to speak, out of the closet and achieve a central importance in social and political debates. (p.13)

Raymond De Young (2011) suggests a positive, forward-looking vision of what I am projecting as the Bioregionalization of Survival:

> as biophysical limits re-emerge, communities will shift their attention from the centrifugal forces of globalization (concentrated economic power, cheap and plentiful raw materials and energy, hyper-consumerism and displaced wastes) to the centripetal forces of localization (widely distributed leadership and authority, more sustainable use of natural energy sources and materials, personal proficiency and community self-reliance).

This is one possible outcome. But other less desirable scenarios are possible too. Ensuring that the Bioregionalization of Survival is progressive will require a vigilant and mobilized civil society armed with knowledge and the capability to put that knowledge to use securing health and wellbeing for local residents.

The Bioregionalization of Survival raises the issue of bioregional justice. Bioregional justice seeks equity and fairness in how a bioregion's assets—including nature's sources and sinks for wastes—are accessed, utilized and sustainably conserved for current and future generations. Bioregionalization of Survival will not necessarily stop people living in one bioregion from exploiting the assets of another bioregion, as currently takes place on a megascale. This raises what will likely emerge as a worldwide transbioregional governance challenge. Herein lies one of the three grand challenges that Friedmann poses for planning theorists. We need a value-based philosophy as a foundation for planning practice and governance. Without this, "we will merely drift with the mainstream, helping to build cities that are neither supportive of life nor ecologically sustainable" (Friedmann 2008, p.211).

The second and third grand challenges for planning theory, to which I turn now, are what Friedmann calls the tasks of adaptation and translation. Planning theory can help "adapt planning practices to their real-world constraints with regard to scale, complexity, and time" (Friedmann 2008, p.248). On the task of translation, Friedmann sees planning theorists

> actively engaged in mining expeditions into the universe of knowledge, on the lookout for concepts and ideas they believe to be of interest in planning education. Their specific contribution to theory is to return from these expeditions to home base and translate their discoveries into the language of planning.
>
> (Friedmann 2008, p.254)

A progressive approach to the maturing field of sustainability science, coupled with bioregional theory, has much to offer those grappling with planning theory tasks of adaptation and translation.

Sustainability science

The defining feature of sustainability science is the emphasis it places on use-inspired research, and the commitment to bridging science (the academy) to society through problem-solving in the real world, with genuine partnerships. Over the past decade an increasing number of universities have begun offering programs in sustainability science. Harvard University's Sustainability Science Program concentrates on advancing scientific understanding of human-environment systems; improving linkages between research and policy communities; and building capacity for linking knowledge with action to promote sustainability. Like *agricultural science* and *health science*, "sustainability science is a field defined by the problems it addresses rather than by the disciplines it employs" (Clark 2007, p.1737).

Infusing bioregional theory into sustainability science amplifies equity and justice concerns, giving rise to a progressive sustainability science with four defining features: (1) it embraces an integrative (transdisciplinary) approach to research that is use-inspired, problem-solving and solutions-oriented; (2) it underscores how regions are a useful scale of analysis for understanding the interaction of local and global dynamics (glocalization) in the study of place-based socio-ecological phenomena, including the coupling of human and natural systems in the (re)production of society's built environment; (3) its proponents share a commitment to creating "knowledge–action collaboratives" that bring together diverse participants in mutually supportive learning networks; and (4) it has a normative and ethical dimension that values the democratization of science and technology and what the National Research Council has called a "transition toward sustainability," improving society's capacity to use the earth in ways that simultaneously "meet the needs of a much larger but stabilizing human population, ...sustain the life support systems of the planet, and...substantially reduce hunger and poverty" (Clark 2007, p.1737).

I shift gears here to illustrate some of these ideas in action. By way of example, I describe how the Center for Sustainability Science, Planning and Design (University of California, San Diego), together with the Global Action Research Center (a nonprofit organization) and local residents in Southeastern San Diego, are advancing a model of rooted community (neighborhood) development in ways that draw upon bioregional theory and sustainability science.

Toward rooted community development

The University of California San Diego Center for Sustainability Science, Planning and Design (hereafter CSSPD) brings diverse people and organizations together to collaboratively study and improve how neighborhoods, cities and bioregions function. Our bioregional approach advances place-based concepts such as foodshed, watershed and "rooted community development."

We think of community in this context as embracing a land ethic. Aldo Leopold offers this insight:

> All ethics so far evolved rest upon a single premise: that the individual is a member of a community of interdependent parts. His instincts prompt him to compete for his place in that community, but his ethics prompt him also to co-operate (perhaps in order that there may be a place to compete for). The land ethic simply enlarges the boundaries of the community to include soils, waters, plants, and animals, or collectively: the land.
>
> (Leopold 1949, p.866)

We advocate this notion of a land ethic which is central to the concept of rooted community.

CSSPD promotes rooted community development through permaculture. Permaculture is a holistic approach that is applied from the local scale of a community garden to broader scales at the urban and regional level (town planning, trade, forestry and farming). Three ethical principles lie at the core of permaculture: care for the earth, care for people and fair share (redistribute surplus according to needs in an equitable and just fashion). Rosemary Morrow spells out the main features of the permaculture approach:

> It is a synthesis of traditional knowledge and modern science applicable in both urban and rural situations. It works with nature and takes natural systems as models to design sustainable environments that provide basic human needs in the social and economic infrastructures that support them. It encourages us, and gives us the capacity and opportunity to become a conscious part of the solutions to the many problems that face us locally and globally.
>
> (Morrow & Allsop 2006, p.5)

CSSPD's rooted community approach aims to bring out aspects of social and political rights which the liberal paradigm has neglected. As Peter Marris (1982) has observed:

> Instead of thinking about social justice only in terms of the equal treatment of equivalent units, it acknowledges the right of each community of people to a familiar habitat, like creatures in the natural world. It recognizes the attachments which bind people to each other and to places, and out of which evolve the unique meaning of each person's life.
>
> (p.121)

Likewise, drawing inspiration from another theorist who thinks in socio-ecological terms, our advocacy of rooted community development challenges "not only economic rationality but also bureaucracies, in ways that encourage political pluralism and the participation by civil society in the management of its productive and vital processes" (Leff 1993, p.63). Our approach to rooted community development calls for new forms of ecological democracy and ecopolity more aligned with the biogeophysical features of our life spaces.

Our community–university partnership pursued a series of strategic initiatives for rooted community development focused on food justice, microenterprise development, youth action networks, watershed management and green infrastructure. Much of the CSSPD's work since it started up in 2009 has focused on neighborhoods and watersheds in Southeastern San Diego and Tijuana, Mexico.

Southeastern San Diego and the Oceanview Growing Grounds

Southeastern San Diego is one of the most diverse communities in San Diego. Located to the east of downtown San Diego, it has a population of approximately 57,000 residents. Over 84% of Southeastern San Diego residents are Hispanic and 78% of the population speaks English as a second language. The community's diversity provides a rich cultural environment, but many of its households struggle financially. Its median household income of US$33,000 is approximately half of the citywide median.

The Oceanview neighborhood in Southeast San Diego consists of about 500 single-family homes with a few apartment complexes and light industry scattered throughout. The area is designated as a food desert (i.e., an area of the city where people lack access to fresh fruits and vegetables). It is also designated as an environmental justice community where poor socio-economic conditions (poverty, unemployment, crime) and pollution impact human health. Over 25% of the children are obese.

Through its partnership with the Global Action Research Center (the Global ARC), the CSSPD established long-term access to a large 20,000-square-foot vacant lot in Oceanview to set up a permaculture garden and a neighborhood-based learning center. The private landowner has leased the land to the Global ARC for $1 per year for as long as the garden continues to function. The site, now affectionately referred to by local residents as the Oceanview Growing Grounds, has two food forests, some raised garden beds and a tool shed.

Over the past three years, CSSPD researchers, local residents and community organizers at the Oceanview Growing Grounds have won a series of small and large grants to pursue permaculture and develop food forests. The most recent grant is from the University of California Office of the President as part of the Global Food Initiative, which facilitated the permaculture project. The center researchers, along with members of The Global ARC and local residents, have worked to critically analyze their activities in urban agriculture (including community gardens, urban farms, food forests, aquaculture and animal husbandry) and evaluate their potential to reduce food disparities and increase food security. The UC Global Food Initiative project was planned in three phases. Phase I involved building the foundation, i.e., securing the land, testing the soil, engaging the community, creating a vision for the garden and building relationships with the City of San Diego, the networks of community gardens, food producers, etc. Phase II deepened the engagement of the local neighborhood in the Oceanview Growing Grounds. The Initiative is now in Phase III, which requires us to lay the foundation for a Neighborhood Food Network, with the Oceanview Growing Grounds serving as a hub for food production and an environmental learning center.

So far, the activities at the Oceanview Growing Grounds offer a promising illustration of a neighborhood-based movement toward rooted community informed by bioregional theory and strengthened by sustainability science. I'll limit the lessons learned thus far at the Oceanview Growing Grounds to conclude with three observations that align with Friedmann's uses of planning theory: (1) The philosophical task: how bioregional theory informed the activities at the site and beyond; (2) The task of adaptation: the ways in which sustainability science has been brought into play; (3) The task of translation: efforts to integrate diverse knowledges to give those involved a more holistic understanding of the situation.

Conclusion

The philosophical task: Friedmann argued that we need a value-based philosophy as a foundation for planning practice. Our experience at the Oceanview Growing Grounds and all the knowledge networking and policy advocacy involved suggests that the bioregional narrative provides a good value-based philosophy based on the concepts of rootedness, attachment, permaculture and bioregional justice. The Oceanview Growing Grounds is located in a watershed containing some of the most polluted water bodies in the country (Chollas Creek and the San Diego Bay). The transformation of the vacant lot into a community garden and food forest not only constitutes vitally needed green infrastructure but provides a real context for the values of bioregionalization for survival. The modification of the site to enable stormwater harvesting, the urban food forestry, the carbon sequestration happening through composting and soil enrichment, and healthy food provisioning all provide concrete expressions of the bioregion philosophy that register at micro-, meso- and macro scales.

Tasks of adaptation and translation: Our work at the Oceanview Growing Grounds and beyond is creating: (a) cyberinfrastructure that community-based organizations can use to clarify and share their priorities for problem-solving and solutions-oriented research; (b) collaborative programs that encourage citizens, scientists, entrepreneurs and others to innovatively pool/share research-based evidence for public benefit; and (c) holistic "connect the dots" approaches to bioregional (urban–rural) sustainability and visualization that integrates otherwise fragmented efforts in the quest for justice, environmental health and good jobs. We've created a Healthy Planning Learning and Action Network (H-PLAN) to advocate for a vision called One Bioregion/One Health (Pezzoli et al. 2014). The One Bioregion/One Health narrative advances sustainability science. It interweaves the emergent discourse in urban and regional planning that focuses on the built environment in relation to health (e.g., urban design for walkability and active living, watershed management for pollution prevention) with the emergent discourse in public health and epidemiology that widens the circle of concern for human health to include human–animal–environment interactions. Together these two discourses shed light on how ecosystem integrity is vital to human as well as non-human health.

John recently referred to the work we are doing in San Diego and Tijuana in a paper titled "Urban Planning under Conditions of Hyper-complexity" (Friedmann 2014). He continues to challenge us to rethink and innovate modes of civic engagement and democratic planning. He might not be convinced of the merits of bioregional theory and sustainability science, but he certainly does recognize the challenges we face in dealing with local–regional–global scales and flows in the 21st century.

Lewis Mumford eloquently argued in *The Culture of Cities* (1938, p.348) that: "The re-animation and re-building of regions, as deliberate works of collective art, is the grand task of politics for the coming generation." In *The Prospect of Cities*, John argues that "a high priority for the century ahead is the rethinking and reconstruction of global governance, the divisions of powers and responsibilities among collective actors, the forms of networking, the territorial and nonterritorial institutions we need for a sustainable planet" (Friedmann 2002, p.17). The bioregional narrative may be one way to think about both these challenges.

References

Beck, U 1992, *Risk Society: Towards a New Modernity*, Newbury Park, London; Sage Publications, California.

Berg, P & Dasmann, R 1977, "Reinhabiting California", *Ecologist*, 7(10): 399–401.

Berry, WE 2012, "It all turns on affection". Paper presented at the National Endowment for the Humanities: 2012 Jefferson Lecture. Available from: <http://www.neh.gov/about/awards/jefferson-lecture/wendell-e-berry-lecture> [16 December 2015].

Clark, W 2007, "Sustainability science: a room of its own", *Proceedings of the National Academy of Sciences*, 104(6): 1737–1738. DOI: 10.1073/pnas.0611291104.

De Young, R 2011, *Localization: A Brief Definition* [online]. School of Natural Resources and Environment, University of Michigan. Available from: <http://localizationpapers.blogspot.com/2011/10/localization-brief-definition.html> [19 February 2016].

Friedmann, J 1979, *The Good Society*, MIT Press, Cambridge, M.A.

Friedmann, J 1987, *Planning in the Public Domain: From Knowledge to Action*, Princeton University Press, Princeton, N.J.

Friedmann, J 2001, "Regional development and planning: the story of a collaboration", *International Regional Science Review*, 24(3): 386–395.

Friedmann, J 2002, *The Prospect of Cities*, University of Minnesota Press, Minneapolis.

Friedmann, J 2008, "The uses of planning theory: a bibliographic essay", *Journal of Planning Education and Research*, 28(2): 247–257.

Friedmann, J 2014, *Urban Planning under Conditions of Hyper-complexity*, unpublished manuscript, School of Community and Regional Planning, Faculty of Applied Science, Vancouver, BC, Canada.

Friedmann, J 2015, *Neighborhood by Neighborhood: Reclaiming our Cities*. Unpublished essay. Available from: <http://www.scarp.ubc.ca/sites/scarp.ubc.ca/files/users/%5Buser%5D/profile/Reclaiming%20our%20cities%20%28new%20version%29.doc> [13 December 2015].

Friedmann, J & Bloch, R 1990, "American exceptionalism in regional planning, 1933–2001", *International Journal of Urban and Regional Research*, 14(4): 576–601.

Fullilove, MT 2004, *Root Shock: How Tearing up City Neighborhoods Hurts America, and What We Can Do About It*, One World/Ballantine Books, New York.

Leff, E 1993, "Marxism and the environmental question", *Capitalism Nature Socialism*, 4(1): 44–66.

Leopold, A 1949, *A Sand County Almanac, and Sketches Here and There*, Oxford University Press, New York.

Marris, P 1982, *Community Planning and Conceptions of Change*, Routledge & Kegan Paul, London; Boston.

Morrow, R & Allsop, R 2006, *Earth User's Guide to Permaculture*, Kangaroo Press, Pymble, New South Wales.

Mumford, L 1938, *The Culture of Cities*, Harcourt, New York.

Pezzoli, K 2000, *Human Settlements and Planning for Ecological Sustainability: The Case of Mexico City*, MIT Press, Cambridge, M.A.

Pezzoli, K, Kozo, J, Ferran, K, Wooten, W, Gomez, GR & Al-Delaimy, WK 2014, "One bioregion/one health: an integrative narrative for transboundary planning along the U.S.–Mexico border", *Global Society*, 28(4): 419–439.

Thayer, RL 2003, *Lifeplace: Bioregional Thought and Practice*, University of California Press, Berkeley.

9 Are social enterprises a radical planning challenge to neoliberal development?

Haripriya Rangan

Introduction

"How would Marx start a business today?"

My friend looked at me with surprise. "Is that a rhetorical question?" she asked, after a fraction of silence.

"It's a hypothetical I've been thinking about," I replied.

"Well," she said, with a little smile, "I hope you find the answer. There's not much by way of his business track record, is there?"

My question hadn't come out of the blue. It was five weeks or more since I'd returned from running my field-based study program on regional sustainability in the Lowveld region of Mpumalanga Province, South Africa. I'd designed and run this program in 2002 as a summer field course in geography and environmental science for both graduates and upper-level undergraduates. Eleven years on, the program was running well. The local government agencies, the community-based organisations, local academics, and activists looked forward to and actively engaged with each new group that I brought on the program. The students found the study experience intensive, grounded, confronting, but also immensely rewarding and personally transformative.

Everything seemed fine, except for one issue that came up a few times during the trip in 2013: the sustainability of the course itself.

In our conversations with members of some community-based organisations, several shared their worries about motivating and recruiting the younger generation to continue the work they were doing and finding the financial resources to keep the organisations running. "We have to find ways of sustaining them to do this work, make it better," said one of them, "otherwise all our efforts will die with us. Maybe you and your students should think of this as a project and come up with some ideas."

I agreed with them. It was an important issue, not just for them, but also for the field-study program. The problem was that it relied solely on me to run it. If for some reason I couldn't do so, then it probably would be taken off the list of courses offered by the university. I didn't know how it would be sustained in the long run.

One of the members reacted to my observation. "This program you have been running is bigger than you or the university," she said. "You must think like us and make a plan to sustain this program for the younger generations."

Soon after returning to Melbourne, some of the graduate students who had been on the trip met up with me. They'd been thinking about the conversations with the community organisation members in South Africa, they said, and wanted to find a way of sustaining the field-study program over the longer term. Would I allow them to work as a group on this project for their final assignment instead of working on individual project proposals? Pleasantly surprised, I agreed.

The students had another request. They wanted to get in touch with some of the alumni of the program. Would I be willing to invite them over for a meeting at my home so that they could share their ideas for the project? With pleasure, I said.

The meeting took place at my home. The students and alumni talked animatedly about the program, how it was radically different from anything they'd done at university, how it transformed the way they thought about international development and sustainability, how it gave them confidence to pursue their different careers, why it needed to continue and be opened up to students from other universities, why more programs like this one needed to be developed. I listened on with fascination from the sidelines.

"What kind of organisation would you set up to sustain such programs?" I asked.

"A social enterprise," said one of them, in decisive tones.

I wasn't sure what she meant. "You mean, like an NGO?"

No, came the vehement answer, it isn't.

"It isn't at all like an NGO, relying on donations to do development projects, or making money through dodgy volunteer programs for clueless students from rich countries who think they're saving some poor Third World community from hell," she declared.

"A social enterprise is a business. It produces something that has social value, sells it at market prices, and invests its surplus in projects that are meaningful to communities instead of returning it to shareholders."

"That's a pretty accurate definition," another said, looking at me. "I reckon it's the best set-up for running such study programs. You don't have to constantly beg for donations to operate, nor rely solely on one university academic like yourself to run the programs till you drop. It's the way to go."

As I listened to their explanations, a random thought crossed my mind. How would Marx react to this idea of a social enterprise? I don't know why it was the first thought that came to me, but there it was. A second question popped up. Was the current enthusiasm for social enterprises an emerging challenge to the prevailing neoliberal *doxa*, or was it just neoliberalism in a new guise? Then, a third thought. Could the social enterprises described by my students fit John Friedmann's concept of radical planning? These questions were roiling in my head when I met my friend the following day.

The logical place to start would have been Marx's writings, but the thought of ploughing headlong into this literature filled me with trepidation. It wasn't easy reading. I feared, once in, I'd get pretty overwhelmed with details and contradictions and not come out with any coherent answer. The second question about neoliberalism and social enterprises seemed a bit easier to tackle, partly because the literature was more recent and likely to be limited. But I decided I would start with the third question, on radical planning, because I knew exactly where to look: in Friedmann's *Planning in the Public Domain*.

So that is where I propose to begin. I will explore how John Friedmann viewed the role of enterprise in the context of radical planning and social transformation, and then look quickly at the literature on social enterprises and consider whether they are extensions of, or radical challenges to, neoliberal development. Finally, I will suggest answers to my opening questions.

Friedmann's meditations on radical planning

All of Friedmann's work on planning has been about bringing critical thinking and knowledge to action, to do things differently from traditional planning so as to improve the human condition, and enable societies to flourish. In *Planning in the Public Domain* (1987), he sets about looking at how this has been done through the agency of three conceptually distinct institutions – state, market, and civil society. Two of the four traditions of planning he outlines are driven from above by the state, either by an enlightened elite or committee of experts who know what is best for the rest of society (social reform), or by government functionaries who make decisions based on scientific reason and the utilitarian principle of the greatest good for the greatest number (policy analysis).

Friedmann's social learning and social mobilisation traditions, in contrast, are driven from below by civil society. Social learning is about producing meaningful knowledge through interaction and practical activity with people in civil society, so that planning becomes an organic process for the benefit of communities. Social mobilisation is about critically examining and challenging the status-quo, resisting state oppression, fighting for social justice, and changing state structures to create new socio-economic environments in which all people can flourish. In both these traditions, planners may or may not be from the elite. They can be in the employ of the state or emerge from civil society as the vanguard of the oppressed masses. Wherever the location of planners, they are distinguished by their commitment to planning that makes sense to, and positive change for, common people and the public domain.

The book offers little detail on the role of economic actors. Friedmann discusses the market in broad terms and does not elaborate on the economic enterprises associated with the four traditions. From his description, the interests of state and market actors appear closely aligned in the social reform and policy analysis traditions. State-led planning in both of these traditions focuses on driving economic growth either by promoting the interests of large-scale owners of capital (market-oriented development) or by intervening and directing economic activity in the broader national interest (state-centred or socialist development). We can infer, somewhat crudely, that the private and public enterprises emerging under these planning traditions are most likely to be large corporate institutions that control substantial amounts of capital and (possibly) employ a lot of people in white- and blue-collar jobs.

It is even more difficult to infer the role of economic actors emerging from radical planning. In the last chapter of *Planning in the Public Domain*, Friedmann discusses the 'mediations of radical planning' – combining social learning and mobilisation – and argues that radical practice must be informed by a transformative theory. Transformative theory, he says, focuses on the structural problems of capitalist society, provides a critical interpretation of existing reality, takes a historical and forward-looking perspective to chart the future course of problems, works out a preferred outcome through emancipatory practice, and develops the 'best' strategy for achieving it in the face of potential resistance from established powers (p.389). As Friedmann suggests, mediation is Janus-faced for radical planners. It requires them to simultaneously look back at transformative theory to shape it to the needs of oppositional practice in local settings, and look forward to create opportunities for groups to critically appropriate such theory and rework it according to their experience and what they want to achieve (p.392).

The mediations of radical planning put radical practice in a contradictory position, standing in one instance alongside civil society groups *in opposition to* state and market, and in the second instance as intermediary *between them* to bring about positive outcomes through transformative theory and practice. Radical planning, from this mediating position, must, on the one hand, work with civil society groups selectively to delink from the state and market and become self-reliant and self-empowered. On the other hand, it needs to deploy transformative theory in realistic terms to enable civil society groups to work with (and within) existing structures of state and market.

How might radical planning achieve selective delinking, self-reliance, and empowerment through these contradictory means? Friedmann invokes the household economy as a cooperative model of working together and pooling time, energy, and skills to secure greater access to the bases of social power (pp.396–397). He mentions the need for radical planners to mobilise these resources to think without frontiers, engage in meaningful action, build networks and coalitions, and focus strategic action through dialogue and mutual learning (pp.398–403). But as he reflects on the dilemmas of radical planning – which include things such as maintaining critical distance, open inquiry, contending with unity of opposites, and struggling against the state for the reassertion of political community in civil governance (pp.407–409) – he arrives at the question of money.

"How shall they finance themselves?" he asks. "Even more to the point, how shall radical planners survive when neither the state nor private foundations pay for their work?" (p.411). He observes that radical practice "does not come dear in terms of money" (ibid.), but what it needs more of is substantial amounts of time, 'sweat equity', and mutual help. Money, if you need it badly enough, he says, "will materialise" through fundraising, government grants, public pension funds, and, if successful, you may even receive substantial support from the public purse (ibid.).

So, reading between these lines, if radical planners are to succeed in their efforts, they need to be able to bring diverse institutions, actors, ideas, and resources together in new ways. They need to be innovative in mediating between civil society and the state. In effect, radical planners need to be entrepreneurs. Social entrepreneurs.

Social innovation and entrepreneurship

It is impossible to think of innovation and entrepreneurship without turning to Joseph Schumpeter's classic work on the role of entrepreneurs in economic development. Schumpeter (1934) saw capitalism as being driven by different cycles of innovation that emerged at critical junctures when there was a crisis in accumulation. He made a clear distinction between invention and innovation. *Invention* was about creating something new, but *innovation* was about bringing the necessary resources together in new combinations, or turning some new idea or invention into a profit-making business. Innovation encompassed not just a new good or a new quality of some existing good, but also new methods of production, new sources for raw materials, new organisation of industry to gain a monopoly position or conversely to break up a monopoly position (Swedberg 2001). Schumpeter proposed that entrepreneurs were innovative because they brought the factors of production (e.g., land, raw materials, technology, labour, money) together in new combinations to break the stagnation of an existing economic cycle and start a new cycle of profit.

Schumpeter regarded entrepreneurs as critical for invigorating capitalist economic development. He saw them not simply operating on the narrow calculus of economic rationality to seek short-term advantage in business, but acting on the basis of an autonomous drive to struggle and create something new for its own sake (Martinelli 2001). Like Berman's (1982) description of Goethe's Faust, Schumpeter's entrepreneurs are radical and revolutionary. They are the intermediaries who place themselves at the centre of relations between investors, manufacturers, technology, and consumers, and take on the risk and uncertainty inherent in creating a successful enterprise.

Although Schumpeter's interpretation of innovation and 'creative destruction' was in part inspired by Marx's work on the dynamics of capitalism (Martinelli 2001), his description of the role of entrepreneurs in economic development has been embraced by non-marxist economists, management theorists, and many more disciplines and professions. 'Innovation' is probably one of the most (over)used terms today by bureaucrats, politicians, business corporations, and universities (almost at par with 'sustainability'), all of whom claim to nurture and promote it in every possible instance (Jessop et al. 2015). 'Innovative disruption' (the latest buzzword coined by the Harvard Business School professor Clayton Christensen) is the order of the day, with every new technology threatening to shake up the status quo and herald a new phase of global economic and social reorganisation. It is in this context that *social* innovation and *social* entrepreneurship have gained attention in recent decades as new ways of addressing social needs.

Social innovation emerged during the 1980s and has since expanded substantially to cover a wide range of activities linked to the public domain. A broad definition refers to it as an activity that creates an improvement in social relations, fostering inclusion and well-being through empowerment processes. The three key features of social innovation include the satisfaction of human need; the improvement in social relations between individuals and groups; and the empowerment of people trying to fulfil their needs (Moulaert et al. 2015). Although one could argue that these features are likely to be found in most planning and development projects, the term emphasises innovations generated from within civil society, rather than by the state, for addressing social problems.

Defourny and Nyssens (2013) observe that the term 'social entrepreneurship' began to be used in relation to the 'third sector' – non-profit and voluntary organisations – often categorised in Europe as the 'social economy'. This 'third sector' was increasingly active in "providing services and goods to persons or communities whose needs were neither met by private companies nor public providers" (p.40). They identify two broad types of social enterprises which they call the 'earned income' and the 'innovation schools'. The first type, earned income, refers to the strategies adopted by various non-governmental organisations (NGOs) in the face of increasing competition for public and philanthropic funding. These organisations may engage in some commercial activities to generate income that supplements the funds they receive from governments or donors to support their social mission. For example, Oxfam, an international development NGO, has shops in many cities that sell artisanal products made by individuals and community groups supported by their development projects in poor countries. Another variant of the earned income type is what Mohammad Yunus, the founder of the Grameen Bank in Bangladesh, describes as a 'social business', which is a "non-loss, non-dividend, fully market-based company dedicated entirely to achieving a social goal" (Cited in Defourny and Nyssens 2013, p.41). These mission-driven businesses may operate either as for-profit or non-profit companies.

The innovation school encompasses entrepreneurs who are more typically Schumpeterian in spirit. These individuals are 'civic' or 'public' entrepreneurs who have the ambition to achieve systemic change; their focus is on outcomes rather than earned income. Such individuals create a new institutional space that exists both in the private for-profit sector and the public benefit sphere (Defourney and Nyssens 2013). There are a growing number of such enterprises, ranging from those that offer technological solutions to ones that offer alternative ways of delivering services. Examples include the well-known M-Pesa system, which was developed in Kenya as a way of transferring money via mobile phones between individuals who did not have access to formal banking (Batchelor 2012); numerous "bottom-of-the pyramid" (Prahalad 2006) products and services in India that are low-cost and which address the needs of poor people; and various businesses that link volunteers with social or environmental programs that provide skill training and other kinds of support services to disadvantaged groups in their communities (Bornstein 2004).

Defourny and Nyssens identify a number of economic, social, and governance indicators that are found in varying combinations in social enterprises (pp.45–46). These include routine 'business' features such as producing goods and services and bearing financial risk; 'social' features combining voluntary and paid work; limited profit distribution; high degree of autonomy in governance; decision-making not reliant on capital ownership; and participatory management by diverse stakeholders. Overall, they see both types of social enterprise as innovative approaches for addressing challenges of poverty, disease, and unequal access to information, skill development, and institutional power.

Neoliberalism in a new guise?

The current enthusiasm for social innovation and entrepreneurship is so hyped that even Professor Pangloss could be forgiven for harbouring a smidgen of cynicism about their virtues. After all, social innovation arose as a concept in the 1980s, a decade when neoliberal ideology gained sway and was enforced in many countries around the world by conservative and authoritarian governments and multilateral agencies like the IMF and World Bank (Harvey 2005). States were forced, on the one hand, to adopt austerity measures and cut back on public-sector employment and social welfare programs and, on the other, to implement liberalisation to lower trade barriers for freer transnational movement of finance capital and corporate investors. Under these conditions, social innovation was a necessity forced on communities and civil society organisations to deal with the wreckage and abandonment by governments and corporations (Friedmann 1992). Social innovation, one can argue, has been the euphemistic justification – using terms like 'human and social capital building' and 'community empowerment' (Peck 2013) – by which many governments reneged on responsibilities towards their populations while defending succour for corporate welfare.

The rise of social entrepreneurship can be similarly viewed in relation to recurrent global financial crises and recessions brought on by the globalisation of neoliberal policies through the 1990s and 2000s. With interest rates close to zero or negative, both finance capital and the people that banks like to call 'high net-worth individuals' have been looking for investment opportunities that will earn their capital more money. Their speculation in complex financial derivatives and global property markets have contributed to enormous instability and stress of which the 2008–2009 global financial crisis was the latest episode. Despite being fully aware of these free-market failures, governments and multilateral institutions alike continue to parrot the neoliberal nostrums of privatisation, deregulation, marketisation, and competitiveness for renewing business cycles and promoting unfettered economic growth.

In the fitful recovery from the global recession and neoliberal gluttony, the current enthusiasm among governments, finance capital managers, and 'angel investors' for promoting all kinds of entrepreneurship reflects the desperation to find new sources of profitable investment. Banks, governments, NGOs, trusts, foundations, and development consultants are falling over themselves to promote microfinance, micro-entrepreneurs and other profit-making bottom-of-the-pyramid solutions (Duvendack et al. 2011). The rise of 'philanthropy consultants' such as Geneva Global and WISE (Wealthy Individuals and Social Entrepreneurs) represents the face of the new philanthro-capitalism that seeks efficiency and profit from altruism (Sen 2015). In sum, the financial crises and pressures generated by neoliberal policies have succeeded in remoulding social innovation and enterprise to service and reinforce the ideological agenda of neoliberal development.

Social enterprises as the means for radical economic transformation

Critical assessments of social innovation and entrepreneurship are necessary because they show how these initiatives have evolved within the ambit of neoliberal ideology and ongoing vagaries of capitalist accumulation. Yet, as John Friedmann points out, critical analysis cannot define the limits of social action; it must also provide a sound basis for pursuing alternative paths of social transformation. Friedrich Engels was a fierce critic of the 'actually existing capitalism' of the 19th century, but he also supported Robert Owen's approach to industrial capitalism, which reinvested profits to improve the living and labouring conditions of his factory workers (Tucker 1978).

My students launched into their group project, a prefeasibility analysis for a social enterprise that would offer field-study programs in South Africa for university students the world over. They produced a comprehensive analysis of the program I ran and outlined the benefits of expanding this experience for students, academics, universities, and local communities in Mpumalanga. We then pooled and raised funds to cover their travel to South Africa to discuss their proposal with local community organisations, academics, small businesses, and government agencies and seek their views on the feasibility of starting up such an enterprise. Local stakeholders were markedly positive in their support. For one, they were already familiar with the format of the current field program and had helped shape it over the years. Second, they saw benefit in being able to define the learning experience for university students as well as draw on their fresh insights and ideas for addressing local and regional problems; this was more valuable to them than deriving any immediate financial benefits from the program. Third, they saw the social enterprise and the programs as the means for mobilising young people in their communities to join in the learning experience alongside students from elsewhere and gain confidence and motivation to find opportunities in their own localities.

The students returned with the heady feeling of knowing they were on the right track with their decision to set up a social enterprise. We settled on a lengthy name – Radical Education for Social, Environment, and Entrepreneurship Development – that formed the acronym RESEED, which aptly represented the aims of the enterprise. The formal paperwork for establishing the company was remarkably instructive. We found that, unlike the USA and UK, which have formally recognised social enterprise categories such as Low-profit Limited Liability Companies (L3Cs) and Community Interest Companies (CICs), respectively, there were no similar choices in Australia; we would either have to incorporate as a for-profit or as a not-for-profit company. As the discussion on RESEED's constitution and organisation unfolded, there was clear consensus among those involved on two issues: the social enterprise would limit profit distribution to reinvestment in communities and environments where the programs would run; and the decision-making power in the enterprise would not be based on the size of capital ownership or investment, but on the collective deliberation of diverse stakeholders – government, civic organisations, businesses, and academics – that collaborated with RESEED to develop and shape new study programs.

Now, as my former students continue to tackle the complexities of getting RESEED underway, their early euphoria has been replaced by the sober recognition that starting up a social enterprise is nothing like the popular stories one hears about technology start-ups. While trial and error and failures among technology start-ups are viewed in positive light by angel investors, social entrepreneurs are unlikely to attract much sympathy or financial backing by presenting a track record of impressive failures to potential investors. RESEED is also not a 'conventional' social enterprise that delivers crucial services to a disadvantaged target group. Instead, it needs to convince investors, universities, academics, and students that its 'business model' for radical education both satisfies the neoliberal pressures they face and provides a learning experience of high value to students and communities.

Two years on since the conversation with my friend, I think I have the answers to my questions. I believe social enterprises do pose a radical planning challenge to neoliberal development. I feel that John Friedmann would be heartened by my former students' commitment to launch radical planning theory into action. I suspect that Marx, were he alive today, might have given RESEED a nod of approval. And I'd like to think that his intellectual comrade, were he around, may have been our first 'Engels' investor.

References

Batchelor, S 2012, 'Changing the financial landscape of Africa: an unusual story of evidence-informed innovation, intentional policy influence and private sector engagement', *IDS Bulletin*, 43(5): 84–90.

Berman, M 1982, *All that is Solid Melts into Air*, Simon and Schuster, New York.

Bornstein, D 2004, *How to Change the World: Social Entrepreneurs and the Power of New Ideas*, Oxford University Press, New York.

Defourny, J & Nyssens, M 2013 'Social innovation, social economy and social enterprise: What can the European debate tell us?' in *The International Handbook of Social Innovation: Collective Action, Social Learning, and Transdisciplinary Research*, eds F Moulaert, D MacCallum, A Mehmood & A Hamdouch, Edward Elgar, Cheltenham, pp. 40–52.

Duvendack, M, Palmer-Jones, R, Copestake, JG, Hooper, L, Loke, Y & Rao, N 2011, *What is the Evidence of the Impact of Microfinance on the Well-being of Poor People?*, EPPI-Centre, Social Science Research Unit, Institute of Education, University of London, London.

Friedmann, J 1987, *Planning in the Public Domain: From Knowledge to Action*, Princeton University Press, Princeton, N.J.

Friedmann, J 1992, *Empowerment: The Politics of Alternative Development*, Blackwell, Cambridge, M.A.

Harvey, D 2005, *A Brief History of Neoliberalism*, Oxford University Press, Oxford.

Jessop, B, Moulaert, F, Hulgård, L, & Hamdouch, A 2015, 'Social innovation research: a new stage in innovation analysis?' in *The International Handbook of Social Innovation: Collective Action, Social Learning, and Transdisciplinary Research*, eds F Moulaert, D MacCallum, A Mehmood & A Hamdouch, Edward Elgar, Cheltenham, pp. 110–130.

Martinelli, A 2001, 'Entrepreneurship' in *The International Encyclopedia of the Social and Behavioral Sciences*, eds NJ Smelser & PB Baltes, Elsevier, Oxford, pp. 4545–4552.

Moulaert, F, MacCallum, D & Hillier, J 2015, 'Social innovation: intuition, precept, concept, theory and practice' in *The International Handbook of Social Innovation: Collective Action, Social Learning, and Transdisciplinary Research*, eds F Moulaert, D MacCallum, A Mehmood & A Hamdouch, Edward Elgar, Cheltenham, pp. 13–24.

Peck, J 2013, 'Explaining (with) neoliberalism', *Territory, Politics, Governance*, 1(2): 132–157.

Prahalad, CK 2006, *Fortune at the Bottom of the Pyramid: Eradicating Poverty through Profits*, Pearson Education, New Jersey.

Schumpeter, JA 1934, *The Theory of Economic Development: An Inquiry into Profits, Capital, Credit, Interest and the Business Cycle*, Harvard University Press, Boston.

Sen, J 2015, 'Commodification of "giving back" in a neoliberal world', *Economic and Political Weekly*, 50(42): 22–25.

Swedberg, R 2001, 'Schumpeter, J.A. (1883–1950)' in *The International Encyclopedia of the Social and Behavioral Sciences*, eds NJ Smelser & PB Baltes, Elsevier, Oxford, pp. 13598–13603.

Tucker, R (ed) 1978, *Marx–Engels Reader*, 2nd edn, WW Norton, New York.

10 Business in the public domain

The rise of social enterprises and implications for economic development planning

Yuko Aoyama

Introduction

My engagement with John Friedmann is perhaps less extensive than most other authors in this volume, as I left UCLA after completing my master's degree. I nevertheless attribute my current interests on governance to his seminal work, *Planning in the Public Domain* (Friedmann 1987). In this chapter I wish to engage with Friedmann's work and further his thinking by focusing on social mobilization, one of four aspects of planning theory he discussed in his book. My objective is to complement John's insights and foresight with contemporary collective actions, which are, in many ways, proposing solutions for the future.

My contribution to this debate is to demonstrate how social mobilization takes place not just in the public domain, but also in the private domain. Contemporary evidence suggests that the state no longer has the monopoly in representing the public domain. I argue that public interests are increasingly represented by hybrid governance that involves civil society organizations, corporations, and a variety of organizations that have dual (social and economic) missions.

Collective action in the public domain

In much of the intellectual history of social sciences, various scholars expended their efforts in articulating analytical distinctions between economy and society, *homo economicus* and *homo reciprocan*, and between state and markets (Polanyi 1944). In *Planning in the Public Domain*, Friedmann begins with a distinction between market rationality and social rationality, the former representing the unrestrained pursuit of self-interest by individuals, the latter representing collective interests and social welfare. His primary focus is to demonstrate a long-standing intellectual history and varying schools of thought that exist about the role of planners in the public sector acting on behalf of society. Planners play a crucial role in facilitating collective action, which involves a number of complex issues, such as allocation of common property resources and management of public goods (Hardin 1968; Olson 1965; Ostrom 2000; Samuelson 1954).

The objective of planning theory, according to John, is to solve a meta-theoretical problem of "how to make technical knowledge in planning effective in informing public actions" (Friedmann 1987, p.22). He distinguishes between normative (what he calls "values") and objective (what he calls "scientific facts") roles of planners in collective action. Planners are situated as specialists with expertise in identifying the means and tools for mediating knowledge and action, whereas politicians are concerned with the general goals of policy ("values").

Friedmann identifies four major schools of planning theory over history; namely, planning as social reform, policy analysis, social learning, and social mobilization. While planning as social reform derives primarily from macrosociology, institutional economics, and political philosophy, planning as policy analysis is largely attributed to the work of Simon (1965) with the ideal-type decision model and bounded rationality. Social learning, according to him, combines Dewey's (1938) process theory of knowledge with Maoist pragmatism, whereas social mobilization refers to direct collective action from below and is historically driven by a diverse collection of "utopian communitarianism, anarchist terrorism, Marxist class struggle, and the neo-Marxist advocacy of emancipatory social movements" (Friedmann 1987, p.83). As a result of these mixed ideological underpinnings, social mobilization typically employs one of the two strategies: politics of disengagement (utopians, anarchists) or confrontational politics (Marxists and neo-Marxists). In many ways, planning as social mobilization is distinctive from the other three schools of thought, as this approach situates planning not primarily as mediation of scientific knowledge, but more as an act of politics.

While the objective of planning is to protect collective interest and mitigate the negative consequences of market rationality, Friedmann also acknowledges the limitations of planning. He is a realist, and states, "it is probably correct to say that in most cases public sector programs are successfully launched only when they are broadly compatible with the interests of corporate capital" (Friedmann 1987, p.21). While the legitimacy of the capitalist state depends on safeguarding public interests, it also depends on the smooth functioning of markets and the prosperity of the private sector. Markets, in turn, cannot function smoothly without effective state regulation (Evans 1995). Thus, markets and states complement one another and making a choice between the two is a choice between "imperfect alternatives" (Wolf 1993, p.64).

I wish to extend John's observation on the role of the corporate capital in the public domain, and consider corporate interests in collective action today by examining stakeholders in the "hybrid domain." In my forthcoming book (Aoyama & Parthasarathy 2016), I seek to address this reality by examining collaborations between states, corporations, non-governmental organizations (NGOs), and social enterprises. Each has undergone significant transformations over the past few decades. In addition, they collaborate and form partnerships to deliver on dual (social and economic) missions. The conceptual boundary between the public and private domains is becoming blurred with the rise of various hybrid entities that combine market and social rationalities.

Although corporate interests in achieving social missions are often understood as part of a neoliberal agenda and therefore a dilution of public interests, such a view is a product of century-old tradition in social sciences that, in my view, has reinforced the conceptual separation between the public and private domains, public and private interests, and state and markets. The reality is that private interests significantly concern themselves with public interests, social action, and in some cases, social mobilization, thereby redefining the boundary between the public and private domains. As such, the concept of what is public and what constitutes public interests is in need of re-evaluation.

In the following section, I offer a brief overview of the rise of the hybrid domain, one that combines aspects of the public and private domains. I then discuss stakeholders of the hybrid domain, with a particular focus on social enterprises. I conclude with how stakeholders can take part in social mobilization through social innovation. By so doing, I critique what has become the basic analytical framework in understanding economic governance—one of state versus markets.

The hybrid domain

My colleague and I conceptualize the hybrid domain as an emerging domain between the public and the private interests that blends aspects of market and non-market principles to generate various forms of coordination and organizations (Aoyama & Parthasarathy 2016). The hybrid domain emerges out of intra-sectoral and cross-sectoral transformation in a new combination of social and economic missions. We observe a gradual transition from bilateral negotiations between the state and the markets to hybrid missions and heterarchical complexity. In some cases, this can be observed in subtle shifts in objectives or articulations of multiple objectives in existing institutions. In other cases, this can be observed in cross-sector collaborations between existing institutions, or the rise of new hybrid institutions that straddle the public and private domains.

The increasing popularity of various instruments such as corporate social responsibility (CSR) initiatives, corporate/private foundations, cross-sectoral collaborations involving firms and NGOs, and the growth of entities such as strategic and leveraged NGOs and social enterprises all point toward the growth of the hybrid domain. The hybrid domain is a shift from shareholder-driven to stakeholder-driven capitalism, and the growing role of civil society organizations working in conjunction with the state as key stakeholders in pursuing social missions. The public domain is being rescaled and its logic is being hybridized as a result of globalization, which, in turn, is blurring and mixing the boundaries between public, private, and civil society organizations.

The hybrid domain is neither dominantly state-driven nor market-driven, but is distinctive in its significant bottom-up feature, in which stakeholders, initially uncoordinated and disparate, gradually emerge and result in articulating highly pragmatic, solution-oriented agendas. Stakeholders in both public and private domains, and in for-profit or non-profit organizations, are coordinating actions in a manner which is not state-directed nor administered. In that sense, the hybrid domain is collective action in itself, one that aims at developing solutions and resolving issues that have broad societal implications. This form of collective action leverages global reach, using technologies, accessing financing, and transferring knowledge and skills that are crucial in scaling up solutions.

Corporations, NGOs, and social finance

Both corporations and NGOs have undergone dramatic transformations in their objectives and organizations in the past decade. Corporations and NGOs are increasingly considered as distinct, yet equally important, stakeholders shaping the hybrid domain (Millar et al. 2004; Ottaway 2001; Warhurst 2005). "Corporate citizenship" is a reflection of growing societal pressures on corporations to behave ethically. The 21st century has been characterized as an era of industry self-regulation, in which corporations must voluntarily adopt social standards and codes of ethics (Haufler 2001). The triple-bottom line advocated by Elkington (1997) combines economic, social, and environmental performance. Corporations are incrementally altering their business practices to ensure that socially responsible practices are reflected in corporate decisions.

Moreover, corporations today are active in charity, in the form of corporate social responsibility (CSR) initiatives. McWillams and Siegel (2001) define CSR as "actions that appear to further some social good, beyond the interests of the firm and that which is required by law" (p.117). CSR initiatives have become increasingly important for corporate leaders and employees alike (*The Economist* 2008). In some cases, some corporations are joining forces with other corporations to collaborate for CSR and forming industry coalitions (Mohin 2012). In others, CSRs are being mandated by the state; for example, the Indian government in 2013 began requiring corporations of a certain size to allocate specific budgets for CSR and to work in partnership with local authorities, business associations, and civil society/non-government organizations.

NGOs increasingly receive grants from the private sector to support their social missions (Doh & Guay 2006; Hess et al. 2002; Rondinelli & London 2003; Vogel 2007; Winston 2002). Moreover, some NGOs have commercialized their strategies and globalized, some bearing "an uncanny resemblance to transnational corporations" (Smillie 1995, p.212). Corporations no longer view NGOs solely as a means to garner social legitimacy, but increasingly as critical sources of knowledge to serve their triple-bottom lines. As corporations find NGOs to be essential partners and sources of knowledge, NGOs can no longer be understood as recipients of corporate charity (Dees 1998; Doh & Guay 2006; Hess et al. 2002; Rondinelli & London 2003; Vogel 2007; Winston 2002). NGOs have become insiders rather than outsider critics of policy-making, and have become well-established stakeholders in the structures and mechanisms of global governance (Scholte 2004).

Social finance, one that bridges the for-profit and the non-profit sectors, is a key feature of the hybrid domain. For example, "impact investment" refers to investments that are "intended to deliver both financial returns and social and environmental benefits" (Rodin & Brandenburg 2014, p.vi). Impact investments serve as intermediaries between investors and social entrepreneurs, providing knowledge and pooling resources for social and environmental causes.

Venture philanthropy is a form of grant-making by private foundations that uses market-based strategies and typically involves equity investment in the private sector, and much like venture capitalism, provides support in areas such as business plan development, ensuring efficiency, and developing measures for reporting progress. Unlike traditional philanthropy, venture philanthropy involves an expectation for a financial return on investment. Entrepreneurial "philanthropreneurs" such as Warren Buffet and Bill Gates have led an initiative called Giving Pledge,[1] which is "a revival and a reinvention of an old tradition that has the potential to solve many of the biggest problems facing humanity today" (Bishop & Green 2008, p.2). The Gates Foundation combines advocacy with schemes to induce innovation and support new social enterprise start-ups while encouraging market-based strategies, financial accountability, and transparency among the NGOs. It has been instrumental in creating collaborative financing schemes and innovating on Product Development Partnerships to support research and development of vaccines for diseases that are considered "neglected" by market forces, such as malaria and tuberculosis prevalent in the global south. These philanthropreneurs are seen as unleashing "philanthrocapitalism" (Bishop & Green 2008; Edwards et al. 2014) and driving "social and environmental progress by changing how business and government operate" (Edwards et al. 2014, p.550).

Social entrepreneurship for social innovation

Some corporations are being established specifically to fulfill social goals. Social enterprises differ from commercial enterprises in sources of funding and expectations for pecuniary versus non-pecuniary compensation. Social enterprises typically combine private sector management practices with social objectives, although a consensus has yet to emerge on a definition (Chell et al. 2010). Generally, social enterprises are for-profit organizations with a dual objective of increasing social value while remaining financially sustainable (Weerawardena et al. 2010). Situated between non-profit organization on the one hand and commercial enterprise on the other, social enterprises are heterogeneous and fall within a broad spectrum (Austin et al. 2006).

Several features of social enterprises include: 1) emphasis on production of goods and services (not relying on advocacy or grants as with NGOs), 2) risk-taking, 3) dependence on paid work (versus volunteers in NGOs), 4) clear community beneficiaries, 5) representation of some kind of collective action/objectives, 6) limited profit-maximization, 7) autonomy from state action, 8) emphasis on stakeholder over shareholder, and 9) participatory management style (Defourny & Nyssens 2013). To accommodate corporations that are actively involved in social causes (Farnsworth & Holden 2006; Moon et al. 2011; Utting & Marques 2010), new legal structures are emerging to allow hybrid organizations, such as the creation of Community Interest Companies (CICs) in the United Kingdom and Low-profit Limited Liability Companies (L3Cs) in the United States. These corporations are not legally liable for profit maximization on behalf of shareholders.

Simms and Robinson (2009) argue that the identity of social entrepreneurs combines both activist and entrepreneur, and this duality leads them to discover, define, and exploit two types of opportunities—issue-based and value-based—with the ultimate objective of enhancing social wealth. Transnational social entrepreneurship refers to an emerging group of skilled immigrants relocating to select locations in the global south to launch start-ups with a strong social mission (Aoyama & Parthasarathy 2016). They represent a new combination of transnational resources—human capital, social capital, technology, and market intelligence—for entrepreneurship that combines social and economic missions.

Social entrepreneurs are well positioned to devise an innovative approach to social value creation. Social innovation refers to innovation for social change (Michelini 2012) designed to satisfy unmet social needs (Van Dyck & Van den Broeck 2013). Social innovation is an outcome of the juxtaposition of a social mission with market logic, enacted either by or in partnership with the private sector. Social entrepreneurship has delivered social innovation in areas such as ethical banking, work integration, and environmental services including recycling (Defourny & Nyssens 2013). Social entrepreneurs function as catalysts in the economy by creating markets for products and services which are typically characterized by either people's unwillingness to pay (i.e., free-rider problem) or their inability to pay.

Implications for economic development planning

In the field of development, partnerships that involve states, foundations, and social finance to serve as private equity funds promoting entrepreneurship are becoming numerous, so much so that the consortium model is emerging as the "new normal" (Salamon 2014). The public and private interests are fused in a new manner that manifests in the changing roles and objectives of these actors. Capitalism itself is adapting to the new social demands, arising out of a rescaled consciousness derived from the hypermobility of people and the global reach of media (mass media and citizen journalism through social networking platforms), which is producing both global empathy (Rifkin 2010) and paranoia. Nevertheless, these stakeholders described in the previous section are providing a greater scope to the hybrid domain, generating diversity in institutional forms and resources, and allowing new areas and scopes for social innovation.

How do we conceptualize planning practice for the hybrid domain? The task ahead for planning theorists is to reflect this reality into planning theory. Many of the conceptual boundaries we have used as building blocks in understanding, analyzing, and proposing future actions in economic development planning are becoming blurred. This poses challenges for future planners and planning theory. For one, the concept of the public domain itself should be re-examined. For another, the role of planners is itself in transition. To effectively engage in social mobilization, planners are increasingly called to take part in collaborations that take place in the hybrid domain, and practitioners already do so on a daily basis.

Partnerships and collaborations among these stakeholders are neither initiated nor mandated by the public domain. Instead, the rise of social innovation that involves private-sector stakeholders suggests, on the one hand, inadequacy or withdrawal of the state in fulfilling social missions, and on the other hand, transformation of capitalism that infuses a greater social mission. The private-sector engagement with social reform suggests a new form of social mobilization, one that operates without entirely divorcing market rationality. To date, the encroachment of market rationality in the social sector is generally viewed as neoliberalism. Without entirely refuting such a claim, we may acknowledge a parallel process, which is motivated by the combination of state *and* market reform, one that seeks efficiency and greater social impacts.

Would it be possible to envision radical planners working hand-in-hand with radical capitalists? These radical capitalists may be heads of large corporations or small social enterprises, engaging in social mobilization. While in the previous conceptualization of social mobilization such engagements may appear paradoxical, their notable leadership positions in the private sector and self-initiated mobilization qualify as direct collective action, if not strictly "from below," but have little to do with state mandates. They are drawn by a number of factors, namely, the desire to make impacts that benefit the greatest number of people, the desire to solve complex problems (particularly in the global south), the lack of patience in moving up the traditional career trajectory or corporate ladder to make impacts, and, finally, role models of technology-entrepreneurs-turned-philanthropists, such as Bill Gates (Microsoft), Jeffrey Skoll and Pierre Omidyar (eBay), and Larry Page and Sergey Brin (Google).

One may argue that corporate involvement in the community has a long history and is nothing new. However, what is distinctive in contemporary corporate involvement in social and environmental causes is that it has largely shed itself of the corporate paternalism of the past, and rarely promotes closed communal action (such as co-ops, which require memberships to receive benefits). Rather, stakeholders today embrace social missions as collectively shared around the globe and collaborate across domains to develop solutions.

Concluding remark

Let me conclude with a personal note. Despite two advanced degrees in planning, I became a geographer. This was a function of my job offers always coming from geography departments. As an economic geographer, I studied mostly industries, innovation, industrial organization, and globalization. My recent interest in governance is a full circle back to my intellectual roots in planning, for which I owe much to John and his work.

When I joined the Graduate School of Architecture and Urban Planning (UCLA) in 1986 as a master's student, John was department chair and my faculty advisor. Although I was intimidated by him, I took his sequence of courses in Third World Development, which was a bold move to say the least for someone without much background in development. If my memory serves me right, I recall not doing very well in the class. As bad a student as I was, John was more than supportive; in fact he had a decisive influence on my career trajectory. John was instrumental in sending me to Paris to experience life in continental Europe, and again instrumental in getting me into the Ph.D. program in City & Regional Planning at UC Berkeley a few years later. He weathered the avalanche of my requests for letters of recommendation.

I still remember pacing for hours in my tiny rented room on Hilgard Avenue in Westwood on an early morning in July 1988, waiting patiently until 9 a.m. to call John and ask for his advice on what to do with this out-of-the-blue offer of an internship at an international organization in Paris.

"Yes, they called me last week for a reference, congratulations!" John responded, happily.

I cautiously inquired, "Does that mean I have to go?"

"Well, what else are you going to do?" he asked.

Just a week before, I had declined a job offer at a consultancy in Los Angeles, conducting energy forecasting for the regional utility company, California Edison, for no other reason than a simple lack of enthusiasm. I had no other job offer.

I inquired further, "Do you think it's an interesting job?"

"Well..." John paused for a moment, and then stated matter-of-factly, "it's a bureaucracy."

So, off I went to Paris. I did not know what he meant then, but I know now. I was truly fortunate to have encountered John very early in my intellectual life.

Note

1 The Giving Pledge (givingpledge.org) currently lists 138 individuals/families who have pledged to dedicate the majority of their wealth to philanthropy (August 2015).

References

Aoyama, Y & Parthasarathy, B 2016, *The Hybrid Domain: Collaborative Governance for Social Innovation in India*, Edward Elgar, New York and London.

Austin, JE, Stevenson, H & Wei-Skillern, J 2006, "Social and commercial entrepreneurship: same, different, or both?", *Entrepreneurship Theory and Practice*, 30(1): 1–22. DOI: 10.1111/j.1540-6520.2006.00107.x.

Bishop, M & Green, M 2008, *Philanthrocapitalism: How the Rich Can Save the World*, Bloomsbury Press, New York.

Chell, E, Nicolopoulou, K & Karataş-Özkan, M 2010, "Social entrepreneurship and enterprise: international and innovation perspectives", *Entrepreneurship & Regional Development*, 22(6): 485–493. DOI: 10.1080/08985626.2010.488396.

Dees, JG 1998, "Enterprising nonprofits", *Harvard Business Review*, 76: 54–69.

Defourny, J & Nyssens, M 2013, "Social innovation, social economy and social enterprise: What can the European debate tell us?" in *The International Handbook of Social Innovation: Collective Action, Social Learning, and Transdisciplinary Research*, eds F Moulaert, D MacCallum, A Mehmood & A Hamdouch, Edward Elgar, Cheltenham, pp. 40–52.

Dewey, J 1938, *Education and Experience*, Simon and Schuster, New York.

Doh, JP & Guay, TR 2006, "Corporate social responsibility, public policy, and NGO activism in Europe and the United States: an institutional-stakeholder perspective", *Journal of Management Studies*, 43(1): 47–73.

Edwards, M, Bishop, M & Green, M 2014, "Who gains, who loses: distributional impacts of the new frontiers of philanthropy" in *New Frontiers of Philanthropy*, ed. LM Salamon, Oxford University Press, Oxford, pp. 539–561.

Elkington, J 1997, *Cannibals with Forks: The Triple Bottom Line of 21st Century Business*, Capstone, Oxford.

Evans, P 1995, *Embedded Autonomy: States and Industrial Transformation*, Princeton University Press, Princeton, N.J.

Farnsworth, K & Holden, C 2006, "The business-social policy nexus: corporate power and corporate inputs into social policy", *Journal of Social Policy*, 35(03): 473–494. DOI: 10.1017/S0047279406009883.

Friedmann, J 1987, *Planning in the Public Domain: From Knowledge to Action*, Princeton University Press, Princeton, N.J.

Hardin, G 1968, "The tragedy of the commons", *Science*, 162(3859): 1243–1248.

Haufler, V 2001, *A Public Role for the Private Sector: Industry Self-regulation in a Global Economy*, Carnegie Endowment for International Peace, Washington, D.C.

Hess, D, Rogovsky, N & Dunfee, TW 2002 "The next wave of corporate community involvement: corporate social initiatives", *California Management Review*, 44(2): 110–125.

McWilliams, A & Siegel, D 2001, "Corporate social responsibility: a theory of the firm perspective", *Academy of Management Review*, 26(1): 117–127.

Michelini, L 2012, *Social Innovation and New Business Models: Creating Shared Value in Low-income Markets*, Springer, Berlin. DOI: 10.1007/978-3-642-32150-4.

Millar, CC, Choi, CJ & Chen, S 2004, "Global strategic partnerships between MNEs and NGOs: drivers of change and ethical issues", *Business and Society Review*, 109(4): 395–414.

Mohin, T 2012, "The top 10 trends in CSR for 2012", *Forbes*, 18 January. Available from: <http://www.forbes.com/sites/forbesleadershipforum/2012/01/18/the-top-10-trends-in-csr-for-2012/#7bb55e424a4c> [14 August 2015].

Moon, J, Crane, A & Matten, D 2011, "Corporations and citizenship in new institutions of global governance", in *The Responsible Corporation in a Global Economy*, eds C Crouch & C McLean, Oxford University Press, Oxford, pp. 203–224.

Olson, M 1965, *The Logic of Collective Action: Public Goods and the Theory of Groups*, revised edn, Harvard University Press, Cambridge.

Ostrom, E 2000, "Collective action and the evolution of social norms", *Journal of Economic Perspectives*, 14(3): 137–158.

Ottaway, M 2001, "Corporatism goes global: international organizations, non-governmental organization networks, and transnational business", *Global Governance*, 7(2): 265–292.

Polanyi, K 1944, *The Great Transformation: The Political and Economic Origins of our Time*, Beacon Press, Boston.

Rifkin, J 2010, *The Emphatic Civilization: The Race to Global Consciousness in a World in Crisis*, Tarcher, New York.

Rodin, J & Brandenburg, M 2014, *The Power of Impact Investing: Putting Markets to Work for Profit and Global Good*, Wharton Digital Press, Philadelphia.

Rondinelli, DA & London, T 2003, "How corporations and environmental groups cooperate: assessing cross-sector alliances and collaborations", *The Academy of Management Executive*, 17(1): 61–76.

Salamon, LM 2014, "The revolution on the frontiers of philanthropy: an introduction" in *New Frontiers of Philanthropy*, ed. LM Salamon, Oxford University Press, Oxford, pp. 3–88.

Samuelson, PA 1954, "The pure theory of public expenditure", *The Review of Economics and Statistics*, 36(4), 387–389. DOI: 10.2307/1925895.

Scholte, JA 2004, "Civil society and democratically accountable global governance", *Government and Opposition*, 39(2): 211–233.

Simms, SV & Robinson, J 2009, "Activist or entrepreneur? An identity-based model of social entrepreneurship" in *International Perspectives on Social Entrepreneurship*, eds J Robinson, J Mair & K Hockerts, Palgrave, London, pp. 9–26.

Simon, HA 1965, *Administrative Behavior: A Study of Decision Making Processes in Administrative Organization* (Vol. 4), Cambridge University Press, New York.

Smillie, I 1995, *The Alms Bazaar: Altruism under Fire: Non-profit Organizations and International Development*, IT Publications, London.

The Economist 2008, "Just good business". Available from: <http://www.economist.com/node/10491077> [14 August 2015].

Utting, P & Marques, JC 2010, "Introduction: the intellectual crisis of CSR" in *Corporate Social Responsibility and Regulatory Governance*, eds P Utting & JC Marques, Palgrave Macmillan, Houndmills, Basingstoke, pp. 1–25.

Van Dyck, B & Van den Broeck, P 2013, "Social innovation: a territorial process" in *The International Handbook of Social Innovation: Collective Action, Social Learning, and Transdisciplinary Research*, eds F Moulaert, D MacCallum, A Mehmood & A Hamdouch, Edward Elgar, Cheltenham, pp. 131–141.

Vogel, D 2007, *The Market for Virtue: The Potential and Limits of Corporate Social Responsibility*, Brookings Institution Press, Washington, D.C.

Warhurst, A 2005, "Future roles of business in society: the expanding boundaries of corporate responsibility and a compelling case for partnership", *Futures*, 37(2): 151–168.

Weerawardena, J, McDonald, RE & Mort, GS 2010, "Sustainability of nonprofit organizations: an empirical investigation", *Journal of World Business*, 45(4): 346–356.

Winston, M 2002, "NGO strategies for promoting corporate social responsibility", *Ethics & International Affairs*, 16(01): 71–87.

Wolf, C 1993, *Markets or Governments: Choosing between Imperfect Alternatives*, MIT Press, Cambridge, M.A.

Part 3

World Cities and the Good City

Contradictions and possibilities

Haripriya Rangan

The 1970s and 1980s were turbulent decades for planners involved in urban and regional development. Many nations faced fiscal crises, state-led planning models were criticised for being ineffective, neither delivering economic growth nor reducing inequality. Neoliberal economic theories gained dominance and were aggressively promoted by multilateral institutions such as the World Bank and the IMF. Globalisation emerged as the portmanteau term for the neoliberal nostrums for nations: free trade, dismantling barriers to transnational capital flows, deregulation, privatisation, stripping back the role of the state in economic welfare. Some scholars were beginning to observe the empirical realities of structural unemployment and deindustrialisation in rich countries and industrialisation in poorer countries (Fröbel et al. 1982), and the emergence of a new international division of labour (NIDL).

As globalisation gathered pace, John Friedmann observed that the neoliberal portmanteau was bringing new factors into the process of urbanisation and regional development in different parts of the world. He set out a research agenda with his student Goetz Wolff for looking at 'world city' formation (1982), and subsequently published a more detailed analysis as the 'World City Hypothesis' (1986). The World City Hypothesis drew together the NIDL and world-systems theories and core-periphery concepts to map out the major cities of the globe that served as the basing points for transnational capital flows and the ensuing influences on urbanisation patterns. This research had enormous influence both within and beyond urban planning, literally generating a whole new sub-field of research on global cities, their economies, labour markets, spatial growth and urban agglomeration patterns, and social inequalities. As globalisation processes have reshaped major cities in countries into mega urban regions, John's interest now centres on how planning might take place in these vast amorphous city systems of concentrated and periurban development.

The essays in this section engage with John's ideas of periurban growth, mega-city regions as urban superorganisms, the politics of property in global cities, and the question of what constitutes 'good city' planning. Michael Leaf comments on the complexity of John's recent thinking about the 'urban superorganism' in the context of Asian cities. Roger Keil discusses the generalised pattern of post-suburbanisation and the need to rethink the concepts of urban fields and suburbs. Ute Lehrer discusses the intensity of high-density residential building in Toronto and the incursions it makes on both the physical reality and cultural meaning of urban public space. Saskia Sassen engages with John's ideas of the post-urban landscape and reflects on the massive build-up and privatisation of urban space occurring in global city-regions. Matti Siemiatycki shows how urban entrepreneurialism through transactive planning methods in Toronto has succeeded in enabling sustainable and socially inclusive planning of the city's waterfront. Mike Douglass draws on John's concept of the Good City to consider the grassroots mobilisation and progressive governance movements emerging in some Asian cities. And Hemalata Dandekar looks at how planners in Mumbai have attempted to envision the city's role in global and regional economic networks and to forge public–private partnerships to achieve shared purpose with poorer communities living near targeted development sites.

References

Fröbel, F, Heinrichs, H & Kreye, O 1982, *The New International Division of Labour*, Cambridge University Press, Cambridge.

Friedmann, J & Wolff, G 1982, 'World city formation: an agenda for research and action', *International Journal of Urban and Regional Research*, 6(3): 309–344.

Friedmann, J 1986, 'The World City Hypothesis', *Development and Change*, 17(1): 69–83.

11 The urban, the periurban and the urban superorganism

Michael Leaf

> If the work of the city is the remaking or translating of man into a more suitable form than his nomadic ancestors achieved, then might not our current translation of our entire lives into the spiritual form of information seem to make of the entire globe, and of the human family, a single consciousness?
>
> (McLuhan 1964, p.61)

That obscure urban object of desire

The world has changed considerably over the course of John Friedmann's writing career, or more to the point here, our understanding of the urban world has shifted considerably during this time. One might imagine this to be due in some part to the influence of John's career, as his writing has sought to explain the urban in its various manifestations. One would therefore expect our overall understanding of global urbanization to have improved over this period, given the attention it has received from John and other scholars. Yet in looking back at John's work in the 1970s on the urban transition in "newly industrializing societies" (Friedmann & Wulff 1975) and comparing it to more recent writing on similar themes, one could be forgiven for concluding exactly the opposite.

The Urban Transition was an extended literature review on what was then labeled the Third World City, divided into "macro-studies" of urbanization processes and "micro-studies" on the nature of urban life. The multiple challenges facing the Third World City were seen as formidable, certainly, but not so daunting as to deter the authors from concluding the book with a "decision-framework" intended to guide urban policy. By the time *The Prospect of Cities* (Friedmann 2002) was published, some three decades later, the scale of these challenges had expanded such that John now wrote about city-regions instead of cities and emphasized the conceptual value of "the urban" over that of "the city." This upward scalar shift was complemented, however, by a simultaneous trend in the opposite direction, focusing in on people and their neighborhood communities by looking at questions of citizenship and the "city of everyday life." Evidently one may attempt to address the growing complexity of cities—or is it the growing understanding of how complex cities are?—by either trying to simplify the synoptic view of the big picture, or, instead, by narrowing in on a smaller, bounded territory within the overall urban field.

Another decade-and-a-half further along and John is not only grappling with complexity, but with "hyper-complexity," as indicated in the title of his, "Urban planning under conditions of hyper-complexity" (2014). The scale of the urban object has ballooned yet again, forcing John to articulate a new term, the "Urban Superorganism" (USO), which he defines as "a hyper-complex, high density, five-dimensional[1] socio-spatial system" (Friedmann 2014). The urban, it appears, is an elusive thing. The more one stares at it, the more opaque it becomes. Opaque but simultaneously fuzzy, indistinct. One is left puzzled trying to understand where the urban leaves off and everything else begins. And when one tries to get inside it, to pick it apart or break it down into its fundamental components, its complexity only seems to increase.

So, what has happened? Has complexity increased along with the size and scale of cities, or is it our perception of complexity that has grown? To put it another way, was the city more "doable" back then, or were urbanists more naïve? In recent years, I have wondered about the city size debates that were still current when I was a grad student in the 1980s. Even by that time the notion of maximum city size—whether derived from presumed limits imposed by physical/infrastructural conditions or from pressures on urban social make-up arising from excessive crowding or scale, or both—had given way to concern for optimum city size, a more relativistic concept that rested on the belief that at some point in a city's growth, its "diseconomies of scale" would begin to outweigh its "economies of scale," thus indicating its point of optimal size. Such concerns for maximum and optimal sizes seem to have vanished into the ether as cities themselves (or rather, city-regions) have grown beyond their presumed maxima and optima. Have questions of city size now been superseded by concern for complexity? Or perhaps the fusing of urban horizons that spatially underpins the formation of USOs, and more conceptually, the planetary spread of urbanism, has simply made the issue of size irrelevant. In this respect, perhaps the main value of the USO derives from the understanding that it is also qualitatively different from that which preceded it. I will return to this issue by the end of this essay; first, however, it is useful to consider certain aspects of periurbanization as it is manifested in Asia, since it is through periurban processes that urban horizons are fused and USOs are brought into being.

The inner-city suburb

Perhaps the most consequential national component of the ongoing global urban transition is that of China, spurred on by sustained rapid economic growth coupled with major institutional changes, most significantly the devolution of administrative and fiscal responsibilities in the nation's administrative system. Such a profound transformation, rapid and spatially extensive as it is, has exposed numerous anomalies in China's urbanization, apparent contradictions or disjunctures that tend to be portrayed by the ever-growing crowds of China urban-watchers as exceptional or unique to the Chinese experience. One such apparent anomaly is what is labeled the *chengzhongcun*, the "village within the city," which is formed when an erstwhile rural village becomes engulfed by an expanding city. As this phenomenon is attributed in part to the administrative distinction between rural and urban lands in China today and related as well to current practices of rural–urban migration, it is generally seen to be a socio-spatial outcome that is distinct to its time and place. But is the collective memory of China's past experiences with urbanization so limited as to overlook precedents to today's *chengzhongcun*?

In one of my first collaborative involvements in China, I worked with colleagues from Zhongshan University analyzing an inner city neighborhood in Guangzhou, named Jinhua, in Liwan District (Wei & Zhou 1997). Jinhua was seen within the municipality of Guangzhou to be an exceptional neighborhood, praised for having overcome its past as a place of degeneracy, social deviance, poverty and criminality to become an orderly and prosperous—and "civilized" (*wenming*)—model neighborhood under the People's Republic. Such characteristics of Jinhua's shady past were understood to have been rooted in its ancient origins as essentially an encampment just outside the wall of the city, a place that accommodated people who were not allowed to stay in the city—itinerant merchants, travelers, those with no valid reason to be in the city after dark. The city had long ago expanded outward to engulf the former village of Jinhua and, when the wall was torn down following the end of imperial China, it became an administratively proper (though perhaps still at that time socially disreputable) part of Guangzhou's urban core.

This practice of using the city wall to exclude undesirables from the city proper is long-standing in China's history. One can look, for example, at Zhang Zeduan's scroll-painting masterpiece *Qingming shanghe tu*, depicting daily life in the Song capital of Bianjing in the early 12th century, to see how the city wall and its gateway functioned as a filter, with in that case a concentration of various small businesses and vendors just outside the gate (Heng 1999). Presumably as Bianjing (now Kaifeng) grew outward over time and the city wall was removed or relocated, this suburban business center of sorts became a proto-*chengzhongcun*.

Thus the *chengzhongcun* in its most basic sense is not unique to our present time, nor is it limited to China. The quarter known as the "36 Old Streets" in Hanoi, so beloved by tourists for its seeming authenticity and expression of traditional Vietnamese urbanity, was formed in a similar fashion, as an encampment of artisans and vendors outside the gates of the ancient Thang Long citadel. The Vietnamese word now commonly rendered in English as "old street" is an archaic term more accurately translated as "guild," indicative of the many small clusters of specialized producers and sellers which characterized this settlement for hundreds of years until French colonial authorities plowed through a series of roads in the wake of the anti-colonial Black Flag rebellion in the late 19th century (Wright 1991).

Nor is this sort of *chengzhongcun* a wholly Asian phenomenon. Although the Parisian neighborhood of Montmartre, to give one of numerous European examples, is now properly incorporated into the city as its 18th *arrondissement*, it began as a *faubourg* (a contraction from *faux bourg*, meaning "false city"[2]), an area of exclusion (and cheap wine) just outside the old wall of Paris—not unlike the *faubourg* of Jinhua in Guangzhou.

Nor is it even necessary to have a wall in order to establish an inner-city suburb of this sort. In the city of Vancouver, the elite neighborhood of Shaughnessy is located at the heart of the residential component of the city, though with a landscape of large houses on very large lots, not unlike other upscale suburban developments of its era. Like the *faubourgs* of Paris, Shaughnessy originated outside of what was then the city proper when it was established by the real estate arm of the Canadian Pacific Railroad in 1907, yet now is considered centrally located because of the expansion of the city around it over the past century.

This diverse set of examples is meant to emphasize that these all began as places apart, territories created by exclusion, whether such exclusion was imposed by others or was the result of auto-exclusion, as in the example of Shaughnessy, by or for elites. These were originally coherent socio-spatial entities—that is, with an understood correspondence between social characteristics and their spatial manifestation—though their social and spatial relations nonetheless may change over time. My argument here is that a principal means—if not *the* principal means—by which urban space has historically been created is through suburbanization of one sort or another. And despite the correspondence between social and spatial forms at the time of origin (which, not incidentally, provides the impetus or rationale for such formation in the first place), socio-spatial correspondence can be a dynamic thing, as seen, for example, in the down-market shift in the inner-ring suburbs of American cities in recent decades, as gentrification has pushed the poor and working classes out of inner-city locales. Although the character of this (sub)urban space may at the outset be differentiated from that of the (old) city proper, there is a reasonable likelihood that in time such suburban space will become integrated with the urban. Even if, as some argue, suburban space is manifestly different from urban space, the process through which urban space is created is fundamentally not different from how suburban space is created, since over time and through historical circumstance, suburban space tends to become urban space.

The periurban and the city proper

Can the same thing be said of periurbanization? Given time and the right circumstances, can the periurb (to coin a term) also become part of the city proper? Periurbanization is a fairly recent neologism, so far only vaguely differentiated from the much older terminology of suburbanization. For the sake of brevity, I will here define periurbanization as the often intricate, if not intimate, intermingling of rural and urban functions, territories and populations at the urban edge and beyond, in contrast to the conventional notion of suburbanization as the outward expansion of the urban into previously unurbanized territories. From such a definition, one could argue that the suburban is actually a subset of the periurban, or, in other words, suburbanization, as conventionally understood, is one of the means by which periurbanization is constituted.[3]

Can the periurban become integrated with the urban, in the way that the *faubourg* of Montmartre is now Paris's 18th *arrondissement* or Jinhua is a model neighborhood of Guangzhou? Presumably, if given enough time and the possibility of socio-economic change, or even socio-cultural change, it would be possible for such integration to occur. But the difference here is with both scale and speed.[4] Considering that the total land area of our planet covered by urbanization may as much as triple in less than four decades, largely due to what we are labeling as periurbanization (and with much of it happening in Asian contexts), it is hard to imagine that such vast territories can be integrated into "the city proper" within a reasonable period of time, as even the provision of basic trunk infrastructure is often problematic (Angel 2008).

Since this teleology of the periurban is so consequential both for the human civilization it contains and for the environment within which it is constituted, perhaps this limited "upgrade potential" should be seen as a characteristic that further differentiates the suburban from the periurban. This is not to imply that the periurban is unchanging. In fact, it is highly dynamic. I would argue that the periurban of today is or will become the urban of the future, though undoubtedly this will be quite different from our historically received notions of urbanity. The conventional understanding of the city proper will give way to some other idea of what it means to reside and work in a large, densely settled territory.

The (peri)urban as technology

It is also highly consequential that these enormous changes in the urban landscape, and more broadly in the landscape of urbanism, are happening in a context of increasing global interconnectivity and technological change. It is well established that technological innovation can foster significant changes in the processes and patterns of urbanization. Elisha Graves Otis's invention of the safety elevator, for example, was a requisite technology for the construction and operations of what came to be called skyscrapers, which in turn transformed the commercial cores of industrial cities in the early 20th century. Technological innovation need not depend on invention *per se* so much as new application of existing technology, as, for example, in what was called the "Colt Revolution" in the formation of Jakarta's extended metropolitan region, referring to the interconnected networks of mini-buses—Mitsubishi Colts—which allowed for the atomized movement of people and goods across the expanding territories of the *desakota* (McGee 1991).

My concern here, however, is not about this linkage between technological innovation and urban change so much as the idea that the city is itself a technology. My starting point for this exploration is with the definition of technology associated with media studies pioneer, Marshall McLuhan, in his book from 1964, *Understanding Media*. Here technology is understood fundamentally as an extension of the faculties of human beings, or in McLuhan's words, "all technologies are extensions of our physical and nervous systems to increase power and speed" (McLuhan 1964, p.90). To give one simple example, eyeglasses, a 13th century technology, are an extension of the human faculty of sight, as they allow a person to see further or more clearly. As an even further extension of our eyes, the much newer technologies of video recording and long-distance electronic transmission in effect allow us to see much further still, from Vancouver to New York, or to Nairobi, or to Jakarta, or to the moon and stars.

For thinking about the urban itself as a technology, one can build upon another example: the idea of clothing as a technology that expands upon the skin that we humans have to protect our bodies from the insalubrities of our surroundings. Following this line of argument, one can therefore look at our houses as further technological extensions of our skin. Carrying this further, we can start to look at the totality of our built environment, our buildings, our cities, not as environment, that is, as something "out there," but rather as an extension of ourselves, in much the same way that one might look at a beehive not as the environment that bees live in, but as an outward extension of what it means to be a bee.[5]

Whether one takes this characterization of the urban as a technology (and therefore an extension of human faculties) to be literal or merely metaphoric, and whether one understands the urban as a single, though complex and multifaceted, technology or as an *ex post* label applied to a disparate collection of technologies, it is nonetheless worth considering how this may contribute to our understanding of (peri)urban processes. As a general observation, it can be argued that this perspective on the urban as a technology brings an additional layer of analysis to those theoretical treatments premised on the understanding of urbanization as a spatially extensive process of socio-economic or socio-cultural transformation delinked from the entity of the city *per se*. For example, one might consider how this technological component of the urban contributes to Brenner and Schmid's conception of "planetary urbanism," a term chosen to indicate the potential for the thorough-going presence of the urban seemingly everywhere (Brenner & Schmid 2011). Or as Brenner described it in another context: "(t)he emergent process of extended urbanization is producing a variegated urban fabric which, rather than being simply concentrated within nodal points or confined within bounded regions, is now woven unevenly and yet ever more densely across vast stretches of the entire world" (Brenner 2013, p.90). In such a conceptualization, the technology of the urban may be argued to be the mechanism by which the processes of extended urbanization (and, more fundamentally, the information flows through which these are conveyed) are expressed across increasingly broad and potentially global territories.

This meta-theoretical interpretation of what might be called teleo-urbanism is by no means novel nor unique to Brenner and Schmid. Louis Wirth, in his influential essay of 1938, *Urbanism as a Way of Life*, argued that urbanism referred to more than just the physicality of the city and as both "a system of social organization" and "a set of attitudes and ideas" could therefore be separated from the entity of the city itself (Wirth 1938, p.19). Such a perspective undoubtedly has even more relevance now, as technological changes since the time of Wirth's writing have greatly expanded the speed and distance over which the underpinning information flows are brought to bear. For one example, one could look at the work of Thompson (2006) in his study subtitled *Urbanism in Rural Malaysia* to see how urbanism, as a socio-cultural characteristic, at least, is manifested in even the most remote village.

The urban as organism

More to the point for our purposes here, however, is how this McLuhanesque understanding of technology can contribute to John's conceptualization of the Urban Superorganism. The choice of terminology is critical here: the USO is labeled as "super" because its size is unprecedented and its territorial extent defies jurisdictional bounding; it is an "organism" because it is seen as having essentially taken on a life of its own, that is, that the basic means by which the USO is created, maintained and reproduced is through self-organization and homeostasis. Or to put it in terms of thermodynamics, the USO in its totality is a negentropic entity, just as all organisms are by definition.[6] In this depiction of what might be considered as a sort of Gaia Hypothesis for metropolitan regions, the idea of the urban as a technological extension of the human species should be understood to be essential, a *sine qua non* of the USO. This is the means by which the negentropy of human life is spatially extended to ultimately encompass the territory of the USO. It is by way of this extension of ourselves through our technology that we are able to form ourselves into a USO, as this is the means by which we scale up from ourselves as individuals to ourselves as an extended, collective entity. In this way, "the urban" may be argued to be fundamentally an expansion of "the human."

And when we extend ourselves through our technology, it is important to understand that at some point we move from being individuals to being part of a collective entity. To facilitate our movement through walking, for example, we extend the protective skin on the soles of our feet through the shoes we wear. And since our shoes are specific to each of us, shoes can readily be seen to be a personal technology. This is in contrast to the further extension of our feet in the form of the hardened surface of the sidewalk, which, as a publicly accessible good, can be thought of as a collective technology. This distinction between personal and collectively accessible technologies may be refined further by differentiating collective technologies according to how restrictive access might be, from, on the one hand, open access, as with the truly unrestricted public spaces in our cities, and on the other, various versions of what economists refer to as "club goods" which can have a wide range of possibilities as to how restrictive (or not) they may be. So, for example, a family's house might be seen as a club good technology, restricted to only the members of the family and their guests, while a gated community, in contrast, would be a club good technology with a much larger club membership.

McLuhan's view of the city as the medium through which the message of human civilization is conveyed is of course utopian. More challenging, and even more utopian, are the implications of technology not just as the extension of our physical selves, but of our cognitive selves. Ultimately the outward extension of our nervous systems and the communications functions they allow are conjectured to hold the potential for the creation of a collective or shared consciousness.[7] Though this point may seem abstract or fanciful, it also can offer us a way to reinterpret the spatiality of the periurban. To what degree can the constrained public realm of the periurban be compensated by the expansion of a shared cognitive realm? For example, a recent rural migrant living locally within the seemingly too large territory of the mega-urban region, the Urban Superorganism, may benefit from increasing linkages through information technology despite limits on their face-to-face interactions in physical space. In other words, the ubiquitous connectivity available through cellphones and the Internet provides alternative mechanisms for societal interaction, creating additional layers of social space for the otherwise cramped inhabitants of the periurban.

What might this mean for our understanding of the periurban as the urban of the future? At the minimum, this requires that we pay attention to the possibility that something as vaguely defined (and vaguely understood) as cyberspace should also be included in our investigation of the public realm in territories such as these. The collective space of our shared consciousness, whether or not through cyberspace, should be understood as an expansion of urban space and investigated in concert with other processes by which urban space expands, including periurbanization. Seemingly, as always with analyses of the future of urbanization, a central concern lies with the potential for social fragmentation and exclusion as urbanization continues apace throughout much of Asia and the rest of the putative developing world. In this respect one might include the caveat that bringing cyberspace into the analysis of (peri)urban space introduces one more possible dimension for societal fragmentation, for splintering cyber-urbanism. But considering the mounting incidences of land-grabbing, dispossession and various other forms of contestation over territory as periurban territories expand across Asia, it is likewise possible that accessibility to our collective shared conscious, our World Brain, will continue to be more open and more democratic than access to the actual physical spaces of periurban growth and consolidation.

Notes

1 In addition to the three spatial dimensions and that of time, John's fifth dimension is a reference to Teilhard de Chardin's concept of the *noosphere*, or the sphere of the mind, seen as a dimension of human thought in parallel with the earth's geological lithosphere and organic biosphere (Friedmann 2014, pp.3–4).
2 Although it is also argued that this is an apocryphal "folk etymology" with *faubourg* more likely derived from the Old French *forsbourc*, a Latin-Frankish amalgam meaning "outside the city" (http://www.etymonline.com/index.php?allowed_in_frame=0&search=faubourg&searchmode=none accessed 21 November 2015). Nonetheless, the persistence of this folk etymology nicely illustrates the depth of bias toward those outside of the city proper, those excluded from urban (and urbane?) society.
3 It is useful to remember that these are not scientifically defined terms. One may also consider the argument (discussed in Leaf 2011) that the terminological distinction between periurban and suburban is in effect about differentiating conditions in the global north from those of the global south, a sort of conceptual apartheid akin to Robinson's (2006) categorical distinction of Global and World Cities from Developmental or Third World Cities.
4 One could also venture a political economy explanation for the persistence of the periurban, in that the "informally" occupied lands of the periurban may function as a relatively low-cost reserve of land for the expansion of proper urbanization from the perspective of both capital and the local state.
5 McLuhan (1964, p.47) attributes this understanding of the city as an extension of our skins to Lewis Mumford in *The City in History* (1961), though Mumford's point of reference was to city walls in particular.
6 Negentropy is a contracted form of negative entropy, a concept introduced by physicist Erwin Schrödinger in a 1943 lecture at Trinity College, Dublin and subsequently published as *What is Life?* (Schrödinger 1945).
7 This conceptualization of a single, shared consciousness resulting from our cognitive extension through electronic media is what McLuhan saw to be the ultimate extension of our collective selves, as indicated in the epigraph to this essay. In writing about this in the early 1960s, he was presaging the Internet, though H.G. Wells had a similar insight in the 1930s about the possibility of creating what he called the World Brain, a repository of all information and analysis that would be freely accessible to everyone and which, by leveling the informational playing field, would be an important step toward achieving world peace (see Wells 1938). In regard to the USO, one can identify parallels between McLuhan's conceptualization and Teilhard de Chardin's noosphere (see note 1).

References

Angel, S 2008, "An arterial grid of dirt roads", *Cities*, 25(3): 146–162.

Brenner, N 2013, "Theses on urbanization", *Public Culture*, 25(1): 85–114.

Brenner, N & Schmid, C 2011, "Planetary urbanization" in *Urban Constellations*, ed. M Gandy, Jovis, Berlin, pp. 10–13.

Friedmann, J 2002, *The Prospect of Cities*, University of Minnesota Press, Minneapolis.

Friedmann, J 2014, *Urban Planning under Conditions of Hyper-complexity*, unpublished manuscript, School of Community and Regional Planning, Faculty of Applied Science, Vancouver, B.C., Canada.

Friedmann, J & Wulff, R 1975, *The Urban Transition: Comparative Studies of Newly Industrializing Societies*, Edward Arnold, London.

Heng, CK 1999, *Cities of Aristocrats and Bureaucrats: The Development of Medieval Chinese Cityscapes*, University of Hawaii Press, Honolulu.

Leaf, M 2011, "Periurban Asia: a commentary on 'becoming urban'", *Pacific Affairs*, 84(3): 525–534.

McGee, TG 1991, "The emergence of desakota regions in Asia: expanding a hypothesis" in *The Extended Metropolis in Asia: Settlement Transition in Asia*, eds N Ginsburg, B Koppel & TG McGee, University of Hawaii Press, Honolulu, pp. 3–25.

McLuhan, M 1964, *Understanding Media: The Extensions of Man*, McGraw-Hill Book Company, New York.

Mumford, L 1961, *The City in History: Its Origins, its Transformations and its Prospects*, Harcourt, Brace and World, New York.

Robinson, J 2006, *Ordinary Cities: Between Modernity and Development*, Routledge, London.

Schrödinger, E 1945, *What is Life? The Physical Aspect of the Living Cell*, Cambridge University Press, Cambridge.

Thompson, EC 2006, *Unsettling Absences: Urbanism in Rural Malaysia*, NUS, Singapore.

Wei, QQ & Zhou, CS (eds) 1997, *The Research on Jinhua Neighbourhood's Renewal in Guangzhou*, Zhongshan University Press, Guangzhou.

Wells, HG 1938, *World Brain*, Methuen, London.

Wirth, L 1938, "Urbanism as a way of life", *The American Journal of Sociology*, 44(1): 1–24.

Wright, G 1991, *The Politics of Design in French Colonial Urbanism*, University of Chicago Press, Chicago.

12 The prospect of suburbs

Rethinking the urban field on a planet of cities

Roger Keil

Introduction

John Friedmann's notion of the prospect of cities, or the urban transition, speaks to the inevitability of the world turning urban (2002). The urban transition is the unstoppable movement from the rural and agricultural to the urban. In this short essay, I will discuss the space in between the rural and the urban, created by suburbanization, and its invisibility in Friedmann's work.[1] While Friedmann sees the urban field (Friedmann & Miller 1965) as the characteristic historical geography of the prospect of cities, he all but overlooks the characteristic form it takes: generalized post-suburbanization by which we refer to the generalized maturation of suburbanization and the spreading of suburban ways of life into the entire urban region: "a process that involves densification, complexification and diversification of the suburbanization process" (Charmes & Keil 2015, p.581).

I will construct my argument through a selective look at Friedmann's work on cities and regions from the past 50 years, first among those his prescient essay with Miller, from 1965, on the "urban field":

> It is no longer possible to regard the city as purely an artifact, or a political entity, or a configuration of population densities. All of these are outmoded constructs that recall a time when one could trace a sharp dividing line between town and countryside, rural and urban man.
>
> (Friedmann & Miller 1965, p.314)

In this short passage, Friedmann unhinged the common views at the time of bounded urbanity and concentric regionalism. The acuity of this observation would come into full relief only much later. Friedmann's observations over the past few decades were cemented by living in some of the most exemplary globalizing urban regions in the western world: Los Angeles, Melbourne, Vancouver. Assuming that those lived experiences influenced Friedmann's thinking, I will read Friedmann's work playfully against that of Henri Lefebvre, another urban visionary, who preceded Friedmann by a generation but did as much for understanding the "urban revolution" we live through today as Friedmann did for the "prospect of cities." Bringing Friedmann into the universe of Lefebvre (or vice versa) also affords me the opportunity to make reference to Paris, often viewed as an important screen against which to project urbanization in the 19th and 20th centuries, as was Los Angeles during the recent *fin de siècle* marking the transition from the 20th to the 21st century.

Envisioning the urban field

So let us begin by reminding ourselves of Friedmann's vision, in the 1960s, first comprehensively developed in a jointly authored piece with John Miller. At the heart of this vision was the rapidly changing urban region. In order to describe a large and interdependent cluster of urban spaces, Friedmann preferred the term city-region: every urban core needs a surrounding regional space to sustain itself (expansion, landfills, airports, housing, industries, recreation, water reservoirs). While concentric in its original imaginary, Friedmann also recognized multimodal and polycentric regional forms that are more common today. It took much imagination in the mid-1960s to see the future urban world evolve because, as Friedmann and Miller note in their pathbreaking essay on the urban field:

> The pattern of the urban field will elude easy perception by the eye and it will be difficult to rationalize in terms of Euclidean geometry. It will be a large complex pattern which, unlike the traditional city, will no longer be directly accessible to the senses.
>
> (1965, p.319)

Decades later, the vision had evolved into a programmatic yet still prospective view of the urban and regional world which now has some statistical reality to it as societies, by conventional standards, are more urbanized. This is what Friedmann has in mind when he speaks today of the prospect of cities. Importantly, in his view, "the urban transition will not be reversed" and "willful attempts at ruralization were … never more than temporary reversals" (2002, p.1). This transition is, of course, not just one of brick and mortar, infrastructures and technologies; it involves urbanization of the world's ways of life: "We are headed irrevocably into a century in which the world's population will become, in some fundamental sense, completely urbanized" (p.2). While "global capital will continue to expand and consolidate its hold over the economy," though, the world is not becoming "culturally homogenized" (ibid.). Expecting creative tension here between capital and place and "local responses to global challenges are decisive for the future of cities" (p.3), Friedmann sees more globalized and more extensive networks of cities and regions arise with stronger linkages among urban regions resulting in an increasingly urban, transnationalized world (p.2). The expansion and consolidation of global capital can be assumed to continue and the urban transition to be completed over the course of this century.

Breaking down urbanization into three distinct but related processes, Friedmann distinguishes demographic, economic and sociocultural change (p.3) to which, surely, today socio-ecological change would need to be added.

In his own right, another urban visionary of the 20th century, Henri Lefebvre, refers to the urban revolution as

> the transformations that affect contemporary society, ranging from the period when questions of growth and industrialization predominate (models, plans, programs) to the period when the urban problematic becomes predominant, when the search for solutions and modalities unique to urban society are foremost
>
> (2003, p.5)

This process is diverse and materializes through a variety of pathways. There is the category of world, or global, cities (very much related to Friedmann's own work) which have been called "basing points" of global capital accumulation (Friedmann 1986; Friedmann & Wolff 1982; Keil, Ren & Brenner 2016). Yet the spatial articulation of economic globalization takes many forms, from small mining towns to industrial districts, from ethnoburbs to financial centers and offshore banking sites, to name just a few (Keil 2011; Keil & Kipfer 2003; Kipfer & Keil 1995; Sassen 2000). Attention, therefore, has to be as much on "ordinary cities" and their bottom-up processes of making the global (Robinson 2006) as on a vast array of "globalizing" cities or "global" cities where the material processes of globalization find their conduit (Brenner & Keil 2011; Luke 2006).

The classical categories of density and diversity, centrality and peripherality have begun to shift in the process of moving towards complete urbanization (Tonkiss 2013, pp.26–59; Keil 2015). In the past, you knew when you were in the city and when you were not. Today, the urban is assumed to be everywhere. The classical, linear model of center-to-suburb urbanization has ceased to be valid in this current phase. Instead, processes of ubiquitous suburbanization (not as mere extensions of a central spatial logic) and post-suburbanization (the maturation of older peripheries) have begun to dominate the push towards urban society. Lefebvre himself recognized that the proliferation of the suburban form and the maturation of the singular *suburb* into a suburban landscape both posed a challenge and formed the foundation for today's urban theory (Lefebvre 1997). Friedmann has also acknowledged that the urban was not going to be found in a distinct and self-contained space and opposite of "the rural" or "the suburban." With regards to urbanization in China, he notes: "In any ontological sense, then, cities are never 'real'. Economic, social, cultural, even physical facets of urbanization extend far into traditionally non-urban areas, transforming both their appearance and mode of life. The city has become a metaphor for the urban" (Friedmann 2006, p.447).

The world that Lefebvre and Friedmann, though separated by a generation, were born into—a European-centered world of dense central (capital) cities like Vienna and Paris—dissipated before their eyes by mid-century. There were two trends, one leading to the regionalization of the city, and the other to global urbanization. Lefebvre and Friedmann became sharp observers of both. Both Lefebvre's and Friedmann's thinking was influenced directly by regional agglomeration, perhaps the most pervasive trend in mid-century urbanization in Europe and North America. Lefebvre viewed suburbanization in Paris as a kraken whose tentacles engulfed the real countryside around Paris and the "unicity" theory that some urban intellectuals had favored in the 1950s: "the historic city exploded into peripheries, suburbs—like what happened in Paris, and in all sorts of places, Los Angeles, San Francisco, wild extensions of the city—the theory of Unitary Urbanism lost any meaning" (Lefebvre 1997). In this sense, the growth of the city into the region and ultimately into the world, into an "urbanized society [that] can only be defined as global" (Lefebvre 2003, p.167), is a material fact in the surroundings of actually existing cities. Ultimately it is a phenomenon that extends beyond to the remote spaces of the vacation resorts in southern France and on the Atlantic coast, which exploded the common notion of "the regional" as a territorial unit, and to the resource economies everywhere around the globe that sustain and provision urban life overall and lastly to nature itself.

For Friedmann, especially in his work on global cities, which was undeniably influenced by living in Los Angeles, the urban region was the core and control center of global economies. In fact, as Hebbert observes, Friedmann and Weaver already talk about the "*world historical forces* of globalism and regionalism" (Hebbert 1984, p.137). This connection remains a constant in Friedmann's thinking beyond the specific Los Angeles experience. A recent analysis of his adopted home region of Vancouver is a telling sign of the elasticity of the city-region idea (Friedmann 2014). He calls this agglomerated space the "city-region," made up of the core city and "a surrounding regional space to sustain itself" (Friedmann 2002, p.3). In the end, though, Friedmann discards this simple core–periphery view of the city-region in favor of a more complex view. Akin to Lefebvre's *tissu urbain*, Friedmann introduces the "skein of the urban" as an operative term marking a process through which "the urban steadily advances across the surface of the earth" (p.6). The metaphor of the interwoven fabric replaces the core and periphery semiotics of previous models. And yet, might we add that the fallacy of much global city theory in Friedmann's wake—despite his explicit mobilization of the "skein of the urban"—has focused unproductively on the core economies of bankers and creatives and eclipsed the in-built hinterworlds of the center, most directly the global suburban. Lefebvre, who had watched Paris sprawl since the 1950s, notes yet another dimension of such hinterworlds when he visits Los Angeles where, after crossing mountain range after mountain range, you still "are and are not in the city" (1996, p.208).

While predicting in his more recent writings that "residual rural activities are disappearing from more and more parts of the world, and that economic urbanization is gaining as the redundant surplus of labor moves from countryside to city in search of a better livelihood" (Friedmann 2002, p.4), Friedmann never fell for a simplistic take on modernization as urbanization. By contrast, as Hebbert (1984, p.141) notes, Friedmann's view of regionalism involves a political and often emphatic notion of rural life where we witness "the direct participation of the rural masses and so enabling them, rather than desk-bound bureaucrats and technicians in a distant capital, to establish programmes that are relevant to local needs in all their real variation" (Friedmann and Weaver 1979, pp.202–203). And while Friedmann clearly rejects the idea of re-ruralization and the historical attempts to make that happen, he honors the problematique caused by the "rural–urban divide" and proposes the concept of "agropolitan development" as a "model of modular urbanization" to understand its significance and possibilities. Still, as was the case with Lefebvre's infatuation with the Pyrenees, there is a strong, but not romantic, relationship in Friedmann's work and life to the non-urban, to the landscape. Yes, he once quipped that the Frankfurt greenbelt was neither green nor a belt. But I have been in regional landscape environments with John where he felt at home, saw the beauty, imagined a future beyond the pitfalls of total urbanization—not least in my own southern German home region where we cruised the countryside and where he spent time at the end of World War II in the service of the American government. Similarly, Friedmann's own weekend island retreat in the Puget Sound sets the counterpoint for an otherwise thoroughly urban life.

Whereas Friedmann originally looked south (to Latin America) in his conjuration of the global city region, Lefebvre had his eyes set on the Chinese revolution. Lefebvre engages with the policy, in his eyes misguided, proposed by some Chinese revolutionaries to push a global rural strategy against the emerging global city in the West. This seemed to make sense as the power of the Chinese Communist Party was based on the peasantry and by extension other non-industrialized countries around the southern half of the globe (Lefebvre 2003, p.112). Similar to Lefebvre's conversation with the Maoist left, Friedmann addresses the development community, a logical interlocutor at a time when urbanization was deemed to be the reserve of an industrializing north and the countryside that of the underdeveloped south. Development dogma attempted to keep the rural masses on the land and away from the urban peripheries of the fast growing cities, but Friedmann pointed out clearly that urbanization would be irreversible (Friedmann 2002). It was what journalist Doug Saunders (2010) would later call "the final wave of rural–urban migration" and could not be stopped by development doctrine.

Friedmann's sensibilities have been shaped by much the same influences: progress *of*, and *through*, urbanization, which pushed on throughout the 20th century and seems unstoppable in the 21st. A man at home in the large-scale, globalized urban region—Los Angeles, Melbourne, Vancouver—he sees the connections of modernization, and urbanization, and perhaps progress to the good society. Yet Friedmann is also a skeptic with reverberations of Walter Benjamin's Angelus Novus who "where we perceive a chain of events, he sees one single catastrophe which keeps piling wreckage and hurls it in front of his feet" (Benjamin n.d.). History as urbanization and modernization appears to have a certain linearity to it. For those in the wreckage that piles up, a degree of submissiveness to the inevitable would be expected. But history is not linear. There are always bends and corners. There are possibilities for agency and change to which Friedmann's work opens our eyes. It is possible to see the particular pathway of urbanization in the 21st century as a version of non-linear history, a spectrum of human opportunity. In recognizing that, Friedmann parts company with Angelus Novus and his historical pessimism and retains an optimism of the mind that is steeped in the deep belief in human enlightenment. Friedmann ultimately remains utopianist in much of what he does and thinks. He states as much in his ideas about the Good City, which "has its foundations in human flourishing and multipli/city" and specifically in "housing, affordable health care, adequately remunerated work, and adequate social provision" (2002, p.118). In contrast to his long-time colleague and frequent intellectual sparring partner, the late Ed Soja (2015), John Friedmann has a mostly aspatial relationship to the urban. Despite his late affection for the work of Lefebvre, and in spite of his professional work as a planner, Friedmann remains an economist first, a thinker who believes in two seemingly opposing things: the *oikos*, or the family household, and the public good. The city almost disappears in between these poles, which are mediated by the city as a political community. The latter is chiefly responsible for making sure that the city is not run like a hotel.

The invisible suburb

Let us now look a bit more closely at Friedmann's idea of the prospect of cities. By definition, a prospect is something that is expected or certain to happen ahead, a mental picture of the future. In Friedmann's view, this prospect is fundamental urbanization "when the distinction between city and countryside would become blurred" (Friedmann 2002, p.131). In contrast to the traditional utopian futurism or utopianism of "the physical, three-dimensional city" (p.118), Friedmann's interest is in "living cities each of which moves along very different historical/cultural trajectories, building and rebuilding itself according to its self-understanding of what it is and would like to become" (p.118). While in conventional terms, this process is imagined as a concentric expansion, it is perhaps ultimately a form of involution in which the urban, as it becomes complete, can only progress when it becomes something that contains its logical opposite: the suburban sort of evolutionary middle-ground between the city and the countryside. Perhaps it is time to recognize, then, that post-suburbanization is now this process of real building of cities and it deserves our full attention. In the remainder of this essay, I will discuss this tendency for urban regions to fold in on themselves, to develop post-suburban form and relations.

Truth be told, Friedmann has no time for the suburbs. In his writing, the suburbs as real places or places of analytical significance seem to never appear. It is almost as if they don't exist in his imagination, despite having lived in some of the most suburbanized cities of the 20th century: Los Angeles, Melbourne, Vancouver. There is one exception, perhaps, in an insightful article Friedmann wrote in 1999 about the re-urbanization of Melbourne following a state planning report with the title "From Doughnut City to Café Society." The article also became a center piece for analysis in his *Prospect of Cities.* Friedmann describes a now familiar process of inner-city gentrification and outer-city decline: "During the post-World War II period, Melbourne expanded rapidly into its outer suburbs, as more and more families were able to realize their 'dream' of a large house on a quarter acre lot. Inner city areas were emptying out and becoming derelict. This is what doughnut city signifies: suburban growth, inner city decline. But by the mid-90s, changes were afoot: empty nesters started to move back into the city, young people tended to marry later, white collar replaced blue collar jobs, and 'yuppies' preferred apartment living close to where they thought the action was. Medium-density developments replaced the quarter acre lot. And so 'Café Society' was born" (Friedmann 2002, p.95). The regeneration of the hole in the doughnut came, however, at the expense of the deteriorating suburban areas.

For Friedmann, this poses a stringent political conundrum of recognition which he takes up in an almost sarcastic, flowery and somewhat uncharacteristic tone given his usually more restrained style of writing:

> The political task of the report ["From Doughnut City to Café Society"] is to persuade Melbourne's opinion makers of its logic. In his public pronouncements, the Minister of Planning had nothing but derisory remarks about the people he called "wheelie binners" (residents of leafy suburbs who roll their garbage containers out to the curb for weekly pick-ups), who are forever "whingeing" (complaining) over the government's lack of attention to their suburban needs. He seemed to be saying, "Why don't they, too, join the trek to the inner city and the glamorous Café Society on the south bank of the Yarra?"
>
> (Friedmann 2002, p.96)

This is, of course, classic Friedmann, who argues with the figure of (central) state versus (dispersed) community power, a figure we know from his metaphorical divide of citadel-versus-ghetto in the polities of the world city. While he surely has no sympathies with the "wheelie binners," Friedmann does recognize their political marginalization in the course of changing Melbourne's image to a center-oriented creative-city blueprint.

Apart from this singular recognition, Friedmann conventionally seems to jump scale directly from the notion of the city to the urban field. While acknowledging the need for dealing politically and administratively with the growth of large urban regions, he tends to view the solutions straddling two poles: the regional level of generalized infrastructure and the lifeworld of the local (urban) community. He did so presciently in his early work with Miller:

> Governments can exercise two modes of influence to hasten the arrival of urban fields: the first is the location of government-financed investments; the second is information. The former is perhaps the more persuasive in the long view. There is a singular opportunity for planning on the scale of urban fields in the design of regional highway and railroad systems, in the location and design of regional airports, in the siting of regional colleges and government-sponsored research institutions, in the distribution of administrative offices, and in the designation and development of public land reserves for recreation. Somewhat less direct controls over location can be used in connection with subsidy programs for the acquisition of second homes as well as for the building of retirement communities and new towns.
>
> (Friedmann & Miller 1965, p.318)

While this section names the parameters of the post-suburban reality in which most living and planning in city-regions now takes place *avant la lettre*, it does not dwell on the specific issues related to emerging demands and needs stemming from that reality.

Remarkably, though, Friedmann early on douses the flames of anti-suburban sentiments and challenges American urban society to accept its periphery as an inevitable part of the future metropolitan world:

> The projected incorporation of the periphery into the urban realm will be accompanied by significant changes in American patterns of living. On the whole, we expect that these changes will be evaluated favorably. Derogatory slogans, such as "sprawl" and "scatteration," bandied about in ideological campaigns, will have to be discarded in any serious search for what it means to live on the new scale. Although not all the consequences can be foreseen now, a few merit closer attention. We shall restrict our comment to only three of them: a wider life space on the average, a wider choice of living environments, and a wider community of interests.
>
> (Friedmann & Miller 1965, p.316).

Friedmann talks about the city-region which he defines as "a functionally integrated area consisting of both a large urban core and contiguous region that serves this city's multiple needs and provides a space for its expansion" (2002, p.22). This emphasis on the city-region—"the whole of the city-region has, in fact, become a new form of urban landscape" (ibid.)—has similarities with Tom Sieverts' *Zwischenstadt* (2003) and Ed Soja's "regional urbanization" (2015). But in contrast to Sieverts and Soja, Friedmann remains sold on some hierarchical image of centrality, both functional and spatial. There is a center that needs expansion and there is a region that will provide satisfaction of needs, all distributed, of course, in a "highly charged political process" (2002, p.25).

This political process itself has its preordained hierarchies of power. It is determined by the center, from the center. In the context of the Melbourne case reviewed briefly above, Friedmann explains that the dominance of the *central* Café Society in the universe of the region is paralleled by the invisibility of the peripheral landscapes of the city-region:

> The rest of metropolitan Melbourne, or 92 percent of the population, are rendered invisible; they are not part of Café Society. They continue to live their ghost lives in the middle and, above all, the outer suburbs, and among them are many immigrants.
>
> (Friedmann 2002, p.96)

Friedmann mocks what he calls a "'trendlet' of migration inversion from suburbs to the inner city" as he finds it patently improbable that the suburban "wheelie-binners" will migrate *en masse* to the Café Society core any time soon. With the Café Society comes the familiar album of images of centrality that eclipses representations of the rhythm of everyday life outside:

> A small number of city landmarks are assimilated to the "official story," becoming icons of city marketing: the Eiffel Tower, Sydney's Opera House, the Golden Gate Bridge, Frank Gehry's Guggenheim Museum Bilbao. But the landmarks of ordinary people … are hidden in the small spaces of everyday life, in backyards and barbershops.
>
> (Friedmann 2002, p.97)

It is naturally understood that this is where Friedmann sees *Aufholbedarf*, the need for some affirmative action to make those unheard stories come alive.

Yet even here, the (post)suburbs, as a specific environment in need of explanation, remain invisible. During a talk given in 2014 at a planning conference in Vancouver, for example, during which Friedmann (2014) extols the push for a regionalized urbanity, the suburbs themselves remain unnamed in this contested landscape. They are just fabric of the city-region, apparently not worthy of special attention. Friedmann is specific regarding suburbs in only few cases. They don't grasp his imagination as places where particular suburban ways of life take shape. Neither does he see suburbanization as a process of city building with its characteristic modalities of state action, capital accumulation and private authoritarianism that characterizes suburbia today (Ekers, Hamel & Keil 2015).

Even in the moment of recognizing the disempowerment of the periphery, Friedmann continues to treat suburbs as young cities and parts of regions. Cities, regions. Nothing in between. He says:

> The 21 so-called suburbs of Metro Vancouver are thus unequivocally growing into complete cities which is what the regional strategy calls for. But in becoming urban in this fuller sense, local authorities must be enabled to deal with the multiple problems generated by this process effectively, fairly and efficiently.
>
> (Friedmann 2014).

Conclusion: looking beyond the prospect of cities

In conclusion, let me raise two issues that re-reading Friedmann's work on the prospect of cities (with implicit references to Lefebvre's notion of complete urbanization) prompted me to note. First, the prospect of cities is fast being realized in this emerging urban century in the post-suburban landscape, in between the center and the periphery of the urban field. It is a world of global suburban constellations (Keil 2013). Friedmann's prospect of cities has to a large degree turned into a post-suburban reality, with particular suburban forms of life, regional infrastructures that connect out to multiscalar networks beyond. These post-suburban lifeworlds are constituted in contradistinction to and in partial autonomy of the (urban) center and the (rural) periphery. This challenges the common notion of urbanization as a process whose prospects have been shaped by 19th- and 20th-century imaginaries of urbanization. Where the centralized industrial cities of Manchester, Chicago or Paris occupied our past projections of where urbanization might lead, we now need to invoke the vast post-suburban landscapes of Los Angeles, Shanghai or Istanbul as guiding models. They should take up more of our attention while we re-envision the prospect of cities for the 21st century.

Second, the urban transition, while unstoppable, is not all-encompassing, and may have to allow space for some quirky reassertions of the non-urban along the way. I am thinking here of the heartland of Friedmann's recent interests: China, where some slow resettlement of abandoned rural villages has begun as urbanites turn their back on the metropolis (Bulard 2015). But the world of urban centers and rural peripheries changes on a global scale, too, as we proceed through the post-suburban century. In a strange reversal of the urban transition, we can now imagine, as does irreverent French novelist Michel Houellebecq in his magisterial *The Map and the Territory* (2012), that vacationing Chinese tourists colonize the French countryside as an entirely de-industrialized *Grande Nation* becomes the destination of alienated sub/urbanites from around the globe. Lefebvre's concern about earlier Chinese preoccupations with the global city echo strongly in this context. Unexpectedly, France, once the metropolitan core of the imagination of planetary urban society, has now become the periphery. A globe of suburbs has swallowed the countryside everywhere, for it to be revived as a global simulacrum in the metropolitan core itself.

Note

1 Acknowledgement: Thanks to Jenny Lugar for her research assistance for this essay.

References

Benjamin, W n.d., "On the concept of history". Available from <http://www.sfu.ca/~andrewf/CONCEPT2.html> [31 December 2015].

Brenner, N & Keil, R 2011, "From global cities to globalized urbanization" in *The City Reader*, eds R LeGates & F Stout, 5th edn, Routledge, London and New York, pp. 666–676.

Bulard, M 2015, "China's villages revive", *Le Monde Diplomatique*, November. Available from <https://mondediplo.com/2015/11/06china> [20 December 2015].

Charmes, E & Keil, R 2015, "The politics of post-suburban densification in Canada and France", *International Journal of Urban and Regional Research*, 39(3): 581–602. DOI: 10.1111/1468-2427.12194.

Ekers, M, Hamel, P & Keil, R 2015, "Governing suburbia: modalities and mechanisms of suburban governance" in *Suburban Governance: A Global View*, eds P Hamel & R Keil, University of Toronto Press, Toronto, pp. 19–48.

Friedmann, J 1986, "The World City Hypothesis", *Development and Change*, 17(1): 69–83.

Friedmann, J 1999, "The city of everyday life: knowledge/power and the problem of representation", *disP*, 35(136–7): 4–11.

Friedmann, J 2002, *The Prospect of Cities*, University of Minnesota Press, Minneapolis.

Friedmann, J 2006, "Four theses in the study of China's urbanization", *International Journal of Urban and Regional Research*, 30(2): 440–451.

Friedmann, J 2014, "Vancouver—21 Suburbs in search of a city". Presented at *Vancouver, Vancouverism and 21st Century Urbanism Symposium*, April 15–16. Available from <https://www.youtube.com/watch?v=CdvDJo9skj0> [6 December 2015].

Friedmann, J & Miller, J 1965, "The urban field", *Journal of the American Institute of Planners*, 31(4): 312–320.

Friedmann, J & Weaver, C 1979, *Territory and Function: The Evolution of Regional Planning*, University of California Press, Berkeley.

Friedmann, J & Wolff, G 1982, "World city formation: an agenda for research and action", *International Journal of Urban and Regional Research*, 6(3): 309–344.

Hebbert, M 1984, "Regionalism versus realism", *Environment and Planning D: Society and Space*, 2: 133–150.

Houellebecq, M 2012, *The Map and the Territory*, trans. G. Bowd, Knopf, New York.

Keil, R 2011, "Transnational urban political ecology: health, environment and infrastructure in the unbounded city" in *The New Companion to the City*, eds G Bridge & S Watson, 2nd edn, Wiley-Blackwell, Oxford.

Keil, R 2013, *Suburban Constellations: Governance, Land and Infrastructure in the 21st Century*, Jovis, Berlin.

Keil, R 2015, "Towers in the park, bungalows in the garden: peripheral densities, metropolitan scales and the political cultures of post-suburbia", *Built Environment*, 41(4): 579–596.

Keil, R & Kipfer, S 2003, "The urban experience and globalization" in *Changing Canada: Political Economy as Transformation*, eds W Clement & LF Vosko, McGill's University Press, Montreal and Kingston, pp. 335–362.

Keil, R, Ren, XF & Brenner, N 2016, *The Globalizing Cities Reader*, Routledge, London.

Kipfer, S & Keil, R 1995, "Urbanisierung und Technologie in der Periode des Globalen Kapitalismus" in *Capitales Fatales: Urbanisierung und Politik in den Finanzmetropolen Frankfurt und Zürich (Capitales Fatales: Urbanization and Politics in the Financial Metropoles Zürich and Frankfurt)*, eds H Hitz, R Keil, U Lehrer, C Schmid, K Ronneberger & R Wolff, Rotpunkt Verlag, Zürich, pp. 61–87.

Lefebvre, H 1996, *Writings on Cities*, Blackwell, Oxford.

Lefebvre, H 1997, "Henri Lefebvre on the Situationist International". Interview conducted and translated by Kristin Ross in 1983; printed in *October 79*. Available from: <http://www.notbored.org/lefebvre-interview.html> [31 December 2015].

Lefebvre, H 2003, *The Urban Revolution*, University of Minnesota Press, Minneapolis.

Lefebvre, H 2014, *Toward an Architecture of Enjoyment*, ed. L. Stanek, University of Minnesota Press: Minneapolis.

Luke, T 2006, "Global Cities vs. 'global cities': rethinking contemporary urbanism as public ecology" in *The Global Cities Reader*, eds N Brenner & R Keil, Routledge, London.

Robinson, J 2006, *Ordinary Cities: Between Modernity and Development*, Routledge, London.

Sassen, S 2000, *Cities in a World Economy*, Pineforge Press, Thousand Oaks, C.A.

Saunders, D 2010, *Arrival Cities: The Final Migration and our Next World*, A.A. Knopf, Toronto.

Sieverts, T 2003, *Cities without Cities: An Interpretation of the Zwischenstadt*, Routledge, London and New York.

Soja, E 2015, "Accentuate the regional", *International Journal of Urban and Regional Research*, 39(2), 372–381.

Tonkiss, F 2013, *Cities by Design: The Social Life of Urban Form*, Polity, Cambridge.

13 Room for the *Good Society*?

Public space, amenities and the condominium

Ute Lehrer

> Cranes crowd the skyline. Those high-rise condos that everyone likes to complain about have brought vivid new life to the streets. The hum and bustle of living city is palpable and it's thrilling.
>
> (Gee 2015)

> The Good Society is a perennial concern. How ought we to build a life in common with each other?
>
> (Friedmann 1979, p.xi)

Introduction

It has become one of the most widely used statements that this century is the urban century, where a majority of people lives in cities. With all this population growth one needs to remember that this demands also a good number of new dwellings. But how to accommodate all this growth? And where? In very few places planners are the ones that actually make these decisions. And it is usually not the public, but the market, or self-help, or a combination of both, which invests capital into particular places in order to build housing and shelter for people. The public plays a role usually, but not always, as a provider for the bare bones of infrastructure. Therefore, planning's role more often than not is focused on where the growth should happen, by developing a policy framework that steers growth into certain areas while hindering it at others (Lehrer & Wieditz 2009). The development and implementation of these growth policies have become a key area for planners of today, and land use planning, together with infrastructure planning, are at the center of all this. The problematic relationship of planning towards the physical aspects of planning, of course, is not something new. Already 30 years ago Allan Jacobs and Donald Appleyard proclaimed that: "City planning is too immersed in the administration and survival of housing, environmental, and energy programs and in responding to budget cuts and community demands to have any clear sense of direction with regards to city form" (1987, p.114).

But the fundamental question of planning remains: How can we build a society that is fair, just and inclusive? How can planners of today plan for cities of tomorrow in order to guarantee a built environment that does not stand in the way of such an ideal society, but rather provides a socio-spatial context that nurtures differences and inclusivity? How can we, as Friedmann is urging us in light of the population growth in cities worldwide, create images of the Good City (2000, p.464)? Friedmann's work reminds us of the necessity of utopian thinking as part of the planning profession, where the ideal is often miles apart from the reality, but that should not stop us from engaging with and pushing forward questions of justice and equality, addressed in the context of what he calls radical practice, or insurgency. Friedmann's utopia is one of social relations and less of built environments—"this is not my domain" (2000, p.471).

The history of planning isn't one with a path paved by lots of successes, and the few that exist occur only within a particular framework, and more often than not, these successes become failures over time due to their inability to adapt to new conditions. Most cities in North America and Europe have examples of social housing complexes that were based on a utopian vision of the Good City. They were built at the height of the modernist period as a response to the ills of the overcrowded 19th-century city, with the promise to guarantee "light, air, opening" to everybody (Giedion 1929) and with that to establish a new and better society, one that would be democratic and just, only to become neglected—socially, politically and financially—over time and to fall into disarray.

This chapter is not about the failure of planning. It's not even about planning *per se*. It rather poses some questions in the context of Toronto's condominium boom: How can we form, as John Friedmann's life work has asked for, a Good Society (or Good City) that is based on mutual respect, on dialogical relations in a non-hierarchical structure? How can we create a city that is just, fair and inclusive when we build concrete structures that disallow a wider engagement of the public? These questions are asked in the context of Toronto's condominium boom. By engaging John Friedmann's concept of the Good Society, which he proposed in the 1970s, I will discuss the condominium boom and its relation to public space in two ways: internalizing amenities on the one hand and encroachment into public space during construction periods on the other.

The condo boom in Toronto and the thirst for urbanity

Since the early 2000s we have seen a massive building boom of condo towers taking place in Toronto, which started in the downtown core, followed by a proliferation into neighborhoods and throughout the entire region. The Condominium is a legal innovation in land tenure, which has been around in Europe for more than a hundred years and arrived in North America in the mid 20th century. In Toronto, we saw a couple of waves of condominium activities and the most recent one, which started in the late 1990s, is the one that is of interest here. Over the last few years, Toronto's condo market is in the international spotlight with statements such as these: "Developers in Toronto are building 97 residential towers—some as high as 92 stories—more than any other city in North America including New York City" (Dmitrieva & van Loon 2015).

The driver for the building boom in Toronto is not primarily caused by speculation, as in many other global cities, but rather it is pushed by demand for shelter, caused by a combination of the constant stream of new immigrants and a need for accommodating lifestyle changes, as well as providing housing for different income levels. The question is open of how these condo towers are transforming fundamental ingredients of an open society, namely amenities or spaces where the public can come together and define and redefine what is possible, and what is not, in that particular moment of that specific society. Most condominium towers have amenities that usually are only accessible to the people who live in the condo tower, and with that a good part of the population is excluded. What was once the pride and the merit of the Modernist period—to provide public amenities to a wide range of the population—has increasingly become internalized inside of the condo tower. In order to have a viable and healthy society, however, one needs not the sameness of the typical condo owner, but a vigorous portion of difference, in practices as well as in opinions.

When I point to forms of homogenization, others see a tendency of opening up towards excitement: "When I left Toronto all those years ago, I was going in search of a wider world. I could never have guessed that when I came back there, the world would come to me" (Gee 2015). This thirst for global-city status can be heard around the world, and it seems to have become part of the political discourse no matter if left, right or center. Politicians call for vibrant cities, pushing forward an agenda that often employs the magical formula of mega projects or spectacles, ideally designed by one of the world's renowned architects, that promises to put a spotlight on a city, and with it, it is believed that the money will flow, first in the form of international investment, and then by economic growth overall. The spectacle goes hand in hand with wanting to build "smart," which these days also means denser and higher cities.

But what kind of urbanism is created through these structures? And what is the role of public space? What about the ideal of a Good Society, a fundamental question that can be found in many cultures throughout history. Urbanism exists, we know it when we feel it, though we can't put our hands on it. But how to define something that is obvious, in front of our eyes, yet not, something that seems to be obfuscated from our view? A widely used definition was established by Louis Wirth in 1938, where he argued that density, size, heterogeneity and distinct forms of social behavior and patterns are at the core of urbanism. This definition allows the researcher to investigate, to measure, to tally up and to map urbanism. But as many have pointed out, this is only part of the story. Urbanism is not just grown out of nowhere. It is embedded into the money economy, which was pointed out as early as 1903 by Georg Simmel when studying modernity in his work on "The Metropolis and Mental Life." And further, as explored by urban thinkers such as Henri Lefebvre, Manuel Castells and David Harvey during the 1970s and 1980s, it is capitalism that produces urban space. This territorialization of capital is the prime engine of both the economy and the society. The city is the site of the market rule and of state practices in which planning is a formally constituting object with assumed civil norms and model citizens (Roy 2011). However, part of urbanism is also a social struggle over urban space, one that Andy Merrifield (2002, p.17) calls "dialectical." In this sense, urbanism is, to quote Ananya Roy, a "political experience, political as it pertains to ... issues of power and conflict" (2011, p.8).

And that's precisely where public space comes in to the discussion. Public space is not homogenous; it contains tensions and is generally conceived as open to greater or lesser public participation. The difference to private space is the rule of access, the source and nature of control over entry to a space, the individual and collective behaviors that are sanctioned in specific spaces, as well as the rules of use (Low & Smith 2006). We can sum it up in the words of Setha Low and Neil Smith who state that: "'Public space' has very different meanings in different societies, places, and times ... its meaning today is very much bound up with the contrast between public and private space" (2006, p.4).

As I have argued elsewhere, public space is not something that exists in itself but continuously has to be negotiated and renegotiated (Lehrer 1998). Just because the land belongs to the City, and therefore even in a market economy could be defined as a good that belongs to all of its citizens via the social agreement of representation, it does not mean that it is truly public. In Toronto, Dundas Square is such an example that demonstrates the limits of public space quite well. The square is often rented out to commercial enterprises for showcasing their products. Also the rules of engagement on the square are clearly defined. Demonstrations, which are the cornerstone of a democracy, can't happen on the square without a permit. If civil society wants to have activities occurring on the square they have to apply through a formal process. The public, in this sense, is orchestrated by the rules of engagement. On the other hand we have places that are private or commercial, such as the living room or the coffee shop, where those demonstrations are planned and in that moment, as I argue, become entities with a public purpose for as long as this activity takes place. In other words, public space takes place in a range of social locations—from the classical park and street to the Internet and social media and everything in between—with the "urban" being the privileged site for analysis. And here, we need to introduce Friedmann's concept of the Good Society as radical social practice.

John Friedmann's Good Society

Throughout most of his life, John Friedmann has been a strong advocate for how to build better societies where power is constantly negotiated and renegotiated. In the late 1970s, at a time when the global economic and political system underwent a major shift towards a neoliberal world order—with an ideology that put the individual above the collective and has the free market economy as its mantra—Friedmann was interested in a positive change of the existing conditions and a more just society. In his belief, a way out of this situation was to build small, local and temporary associations, or sodalities as he called them: "'good societies', small in the numbers of its members, bonding through interpersonal relations of dialogue, non-hierarchical in structure, and oriented towards struggles in the street, the law courts, academia, and democratic elections" (Friedmann 2011, p.51). The motivation to strive for a Good Society, as Friedmann states, is "because we are unable to bear the world's absurdity" and therefore start to revolt, which then becomes a struggle for meaning, meaning over "significant relation to self and to others, and to the environment in which we move, both physically and in spirit" (1979, p.8).

Dialogue is at the center of the Good Society, with each person being a questioner and a responder alike. The problem, as Friedmann sees it, is that the Good Society has to function within a different system, namely that of the state and societal planning, which have hierarchy and power as their ordering principles. This means that two different systems are trying to get into a dialogue with each other. The Good Society model is based on the understanding that every participant is both a "questioner and a responder alike," while the state and social planning represent a system that believes in hierarchy and power. Not everybody has equal voice at each step of the way. Because it refuses hegemonic power, there is a permanent struggle for the Good Society to assert itself within the other system, to be in opposition of it, so as to open up and advance into new territories. In contrast to state and social planning, the Good Society does not want to acquire power for itself, nor does it want to abolish the state because that would have a totalizing effect. Instead, it stands dialectically "in opposition to the world of social planning and the state" (Friedmann 1979, p.14), not dialectically in a Marxian sense though, rather in the Chinese tradition of Yin and Yang, where the idea of unavoidable historical progress is absent and where the "unity of opposites" is in continuous and dynamic tension with each other. Friedmann calls it "radical social practice."

The Good Society is temporal and gets created in moments, it is time sensitive and it is constantly socially produced. "The project of the Good Society is to open up and expand the spaces for dialogue in a society that is subject to the hegemonic powers of large corporations and the state." The good society "is a temporary social formation which, lacking a territorial base of its own, *exists exclusively in its actual practices*. Its space is the space of social relations" (Friedmann 2011, p.58; emphasis added).

Therefore, the Good Society does not need a specific container, neither a building nor a public open space, but it is produced through actual practices. The place of the Good Society is "the street, the factory, the neighborhood, the school ... These are its physical settings. But they do not define nor limit the Good Society" (Friedmann 1979, p.xiii).

This understanding of the social production of the Good Society is similar to what I argued above in regards to public space (and in Lehrer 1998).

While small in size (as Friedmann suggests it contains between five and 12 members), the Good Society should not be mixed up with the family unit. In order to be part of it, the family would need to

> break down the barriers between the private and public realms, it must cease to be a place for the accumulation of possessions, for the practice of exclusiveness, for the mere reproduction of social relations. It must instead become a place for the transforming practice of dialogue among its members, each of whom is a dyadic being, free and independent, accepted as an equal and in his difference, or hers, from every other member and by each.
>
> (Friedmann 1979, p.xiv)

It almost sounds apologetic when Friedmann states: "To those who fail to be involved, it does not usually disclose itself. You will find it only in practice ... now here, now there, wherever you are and whenever you are prepared to join in its work" (1979, p.xiii).

The quest might be utopian, but utopia in Friedmann's thinking is a "normative theory: a vision of how social relations ought to be arranged, and how we should proceed to structure them" (1979, p.xi). It comes with discipline and commitment for a future with hope, challenges and transcendent possibilities. Some 10 years later, Friedmann picks up the importance of utopia again, in a response to Castells' trilogy on the network society, where he argues that utopian vision is important for building a city that is informed by values and therefore is justifiable. Utopia is needed to correct injustice (Friedmann 2000).

Is there a place in Toronto's condominium for the Good Society?

While John Friedmann's work speaks very little to the role of the built environment in urban planning processes—in fact he rejects addressing urban form directly (see above)—I nevertheless want to take up the challenge and argue that the form of, and the practices in, the built environment are more, or less, conducive for moments of the Good Society. I discuss this within the context of two areas where the quest for the Good Society might find a material container: first, the common areas in a condominium or what normally is called amenities, and second, the space outside of the condominium: the street and open spaces.

The typical condominium building in Toronto is a high-rise building with individual units, common areas such as rooftops, party rooms, swimming pools and so on, a lobby and sometimes additional space for retail. Occasionally, there are internal or external parks, and often some sort of open space. Almost all of them have exercise rooms, and a good number have terraces, lounges, BBQ areas, party rooms and reflection pools. Curiosities such as a rock-climbing wall, a wine-tasting room, or a dog-washing area are appearing on the list of amenities in the sales brochures, as is the yoga room. Those that are part of the condominium have access to these amenities, either as owners or renters, or as guests.

There are two sides to the sales pitch promoting lifestyle and amenities. It internalizes amenities that under a Keynesian state were public—the swimming pool for example—and with that, privatizes them. This means that this cooptation creates environments where people no longer have to leave their homes to use public amenities and hence minimizes their chances of encountering people that are different from them. One wonders what impact this privatization of amenities has on the understanding of the public. As a result will cities such as Toronto see less and less political support for public amenities, for instance swimming pools? Or does the existence of common areas, with all their internal contradictions and conflictual elements (noise, smoke, social practices, etc.), have the potential to create temporary social formations that have a political aspect to them and therefore are forms of the Good Society, where visions for a better, more just and inclusive city are developed in small groups of five to 12 members?

Whereas the first discussion of the condominium looked at the internal aspects of a condominium, the second one goes outside, to the street level. When a condominium gets constructed, the first sign of the imminent transformation is a fence that marks the territory, but also protects the public from any danger. However, one also could argue that the construction fences that are going up in the middle of sidewalks are an encroachment into the public space (see Figure 13.1). People have to continuously navigate around them, sometimes increasing the risk of accidents. While there are regulations in place for these walls—for example advertisement is limited to the companies that are associated with the site in one way or another—they are also part of the public realm. Because of the sheer amount of construction sites in some neighborhoods, this has also reached the political realm. Beautification strategies of changing the construction walls were successfully put forward by local councillors and led to new types of boardings for some of the construction sites, or to the request for creative work along the walls executed by artists or by the local community.

The board-fencing problem is temporary and lasts just as long as construction is going on. What is permanent and only accessible after construction is done are passageways, small pocket parks and other open spaces that are publicly accessible but privately owned (POPS, as they are called in the literature). They have become more and more a feature of Toronto's condo landscape. As laudable as it is that the developer agrees to have part of the privately owned land open to the public, often in exchange for more height

Figure 13.1 Extrusions into public space
Source: Ute Lehrer

and density, there are two problems: the first one is that social practices on that land are regulated by the owner of the land and enforced by private security. This usually entails that loitering is not allowed and that the public space will be closed during certain hours. The second problem is similar to the internalized swimming pool: the political will to pay towards public parks, or more generally, to pay municipal taxes, is reduced when one has access to open spaces right at home.

So where is the realm of the Good Society here? Is the condo tower more or less conducive to have moments of a Good Society evolve in it? And why should a condominium tower be more prone to creating the right envelope for it than other forms of housing? The discussion is inconclusive.

Conclusion

Are we moving in the direction of the Good Society as John Friedmann's life work has been trying to convince us? The concept of the Good Society is, as Friedmann says, "a spiritual and moral inquiry addressed to those who, by acting in the world, endeavor to find new pathways of our collective future" (2011, p.58). The reasons for choosing this text are its non-linear way of writing and the fact that it gives the reader space and contemplation in order to engage with the complexity of contemporary cities: from the contradictions of growth to urbanism as a political experience, from the social construction of public space to the vision of an ideal society, from the internalization of public amenities to increased privatization, from condominium building to the city.

In the context of Toronto, one needs to ask what kind of city is being created? Is the city that Marcus Gee encountered when he came back to Toronto a better city? Or is Toronto going the way of New York, where one blogger, after seeing a series of pictures from the subway of the 1980s, lamented:

> I grew up in the Big Apple, remember this period well. ... It wasn't half as bad as often depicted. NYC was such a fun, creative and exciting place, all the way up to around 2002 or so. It's sadly become a shell of itself. Everything that was unique has been sucked dry.
>
> (Cucci 2013)

As for Toronto, the collective willingness to pay for the maintenance of public parks and public swimming pools, which are especially important in dense urban structures, might shrink given that the usual condo owner has their own little open space with some "green space" as part of the condominium structure.

It is quite possible that the internalization of a wide range of amenities will continue what has been described as splintering urbanism: where some people have access while others are excluded from the benefits of social infrastructure. Just to make the point clear, it is not the planning department of the city that is to blame for this tendency but our collective willingness to pay for amenities that should serve everybody, and not only those that can afford them. So, let's face it: while the condominium internalizes a lot of amenities, we should still make sure that we, as a collective, understand the importance of spaces that allow spontaneous communities to evolve. This, of course, needs not only the political will but what John Friedmann would call the Good Society: dialogue, visions, possibilities, radical practice; people engaging with each other for a better life and to balance out those that are in power.

References

Cucci, J 2013, "NYC Subways in the 1980s were no jokes", *The Roosevelts*, 23 October. Available from: <http://www.rsvlts.com/2013/10/23/nyc-subways-in-the-1980s-were-no-joke-47-photos/#9> [21 February 2016].

Dmitrieva, K & van Loon, J 2015, "Is Canada the New Switzerland? Safe reputation abroad seen driving Toronto's condo boom", *Bloomberg News* 22 May. Available from: <http://business.financialpost.com/personal-finance/mortgages-real-estate/is-canada-the-new-switzerland-safe-reputation-abroad-seen-driving-torontos-condo-boom> [10 January 2016].

Friedmann, J 1979, *The Good Society*, MIT Press, Cambridge, M.A.

Friedmann, J 2000, "The Good City: in defense of utopian thinking", *International Journal of Urban and Regional Research*, 24(2): 460–472.

Friedmann, J 2011, *Insurgencies: Essays in Planning Theory*, Routledge, London.

Gee, M 2015, "The Toronto I left isn't the city it's become. Life is happening right here", *The Globe and Mail* 9 October. Available from: <http://www.theglobeandmail.com/news/toronto/the-toronto-i-left-isnt-the-city-its-become-life-is-happening-right-here/article26759564/> [10 October 2015].

Giedion, S 1929, *Befreites Wohnen. 85 Bilder erläutert von S. Giedion*, Orell Füssli, Zürich.

Jacobs, A & Appleyard, D 1987, "Toward an urban design manifesto", *Journal of the American Planning Association*, 53(1): 112–120.

Lehrer, U 1998, "Is there still room for public space? Global cities and the privatization of the public realm" in *Possible Urban Worlds*, ed. International Network for Urban Research and Action, Birkhäuser, Basel, Boston, pp. 200–207.

Lehrer, U & Wieditz, T 2009, "Condominium development and gentrification: the relationship between policies, building activities and socio-economic development in Toronto", *Canadian Journal of Urban Research*, 18(1): 82–103.

Low, S & Smith, N (eds) 2006, *The Politics of Public Space*, Routledge, London.

Merrifield, A 2002, *Dialectical Urbanism: Social Struggle in the Capitalist City*, Monthly Review Press, New York.

Roy, A 2011, "Urbanism, worlding practices and the theory of planning", *Planning Theory*, 10(1): 6–15.

Sassen, S 2001, *The Global City: New York. London, Tokyo*, 2nd ed., Princeton University Press, Princeton, NJ.

Simmel, G 1903, "The metropolis and mental life" in *The Sociology of Georg Simmel*, trans. and ed. KH Wolf, The Free Press, New York, pp. 409–424.

Wirth, L 1938, "Urbanism as a Way of Life", *The American Journal of Sociology*, 44(1): 1–24.

14 The escalating privatization of urban space meets John Friedmann's post-urban landscape

Saskia Sassen

In his recent work on China, John Friedmann (see especially 2013; also 2005, 2006) gives us a brilliant and visionary interpretation of a condition he names the post-urban. He uses the term "post-urban era" to capture

> a period of transition during which many single-centered urban regions are gradually absorbed by and incorporated into a polycentric urban system that extends over a relatively compact, densely populated area and is home to multiple millions, as many as upwards of 50 million or more. Such a region can no longer be called a city in any conventional sense; it is an unprecedented form of the human habitat.
>
> (Friedmann 2013, p.2)

Friedmann observes that one marking feature of this emergent condition is the loss of the "periurban zones" that have traditionally existed alongside cities. As a result, the remaining agricultural or other rural production that survives the rapid urban expansion becomes industrialized—the only way to survive the urbanizing onslaught. I find this a brilliant insight by Friedmann. In the case of major urban centers in a polycentric region, "neighboring periurban areas begin to interpenetrate, forming a continuous urban skein," a process Friedmann refers to as "a fusion of urban horizons" (Friedmann 2013, p.2).

No matter the multiple urban nodes in this vast landscape, there is an infrastructural grid that links them to "each other and to the world." That grid consists of familiar transport modes but also electronic networks. One overall impact is to enable all sorts of mobilities that eventually begin to have the effect of reducing space–time distances.

But this is not simply Gottmann's spatially understood megalopolis. This post-urban landscape is a complex multilayered entity that is interactive and, mostly, responsive to those interactions. Notable examples are the Yangtze River Delta, the Pearl River Delta, the Tokaido region in Japan, and the emerging post-urban region centered on Mumbai (Friedmann 2013; see also Salingaros 2002).

Here we begin to get to the heart of Friedmann's argument: This socio-spatial condition is new—we have not seen this in earlier periods, thus neither can our existing categories capture it adequately. Friedmann identifies two, of possibly many more, key variables as critical. One is that this post-urban condition needs to be understood "not only as a physical artifact in three dimensional space but additionally as a *densely patterned, dynamic socio-cultural, economic, and political set of interdependent systems* that are constituted of tens of millions of interactive decision-making units" which range from households to powerful governmental entities "connected in various ways to each other via a *fourth dimension* of face-to-face and electronically mediated *communications and exchanges* across different scales" (Friedmann 2013, p.3; emphasis added). In terms of planning, this can open new ground but also raise problems of all sorts.

The second critical element is "the sphere of self-reflective thought" which can seem chaotic, "but it is actually helping to give shape to complex new patterns in the material world, as millions of actors incrementally adjust their decisions according to *error-correcting feedback and other information*" (Friedmann 2013, p.4; emphasis added).

Friedmann posits that the above features are the

> outlines of a partially *self-organizing human system* that conforms to given parametric constraints that are themselves undergoing constant revision, extensions, and contractions. *An urban super-organism can thus be understood as a high-density, four-dimensional spatial system* where a change originating at any point tends to ripple through the system, producing unanticipated changes, both small and large, at many other points.
>
> (Friedmann 2013, p.4; emphasis added)

This is an enormously exciting and visionary conceptualizing of both the deeper meaning of a post-urban condition and the survival dynamics ensuring fluidity. In my reading, it also harkens back to some of his earlier work on territory (Friedmann 1978, 1981) and, while less explicitly, in his agenda-setting work on World Cities (Friedmann 1995). I (Sassen 2013a, 2013c) find that the category of the territorial is ascendant today in ways that contest the more classic category of the nation-state (see also, for a Chinese perspective, Xu and Yeh 2010).

I can see, and accept, Friedmann's interpretation of a post-urban condition and, importantly, his analysis of the features that give it a capacity for survival. It is satisfyingly complex and has extraordinary potential for re-inventing mega-urban regions.

My concern is with emergent forces that can become powerful obstacles to this type of complex, always mobile or changing, and partly self-adjusting system. Friedmann's observations about the specific ways in which planning matters in this "post-urban" phase are important. But my question is, are they enough to counteract the obstacles?

In what follows I focus briefly on one major and escalating negative obstacle to this fluidity. It is the rapidly surging trend in many parts of the world of large-scale corporate buying of properties. I argue that at the current scale as instantiated in the leading 100 cities that are the object of such investment, this amounts to the privatizing of massive pieces of a city. That, in turn, raises a question as to whose city it is.

Who owns the city?

Is the type of fluidity Friedmann emphasizes as a key to a workable post-urban future threatened by the massive foreign and national corporate buying of whole pieces of cities? These acquisitions tend to eliminate urban tissue (little streets and squares, mixed small-scale uses, smaller public government offices, etc.) and they turn whole areas of a city and their larger metro areas into what are basically massive enclaves of office towers. This remaking of urban space away from smaller scales and footprints could function as a massive barrier to the type of mechanisms Friedmann emphasizes as enabling a type of reasonable urbanity even in the kinds of large urban geographies he describes.

And the scale of these corporate investments is large and growing. Taking just the last two years, from mid-2013 to mid-2014, corporate buying of existing properties reached over US$600 billion in the top 100 recipient cities of the world, and rose to over US$1 trillion from mid-2014 to mid-2015 (see Table 14.1; Cushman & Wakefield 2014). These figures include only properties of a certain size: one measure is that the minimum price is US$5 million in the case of New York City. In short, these are significant properties when it comes to cost and size; further, those US$600 billion exclude many acquisitions that do not quite reach those minimums but can also be quite "significant."

These figures exclude similarly large amounts going to the buying of urban land for site development.

I would add that these developments also further constrain the options for poor and modest-income urban residents. I conceptualize cities as complex but incomplete systems, and it is this that gives them their long lives and the capacity to outlive far more formal and powerful actors, from kings to corporations (Sassen 2013b, 2014). Further, in this mix of complexity and incompleteness also lies the possibility for those without power to acquire a certain complexity in their powerlessness, to be able to assert "We are here," "This is also our city." Or as the legendary statement by the fighting poor in Latin America puts it "*Estamos Presentes*": We are present. It is in cities to a large extent where the powerless can make a history, a culture, an economy, even if mostly in their neighborhoods; eventually each one of these can spread to a vaster urban zone as "ethnic" food, music, therapies, and more. All of this cannot happen in an office park, no matter its density; these are privately controlled spaces where low-wage workers can work, but not make. Nor do those without power get to make a history in plantations and mines today. In the past, these were spaces where powerless workers

Table 14.1 Total investment volumes in top 50 recipient cities (Q3 2014 to Q2 2015)

Metro	*Volumes (US$)*	*Growth**
1. New York	74,799,870,615	36.3%
2. London	55,206,679,357	13.4%
3. Tokyo	37,971,179,153	0.7%
4. Los Angeles	37,457,376,509	14.4%
5. San Francisco	32,355,485,613	35.9%
6. Paris	22,955,312,136	–0.2%
7. Chicago	20,036,200,994	39.4%
8. Washington	18,515,548,212	29.5%
9. Dallas	16,296,780,618	13.4%
10. Atlanta	16,022,394,226	60.7%
11. Miami	15,949,703,541	74.5%
12. Boston	15,365,776,426	43.2%
13. Hong Kong	14,447,415,389	4.9%
14. Sydney	14,075,615,656	7.9%
15. Houston	12,365,902,892	–6.2%
16. Berlin	11,814,090,834	–6.2%
17. Seattle	11,609,540,148	31.9%
18. Melbourne	11,078,147,297	33.1%
19. Frankfurt	9,845,334,528	14.4%
20. Phoenix	9,312,751,061	53.5%
21. Denver	9,029,533,977	19.6%
22. Austin	8,046,028,787	45.3%
23. Shanghai	7,978,366,830	–19.6%
24. Amsterdam	7,942,738,059	13.3%
25. Munich	7,271,540,067	9.9%
26. San Diego	7,251,264,452	–0.3%
27. Madrid	7,097,274,018	164.3%
28. Orlando	6,981,214,900	55.1%
29. Stockholm	6,338,824,520	–20.7%
30. Hawaii	6,048,702,620	48.5%
31. Osaka	5,839,892,968	26.1%
32. Hamburg	5,794,518,685	23.7%
33. Toronto	5,780,113,060	–23.9%
34. Singapore	5,575,750,013	–24.4%

Metro	*Volumes (US$)*	*Growth**
35. Beijing	5,408,756,455	–25.9%
36. Brisbane	5,368,732,014	39.2%
37. Philadelphia	5,333,247,720	–22.0%
38. Seoul	5,264,240,793	–16.0%
39. Nanjing	5,190,516,937	142.6%
40. Minneapolis	5,098,620,802	64.1%
41. Raleigh/Durham	4,867,567,697	86.1%
42. Charlotte	4,763,778,197	46.2%
43. Tampa	4,763,108,826	55.5%
44. Portland	4,459,699,959	91.5%
45. Milan	4,258,359,663	142.1%
46. Dublin	4,257,624,236	–3.7%
47. Oslo	4,250,853,127	92.7%
48. Manchester	4,224,580,070	25.2%
49. San Antonio	3,727,740,580	58.7%
50. Birmingham (UK)	3,708,838,018	27.4%

Source: Cushman & Wakefield 2014, based on information from Real Capital Analytics, Oxford Economics, Guardian News and Media Ltd., The World Economic Forum, Urban Land Institute

*Compared to previous 12 months

could gain that complexity in their powerlessness by the sheer concentration of their numbers, and often succeeded in gaining some rights and protections. But now control in such spaces has become *de facto* "militarized," with hired armed guards in control. Thus today it is in cities where that possibility of gaining complexity in one's powerlessness can happen—in our large, messy and somewhat anarchic cities—because nothing can fully control such diversity of peoples and engagements. If the current large-scale acquisitions and site developments continue, we will lose much of this type of making that has given our cities their cosmopolitanism—because what we call cosmopolitanism at the center is the stylized version of what actually originates in thick local cultures (Sassen 2013a, 2014).

When I ask myself where today's frontier zone is, my answer is: in our large cities. The frontier is a space where actors from different worlds have an encounter for which there are no established rules of engagement. In the old historic frontier this led to either negotiation with indigenous peoples or, mostly, to their persecution and oppression. The frontier space that is today's large, mixed city offers far more options. Those with power to some extent do not want to be bothered by the poor, and the mode is often to abandon them to their own devices; in some cities (for instance US and

Brazilian cities) there is extreme violence by police, but this can often become a public issue, which is something, perhaps a first step in longer trajectories of gaining at least some rights. Yet, it is in cities where so many of the struggles for vindication have taken place and have, in the long run, partly succeeded.

All of this is pertinent to Friedmann's vision of a manageable post-urban space. It is with this larger context in mind that I turn to the "innards" of this new phase in city buying.

What is different in today's corporate buying of urban properties?

It is easy to explain the post-2008 investment surge as more of the same. After all, the late 1980s also saw rapid growth of national and foreign buying of office buildings and hotels, especially in New York and London. I wrote about this in *The Global City*, notably the fact that over half of the buildings in the City of London were foreign owned at the height of that phase. Financial firms from countries as diverse as Japan and the Netherlands found they needed a strong foothold in London's city to access European capital.

There is then something familiar in this current post-2008 surge in acquisitions.

But an examination of the current trends shows some significant differences and points to a whole new phase in the character and logic of foreign and national corporate acquisitions (Sassen 2013c, 2014). Let me add that I do not see much of a difference in terms of the urban impact between national and foreign investment. The key fact here is that both are corporate and large-scale: this is what is critical.

Four features stand out.

One is the sharp scale-up in the buying of buildings, even in cities that have long been the object of such investments, notably New York and London. Around the world there are about 100 cities that have become significant destinations for such acquisitions. Indeed the rates of growth are far higher in some of these than they are in London and New York, even if the absolute numbers are still far higher in the top-tier cities. For example, *foreign* corporate buying of properties from 2013 to 2014 grew by 248% in Amsterdam/Randstadt, 180% in Madrid, and 475% in Nanjing. In contrast, the growth rate for New York was a bit over 68.5%, 37.6% for London, and 160.8% in Beijing, just to mention the major cities in the concerned regions.

The second feature that stands out is the extent of new construction. In the older period of the 1980s and 1990s it was often about acquiring buildings: notably high-end Harrods in London and Saks Fifth Avenue in New York, and trophy buildings such as Rockefeller Center in New York. In the post-2008 period, much buying of buildings is to destroy them and to replace them with far taller and far more corporate and luxurious types of buildings—luxury offices and luxury apartments.

The third feature is the spread of mega-projects with vast footprints that inevitably kill much urban tissue: little streets and squares, density of street-level shops and modest offices, and so on. These mega-projects raise the density of the city, but they actually de-urbanize it. Their large footprints commandeer and erase stretches of urban tissue and privatize it. A kind of private walled domain installs itself where there used to be all kinds of small-scale urban space. Office parks, luxury apartment buildings, and even malls, which are meant to draw consumers, now have private guards in control of access. Cities have long had high-rise buildings and they can add vibrancy and life to an area. But today's mega-projects are not quite like that.

It is this type of trend that has led me to the notion that density is not enough to have a city. It fits the argument I have made elsewhere (Sassen 2013a) that the city has "speech"—it tells us what works and what does not. But we have difficulty understanding its speech. Now these new kinds of mega-projects are actually screaming at us the fact, easily overlooked in much commentary about cities, that density is not always urbanity.

A fourth feature is the acquisition of whole blocks of underutilized or dead industrial land for site development. Here the prices paid by buyers can get very high. One example is the acquisition of a vast stretch of land in New York City (Atlantic Yards) by one of the largest Chinese building companies. It is now land occupied by a mix of modest factories and industrial services, modest neighborhoods, and, more recently, artists' studios and venues as these were pushed out of lower Manhattan by large-scale developments of high-rise apartment buildings. This very urban mix of occupants will be thrown out and replaced by 14 formidable luxury towers for residences. Also here we see a sharp growth of density that actually has the effect of de-urbanizing that space. It will be a sort of *de facto* "gated" space with lots of people. It will not be the dense mix of uses and types of people we think of as urban. This type of development is taking off in many cities, mostly with virtual walls, but sometimes also with real ones. I would argue that with this type of development the virtual and the actual walls have similar impacts on de-urbanizing pieces of a city. (An interesting observation by Haripriya Rangan is that this kind of massive complex of high-rise housing can be seen as a verticalizing of suburbia, with its homogeneity of occupants and uses, and absence of dense street activity, and mixed economic life.)

This proliferating urban gigantism has been strengthened and enabled by the privatizations and deregulations that took off in the 1990s across much of the world, and have continued since then with only a few interruptions. The overall effect has been a reduction in public buildings and an escalation in the amount of large corporate private ownership. This brings with it a reduction in the texture and scale of spaces previously accessible to the public—a space that was more than just public buildings. Where before there was a government office building handling the regulations and oversight of this or that public economic sector, now there might be a corporate headquarters, a luxury apartment building, or a mall.

By way of conclusion

The global geography of extraction that has long been part of economic development in the history of the West has gone well beyond its traditional association with plantations and mines, even as these are also expanding. Today these modes of extraction have been extended and made more brutally efficient. While not new, what stands out is the sharpening and corporatizing of extraction—this is not the quasi-heroic developer/explorer of an earlier period, but a corporate firm which needs no courage, just capital.

And now that corporatizing of access and control, and increasingly even ownership, has extended not only to the high-end urban sites, but also to the land from beneath the homes of modest households and government offices, we are witnessing a historic unusually large scale of corporate buying of whole pieces of cities. The mechanisms for these extractions are often far more complex than the outcomes, which are often quite elementary in their brutality.

Sharp changes in the ownership of urban land are leading to a new type of urbanization in a growing number of major cities. One key transformation is a shift from mostly small private to large corporate modes of ownership, and from public to private. This is a process that takes place in bits and pieces, some big and some small, and to some extent these practices have long been part of the urban land market and urban development. But, as I have explained here, the scaling and the amount of urban tissue destroyed has taken matters to the other side of the curve—it is no longer simply what cities have always undergone: destruction and rebuilding. The spread of mega-projects with vast footprints inevitably kills much urban tissue: little streets and squares, density of street-level shops and modest offices, and so on. These mega-projects raise the density of the city, but they actually de-urbanize it. Their large footprints commandeer and erase stretches of urban tissue and privatize it.

These trends suggest that at the current scale of acquisitions, we are actually seeing a systemic transformation in the pattern of land ownership in cities, one that alters the historic meaning of the city. Such a transformation has deep and significant implications for equity, democracy, and rights. This is particularly so because what was smaller and/or public is becoming larger and private. And even if this transformation comes with local government support, such shifts are privatizing more and more urban space if only because of the typically vast footprint of these private projects. The trend is to move from small properties embedded in city areas that are crisscrossed by streets and small public squares to projects that erase much of this public tissue of streets and squares via mega-projects with large, sometimes huge, footprints. This privatizes and de-urbanizes city space no matter the added density.

Large cities have long been complex and incomplete. This has enabled the incorporation of diverse people, logics, politics. A large mixed city is a frontier zone, where actors from different worlds can have an encounter for which there are no established rules of engagement—a zone where the powerless and the powerful can actually meet. This also makes cities spaces of innovations, small and large. And it is a place where those without power get to make a history, a culture, an economy—even if they do not necessarily become powerful they produce components of a city, leaving a legacy that adds to the cosmopolitanism of a city.

These are some of the positive features I also find embedded in the urban megaspace, or superorganism, given his focus on biology, that Friedmann describes with his notion of a post-urban that is fluid and can change, enabling multiple adjustment mechanisms that can generate a reasonable urban life, even in urban tissue that together covers the equivalent of many cities and thereby generates a region with 50 million or even 100 million residents.

My question to Friedmann is whether the negative force of mega-projects which contributes to a de-urbanizing of that space could not be a major structural obstacle to that fluidity. We can think of this again, as a curve: to some extent a strong city can survive a few mega-projects but might not if such mega-projects proliferate and become larger and larger. My focus here is on the latter of these conditions—an excess proliferation of mega-projects that are destroying too much urban tissue. While my focus is on cities that are major recipients of such corporate investment, and most cities in the world are not such types, Friedmann's extended fluid space is likely to contain many such mega-projects.

I like the notion of a fluid, complex space with multiple dynamics that can keep adjusting towards formations marked by city-ness (cf. Sassen 2013a).

It seems to me, and I wonder what Friedmann would say, that this mix of complexity and incompleteness that marks cities ensures a capacity to shape an urban subject and an urban subjectivity. The urban subject is one that can override the religious subject, the ethnic subject, the racialized subject, and, in certain settings, also the differences of class. There are moments in the routines of a city when we all become urban subjects. Rush hour is one such mix of time and space where we all function as urban subjects, and we all belong—rush hour masses running to catch public transport. So is air pollution or smog, or asymmetric war as it urbanizes war.

But today, rather than a space for including people from many diverse backgrounds and cultures, our global cities are expelling people and diversity. The new owners, often mostly part-time inhabitants, are very international but that does not mean that they represent many diverse cultures and traditions. They are astoundingly homogeneous no matter how diverse their countries of birth and languages. The processing of so much difference via a complex global corporate project is in itself an admirable capacity, if only it were put to better use. This is not quite the "urban subject" that our large, mixed cities have historically produced. This is above all a global *corporate* subject. And it is also a subject that has little connection to the traditional upper classes in cities, for whom the city was "their" space for representing their power, culture, sophistication—all understood as positives for them, and to some extent they contribute to the making of many grand public buildings.

Much of urban change is almost inevitably predicated on expelling what was there. Since their beginnings, whether 3,000 years ago or 100, cities have kept reinventing themselves, and that means that there were winners and losers. Urban histories are replete with accounts of those who were once poor and quasi-outsiders, or modest middle classes, that gained ground—because cities have long accommodated extraordinary variety.

But the large-scale corporate buying of, literally, urban space in its diverse instantiations introduces a de-urbanizing dynamic. It is not adding to heterogeneity and diversity. It literally brings a whole new formation into our cities—in the shape of multiple massive high-rise luxury implants. One way of putting it is that this new set of implants contains within it a logic all its own, one that cannot be urbanized in the specific/idiosyncratic terms of a given city—that is, it cannot be tamed into becoming part of the logics of the city where it inserts itself. And this, it seems to me, is also a major obstacle to the type of fluidity that Friedmann sees as a potentially positive force in the re-making of urban space, so that vast endless stretches of built-up terrain can actually reshape themselves into a new type of urbanity. What I describe here is a negative force that could mess up that fluidity.

References

Cushman & Wakefield 2014, *Winning in Growth Cities 2014/2015. A Cushman & Wakefield Capital Markets Research Publication*. Available from <http://www.winningingrowthcities.com> [20 November 2015].

Friedmann, J 1978, "The spatial organization of power in the development of urban systems" in *Systems of Cities*, eds LS Bourne & JW Simmons, Oxford University Press, New York, pp. 12–50.

Friedmann, J 1981, "The active community: toward a political-territorial framework for rural development in Asia", *Economic Development and Cultural Change*, 29(2): 235–261.

Friedmann, J 1995, "Where we stand: a decade of world city research" in *World Cities in a World-system*, eds PL Knox & PJ Taylor, Cambridge University Press, Cambridge, pp. 21–47.

Friedmann, J 2005, *China's Urban Transition*, University of Minnesota Press, Minneapolis.

Friedmann, J 2006, "Insights into planning in three East-Asian cities", *The Town Planning Review*, 77(3): 339–344.

Friedmann, J 2013, "Is China moving into a post-urban era? Some challenges for planners". Invited lecture to Shanghai Bureau of Planning. Unpublished.

Salingaros, NA 2002, "Development of the urban superorganism", *Katarxis No. 3*. Available from: <http://www.katarxis3.com/Salingaros-Urban_Superorganism.htm> [8 June 2013].

Sassen, S 2013a, "Does the city have speech?", *Public Culture*, 25(2): 209–221.

Sassen, S 2013b, "A focus on cities takes us beyond existing governance frameworks" in *The Quest for Security: Protection without Protectionism and the Challenge of Global Governance*, eds M Kaldor & JE Stiglitz, Columbia University Press, New York, pp. 238–259.

Sassen, S 2013c, "When territory deborders territoriality", *Territory, Politics, Governance*, 1(1): 21–45.

Sassen, S 2014, *Expulsions: Brutality and Complexity in the Global Economy*, Belknap/Harvard University Press, Cambridge, MA.

Xu, J & Yeh, AOH (eds) 2010, *Governance and Planning of Mega-city Regions: An International Comparative Perspective*, Routledge, London.

15 Urban entrepreneurship through transactive planning

The making of Waterfront Toronto

Matti Siemiatycki

Introduction

In 1993, John Friedmann published a widely cited commentary outlining his vision of a future direction for planning. He called it "Toward a non-Euclidian mode of planning" (Friedmann 1993). This commentary built on his groundbreaking theory of transactive planning developed in *Retracking America* (1973), and his philosophy for mobilizing knowledge into action in *Planning in the Public Domain* (1987).

For Friedmann, the old style of Euclidean planning was rooted in 19th-century views of planning as a form of engineering science. In the old planning style, the assumption is that decisions are being made rationally and comprehensively. The objective of planning, from this perspective, is developing long-term plans, simulations and blueprints based on advanced analytic methods. This gives decision-making a sheen of scientific rigor.

Yet this old model of planning is particularly unsuited for turbulent times, and contexts where organizations and individuals are in a constant state of flux. In Friedmann's proposed non-Euclidean model, planning is less about developing plans and preparing documents to chart a long-term course, and more a way of bringing knowledge to bear on action in the here and now. To achieve this end, Friedmann argued for an approach to planning that privileges the immediate timeframe and the local or regional scale. It has five key characteristics:

1 *Normative* and infused with values about inclusiveness, respect for the natural world, fairness and equality.
2 *Innovative* in the sense that it is entrepreneurial and looks for creative solutions. Friedmann (1993, p.483) suggests that "innovative planning requires great skills in negotiation, mediation, and the art of compromise. It is a form of planning that, like entrepreneurship in the private sector, is prepared to take risks, even while remaining publicly accountable."
3 *Political* by considering the strategies necessary to implement innovative plans and overcome opposition from people who feel they are left worse off.

4 *Transactive* by drawing affected people into the planning process from an early stage, and engaging in mutual learning by respecting both expert and experiential knowledge.
5 *Social learning* realized through open deliberations, critical evaluations of past initiatives and a willingness to correct course as new information is presented. This requires leadership that is not afraid to make mistakes and a political culture that is not out to score partisan points at every turn.

Overall, Friedmann's recipe for a new non-Euclidean, transactive type of planning is infused with a sense of hope and optimism about the human capacity to work out differences in the service of realizing collective action. Transactive urban planning is about being entrepreneurial in the true sense, taking on the risk of bringing people and capital together in innovative ways to generate new forms of profit that deliver broad public benefit. This recipe for a non-Euclidean approach to planning may sound ideal, even idealistic, but is it really realistic?

Over the years, entrepreneurial urban governance has been roundly criticized. It has been closely tied to elite-led civic boosters and the remaking of cities in their image. Through close partnerships between public- and private-sector institutions, entrepreneurial redevelopment initiatives commonly result in the construction of sites of spectacle, such as revitalized waterfronts or entertainment districts, aimed at making cities more competitive and boosting them up the world cities rankings. In these regeneration zones, an attractive public realm may be remade surrounding luxury real-estate developments, high-end shops, leisure facilities and cultural institutions. However, issues of social inequality and exclusion persist or are even exacerbated by privately owned public spaces, limited affordable housing provisions, and different forms of gated communities. Such entrepreneurial public–private redevelopment is typically highly speculative and set up in ways that the public bears much of the risk while the private sector captures an outsized share of the reward (Harvey 1989; Ponzini & Rossi 2010).

A further challenge to a transactive approach to planning is that political discourse is more polarized than ever. As William Brett (2013) explains, there is a growing entrenchment of popular movements across the ideological spectrum around the world that set up a binary opposition between a "morally pure" people and a vilified political, financial, or technocratic elite. Conflicting factions find it difficult to agree on a common set of facts, let alone agreeable policy directions. Political point scoring has become the order of the day. And new modes of communicating and engaging people, including the rise of social media, have powerfully given voice to marginalized groups, but also serve as an amplifier and an echo chamber for the most base-level perspectives, some of which are reactionary and hateful. In this adversarial planning environment, there are few shades of grey, little interest in social learning about other perspectives, and no room for compromise. In these polarized and conflictual social contexts, can a transactive, non-Euclidean model of planning really succeed?

Making non-Euclidean planning work

In fact, Friedmann's model of non-Euclidean planning, predicated on urban entrepreneurialism and transactive engagement, may provide the best chance of making and implementing plans in polarized milieus characterized by a deep cynicism in elite institutions. In the remainder of this essay, I will provide a brief case study of the regeneration of Toronto's derelict, post-industrial waterfront at the turn of the 21st century as an example of the promise and pitfalls of a transactive approach to planning. This case study is based on scholarly and secondary documentation that sets out the history of Toronto's waterfront development. It also draws on my personal experience as a member of the board of directors of Waterfront Toronto, the government crown corporation responsible for waterfront regeneration, between 2009 and 2013, a critical time in the undertaking of the initiative.

A history of gridlock on the waterfront

Struggles over the purpose and identity of Toronto's waterfront go back over a century, as do plans for its development and revitalization. Toronto is located on the shore of Lake Ontario. From the mid-19th century the waterfront district became a significant site for industrial activity, including heavy industry such as tanneries, refineries and energy production plants.

However, as the viability and presence of industrial activity on Toronto's waterfront diminished in the mid-20th century, the redevelopment of the area was slow and fragmented. A key impediment to large-scale, master-planned redevelopment were tensions and competing interests between the many federal, provincial and municipal government agencies and departments that had responsibility for governing various aspects of the waterfront. To make matters more complicated, land ownership was fragmented between the different government agencies, as well as numerous private landholders (Eidelman 2011). The result was political gridlock and the lack of coherent development activity.

In the absence of a comprehensive waterfront redevelopment plan, public land along the water's edge and in the surrounding areas was incrementally sold off to private developers for industrial and, later, residential and commercial developments. This strategy had the effect of creating a patchwork waterfront with multiple uses that often conflicted. In the central waterfront area where most of the redevelopment had occurred, prized public access to the water's edge was blocked in multiple locations with industrial plants and a "concrete wall" of tall luxury condominium towers. This was a major source of public dissatisfaction. To the east of downtown, by contrast, little development had occurred and the area remained a mix of active and derelict industrial uses. And across the entire waterfront, the transportation landscape was orientated towards motor vehicle traffic and was uninviting for transit users, cyclists and pedestrians. Despite half a century of revitalization efforts, conflicting interests, the lack of meaningful community engagement about what the waterfront should be, and competing jurisdictional responsibility resulted in a waterfront that at the end of the 20th century was physically uninviting and an afterthought in the mental map of the city for most Torontonians.

Breaking the cycle through transactive planning

The turn of the 21st century began a new era for Toronto's waterfront redevelopment, which coalesced around a new vision for the area and, perhaps more importantly, a new way of undertaking planning. This vision was set out in the final report of the Toronto Waterfront Revitalization Task Force (2000), which comprised senior government officials and private sector leaders. Importantly, the vision articulated by the task force strongly emphasized revitalizing the waterfront as a means to boost the city's global economic competitiveness and world-class city credentials, a common preoccupation for Toronto civic boosters and a driver of elite-oriented waterfront revitalizations worldwide. However, the task force also set out a model of institutional cooperation that encouraged urban entrepreneurship in the service of achieving broad social, environmental and economic benefits by sharing risk and engaging broadly with diverse stakeholder communities. Indeed, Friedmann's core tenets for a non-Euclidian approach to planning—being innovative, normative, political and transactive—featured strongly in the planning model that ultimately broke the gridlock on the waterfront.

Innovation

A key first step was the inauguration of a new special-purpose organization that was deliberately designed to be entrepreneurial and break through the roadblock of the entrenched interests and jurisdictional conflicts that had hindered previous waterfront development. On October 19, 2000, the Prime Minister of Canada, the Premier of Ontario, and the Mayor of Toronto stood together to announce the formation of the Toronto Waterfront Revitalization Corporation. The TWRC, later rebranded as Waterfront Toronto, was designed as an action-orientated urban development corporation that would usurp or cut through the clutter of the many existing government agencies and departments in the area. It had a mandate to devise a master plan for the massive waterfront precinct, develop local infrastructure and undertake environmental remediation. This mandate is encompassed in a broader public policy goal, which Waterfront Toronto CEO John Campbell (2014) explains is to:

> Leverage the infrastructure project to deliver key economic and social benefits that enable Toronto to compete aggressively with other top-tier global cities for investment, jobs and people.

The Corporation was governed by a board of directors of private citizens appointed by the three levels of government, and capitalized at CAD$1.5 billion by equal contributions of CAD$500 million from each shareholder. But this start-up funding was only a fraction of the estimated CAD$17 billion that it would cost to develop the city's entire waterfront precinct. To bridge the gap, Waterfront Toronto was set up as a public–private partnership. The government contributions were to be spent to take on risks that the private sector would not otherwise do on their own: assemble privately held plots, remediate polluted land and invest in infrastructure upgrading such as flood protection, parks and sewers. Once this land was assembled and cleaned, and services upgraded, it would be sold at a higher price to private developers. The developers would then bear the construction and market risks associated with building and selling new residential or employment facilities. As part of the land sale agreements, Waterfront Toronto would negotiate public interest covenants regarding building heights, design quality, environmental standards such as LEED certification, and non-market housing provision. Any profits that Waterfront Toronto accrued from the land sales would be reinvested into future infrastructure and remediation projects, creating a virtuous cycle. This model of redevelopment, and the Corporation's governance structure with a private citizen-led board of directors, encouraged Waterfront Toronto to be entrepreneurial while removing decisions from the daily political dynamics at each level of government.

Taking a normative stance

To be sure, the centralized urban redevelopment corporation model chosen for Waterfront Toronto, with its entrepreneurial inclinations and aspirations of encouraging global competitiveness, have garnered considerable criticism. Scholars such as Lehrer and Laidley (2008, p.796), for instance, contend that Waterfront Toronto's policy objectives reflect a neoliberal political imperative for waterfront redevelopment centered on promoting elite-oriented economic growth while perpetuating "inequality and disenfranchisement through the passive but specific exclusion of particular communities and groups." Eidelman (2011) argues that the presence of a powerful central crown corporation with a private citizen-led board of directors may weaken democratic accountability over decision-making. These critiques echo the challenges made of many waterfront redevelopments globally, in particular that they have been overwhelmingly developed as residential and consumption enclaves for a wealthy global elite (see Holden et al. 2015).

One way that Waterfront Toronto has responded to such critiques and aimed to avoid the pitfalls of other entrepreneurial redevelopment initiatives internationally is through the implementation of a normative vision for a revitalized waterfront. This vision mingles aspirational rhetoric about a waterfront redevelopment initiative that improves Toronto's international status, with a strong set of values promoting inclusivity, environmental sensitivity and high-quality place-making. Senior executives within Waterfront Toronto have been acutely aware of the elite-dominated developments that have been the outcome of waterfront redevelopments globally, and have explicitly argued against this path for Toronto. As Meg Davis, Waterfront Toronto's Senior Vice President, explains,

> It shouldn't be a place just for the uber-rich...we want it to be a place for families, for people of all ages and stages of life. We want seniors living down here, we want families of all incomes living down here and that's the goal that we've been working on.
>
> (Davis 2013)

This normative vision of an inclusive, sustainable, attractive waterfront has translated into the tangible plans and projects implemented by Waterfront Toronto since its inception. It has also been integrated into the programming of space in buildings by public- and private-sector landowners along the waterfront. Key common features of these plans are an orientation towards prioritizing transit and non-motorized modes of travel, inclusivity and design excellence. In the built-up central waterfront area, Waterfront Toronto undertook a $130 million redevelopment of the main high street, Queen's Quay Boulevard. This involved reducing the width of the road from four to two lanes of general-purpose car traffic and reallocating the space to a transit-only right of way, multi-directional bicycle paths and a widened pedestrian sidewalk. The *Toronto Star* newspaper's urban affairs critic summed up the significance of this urban intervention when the revitalized street opened in 2015:

> Perhaps for the first time, the city has built a thoroughfare for everyone. That means pedestrians, cyclists, skate boarders, roller bladers, babies in strollers, transit passengers, wheelchair users and, yes, drivers.... In Toronto, that makes it a radical intervention. It strikes at the heart of a city that measures its success by vehicular congestion rates.
>
> (Hume 2015)

Further to the east, where the derelict industrial lands are being redeveloped, Waterfront Toronto has designated a mix of land uses that will provide diversity in the area. Alongside market condominiums and office developments, there is a new community college campus on the water's edge accompanied by student housing, ensuring a youth presence in the area. One particularly important program offered by the college at its new waterfront campus is Dental Health, which houses a large low-cost public dental clinic on its premises that attracts patients from across the city.

At another site on the waterfront, a partnership between the City of Toronto, Waterfront Toronto, a major developer and a non-profit arts agency has delivered 80 affordable rental units mandated for artists, which will be owned by the city. In the eastern part of the site, a new social-housing complex owned by the Toronto Community Housing Corporation was among the first residential buildings to open in the area, across the street from market condominium buildings. And throughout the area, Waterfront Toronto has aimed to encourage the cultivation of an "intelligent community." It struck a deal with a private service provider to wire the entire waterfront area with ultra-high-speed broadband Internet and make it accessible to all residential and commercial businesses at a fixed below-market price. Importantly, the deal provides tenants in the area's social housing buildings with the same access to ultra-high-speed Internet service at a highly discounted price.

Finally, ecological sensitivity and high-quality public realm and building designs are key features of the plans. Waterfront Toronto established minimum green building requirements and developed an on-site soil recycling facility to minimize the trucking of contaminated construction materials to landfills. In 2005, the Corporation instituted Toronto's first design review panel to ensure that high standards for architecture and urban design are met. Waterfront Toronto has designated a wide, continuous public boardwalk along the water's edge—correcting one of the public's primary criticisms of earlier generations of waterfront development in Toronto. And it has built public parks throughout the district in advance of the opening of new private developments. A number of these parks have been commissioned through international design competitions and include facilities for users of all ages such as child play structures, a skateboard park, an outdoor cooking oven and seating for the public to engage with the ongoing theater of the harbour. Once built, these parks are owned and operated by the City of Toronto, ensuring universal public access. Through its engagement as the master planner for the district, Waterfront Toronto has actively translated a normative set of values into a built community.

Learning through engagement

Importantly, this vision of an inclusive, environmentally sensitive, attractive waterfront and the normative values it entails were not imposed top down on Torontonians by Waterfront Toronto. Rather, Waterfront Toronto's vision and the subsequent plans they produced have been created through an extensive and meaningful process of civic engagement carried out over a number of years. Waterfront Toronto has undertaken hundreds of public meetings in large venues and with small groups to learn about the diverse desires for a community that includes multiple publics.

These consultations have spanned the various phases of the project. They began from the Corporation's origins when debates were still ongoing about the overall vision for the waterfront. As Waterfront Toronto CEO John

Campbell explained in an interview with the Canadian Broadcasting Corporation (2010), consultations at this stage began without preconceived notions, "from the ground up, starting with a blank slate…Tell us what you like about your neighbourhood, what you don't like." As plans took shape, more detailed discussions were initiated about the urban design character of the individual precincts along the waterfront, and have followed through to highly specific discussions about the design and construction approaches for individual projects.

Waterfront Toronto's approach to consultation broke with the "decide and defend" model of public engagement that had characterized the history of waterfront planning in Toronto. Instead it saw the community as a resource that, could be tapped to bring forward new ideas that improve the plans. One paradox for an organization that prizes meaningful community engagement is that, especially during its early years of operation, Waterfront Toronto was criticized for a lack of transparency in reporting on the details of how the Corporation spent public money or made decisions. Although the Corporation released audited financial statements annually and meeting minutes, some Toronto City Councillors at times complained about difficulties obtaining a thorough public accounting of the purpose of contracts or their cost (Lehrer & Laidley 2008).

Despite issues about transparency, the meaningfulness and effectiveness of Waterfront Toronto's community consultation and engagement efforts are widely acknowledged in the city, resulting in a high level of support for the Corporation and its plans. For a high-profile public crown corporation like Waterfront Toronto that is working in the spotlight of the public eye, meaningful community engagement is the product of enlightened self-interest. Deep, meaningful, ongoing engagement with multiple publics brings forward new perspectives that improve the quality of plans, and increases community "buy-in." While it may take longer at the outset, it reduces conflicts and speeds up implementation in the long run. At the same time, for a crown corporation with three political masters in the municipal, provincial and federal governments, Waterfront Toronto is especially vulnerable to political shifts that at any time could result in calls for a new direction or the dissolution of the Corporation altogether. In this context, it is critical that the vision for the Toronto waterfront developed by the Corporation meaningfully reflect the interests and ideas of the community and the different levels of government involved. If key stakeholders trust the Corporation and respect the work it is doing, then it will be more difficult to unsettle its direction should any of the three government shareholders in Waterfront Toronto try to impose their own plans unilaterally.

Getting political

Indeed, Waterfront Toronto's vision and mandate came under acute threat when the political winds shifted at Toronto city hall, highlighting the importance of political constituency building as an act of urban planning. In the fall of 2010, Torontonians elected Rob Ford as Mayor of the City of Toronto, who was closely supported by his brother, a newly elected city councillor. Mayor Ford ran on a right-wing populist platform characterized by the slogans "stop the gravy train" and "stop the war on the car." These positions put him distinctly at odds with the vision and plans for the waterfront redevelopment put forward by Waterfront Toronto.

From the outset of his term in office, Mayor Ford and his council supporters were highly critical of Waterfront Toronto; the Mayor's brother councillor Doug Ford called the waterfront project "one of the biggest boondoggles the feds, the province and the city has ever done." They felt that the emphasis on high-quality urban design in the streetscapes and parks developed by Waterfront Toronto were unnecessary indulgences that the city could ill afford. And they argued that high-density showcase redevelopments would generate far greater financial returns and global recognition than the mid-density, inclusive, transit-orientated mixed-use plans proposed by Waterfront Toronto. Instead, they floated plans for a mega-casino and luxury resort, a major new professional sports stadium, and a massive shopping mall on the waterfront. Conversely, they criticized plans for the city to pay to fund social housing projects in the waterfront district when the area had some of the most expensive and coveted land in the city. For Waterfront Toronto, then, a key challenge was to balance its position as a non-partisan crown corporation with three levels of government as its equal shareholders, with the need to act strategically to navigate the shifting political landscape. This required leveraging the Corporation's diverse community of supporters in order to realize the implementation of its vision.

Importantly, at crucial moments of tension where competing schemes were proposed by local politicians, Waterfront Toronto had a bevy of supporters that mobilized to defend the plans that had been painstakingly produced with extensive stakeholder input. Many of the local community groups and planning experts that had been part of developing Waterfront Toronto's plans through years of civic engagement would consistently come out publicly as strong supporters of the Corporation and its vision.

And behind the scenes, the other levels of government that were shareholders and significant funders of Waterfront Toronto intervened to preserve a plan that they had invested heavily in, financially and politically. At one especially critical moment, when Councillor Ford announced a high-profile proposal to substantially redraw the waterfront land use plan with one that was far more auto- and elite-oriented, the Federal Minister of Finance and a close ally of the Mayor's family personally intervened. He convened a private meeting with the Mayor, his councillor brother and Waterfront Toronto executives to express how committed he was to the Corporation's plans and to broker a detente.

Waterfront Toronto was ultimately able to withstand the political challenges to the implementation of its plans brought forward during the Ford mayoralty, in large measure because of the social and political capital it had accrued with its government shareholders and the community at large. This capital was built through extensive and meaningful civic engagement so that diverse communities felt a level of ownership of the Waterfront Toronto plans. And it resulted from the building of trust with citizens and in key corridors of power in the ability of Waterfront Toronto to deliver on its promised mandate.

Conclusion

More than two decades on from his initial invocation for a non-Euclidean model of planning, the aspirational and optimistic quality of Friedmann's ideas remain strong. Yet in a context of hyper-polarization in public discourse around planning decisions, a key question is whether exercises in non-Euclidean planning can actually deliver results? As illustrated in the case study above, Waterfront Toronto embraced most of the key tenets of a non-Euclidean approach to planning: the Corporation was entrepreneurial, normative, transactive, and politically strategic to overcome opposition from ingrained interests.

Indeed, the Waterfront Toronto case study provides a key insight about urban entrepreneurship in the public interest. While entrepreneurialism as an approach to urban governance has been widely critiqued for a lack of public accountability and promoting unequal development, it is the complementary actions of being both entrepreneurial *and* transactive planning processes that contributed to Waterfront Toronto's success during the first decade and a half of the 21st century. The Corporation's entrepreneurial mandate encouraged it to identify public–private partnership opportunities, assume risk where appropriate, and marshal public resources to redevelopment initiatives. Yet this entrepreneurialism was predicated on deep, meaningful, ongoing civic engagement with a broad range of political, business and community stakeholders. This ensured that the plans being developed encompassed the values and ideas of multiple communities about what should be built, and had the political legitimacy to endure changes in government. As such, through transactive planning, urban entrepreneurialism was employed in the service of the public interest.

The case of waterfront planning in Toronto also highlights the barriers to fully implementing successful entrepreneurial urban governance. In particular, social learning based on openness and learning from past mistakes is the most challenging non-Euclidean planning ideal for goal-orientated organizations to implement. Under the glare of intense scrutiny, with rival government agencies and a highly partisan political milieu, Waterfront Toronto was constantly under threat of being found inadequate and shut down. This created the need for the corporation to constantly demonstrate its worth to its political sponsors and the general public. And it provided the context for an environment where a lack of information transparency has been a source of criticism at times. While social learning by embracing and learning from failure has become a common mantra in entrepreneurial private-sector organizations such as high-technology start-ups, it remains a challenge in highly politicized public planning environments. This makes meaningful social learning a difficult concept for many entrepreneurial planning organizations to fully realize, regardless of how effective a strategy it may be.

References

Brett, W 2013, "What's an elite to do? The threat of populism from left, right and centre", *The Political Quarterly*, 84(3): 410–413.

Campbell, J 2014, "John Campbell speaks to the Toronto Region Board of Trade", *Waterfront Toronto* 27 October. Available from: <http://blog.waterfrontoronto.ca/nbe/portal/wt/home/blog-home/posts/john+campbell+speaks+to+the+toronto+region+board+of+trade+01> [12 November 2015].

Canadian Broadcasting Corporation 2010, "Civic muscle: a civic institution that gets it." Available from: <http://www.cbc.ca/toronto/features/torontovotes2010/civic-muscle5.html> [12 November 2015].

Davis, M 2013, "Toronto, the waterfront and world-class status", *Cityzen Developments* 3 July. Available from: <http://blog.mycondomylife.com/cityzen-developments/2013/07/in-this-second-part-of-our-three-part-waterfront-revitalization-serieswere-looking-at-the-status-of-toronto-as-a-world-class.html> [9 August 2016].

Eidelman, G 2011, "Who's in charge? Jurisdictional gridlock and the genesis of Waterfront Toronto" in *Reshaping Toronto's Waterfront*, eds G Desfor & J Ladley, University of Toronto Press, Toronto, pp. 263–286.

Friedmann, J 1973, *Retracking America: A Theory of Transactive Planning*, Anchor Press, New York.

Friedmann, J 1987, *Planning in the Public Domain: From Knowledge to Action*, Princeton University Press, Princeton, N.J.

Friedmann, J 1993, "Toward a non-Euclidian mode of planning", *Journal of the American Planning Association*, 59(4): 482–485.

Harvey, D 1989, "From managerialism to entrepreneurialism: the transformation in urban governance in late capitalism", *Geografiska Annaler. Series B, Human Geography*, 71(1): 3–17.

Holden, M, Scerri, A & Esfahani, AH 2015, "Justifying redevelopment 'failures' within urban 'success stories': dispute, compromise, and a new test of urbanity", *International Journal of Urban and Regional Research*, 39(3): 451–470.

Hume, C 2015, "New Queens Quay: a redesign for everyone", *Toronto Star*, 22 June, p. GT.2.

Lehrer, U & Laidley, J 2008, "Old mega-projects newly packaged? Waterfront redevelopment in Toronto", *International Journal of Urban and Regional Research*, 32(4): 786–803.

Ponzini, D & Rossi, U 2010, "Becoming a creative city: the entrepreneurial mayor, network politics and the promise of an urban renaissance", *Urban Studies*, 47(5): 1037–1057.

Toronto Waterfront Revitalization Task Force 2000, *Our Waterfront: Gateway to the New Canada*, Toronto Waterfront Revitalization Corporation, Toronto.

16 From good city to progressive city

Reclaiming the urban future in Asia

Mike Douglass

Planetary urbanization without cities

In the first decades of national independence after World War II the idea of the city in most of East and Southeast Asia was constructed by newly created developmental states that promised gains in material welfare in exchange for compliance to centralized authoritarian rule (Woo-Cummings 1999). Stunning records of economic growth were achieved in several "tiger economies." However, by the 1980s, urbanization and the rise of civil society witnessed rising contestations over negative impacts and uneven distribution of benefits that resulted in democratic reforms in several countries. Along with these reforms, cities also began shifting from command economies toward what Friedmann (1962, p.76) summarizes as "a form of collective life" and as a polis of participatory public decision-making.

Global neoliberalism also appeared in Asia in the 1980s. Promoted and enforced by powerful international lenders, corporatization of government began to substantially limit the scope of government in pursuing remedies to social concerns. Deregulation of control over urban land development, accelerating privatized public spaces, and blurring corporate–government lines through "public–private partnerships" all contributed to a new era of corporatization of cities that proceeded without political accounting (Flyvbjerg et al. 2003). Corporatization recast the city as an ultra-competitive engine of growth socially justified by a simplified version of trickle-down economics (Economist Intelligence Unit 2012).

Corporatization is radically transforming cities and city systems, locally and globally. Friedmann's (1986) seminal contribution on the emergence of world cities as basing points for corporate decision-making through global urban networks sparked a new field of research on the globalization of urbanization (Sassen 1991; Taylor 2000). The coupling of city and nation that had seemed so obvious in the 1960s was supplanted by writing on the denationalization of urban space (Sassen 2003). Friedmann (2002) went further by postulating that the world was increasingly composed of *de facto* city-states directly embedded in the global corporate economy. These formulations also highlight the destruction by corporatization of "the city's lived spaces" of social meanings and community bonds (Friedmann 1999, p.4). Sassen (2015, p.1) extends this theme by stating that corporate mega-projects are eliminating the "urban tissue" of publicly accessible spaces, concluding that corporatization is "de-urbanizing" citymaking as it "alters the historic meaning of the city."

While Brenner and Schmid (2014) proclaim that we have entered an era of planetary urbanization that incorporates every corner of the world into a global urban matrix, inspection on the ground reveals the paradox that corporatization is not producing cities as historically understood to be spheres of social and political action. Many scholars have coined terms for this condition: geographies of nowhere (Kunstler 1994), the city as a theme park (Sorkin 1992), secessionary urban spaces (Graham & Marvin 2001), de-socialized spaces (Gleeson 2006), and globopolis (Douglass 2009). This is the context in which in some instances grassroots mobilizations are capturing urban government to reclaim cities as progressive theaters of social and political action.

From the good city to the progressive city

The good city

Big data on protests find that politically significant protests globally reached a record number over the past decade (Carothers & Youngs 2015). In Asia these contestations are increasingly urban-based and focus on the seven faces of corporatization identified in Table 16.1. These include privatization of basic services and public spaces; dispossessions of land and assets for mega-projects; displacement of local shops and public markets by chain stores, mini-marts, shopping malls, private new towns in town and in periurban areas that eliminate entire urban districts and villages; and precariatization of labor (Douglass 2014).

Friedmann (2000) brings these issues together by proposing the idea of "the Good City," which is both a vision for the future and a framework for critically assessing "structural problems of capitalist society viewed in a global context" (Friedmann 2011, p.62). The central purpose of his Good City is human flourishing, which is to be supported by four pillars: socially adequate housing, affordable healthcare, adequately remunerated work, and adequate social provisioning of all of these services to the "weakest citizens" (Friedmann 1987). The Good City is animated by an active civil society capable of capturing processes of governance that "becomes coextensive with… 'the city of everyday life'" (p.469).

Our formulation for research on progressive cities in Asia adopts major elements of the Good City while modifying it in several ways (Figure 16.1). First, we consolidate his four pillars into a single pillar of distributive justice, which is left open to many other elements of the material conditions for human flourishing to be determined city by city. Second, we add

Table 16.1 The seven faces of corporatization of cities in East and Southeast Asia

Dimension/Face	*Main characteristics*	*Impacts*	*Examples*
1 *Corporatization of government*	Deregulation; privatization of public institutions, services, land; public–corporate partnerships	Unequal access to basic urban services, uncoordinated land use planning	Privatization of higher education, water, transportation, postal services; private new towns on prime agricultural land
2 *Appropriation of public space*	Selling public land to corporations for private use	Permanent loss of public spaces	Loss of public parks, promenades, public markets, streets and lanes
3 *Land dispossessions*	Government-assisted taking of land for corporate projects	Loss of neighborhoods, homes, cultural spaces, livelihoods, social support networks	Peri-urban land grabs, use of eminent domain to evict residents from low-income neighborhoods
4 *Mega-projects*	Huge spatial footprints, wholly privatized spaces, massive displacement of pre-existing uses and activities	Elimination of the "urban tissue" of lanes, common spaces, spaces of daily encounters, civic spaces, political gathering places	Mega-malls, tourism complexes, very tall buildings, sites for global spectacles such as the Olympics, business hubs, "smart" U-Towns
5 *Replacement of local business*	Replacement of locally owned shops by corporate chains and franchises	Loss of sociability of local economies; immense economic leakages from localities	Big-box stores, shopping malls, mini-marts, food franchises, chain stores
6 *Corporate housing and new towns*	Exclusive enclaves with limited or no public access or public spaces	Accentuates social inequalities and class/ethnic divisions	Peri-urban housing enclaves, eco-cities and new towns in Asia
7 *Labor relations*	End of life-time employment; precariatization (sub-part-time work); withdrawal of pensions and other benefits from employees	Perpetually impermanent employment; lack of savings or retirement support; incomes below levels needed for maintaining basic levels of living	End of life-time employment in Japan; precariatization of labor in Korea following 1998 IMF crisis

Source: Mike Douglass

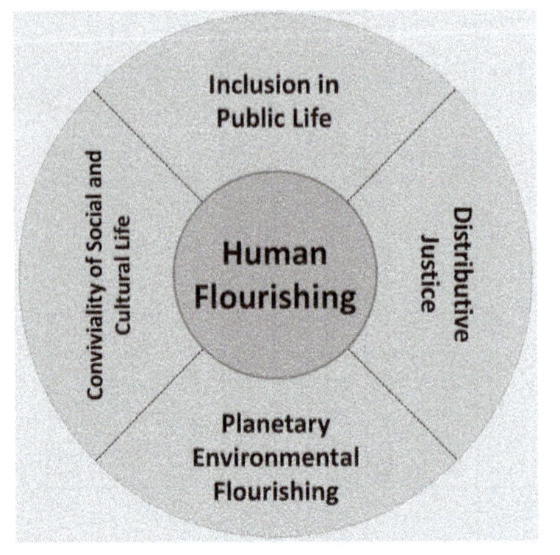

Figure 16.1 The four pillars of human flourishing in progressive cities
Source: Mike Douglass with reference to Friedmann 1987, 2000, 2002, 2011

"conviviality" of social and cultural life as a pillar. Third, we include a pillar representing concern for human relations with nature and the planetary biosphere. In focusing on contextual variations in cities in Asia, we have the explicit aim to bring the local state fully into research on cities. In addition to these differences our reason for using progressive cities instead of "good cities" is to focus on processes as well as outcomes and to acknowledge progress in motion rather than only outcomes.

Progressive cities

When applied to cities, the term "progressive" has been used in contradictory ways (Atkinson & Jorgensen 2014; Papayanic 2004). The concept put forth here centers on Friedmann's Good City concept or "human flourishing" as a "fundamental human right" to the "full development of intellectual, physical and spiritual potentials in the context of wider communities" (Friedmann 2000, p.466). Friedmann draws from Aristotle's concept of *eudaimonia*. Many social philosophies have similar, if not the same, core elements (Lacey 2015). Confucianism, for example, speaks of human flourishing as "learning to be human" through continuous "creative transformation" of the self in "an ever-expanding network of relationships" (Tu 1993, p.142). In contrast to "happiness" as a state of satisfaction, human flourishing "conveys the idea of a process, of both a personal project and a goal for humanity" (Triglav Circle 2015, p.1).

Cities cannot produce human flourishing as such, but they can provide supporting conditions for people to experience it through what Friedmann calls the space-forming, space-contingent processes of citymaking, here identified as the four pillars of inclusion, distributive justice, conviviality, and environmental sustenance.

Inclusion in the social and public life of a city is axiomatic for human flourishing. Unless people who reside in cities are included in public decision-making, the uses of political power will continue to marginalize and ignore the voices of many. Of particular interest are the spaces in which people can gather socially at arm's length from both the state and private commercial interests (Ho & Douglass 2008).

Inclusion also draws from contributions to reconceptualizing the concept of cosmopolis by Sandercock (2003) as a grassroots process, which, as explained by Conley (2002, p.129), is the world as city in which inhabitants "can assert their differences and negotiate them in a productive and affirmative way." Not only for and by its "citizens," inclusion equally welcomes "the stranger" (Holston 2001).

Distributive justice has many building blocks, including Harvey's (1973) landmark *Social Justice and the City*, Lefebvre's (1991) right to the city, and Soja's (2010) spatial justice. Friedmann's (1992) writing on *Empowerment* brings together another tradition of self-empowerment of marginalized, oppressed, and dispossessed people. Each concept contains elements of resistance as well as cooperation, the creation of new spaces, and pursuit of alternative community projects (Friedmann 2011).

Conviviality. In giving urban dimensions to Ivan Illich's (1972) treatise on conviviality, Lisa Peattie (1998) emphasizes the human desire to be creative and gain self-awareness that is validated through interpersonal relations. She places it at the center of citymaking, where "conviviality is, indeed, the very nourishment of civil society itself" (p.250). It thrives in shared public and common spaces. Conviviality is a fundamental source of social trust that is the lubricant of cooperation.

Recasting *human relations with nature* ranging from supporting the resilience of city ecologies to expanding spaces for the reproduction of the planetary biosphere is critically important to the survival of humanity (Duara 2014). This is not only manifested in global climate change but also in most cities in Asia where air, land, and water pollution are among the highest in the world and where anthropogenically driven environmental disasters are now occurring at unprecedented scales and frequencies (Douglass 2016).

As underscored in Friedmann's Good City, the intention of a progressive-cities framework is not only to provide a vision of the future. It is also meant to provide a framework for assessing cities today. Research on progressive cities in East and Southeast Asia was initiated in 2013 to use our framework for this purpose.

The rise of progressive cities in East and Southeast Asia

During the early post-colonial decades of the mid-20th century in Asia, progress was placed in the care of developmental states supported by international organizations such as the United Nations and the World Bank. With few exceptions, these states adopted a model of government that promised high rates of economic growth in exchange for maintaining authoritarian regimes, which were also kept in place by active use of police powers. This model prevailed into the 1980s when it began to be supplanted by a hybrid neoliberal–neodevelopmentalist formulation of unfettered global corporatization as the high road for human progress.

Principal drivers of this shift were international lending institutions, notably the World Bank, the International Monetary Fund, and the Asia Development Bank. By the 1990s the World Bank was already demanding privatization and full cost recovery of public services, which at its peak reached nearly 90 percent of its loans worldwide (Grusky 2001). Although the 1998 Asian financial crisis directly involved just a few countries, its impacts spread throughout East and Southeast Asia. National economies recovered over varying time spans, but a longer-lasting effect was the spread of neoliberal policy regimes throughout most of Asia (Siregar 2004).

A major dimension of policy shifts was the ending of the strong protection of cities from global competition. Urban development was recast as a competitively global pursuit rather than being contained within national development as it was in the past. As a result, the urban problematics facing cities in Asia's open economies became more similar to, rather than sharply differentiated from, those of other world regions (Sassen 2015). Income inequalities, precariatization of labor, use of low-wage foreign workers, environmental degradation, and environmental disasters all increased to new levels. With unprecedented increases in global corporate mega-projects, spaces of public life also began disappearing, and urban design was overtly used to contain and marginalize democratic freedoms through gating, surveillance, the pervasive setting up of security barriers, and landscaping to control foot traffic (Douglass 2014).

The rise of civil society accompanying urbanization in Asia and the world is pushing back against these trends (Friedmann 1998, 2011). Cities became the focus of new rounds of political activism for resolving the many issues of daily life, livelihood, environment, and access to the public sphere. In some cities inclusive grassroots mobilizations have been able to reach into the mayor's office to generate progressive policy agenda.

In the context of the twin processes of corporatization and citizen activism to (re)claim cities that seemed to be making headway in some cities, we initiated a research project in Asia and Europe in 2013 using the progressive cities framework detailed above. In East and Southeast Asia candidate cities were chosen through round-table discussions among scholars doing urban research, which resulted in the selection of Seoul, Busan, Taipei, Hong Kong, Chengdu, several cities in Japan, Surakarta, and Surabaya. Two key research questions headed a number of subsequent inquiries: (1) In what ways, if any, is the governance of the city progressive? (2) How did progressive governance politically emerge?

Although the initial assumption was that progressive cities could only be found in countries in which democratic reforms and devolution of power to city levels had occurred, research found that progressive actions occurred in other settings as well. In Chengdu, for example, the adoption of participatory budgeting (PB), an innovation originating in Porto Allegre, Brazil, manifests aspirations for inclusive governance and distributive justice (Cabannes & Ming 2014). As underscored by Friedmann for China in general, PB in Chengdu has been an endogenous process without any international support; it is locally designed and embedded in local political and administrative processes. From 2009 to 2012 more than 40,000 projects in more than 2,300 villages were implemented, making it the largest PB program in China and one of the largest in the world. Of particular interest to the discussion on civil society mobilizations, PB in Chengdu began in villages of Chengdu, which is a city extending more than 100 kilometers into its rural periphery and where social identities are reportedly stronger than in the city proper (Friedmann 2005).

With half of its population in rural communities, PB was made possible by municipal reforms of 2007 that sought to reverse the widening rural–urban divide in quality of life and income from livelihoods. The reforms included rights to communal land and private ownership of housing and agricultural land, which had become major sources of rural unrest caused by dispossessions of land for large-scale public and corporate projects. PB is officially stated to be a democratic process of decision-making by village people. Projects selected through autonomous village councils cover basic infrastructure for marketing of fresh food; maintaining irrigation and flood control; cultural, literacy and fitness programs; village radio and cable TV; and village administration of public services such as solid waste collection. Residents in each community have the power not only to decide on the use of public money but also to control it through community-led mechanisms of monitoring (Cabannes & Ming 2014).

As part of the pilot reform on integrated and balanced development between rural and urban areas in the Chengdu Municipality, the city developed policies and regulations to include local villagers in decision-making, monitoring, and evaluating village-level public services projects. Fundamental to this has been the establishment of a new village-level governance mechanism, the village council, to regulate the allocation of village public services funds. Each village council generally has a dozen or more members elected by and from among local villagers, who then go on to form a democratic finance management group and a budget oversight group.

While Friedmann's research on China has been criticized for being overly optimistic about civil society (Walcott 2007), this criticism suffers from a narrow view that civil society only exists if it is politically engaged in public decision-making. The position here is in agreement with Friedmann (1998) that civil society, defined as the organized face of society, is mostly for itself rather than politically motivated. As such, China and Asia in general have rich histories of organized civil society, even if politically suppressed. At the same time, Friedmann might also underestimate the capacity of civil society to politically engage and effectively pressure government for change at local levels. He (Friedmann 2005) states that social organizational capacities were severely dampened by government during and after the Maoist era political processes and further compromised by massive rural–urban migration. However, evidence from Chengdu supports O'Rourke's (2003) discovery in Vietnam that top-down command planning can be community driven. This is most likely at local levels where government officials are visible and cannot so easily shield themselves from social pressures.

Research on Taipei illuminates how grassroots movements resulted in the preservation of vernacular heritage and the establishment of a community museum, which emphasizes the importance of conviviality through place-making (Ho 2015). In Busan, South Korea, government stopped slum demolitions in favor of a government-community partnership that generates new livelihoods through community engagements in the arts and artisanal production (Joo 2015). In Japan, city and local governments are promoting participatory art festivals as a way of sustaining the vitality of cities that are experiencing depopulation (Koizumi 2015). The triple disaster in Tohoku, Japan in 2011 also resulted in innovations in local governments for more inclusive decision-making (Aoki 2015). In Indonesia, democratization following the ouster of President Soeharto in 1998 and subsequent radical devolution of state power has seen the election of progressive mayors in such cities as Surakarta and Surabaja (Padawangi 2015). The popular support of Joko Widodo, then Mayor of Surakarta and now President of Indonesia, came from grassroots engagements to upgrade slums and provide land titles to relocated families, engaging government and vendors to resolve disputes over access to public space, curtail corruption, and revive cultural traditions (Majeed 2012).

Seoul presents the most thorough shift from neoliberal to progressive governance. A snap election in 2011 selected an activist lawyer who had never held elected office previously and who ran as an independent candidate. The election was the outcome of the city's long experience with grassroots political movements that had been unable to counter the power of national political party structures. The new mayor, Park Won-soon, immediately set up hosts of citizen councils and direct representation in government decision-making. He cancelled the city's mega-projects that had created a huge debt burden to the city, and he pushed through legislation to stop wholesale evictions accompanying corporate projects. Concerning the environment, his plan to cut energy consumption by one nuclear power plant was achieved in just three years (Cho 2014, 2015). In 2014 he was re-elected by the widest margin of any candidate running for office across the nation (Cho 2014).

The point to emphasize is not that a "magic mayor" changed the political landscape, but rather that the urban culture of Seoul produced the opportunity for a dynamic leader to be elected when an opening in the political system appeared. As Clavel (1986) found with the history of progressive cities in the U.S., the progressive governments that have emerged in Asia have originated from grassroots mobilizations of citizens aspiring for political change and for new values of city life.

Conclusions

The rise of civil society and insurgencies are everywhere, confronting city governments to be more inclusive, just, supportive of social and cultural life, and environmentally responsible. Progressive city governments are appearing in response in many quarters of the world (Goldberg 2014; Harvey 2012; McGuirk 2014).

The idea of progressive cities rising in East and Southeast Asia can be met with skepticism. Local governments remain underfunded, understaffed, and without significant political power in many countries. Even where democratization and devolution of state power to city levels have occurred, cities differ significantly in terms of local political culture and histories of social activism. However, when city hall is breached, our research shows that the unexpected can and does occur.

Whether such government can be sustained is always in question. As Friedmann (2000, p.470) observes, "good governance always hangs on slender threads." However, our research reveals greater promise for progressive governments to persist than might be apparent. The principal reason for optimism is that they emerge from longer histories of grassroots activism that have developed locally progressive cultures and activist capacities that are more enduring than the tenure of a single elected official. In any case, popular aspirations for progressive city governance are more apparent than previously imagined in Asia and globally. Whether they can push through social, political and economic barriers to institute progressive governance is a question worth pursuing in these times of corporatization that is swiftly undermining the idea of the city as a sphere of social life and participatory governance.

References

Aoki, N 2015, "A tsunami-ravaged town becomes progressive to survive and revive". Presented at the *International Symposium on the Rise of Progressive Cities East and West*, Paris Sorbonne University, May 11–12.

Atkinson, S & Jorgensen, J 2014, "From progressive planning to progressive urbanism: planning's progressive future and the legacies of fragmentation", *UW Tacoma Digital Commons*. Available from: <http://digitalcommons.tacoma.uw.edu/cgi/viewcontent.cgi?article=1000&context=conflux> [25 January 2016].

Brenner, N & Schmid, C 2014, "Urban worlds – the 'Urban Age' in question", *International Journal of Urban and Regional Research*, 38(3): 731–755.

Cabannes, Y & Ming, Z 2014, "Participatory budgeting at scale and bridging the rural–urban divide in Chengdu", *Environment & Urbanization*, 26(1): 257–275.

Carothers, T & Youngs, R 2015, "The complexities of global protests", *Carnegie Endowment for International Peace*. Available from: <http://carnegieendowment.org/2015/10/08/complexities-of-global-protests/iint> [19 February 2016].

Cho, MR 2014, "The governance of the Park Won-Soon administration: a performative governance for a progressive city", *Journal of Daegu Gyeongbuk Studies*, 13(2): 1–9 (in Korean).

Cho, MR 2015, "Progressive city in the making? The Seoul experience", *International Symposium on Making a Progressive City: Seoul's Experience and Beyond*, Seoul City Hall, 15 October.

Clavel, P 1986, *The Progressive City*, Rutgers University Press, New Brunswick, N.J.

Conley, V 2002, "Chaosmopolis", *Theory, Culture & Society*, 19(1–2): 127–138.

Douglass, M 2009, "Globopolis or cosmopolis? – Alternative futures of city life in East Asia", *Studies in Urban Humanities*, 2: 67–115.

Douglass, M 2014, "After the revolution: from insurgencies to social projects to recover the public city", *International Development Planning Review*, 36(1): 15–32.

Douglass, M 2016, "The urban transition of disaster governance in Asia" in *Disaster Governance in Urbanising Asia*, eds M Miller & M Douglass, Springer, Singapore, pp. 13–43.

Duara, P 2014, *The Crisis of Global Modernity: Asian Traditions and a Sustainable Future*, Cambridge University Press, Cambridge.

Economist Intelligence Unit (EIU) 2012, *Benchmarking Global City Competitiveness, The Economist*, London.

Flyvbjerg, B, Nils, B & Werner, R 2003, *Megaprojects and Risk: An Anatomy of Ambition*, Cambridge University Press, Cambridge.

Friedmann, J 1962, "The city in history", *The Town Planning Review*, 33(1): 73–80.

Friedmann, J 1986, "The World City hypothesis", *Development and Change*, 17(1): 69–83.

Friedmann, J 1987, *Planning in the Public Domain: From Knowledge to Action*, Princeton University Press, Princeton, N.J.

Friedmann, J 1992, *Empowerment: The Politics of Alternative Development*, Blackwell, Cambridge, M.A.

Friedmann, J 1998, "The new political economy of planning: the rise of civil society" in *Cities for Citizens: Planning and the Rise of Civil Society in a Global Age*, eds M Douglass & J Friedmann, John Wiley & Sons, Chichester, pp. 19–35.

Friedmann, J 1999, "The city of everyday life: knowledge/power and the problem of representation", *disP*, 35(136–7): 4–11.

Friedmann, J 2000, "The Good City: in defense of utopian thinking", *International Journal of Urban and Regional Research*, 24(2): 460–472.

Friedmann, J 2002, *The Prospect of Cities*, University of Minnesota Press, Minneapolis.

Friedmann, J 2005, *China's Urban Transition*, University of Minnesota Press, Minneapolis.

Friedmann, J 2011, *Insurgencies: Essays in Planning Theory*, Routledge, London and New York.

Gleeson, B 2006, "Desocializing space: the decline of the public realm in western Sydney", *Social & Cultural Geography*, 7(1): 19–34.

Goldberg, M 2014, "The rise of the progressive city", *The Nation* 2 April. Available from: <http://www.thenation.com/article/rise-progressive-city/> [15 March 2015].

Graham, S & Marvin, S 2001, *Splintering Urbanism: Networked Infrastructures, Technological Mobilities and the Urban Condition*, Routledge, London.

Grusky, S 2001, "Privatization tidal wave – IMF/World Bank water policies and the price paid by the poor", *The Multinational Monitor*, 22: 9. Available from: <http://multinationalmonitor.org/mm2001/01september/sep01corp2.html> [26 January 2016].

Harvey, D 1973, *Social Justice and the City*, Edward Arnold, London.

Harvey, D 2012, *Rebel Cities: From the Right to the City to the Urban Revolution*, Verso, New York.

Ho, KC 2015, "Taipei: a city of protest and a city of progress", *International Symposium on Making a Progressive City: Seoul's Experience and Beyond*, Seoul City Hall, 15 October.

Ho, KC & Douglass, M (eds) 2008, *International Development Planning Review*, Special Issue on "Globalisation and livable cities: experiences in place-making in Pacific Asia", November.

Holston, J 2001, "Urban citizenship and globalization' in *Global City-regions*, ed. AJ Scott, Oxford University Press, New York, pp. 325–348.

Illich, I 1972, *Tools for Conviviality*, Espirit, Paris.

Joo, YM 2015, "Towards progressive governance in a developmentalist metropolis: the case of slum regeneration policy in Busan, South Korea", *International Symposium on Making a Progressive City: Seoul's Experience and Beyond*, Seoul City Hall, 15 October.

Koizumi, M 2015, "Governance with a creative citizenry: public art projects for cultural vitality in Japanese cities", *International Symposium on Making a Progressive City: Seoul's Experience and Beyond*, Seoul City Hall, 15 October.

Kunstler, JH 1994, *The Geography of Nowhere*, Touchstone, New York.

Lacey, H 2015, "Food and agricultural systems for the future: science, emancipation and human flourishing", *Journal of Critical Realism*, 14(3): 272–286.

Lefebvre, H 1991, *The Production of Space*, Blackwell, Oxford.

Majeed, R 2012, *Defusing a Volatile City, Igniting Reforms: Joko Widodo and Surakarta, Indonesia, 2005–2011*, Princeton University, Innovations for Successful Societies, Princeton, N.J. Available from: <http://successfulsocieties.princeton.edu/sites/successfulsocieties/files/Policy_Note_ID199.pdf> [22 December 2015].

McGuirk, J 2014, *Radical Cities: Across Latin America in Search of a New Architecture*, Verso, New York.

O'Rourke, D 2003, *Community-driven Regulation*, MIT Press, Boston.

Padawangi, R 2015, "Constructing progressiveness: the complexity of progressive cities in Surakarta and Surabaya", *The International Symposium on the Rise of Progressive Cities East and West*, Paris Sorbonne University, May 11–12.

Papayanic, N 2004, *Planning Paris before Haussmann*, Johns Hopkins University Press, Baltimore.

Peattie, L 1998, "Convivial cities" in *Cities for Citizens: Planning and the Rise of Civil Society in a Global Age*, eds M Douglass & J Friedmann, John Wiley, London, pp. 247–253.

Sandercock, L 2003, *Cosmopolis II: Mongrel Cities of the 21st Century*, Continuum, London.

Sassen, S 1991, *The Global City: New York, London, Tokyo*, Princeton University Press, Princeton, N.J.

Sassen, S 2003, "Globalization or denationalization?", *Review of International Political Economy*, 10(1): 1–22.

Sassen, S 2015, "Who owns our cities – and why this urban takeover should concern us all", *The Guardian*, 24 November. Available from: <http://www.theguardian.com/cities/2015/nov/24/who-owns-our-cities-and-why-this-urban-takeover-should-concern-us-all?CMP=share_btn_tw> [19 February 2016].

Siregar, PR 2004, *World Bank and ADB's Role in Privatizing Water in Asia*. Available from: <http://cadtm.org/World-Bank-and-ADB-s-Role-in> [26 January 2016].

Soja, E 2010, *Seeking Spatial Justice*, University of Minnesota Press, Minneapolis.

Sorkin, M 1992, *Variations on a Theme Park: The New American City and the End of Public Space*, Noonday Press, New York.

Taylor, PJ 2000, "World cities and territorial states under conditions of contemporary globalization II: looking forward, looking ahead", *GeoJournal*, 52(2): 157–162.

Triglav Circle 2015, *Human Flourishing and Social Justice*. Available from: <http://www.triglavcircleonline.org/2005/12/human-flourishing-and-social-justice/> [15 August 2015].

Tu, WM 1993, "Our religions" in *The Seven World Religions Introduced*, ed. A Sharma, Harper, San Francisco, pp. 139–227.

Walcott, SM 2007, "*China's Urban Transition*, by John Friedmann", *Economic Geography*, 83(4): 445–446.

Woo-Cummings, M (ed.) 1999, *The Developmental State*, Cornell University Press, Ithaca, N.Y.

17 Transactive planning and the "found space" of Mumbai Port lands

Hemalata C. Dandekar

The context

Planning for Mumbai's port lands encompasses decades of analysis, deliberation and stalemate. Under a neoliberal, public–private partnership-driven model to spur economic development, the Central Government of India currently appears poised to "liberate" locked up port lands for civic use and for private speculation. A Mumbai Port Land Development Committee[1] report suggests ways to put some 1,800 acres of prime waterfront land, currently controlled by the Mumbai Port Trust (MbPT), to uses that benefit both the city and port. Representing as this does about one-eighth the total land area of the City of Mumbai, and strategically placed as a narrow strip edging the entire eastern coast of the city peninsula, the port land offers an opportunity to revitalize and reinvent the city.

Current planning to repurpose Mumbai Port lands is, as it has been in previous attempts, highly contested. The need to think at all levels—global, national, regional and at the same time local—is essential if Mumbai is to attain (or, as some claim, retain) world city status. A collaboratively planned revitalization is critical but seemingly unattainable. A variety of stakeholders—local to national levels of government, local to multinational business, developers, city residents, labor unions, non-profits, and a myriad of other constituencies of this multicultural Indian metropolis—are in the fray over its repurposing and future occupancy. The contemporary ideal of planning for the public good is poignantly salient, as are the prospects of a land-short city aspiring to attain (or retain) world city status.

The stakes are high in the deliberation over the future use of this "found" land which it is anticipated will soon be "liberated" from port trust control. The heterogeneous activities involved in planning in market situations detailed some decades ago by Friedmann (1987, pp.25–29, see particularly Chart 1) are palpably at play. Civic groups and organizations, labor unions, and many different levels and branches of government are engaged in an activity in which market rationality and social rationality vie for dominance. As Friedmann notes (p.25), in a market society (such as the Indian) "the central coordination of all planning activities is patently impossible." But, as he further notes (p.28, point 8), the planning effort needs to "restrain market rationality in the name of social interests." This observation is pertinent in Mumbai around the deployment of government-controlled port land.

Planning for port land involves negotiating between fundamentally conflicting agendas. They are reflected in the goals set for the 2014 Development Committee by the Union Minister of Shipping, which include "building world-class cruise terminals, new waterways projects, a 500-room floating hotel, 3–4 floating restaurants, a Ferris Wheel on the lines of London Eye and marinas and jetties to promote intra-city water transport in Mumbai" (*The Hindu* 2014) as well as meeting the need for social housing to alleviate the chronic housing shortage of the poorest in the city who live in informal settlements throughout the metropolis. The estimated land value (11.25 billion US dollars) is identified as the source of collateral for development projects to be executed on a BOT (build, operate, transfer) basis. The committee reportedly recommended that 1,000 of the 1,860 acres be made available to Mumbai city to serve as a transportation hub (40% of the land) and a green lung (30% for open spaces). The draft report recommends creating an autonomous implementation authority—the Mumbai Port Land Development Authority—that is financially and administratively empowered to overhaul port land and curtail port operations to make more land available for city use (see Purohit 2015). There is speculation over how much land will actually be released, where, for what civic purposes and, most importantly, if there will be an entity with the overriding authority to act. The committee report has yet to be released to the public.

Regardless of when, and if, this report results in implementation, the committee efforts highlight the difficulties of planning Mumbai's port lands so as to balance both humanistic and technical/analytical assessments and to propose interventions that result in action. Bridging the divide between a focus on economic efficiency/technical rationality and on social equity/access is challenging. And predictably, these plans come into headlong conflict with the power structure that underpins big city politics as the stakes over who gains control over land are astronomically high.

Stepping back from this to contemplate the larger cycles of action and reaction, the accommodation to center/periphery shifts in power that underlie land use decisions in key areas of world cities is facilitated by being viewed through the framework that Friedmann (1987, pp.74–75) provides of alternative planning approaches and their underlying premises.[2] Planning for world cities must take cognizance of regional and national wellbeing as well as the local, and develop cross-sectoral agreements to act. In democratic societies, where a myriad of actors have voice and stake, achieving a strategic plan for action and bringing it to implementation is challenging and fraught with contradictions as attested in the current contestation over visions for Mumbai's port lands. These constituencies might achieve a shared purpose and balanced action by "bridging the communications gap" eloquently described as transactive planning (Friedmann 1973, pp.171–193) and elaborated by various theoreticians of communicative practice (Forester 1988; Krumholz & Forester 1990), which has yet to be tried in efforts to find common ground between different stakeholders in Mumbai. The approach has been used, and successfully, in surfacing the needs and priorities of particular constituent groups such as, for instance, residents of informal settlements. But such an approach has not been attempted in the overview deliberations of all the varied entities, holding divergent goals that have a stake and leverage in Mumbai's waterfront.

MbPT: a brief history

Mumbai Port has declined in the face of competition from a new port that is located directly across the bay in Mumbai harbor. Prime waterfront land has been left underutilized allowing a mélange of uses to permeate, including shanty towns and squatter settlements which have become sites of illegal underworld activities, and non-conforming industries and businesses which have obtained long-term leases for their enterprises. Starved for suitable development sites the city covets port lands but has no jurisdiction as the MbPT holds that power. Mumbai City, Port and the metropolitan region are losing their regional and national dominance as the pivotal node for export and import flows of goods and as a center for industry and manufacturing. This is partly due to the inadequate infrastructure of the city and resulting congestion and inefficiencies. Attaining a new city-port synergy is publicly acknowledged as critical by a diverse set of stakeholders who see the need for a city fabric that supports the reinvented base of the city economy. Pragmatic intra-government negotiations and planning processes that include private and third-sector stakeholders is required if port and city are to reach a new, productive and sustainable equilibrium.

The need for creative, inclusive planning intent and, more importantly, processes to achieve it is certainly recognized. But the capacity and will to act have been hard to garner and, more importantly, to implement. Insight from communicative processes, specifically as first delineated by Friedmann as dialogue which allows the exchange of professional and experiential knowledge, has offered guidance within constituencies, just as it has had resonance and been effective in planning processes at the local level in the U.S.[3] But their efficacy and relevance in the messy, politically fragmented, power-defined, hierarchically structured planning discourse in contexts such as Mumbai city/port land negotiations are untested and may be worth exploring given that successive efforts to plan and deploy these lands have stalemated and languished.

Colonial Mumbai: The evolution of Mumbai City was intricately intertwined with its location on the western coast of India and its significant geographical asset: a sheltered port. Mumbai's development during the British colonial period was intrinsically related to its ties, of trade, of commerce, and of economy, as well as of administrative connections with

London. The dendritic transportation and communication infrastructure built by the British government emanated from Mumbai City into the productive agricultural, labor-rich hinterland of the Deccan Plateau. The regional connections enabled economic growth through trade and also helped fuel industrial production in the core of the colonial city. The viability of Mumbai today continues to be linked with trade and finance but is no longer heavily dependent on the old port. Expansion of transportation infrastructure, primarily rail, road and, more recently, highway networks, has been a key factor in facilitating new regional and national connections that have kept flows in flux and, inevitably, moving away from Mumbai's downtown as the epicenter of the region.

The core–periphery spatial systems approach (Friedmann & Wulff 1975, pp.11–12) serves an important heuristic purpose in helping to sort out these emerged relationships that are inherently imbalanced and conflicting. Mumbai City aspires to be a world city and to continue to play a leading role in the economy of India. As congestion, a declining quality of life, and lack of amenities cause it to lose ground, access to port lands is perceived as key to remediation and to reinventing the city. The contestation, quite predictable given the multitude of stakeholders and the high rewards for prevailing, is over the nature and intent of this reinvention.

Post Independence: The expansion of Mumbai's port continued after Indian Independence, well into the 1970s in particular segments of its operations, such as petroleum (not an ideal activity to be located near a major population center), but the port's long-term viability has been in question. Between 1988–96 facilities to handle crude oil, petroleum, liquid chemicals and petroleum products were developed, including: four oil berths capable of handling large tankers; a modern jetty; and a number of new upgraded pipelines. This expansion helped handle imported petroleum and chemical products needed by petrochemical industries that had located on the shores of Mumbai and Navi Mumbai. With a total of 63 anchorage points the port was the largest in India, handled the highest amount of cargo and employed some 40,000 workers directly and many more indirectly. Jawaharlal Nehru Port (JNPT), the new port across the bay that enjoys significant transportation and locational advantages and lower land costs, started competing operations in 1989.

Post-liberalization globalization: A new policy of globalization, privatization and liberalization, charted by the Central Government in the 1990s, created major challenges to both Mumbai city and port. Mumbai First[4] advocated for public–private partnerships to create a city that would be a competitive player in the global economy and would reinvent its base economy through a variety of transformations of industry and product. Its 2010 Concept Plan for Mumbai Metropolitan Region visualizes ambitious development of the physical infrastructure of the city-region including large-scale land reclamation and creation of new islands of "artificial land" in Mumbai Harbor. It envisions a shift in the city economy to tertiary services with a high emphasis on skilled human capital and a high rate of growth in Business Services and 24% employment in the Secondary Sector.[5] These projections and the State Government's initiatives to grow IT services drew attention away from the old manufacturing, chemicals, and trade economy for which the port was a key infrastructure. Traditional industries that had flourished within the city, such as textiles, have declined and financial and other services have grown. The long-term viability of this service economy largely rests on the city's ability to provide high-end financial and IT services and cater to other competitive sectors, such as diamond cutting and trade, that build on available highly skilled labor, and to facilitate construction of infrastructure. In this new economy, the need to develop a symbiotic relationship between the port and the city has emerged with greater urgency.

Repurposing Mumbai Port lands

Land for housing, service provision, and commerce is acutely short in Mumbai city. And the underutilized Mumbai Port lands have been documented and mapped in great detail to find space that can remediate this reality.[6] Visionary land use plans for repurposing it to alleviate congestion and to revitalize the city are many. This work has also highlighted how the MbPT land, infrastructure and the potential amenity of additional, accessible waterfront offers an opportunity to "mend" or enhance the urban fabric of downtown Mumbai and improve the quality of life in Mumbai city (see for example Mehrotra et al. 2005). The eastern waterfront has been effectively locked away and inaccessible to most civilian activities for the last century, literally "walled off" from the daily life and the hustle and bustle of Mumbai city life and its commercial economy. Commuters on the Harbor Railway that edges the docklands only glimpsed the dilapidated, discarded buildings, warehouses and infrastructure of the port area. To the working Mumbaite commuting to work downtown, the eastern dock area was a mysterious no-entry land. However, under pressure, the MbPT has provided a strip of land for a new, 10-mile-long Eastern Freeway that runs above the existing main port road, parallel to the Harbor Railway. This recently completed elevated road provides much clearer views of the port area and serves to underscore the dichotomy between the dense city fabric of Mumbai City to the west and the underutilized Mumbai Port lands to the east. This visible contrast has strengthened the city resolve, now backed by popular sentiment, to press MbPT to open up the eastern waterfront for the benefit of the city.

Due to its geography, history and strategic location, Mumbai Port lands represent an asset that is highly contested. Visions for their reuse range from amenity-based, high-end leisure activity to those offered by the MbPT for increasing port activity at strategic waterfront sites. Numerous constituencies have a stake in the outcomes of these land-development decisions. Industrial facilities, the dock infrastructure, related storage and processing areas and buildings, illegal squatter settlements, and underworld activities have infiltrated these areas and claim rights to them. In 2002, 11 government, 17 private, five NGOs and 10 labor groups were stakeholders in this area (Mehrotra et al. 2005, p.8). They hold contradictory positions on how Mumbai's eastern waterfront docklands, industrial infrastructure, buildings and utilities need to be repurposed for optimizing their economic, social or civic usefulness in the global economy.

Alternative plans reflect the diverse vested interests of these stakeholders. For example, they range from a proposal by the MbPT to refurbish the old port infrastructure to modernity and return it to its primary purpose as an entry port for goods and people, to NGO claims for lands, some already occupied by squatter settlements, to create social housing for the poor. All have legitimacy and a rationality that is consistent within their internal frameworks. But lost in this contestation is the issue of what is needed in the new global economy to jump-start and support all constituencies that occupy the heart of a city that is in economic transition, one in physical distress and manifesting a decaying quality of life, overcrowding, lack of maintenance and overloaded infrastructure. Historically the east dockland waterfront successfully serviced the city and maintained its competitive edge during the industrial period. It is poised to be able to play a similar role in the new knowledge and service economy of the 21st century if planning processes can be aligned to enable this role.

Finding the port and city symbiosis: The potential of the eastern waterfront to play a key role in integrating the Mumbai Region with nodes of economic activity, people, manufacturing and transportation infrastructure is clearly illustrated in many concept designs that have been developed over decades. They evoke and reference a diverse range of examples, including San Francisco, Lisbon, Rotterdam, New York and Baltimore. London's docklands, particularly the now well-known case of the Canary Wharf and India Docks, the main receiving point of bulk goods from Mumbai during colonial times and now transformed to office, commercial, service and housing usage, are noted as offering a particularly salient approach. The experience of these cities is instructive in revealing what is possible but has limited direct utility. In land use planning, success is based on the technical, spatial, geographic parameters, resource base and overall configuration of a particular landscape and what it logically allows. And case examples of what has worked elsewhere, in similar landscapes, can provide guidance.

However, most case studies do not explicate how making changes in key infrastructure is a politicized, power-based activity in which technical rationality plays a role, but does not usually determine decisions. Long-standing interests, timing and political clout are important signifiers and they vary greatly according to place, point in history and context. In Mumbai these different viewpoints are argued in the popular media, through journalistic fact finding and positing of arguments, through inter- and intra-government sector deliberations and through the elected political/administrative process which is opaque and not driven by systemic grassroots citizen participation in a structure of regular engagement in decision-making. The question of if, and where, such discourse and dialogue between diverse constituencies may be created is rarely addressed in the existing planning process.

Land use ideals: The value of government-owned land in the Mumbai Port area and the possibilities inherent in selling or leasing just some of this land to provide the capital needed for infrastructure and other investments has been carefully analyzed. A World Bank study (Peterson & Thawakar 2013) estimates that utilizing some 200 hectares (494 acres) can provide the capital needed for the redevelopment effort projected for both the city and the port areas.[7]

The preservation and adaptive reuse of the historic, cultural and architectural fabric to celebrate the narrative of the old city and port has also garnered attention and it has been noted that attending to this patrimony will enable successful economic redevelopment strategies centered on tourism. That revitalized downtowns and adaptively reused historic buildings provide a cachet and legitimacy to multinational industries that appropriate these sites for their facilities has informed significant investments in Mumbai city and are evident in the Ballard Estate area of Mumbai adjoining the entryway to MbPT lands (see Mehrotra 1998). Capital needed to finance investments in critical infrastructure and to create the environment and synergy that would allow private capital to flow into the city to improve the physical fabric now appears to be at hand. The complexity and challenge lies in creating a vision and an approach that will work in a society that is a functioning democracy, one in which economic revival which results in gentrification, takings, and removal and relocation is constrained and tempered by laws that protect rights of low-income slum residents and the middle class to land tenure and access to shelter. It is a society in which there are stakeholders that demand a development that meets the needs of the poor, the working, and the middle classes. The government must listen if a sustainable future is to be attained. In this effort, a structure of tiered decision-making, vested in the local, and consensus building around land use decisions that are guided by a general plan, as one finds in the culture of decision-making at the local level in the U.S., would be conducive. But it is not the norm in Mumbai's planning structure. This raises the question of whether communicative planning and other approaches that require some erasure of power differences in discourse can transfer across socio-political boundaries and cultures, even in systems such as India's that self-label as practicing democracies.

In the democratic structure of Indian politics and the multicultural, variegated (differentiated by caste and class) society of Mumbai, an approach to redevelopment of the historic dock lands might benefit from involving communication that underscores that all parties have a stake and can have a share in the benefits. Efforts at such communications and structures that can be relied on for communicative action to be developed across sectors are worth exploring. Planning and decision-making to date has largely involved experts—government entities, business, labor unions, NGOs representing squatter settlements. Planning deliberations and outcomes have played out in a highly political decision-making system. Plans and visions for reconfiguring the region have been in play for at least the last 50 years (see, for example, Correa et al. 1965). Some of these—the concept of a twin city for instance—were implemented. But none of the many current plans for MbPT lands will be directly adopted on the basis of their technical rationality and worth. Political pressures on the process and the decision-makers are formidable. Decisive action is needed as the city inexorably loses ground to more agile actors elsewhere. It requires that a strong political will and leadership emerge in Mumbai (as it has in cities such as Hyderabad and Ahmedabad), one which is backed by popular support garnered through effective mass communication that convinces, cajoles or defies all other authorities and elicits cooperation. Although in other seemingly more successful Indian cities grassroots communicative planning around local land use decisions has not been notable, in Mumbai, with its history of strong vested stakeholder groups, efforts to launch trust-building discourse may be the way to gain momentum and break through stagnation.

Some reflections

It appears that, as in other Indian cities that have succeeded in infrastructure development and self-reinvention, the Mumbai dock land repurposing will involve compromise and accommodation and probably result in *ad-hoc*, neoliberal, and somewhat piecemeal actions. But it will be guided to a greater or lesser extent by an overall development concept that has been shaped to respond to conflicting claims and visions. A good planning process that is inclusive, that incorporates both a regional sensibility, and a local, grounded sense of stakeholders, roles and history will require finding the critical balance between life space and economic space that Friedmann (1988) has eloquently articulated in essays which delineate its many forms. In later writing the reference to the true wealth of cities as vesting in the human, social, cultural, intellectual, natural, environmental and urban assets (Friedmann 2007) rings true for Mumbai. It can help identify the activities and functions that might best be located on the eastern waterfront so as to draw on and strengthen the traditional city center and create a "city heart" which also embraces the port and the eastern dock yard area as a key element of the city past and the city present. Such a planning process may prove to be inclusive of, and able to mediate between, the desires of the diversity of stakeholders who have claims and rights to the city.

Notes

1 The committee was chaired by a former Chairperson of the Mumbai Port Trust (MbPT) and appointed by the Union Minister for Shipping Road Transport & Highways to whom MbPT reports. It was charged to look into ways of

transforming the overall use of port land and to suggest ways and means to put some 1,800 acres, controlled by the MbPT, to effective use. Its work represents the most recent of many attempts by government to plan for the revitalization and use of this strategically located land.

2 Particularly helpful in thinking about these relationships and understanding the viewpoints of those involved in this contestation is provided in the descriptions of the intellectual traditions of planning articulated by Friedmann (1987, pp.54–85).

3 A conceptual ideal of successful communication between technical planners and others is provided in Friedmann (1981) and Schön (1983).

4 Consisting of a consortium of business interests working in collaboration with the Mumbai Chamber of Commerce, Mumbai First was established in 1994 in association with the British Council and drew inspiration from London First as a think tank to foster relationships between major stakeholders. See http://www.mumbaifirst.org/.

5 See p.6 of the 2010 Concept Plan power point at http://www.mumbaifirst.org/ which states that Bombay First drew inspiration from the emergence of London First and the ways that it assumed the role of facilitating the restructuring of London through various public–private partnership initiatives.

6 Mehrotra et al. (2005) document in some detail the sub-optimal use of port land (see in particular p.12) and the potential of real estate development that would complement the city fabric and alleviate some constraints and challenges (see in particular p.25).

7 Peterson and Thawakar (2013, p.15) note that just 200 hectares managed over the long run, according to economic and urban development principles, can provide the financing for redevelopment activity. They advocate managing port land as a coherent estate, where genuinely surplus land is identified, and land values can be converted from time to time into critical infrastructure investments.

References

Correa, C, Mehta, P & Patel, S 1965, "Planning for Bombay – patterns of growth, the twin city, current proposals", *Marg, A Magazine of the Arts*, 3, June: 29–56.

Forester, J 1988, *Planning in the Face of Power*, University of California Press, Berkeley.

Friedmann, J 1973, *Retracking America: A Theory of Transactive Planning*, Anchor Press, New York.

Friedmann, J 1981, "The transactive style of planning", *Retracking America*, Rodale Press edn, Emmaus, Pennsylvania, pp.171–193.

Friedmann, J 1987, *Planning in the Public Domain: From Knowledge to Action*, Princeton University Press, Princeton, N.J.

Friedmann, J 1988, *Life Space and Economic Space: Essays in Third World Planning*, Transaction Publishers, New Brunswick, N.J.

Friedmann, J 2007, "Reflections on place and place-making in the cities of China", *International Journal of Urban and Regional Research*, 31(2): 257–279.

Friedmann, J & Wulff, R 1975, *The Urban Transition: Comparative Studies of Newly Industrializing Societies*, Edward Arnold, London.

Krumholz, N & Forester, J 1990, *Making Equity Planning Work: Leadership in the Public Sector*, Temple University Press, Philadelphia.

Mehrotra, R 1998, "Bazaars in Victorian arcades: conserving Bombay's historic core" in *City Space + Globalization: An International Perspective*, ed. HC Dandekar, College of Architecture, University of Michigan, pp.46–53.

Mehrotra, R, Joshi, P & Paul, A 2005, *A Study on the Eastern Waterfront of Mumbai*, Urban Design Research Institute, Mumbai.

Peterson, GE & Thawakar, V 2013, "Capturing the value of public land for urban infrastructure: centrally controlled landholdings", *Annual World Bank Conference on Land and Poverty*, The World Bank, Washington D.C., 8–11 April.

Purohit, K 2015, "Report on Mumbai's port land use given to Centre", *Hindustan Times* 9 January, 21: 22. Available at: <http://www.hindustantimes.com/mumbai/report-on-mumbai-s-port-land-use-given-to-centre/story-45efgoIteLshAm3tinWaLN.html> [11 August 2016].

Schön, DA 1983, "From technical rationality to reflection-in-action" in *The Reflective Practitioner: How Professionals Think in Action*, Basic Books, New York, pp. 21–69.

The Hindu 2014, "Panel set up on Mumbai Port land use", 26 June. Available at <http://www.thehindu.com/business/Industry/panel-set-up-on-mumbai-port-land-use/article6152323.ece> [11 August 2016].

Part 4

Social learning, communities, and empowered citizenship

Jacquelyn Chase

This section takes much inspiration from John Friedmann's turn toward a transactive model of planning that was introduced in *Retracking America* (1973).

Ironically, the title *Retracking America* does not hint at the generations of students who would seek John's mentorship for their research around the world. But it was his many years of development work abroad that led him to rethink planning as the preserve of experts. John had already clarified his skeptical stance on development when he advocated putting the planner's expertise at the service of poor regions; but transactive planning signaled something new in the practice of planning, not just in its object.

Four of these essays are case studies that reflect our personal relationships to different kinds of communities over years, if not decades. These relationships are part of our teaching, research and service. These entanglements are complex and sometimes messy, but here we relate conceptual insights that our engagement with these diverse situated contexts has gifted us.

A common theme in the case studies is the effort by communities to define and secure a life space in an era of neoliberal hegemony. Communities face pressure to privatize and market almost every aspect of life and it is interesting to see how they mobilize old and new sources of capital (social, financial, natural) to protect non-market spaces of life. Three of the four case studies show that alternative development is a useful frame for understanding rural and urban poverty in the United States.

In the first essay, Hibbard bases his two cases in "Indian country" in Oregon and Alaska on the principle of diversity and on the troubled relationship to assimilation policies that Indians have faced. The cases show a selective linking to the market for raw materials, but underscore the persistence of subsistence—something that grounds all planning discourse and action in the two communities to a cultural and ecological life space.

Isaac's essay follows with three projects in New Mexico. Like Hibbard, she notes the legacy of imperial relations among minority communities. In her evaluation of capacity, she refers to the residue of these relations as "imperial assets." She provides the example of predatory lending as a kind of negative capacity that communities can confront as part of "shared community problems."

Next, Winkler's contribution focuses on the concrete outcomes of a resident-led informal housing project in post-apartheid South Africa. She describes the solidarity of her students with members of the community who would have been left out of the project as originally designed by local planners. The reorientation led planners back to the drawing board to revisit their plans.

My essay follows with a discussion of planning in a stigmatized and stereotyped kind of community in rural America. It discusses how the property rights sentiment of the American rural west does not explain resistance to local planning. Instead, private property can serve community needs, such as fire safety and recovery, and thus has helped create a diverse and inclusive working landscape and life space in this poor exurban area.

Would any of us have studied planning without John's encouragement to engage emotionally with the subjects of our research? As Erfan's creative and very personal essay on love implies, we can welcome love (and other strong emotions) into planning because we have heard John's enigmatic appeal that "to travel to what is farthest, we must go by the path that is nearest" (1979). We have listened to his invitation to practice a "heightened knowledge of the self; an increased capacity for learning…[and] a heightened capacity for empathy" (Friedmann 1973, p.20).

References

Friedmann, J 1973, *Retracking America: A theory of transactive planning*, Anchor Press, New York.

Friedmann, J 1979, *The Good Society*, MIT Press, Cambridge, M.A.

18 Development in Indian country

Empowerment, life space and transformative planning

Michael Hibbard

> Throughout much of the world, ordinary people ... are struggling for survival with human dignity ... to construct a new order in which livelihood, the object of economics, will be subordinated to the broader and more encompassing values of life itself.
>
> (Friedmann 1988, p.xi)

Introduction

Development planning has characteristically sought to address the "deficiencies" of rural regions, such as underemployment and economic insecurity, weak schools, and inadequate infrastructure. The aim has been to introduce the high mass-consumption market economy to rural areas, through some combination of absorbing "surplus" rural labor, bringing industrial production to agriculture and natural resource extraction, and providing advanced infrastructure and services.

But many rural peoples, communities, and regions resist the idea that they are deficient and need to be "developed" in the conventional sense. They accept a reduced material standard of living because they value a rural lifestyle: physical characteristics such as lower population density and closeness to nature, and rural cultural and social influences on their lives (Hibbard & Lurie 2013; Horlings & Marsden 2014).

John Friedmann has been a central figure in the critique of conventional development planning and is responsible for an important set of closely related alternative development ideas. He was among the first scholars to recognize the tension between economic space and life space in development planning (Friedmann 1983). He further observed the wide variation in what is valued across the life spaces of different peoples and the importance of empowerment to enable them to be successful on their own terms (Friedmann 1992). And he identified and explained transformative planning, an approach to tackling the institutional structures that prevent or enable empowerment (Friedmann 1987). This chapter draws on the development experience of two Native American[1] communities, one in Alaska and one in Oregon, to probe Friedmann's ideas on empowerment, transformative planning, and the negotiations between life space and economic space.

Development planning—the emergence of an alternative

The conventional rural development planning model emerged in the late 19th century. Its purposes were to manage primary resources such as soils, forests, minerals, and water so as to supply the food, fiber, lumber, minerals and other primary commodities essential to developing national economies; and provide permanent occupations, homes, and communities in rural regions (MacKaye 1919). Reaching its peak in the post-World War II era, it held that the only thing needed for progress toward "development" was the right kind of program (Hirschman 1981). Well-known examples include the irrigated agricultural communities of a century ago in the settler societies of Australia, Canada, and the U.S.; large-scale river basin developments around the world, from the 1920s to the present; and current efforts to "urbanize the countryside" in China.

By the 1970s, scholars led by Friedmann began to challenge the notion of a universal approach to development. They maintained that the point of development planning should not be maximizing aggregate demand but responding to local social, cultural, and environmental circumstances (Friedmann 1992; see also, e.g., Goulet 1971 and Scott 1985). While this alternative view did not completely displace the conventional view, it had a powerful influence. There is broad recognition that successful development entails local people having an effective voice in their own affairs, grounded in the local culture and its institutions and addressing essential needs as understood in the local culture (Friedmann 1988).

Friedmann's observations about the possibilities for alternative development—empowerment and transformative planning, life space and economic space—emerged from his investigations of real forms of practice, from his work on the Tennessee Valley Authority in the 1950s to China in the 2000s (Friedmann 2002). He had a major role in moving the field away from an idealized rational planning model toward careful study of what planners actually do and reflection on the effects of their actions. It led to a new approach to planning scholarship: fine-grained, interpretative case studies informed by concepts from social theorists (Innes & Booher 2015).

Thomas Kuhn (1987) observed that a discipline without a large number of thoroughly executed case studies is a discipline without systematic production of exemplars, and that a discipline without exemplars is an ineffective one. Given the role of case studies in planning scholarship, this chapter explores the application of Friedmann's ideas of alternative development in a new context. The isolated, sparsely settled, deep rural setting of most Native American communities makes for an instructive contrast to the sites of most planning scholarship. The position of American Indian and Alaska Native communities as "internal colonies" within the U.S. bridges the experience of rural communities in the global north and south. Finally, the approach of the U.S. in dealing with Indian and Alaska Native communities closely tracks the evolution of development planning broadly.

The Indians' "white problem"[2]

The presence of indigenous peoples presented a serious challenge to European colonizers of what is now the United States of America. At best, white settlers viewed Indians as innocents in need of assimilation; at worst, they were seen as a menace to be exterminated. Whatever the case, "the Indian problem" presented whites with a three-part challenge: how to secure access to Indian land and other resources; how to transform Indians into non-Indians; and how to maintain effective control over Indian groups, how to systematically contain them. In the Indian view, the situation was the Euro-American or "white problem," the mirror image of the Indian problem: how, in the face of invasion, conquest, and loss of power, to maintain or regain control over resources, especially land; how to maintain particular sets of social relations and more or less distinct cultural orders; and how to have some measure of political autonomy. Tracing the working through of the Indian problem and the white problem sheds much light on the evolution of development planning.

Once the policy of physical extermination ended in the 1880s, when Indian peoples were no longer able to resist colonization, an assimilationist approach to Indian policy emerged. Grounded in the emerging rural development planning model, it endeavored to assimilate Indian peoples into mainstream culture by breaking up reservations and making Indians into individual landowners, small-business operators, commercial farmers, and wage workers. It assumed that Indian social groupings and cultural identities would be absorbed and disappear into the larger society. Assimilationist approaches alternated with more culturally sympathetic policies and programs for nearly one hundred years but ultimately they were discredited and largely reversed.

The indispensable factor in Indians' resistance to assimilation has been their empowerment (Friedmann 1992) through tribal sovereignty. U.S. legislation and case law generally support the view that tribal governments are, in an important sense, sovereign nations that have a "special" government-to-government political relationship with the U.S. government. They have inherent powers of self-government and can create their own laws and policies, control their own land and resources, maintain their cultures, and uphold their political autonomy—in short, deal with the white problem.

Tribal communities have been most successful in reinforcing the principle of sovereignty through the practice of what Friedmann (1987, 1992) called "transformative planning." A growing body of scholarship argues that planning is concerned not solely with the codified knowledge of formally trained professionals but also with local or community knowledge (Innes & Booher

2015). In this view, a tribal community is not the passive recipient of conventional development plans and programs. It is resilient and can actively resist, interpret, and negotiate, albeit often in subtle ways; ultimately, it can fashion its own plans based on its own culture, values, and aspirations (Ugarte 2014).

Transformative planning in Indian country assumes the principle of sovereignty. It entails the community itself identifying and implementing strategies for reaching its own self-identified goals. An aspect of that has been the encounter between economic space and life space. As Friedmann points out, economic spaces are abstract—nodes of production and consumption and the linkages between them, flows of capital, labor, commodities, and information. Life spaces are concrete, bounded, territorial places, "the ground on which the history of a people is enacted," "people organized for a life in common" (Friedmann 1988, p.96). Both are necessary, but for rural people, especially Indigenes, economic space has been a vehicle for demolishing life spaces.

For tribal communities in the United States the white problem has always been about how to maintain economic space and life space—sovereignty and the associated control of land and resources, preservation of culture, and the means as well as the right to effective self-government. In Friedmann's terms, it is about empowerment and the practice of transformative planning.

Transformative planning in Indian country

To probe the nature of development planning in Indian country I tell (some of) the story of two communities with which I have been involved: the Confederated Tribes of Warm Springs, Oregon and Kake, Alaska. I use these cases not because they are typical—they aren't—but because they are helpful in illuminating transformative planning.

The Confederated Tribes of Warm Springs

The Confederated Tribes of Warm Springs was created by treaty with the U.S. government in 1855. The Indian signatories represented various bands of the Warm Springs and Wasco tribes. They ceded a huge tract of land but reserved a substantial portion for their reservation. They also reserved the right to fish, hunt, forage, and pasture stock in their accustomed places on the ceded lands. They were joined in the early 1880s by a smaller group of Paiutes. These three federally recognized tribes constitute the Confederated Tribes of Warm Springs (CTWS).

The tribes escaped much of the harmful effects of assimilationist policies and programs, primarily because of their remote location and lack of attractive agricultural land. Like most reservations, the tribes govern themselves under the terms of their own Constitution and bylaws, initially adopted in 1938. The governing body, the Tribal Council, consists of eleven members:

the chiefs of each of the three tribes are lifetime members and eight members are elected for three-year terms. Tribal Council meetings are open to all tribal members.

In addition to the Tribal Council, major decisions are deliberated at General Council meetings where all tribal members have the opportunity to voice their views. Regular General Council meetings are held annually; special General Council meetings are held as necessary, to discuss political, economic, and social issues affecting the tribes, such as major development projects. Most General Council meetings are called by the Tribal Council but any tribal member can call a meeting.

Their approach to self-government reveals a great deal about the values and priorities of the CTWS. First, the reservation itself has important meaning. Unlike the case of many indigenous peoples who were "relocated" to distant places, the reservation is a part of the traditional homeland of the Warm Springs and Wasco peoples. They "reserved" it to themselves in the 1855 treaty. For them and for the Paiutes who joined them later, the reservation is imbued with a variety of tangible values as a source of subsistence (hunting, fishing, gathering). Of at least equal importance, it also has vital intangible values—belonging, attachment, beauty, and spirituality—elements of life space. Protecting their reserved lands and their resource rights on their ceded lands is a crucial community goal.

Second, there is a strong CTWS identity. The durability of traditional customs indicates a deeply held attachment to their heritage. More concretely, it is embedded in the reservation's governmental structure and processes. Each of the three tribes retains its own voice in the Tribal Council, yet they work collectively for the community as a whole. The General Council meetings give voice to the collective membership.

Third, there is great interest in assuring the future of the tribes. In the words of a 1944 Bureau of Indian Affairs report, the tribes are "convinced of the necessity of planning as a means of developing and safeguarding their properties" (Bureau of Indian Affairs, 1944, part 2, Section I, p. 2).

In sum, the CTWS are characterized by a strong communal orientation to the protection of their land, their resources, and their distinct cultures, and to the betterment of the community as a whole. Their approach to planning has tried to take all that into account as it has evolved over the last seventy-five years.

A planning program focusing on the preservation and management of the CTWS land base and other resources was instituted by the Bureau of Indian Affairs (BIA) in 1940. Then, in 1958, the tribes received substantial cash settlements in two land disputes. Through a series of General Council meetings they decided to make a small per capita distribution but retained the bulk of the settlement funds in the tribal treasury, to be used for development.

The first product of that decision was a development plan prepared by consultants rather than the BIA. Characteristic of conventional development planning, the plan focused on economic space. It consisted of an inventory of reservation resources and suggestions as to how they might be exploited for economic growth. Its emphasis was on timber production and tourism. Implementing the plan, the tribes purchased a number of assets on the reservation, including a wood products manufacturing plant and land that has since been developed into a major resort with a hotel and convention center, a small casino, and a golf course. The tribes also own and operate a hydroelectric generating facility that sells power to cities off the reservation. The revenues from these activities enhanced the tribal government's financial position and enabled them to build strong services for their members.

Subsequent plan updates in 1969–1970 and 1983, also prepared by outside consultants, focused on infrastructure and public facilities. However, the 1983 update was a turning point; it included the tribes' life space—social and political development and cultural and human resources. A tribal language program, an early childhood learning center, a museum, and new health clinic were all implemented.

The 1983 update involved a high level of public participation and when the CTWS planning office designed a process for future plan updates, they sought to produce the same level of buy-in or ownership. It is an ongoing process open to all tribal members, including widespread involvement of tribal officials at all levels of all departments.

To sum up, the CTWS community has always been highly engaged in governance. There is no clear separation between the government and the people. Planning and policy decisions are community decisions, with all major decisions brought to General Council. Despite that, the first several iterations of development planning at Warm Springs relied almost exclusively on expert outsiders, initially the BIA and then consultants. Those plans concentrated on economic space, growing the market economy of Warm Springs. But the 1983 update broke new ground. It opened the process to the general membership and spoke to issues of life space as well as economic space. One result has been that subsequent planning processes have been designed and carried out by the tribes' own planning office rather than by consultants. This approach to transformative planning embraces explicit concern with tribal and community control of the planning process.

Kake

Kake is a Tlingit community located on the northwest shore of Kupreanof Island in southeast Alaska. Southeast Alaska is an archipelago, a series of closely scattered islands accessible only by boat and, in modern times, airplane. Until the 1870s, the Tlingit and other southeast Alaskan tribal peoples relied on the bounty and variety of natural resources available locally to fashion their living and societal structure, with little outside influence. This changed after the United States purchased Alaska from Russia in 1867. Although the Tlingits never signed treaties or sold their land, non-Natives began taking possession.

The area around what is now Kake was a traditional summer gathering site for the Keex' Kwaan (Kake) Tlingits, a base for fishing, hunting, and preserving their take. As white settlement encroached, Kake gradually became a permanent settlement for the Keex' Kwaan. In 1906, processors from "outside" (outside Alaska, in Alaskan parlance) opened a commercial salmon saltery in Kake. This marked the beginning of the community's involvement with conventional development, with production for export. Another outside company built a salmon cannery on the site of the saltery in 1912. At about the same time, Keex' Kwaan tribal elders established the Kake municipal government.

In 1910 the U.S. Congress passed the Organized Village Act, under which Alaska communities could set up a form of municipal self-government. Native villages were generally excluded from participation because Native people were not U.S. citizens. However, there was a provision by which Natives could become citizens. Kake's elders applied for and received U.S. citizenship and obtained a municipal charter. They made a conscious decision to give up their traditional system of governance and adopt the formal American system. Kake was apparently the first Native community in Alaska to take this assimilative step. The Kake city government continues to operate under the laws of the State of Alaska, providing infrastructure and other typical municipal services.

The global demand for canned salmon was robust and, by 1920, over one hundred canneries were operating in Alaska. Like most in Alaska, the financial situation of the Kake cannery was always precarious, undercapitalized and operating on thin margins. It changed hands at least four times—all the owners were outside companies—prior to its acquisition by the Organized Village of Kake (OVK) in 1948.

OVK is the federally recognized tribal government of the Keex' Kwaan, formed in 1948. It advocates for and protects the Keex' Kwaan's customary and traditional fishing, hunting, and gathering areas that the tribe historically inhabited and utilized. It also provides many social service and educational programs for its members and the overall community of Kake.

One of the first acts of OVK was to buy the cannery, which at the time had been closed down by its outside owners. OVK operated the cannery until the late 1970s when, along with many other Alaskan canneries, finances and changing market conditions forced its final closure.

A second resource extraction industry, logging, came to southeast Alaska at about the time the Kake cannery closed. The Alaska Native Claims Settlement Act (ANCSA) of 1971 transferred 11% of Alaska's lands to native groups as compensation for lands taken. The land was administered through local "village" corporations and regional corporations. Tribal members became shareholders in their village and regional corporations and the Native corporations were mandated to make a profit from their lands. Thus, the Keex' Kwaan are shareholders in the Kake Tribal Corporation (KTC) and the Sealaska Regional Corporation.

The primary business of KTC, established in 1975, was forest products. It received title to substantial forest holdings around Kake and created numerous jobs through clearcutting their timberland and selling logs and wood pulp on the global market. When Kake's timber allocation was harvested, KTC was forced to declare bankruptcy in 1999. By 2004, all logging operations were discontinued; the corporation remains insolvent.

In short, for a century, Kake was something of a success story in terms of conventional development. The global demand for their resources, first salmon and then timber, provided a solid economic base for the community. Admittedly, there were problems. Like all natural resource work, it was seasonal and somewhat irregular, depending on market conditions. The cannery was owned by a series of outside firms for the first three decades of its existence. The work itself was grueling and often dangerous. Nevertheless, these economic opportunities provided a substantial material standard of living for the Keex' Kwaan.

With the loss of the cannery and then the timber industry the economy of Kake collapsed. Between 2002 and 2005 the population of Kake fell from over 800 to less than 500, as at least 150 working-age residents and their families were forced to leave the community in search of employment. These conditions also brought confusion, distraction, and threats to the way of life of Kake residents.

The virtual disappearance of the natural resource economy reinvigorated ongoing local conflicts over economic versus life space—social, economic, and environmental values and what it means to be Keex' Kwaan.

In the winter of 2004, as logging was winding down, Kake's three governmental entities began efforts for a collective response to the community's crisis. It was difficult and contentious, brought about only because of the failure of the local economy. The three organizations with governance responsibilities in Kake make for a complex administrative framework; the city government, OVK, and KTC have different but overlapping missions and responsibilities. Moreover, they have different orientations toward development. KTC is by definition a supporter of conventional development. It is a for-profit corporation tasked with making money for its shareholders. OVK is the guardian of the Keex' Kwaan's cultural heritage, the people and their traditional territory. The city is the provider of basic services such as infrastructure and public safety. Although they are all bottom-up, endogenous organizations, they had difficulty communicating with one another and cooperation was problematic because of a perception that they were engaged in a zero-sum game in which success for one organization could only come at the expense of another.

Their joint effort resulted in formation of the Comprehensive Economic Development Strategy (CEDS) committee that included leaders from all three groups—the City Mayor, the Executive Director of OVK, and the Vice President of KTC—along with other important figures such as the school superintendent and the head of the newly formed small business association.

The CEDS committee used a variety of processes, including "town hall" meetings open to all, to identify criteria by which to screen proposed socio-economic development projects. The final criteria were evenly balanced between economic space (job and business creation) and life space (conserving and restoring the environment and protecting and strengthening Tlingit culture). However, as things improved in Kake and the sense of crisis lifted, the community became more sensitive to the importance of life space.

An open-ended question in a 2009 household survey by the University of Oregon (Hibbard et al. 2010) asked respondents about "the things we most need to preserve in our community." Forty-nine percent said that preserving Tlingit culture is important; a further 21% responded that preserving the Tlingit language is important; and 17% mentioned the subsistence lifestyle—hunting, fishing, gathering. When asked what the community should change, 15% felt that increasing the amount and availability of employment is important. The responses suggest that economic space is important, but life space, the preservation of Tlingit culture and language, is the overwhelming priority.

A more concrete example comes from looking at their cash versus the subsistence economy. It is a truism that Keex' Kwaan (and other Alaska Native) culture is so bound up with subsistence that it is impossible to have the one without the other; being Native Alaskan means living a subsistence lifestyle. But however deep-felt its cultural meaning, it is not nostalgia or sentimentality that guides the Keex' Kwaan toward subsistence. On a functional level, everyone who lives in Kake depends in part on subsistence. It is an important cultural practice: a way of living in the world, of bringing children into the community, and of honoring the elders, as well as a source of food and other resources necessary for survival.

Not everyone engages in subsistence activities but everyone receives the produce of subsistence, through trade, gifts, and the like. The reverse is also true; everyone depends on the cash economy. As important as it is, there are things subsistence cannot provide, and households continue to find ways to generate income—from self-employment, seasonal and part-time work, remittances from family members living away, and from transfer payments. Moreover, the infrastructure that enables subsistence depends on the cash economy. Subsistence activities require boots and bush clothes, buckets and clam shovels, boat motors and fishing gear, guns and ammunition, smoke houses and canning equipment.

To sum up, the collapse of Kake's fishing and then timber economy left little choice but to explore alternative development options. An important result has been the emergence of what John Altman (2011) calls the hybrid economy, in which subsistence is viewed as a co-equal with the cash economy (income from work, remittances, and transfer payments). In that formulation the veneration of Tlingit values and lifeways makes it difficult to draw a distinction between life space and economic space. The effect in Kake is that people are willing to accept a lower material standard of living in exchange for the benefits of living the Tlingit way.

So what?

Drawing on Friedmann's observations, the Warm Springs and Kake cases illustrate that: 1) not all peoples, communities, and cultures have the same ambitions for themselves; 2) the life space of subjugated groups is at risk because of the overwhelming emphasis on economic space in conventional development planning; but 3) transformative planning offers subjected groups the ability to resist and maybe even to take action on their own behalf.

Early on, both communities emphasized conventional development, strengthening economic space at the sacrifice of life space. In Warm Springs this was primarily the result of a strong federal push. In Kake it was market pressure. Eventually, both communities recognized the threat to their life space and acted to save it: Warm Springs by incorporating concern for life space into their planning process and Kake by explicitly adopting the hybrid economy. Both communities embraced transformative planning, though not necessarily in ways anticipated by Friedmann. In his formulation, transformative planning is the process of identifying and implementing strategies for transforming the structures of oppression, "collective self-empowerment" (Friedmann 1987, p.389). But who is the planner? In these cases the oppressed community itself developed a consciousness of its oppression and strategies for responding: Warm Springs through the General Council and Kake by forming a community-wide institutional coalition.

Indigenous survival in the face of the white problem is an ongoing challenge. These cases demonstrate that while the challenge is substantial it is not insurmountable. Through transformative planning, indigenous peoples have achieved meaningful control in negotiating the tensions between economic space and life space.

Notes

1 I will generally use the terms "American Indian" or "Indian" and, in the case of Alaska, "Alaska Native" or just "Native" (Alaska Natives include Indians, Aleuts, and Eskimos). I do so for two reasons. First and most important, these are the terms most often used by the descendants of the aboriginal inhabitants of the contemporary U.S. to identify themselves. Second, they are standard within the federal laws and policies that define the unique and distinct position of "American Indians" and "Alaska Natives" vis-à-vis their political status and relationship to the federal government. Similarly, my use of "tribe" and "Indian tribe" follows standard practice in federal Indian law and policy and in the self-description of many Indian communities.

2 This and the following sections are based on Hibbard 2006, Hibbard 2016, and Lane and Hibbard 2005.

References

Altman, J 2011, *Alternate Development for Indigenous Territories of Difference*, CAEPR Topical Issue No. 5. Australian National University Center for Aboriginal Economic Policy Research, Canberra.

Bureau of Indian Affairs 1944, *Reservation Planning: Warm Springs Reservation Program*, Warm Springs Agency, Warm Springs, OR.

Friedmann, J 1983, "Life space and economic space: contradictions in regional development" in *The Crises of the European Regions*, eds D Seers & K Öström, Palgrave Macmillan, UK, pp. 148–162.

Friedmann, J 1987, *Planning in the Public Domain: From Knowledge to Action*, Princeton University Press, Princeton, N.J.

Friedmann, J 1988, *Life Space and Economic Space: Essays in Third World Planning*, Transaction Publishers, New Brunswick, N.J.

Friedmann, J 1992, *Empowerment: The Politics of Alternative Development*, Blackwell, Cambridge, M.A.

Friedmann, J 2002, *The Prospect of Cities*, University of Minnesota Press, Minneapolis.

Goulet, D 1971, *The Cruel Choice*, Atheneum, New York.

Hibbard, M 2006, "Tribal sovereignty, the white problem, and reservation planning", *Journal of Planning History*, 5(2): 87–105.

Hibbard, M 2016, "Development planning with cultural integrity: self-determination, multifunctionality, and the hybrid economy in Indian country", *Journal of Planning Education and Research*, DOI: 10.1177/0739456X15612200 [2 November 2015].

Hibbard, M & Lurie, S 2013, "The new natural resource economy: environment and economy in transitional rural communities", *Society and Natural Resources*, 26: 827–844.

Hibbard, M, Adkins, R & Onyschuk, S 2010, *Results and Analysis of the 2009 Comprehensive Economic Development Strategy (CEDS) Committee Kake Household Survey*, University of Oregon Institute for Policy Research and Innovation.

Hirschman, AO 1981, *Essays in Trespassing: Economics to Politics and Beyond*, Cambridge University Press, Cambridge, M.A.

Horlings, LG & Marsden, TK 2014, "Exploring the 'new rural paradigm' in Europe: eco-economic strategies as a counterforce to the global competitiveness agenda", *European Urban and Regional Studies*, 21(1): 4–20.

Innes, JE & Booher, DE 2015, "A turning point for planning theory? Overcoming dividing discourses", *Planning Theory*, 14(2): 195–213.

Kuhn, TS 1987, "What are scientific revolutions?" in *The Probabilistic Revolution, Vol. 1: Ideas in History*, eds L Kruger, LJ Daston & M Heidelberger, MIT Press, Cambridge, M.A., pp. 7–22.

Lane, MB & Hibbard, M 2005, "Doing it for themselves: transformative planning by indigenous peoples", *Journal of Planning Education and Research*, 25(2): 172–184.

MacKaye, B 1919, *Employment and Natural Resources*, Department of Labor, Office of the Secretary, Government Printing Office, Washington, D.C.

Scott, JC 1985, *Weapons of the Weak: Everyday Forms of Peasant Resistance*, Yale University Press, New Haven.

Ugarte, M 2014, "Ethics, discourse, or rights? A discussion about a decolonizing project in planning", *Journal of Planning Literature*, 29(4): 403–414.

19 Operationalizing social learning through empowerment evaluation

Claudia B. Isaac

My personal journey with social learning

This chapter explores how three examples of my planning practice illuminate how John Friedmann's social theory can inform participatory community development work. My approach to planning aligns with the social mobilization paradigm. To use Friedmann's terminology, this is a conflict centered approach that challenges many of the collaborative themes of social learning (Friedmann 1987). Nonetheless, many elements of social learning theory have proven very useful in my practice.

The social learning practice is rooted in community-based participatory research. It envisions working with community-based organizations that seek to transform entrenched inequities built into social and economic systems. I frame work with these organizations in a conception of "planning as pedagogy," using pragmatic, deliberative, and communitarian approaches, all of which are informed by (explicitly and implicitly) Friedmann's social learning theory (Healey 2011). My clients are deeply grounded in a commitment to social movement activism for revolutionary structural change. They engage geographically and culturally defined communities in asset-based development, a practice that builds economic capacity through identification and nurturing of pre-existing community capabilities. This practice in turn requires the self-expansion of community and organizational capacity in order to confront structural and political conditions that limit community well-being. These approaches combine with a methodology called empowerment evaluation (Fetterman 1996). This methodology resonates with key themes in Friedmann´s exploration of social learning as a methodology for positive social transformation and draws explicitly on Dewey as illuminated by Friedmann (1987).

Empowerment evaluation uses community-based and participatory processes to help organizations analyze their own practice and make data-driven adjustments to their programs. Central to the methodology are activities that bring to the surface the local knowledge of program and organization participants to understand, critique, and then transform their own practices. The community-based organizations all convene to advance racial, class, and gender justice agendas. I have lent my assistance to organizations with methodologies that ensure the quality and rigor of community-generated knowledge to increase the likelihood of social justice outcomes from their work.

So, despite my unease with social learning's casting of social transformation and empowerment as an essentially collaborative practice, I share Friedmann's insistence on positive social transformation as a central function of planning practice, and I agree with him that incremental, place-based social movements can advance transformative goals. I also agree that life space and economic spaces are intimately related (Friedmann 1992). These require balanced attention in the development planning process, particularly as place-based movements seek to transform both neoliberal and Keynesian economic structures that undermine community self-determination and their capacity to empower themselves.

The operationalization question in social learning planning

The cases described here demonstrate how collaborative, transgressive, and community-based planning processes are made possible by rigorous community inquiry. Indeed, alternative development requires practices that allow community members to not only learn from each other through deliberation, but also to develop the critical skills to assess the quality of their activities. As such, this chapter attends to how planners (professional and grassroots) engage the concepts of capacity and resiliency to enable community sustainability and self-determination through self-assessment.

The organizations that I discuss here all contribute to the conversation about community health and vitality through community-based analysis of global, regional, and local conditions and of the socio-economic and spatial inequalities that shape local conditions. These examples also offer a tool box of collaborative, redistributional, and strategic means of preserving desired conditions. The approach to planning builds on existing community strengths and assets while pushing back against forces that undermine the well-being of the community.

Community capacity

The cases discussed here include an evaluation of a domestic violence prevention program; a community land trust; and a farmer training program. Friedmann's (1992) discussion of the role of civil society in social and political empowerment informed all of these projects. His conception of emergent civil society as a grassroots form of resistance to exclusionary and oppressive state and corporate institutions has helped shape the approach I have taken with my clients to build community capacity. In particular, Friedmann's mapping of the *intersections* of civil society, corporate society, and the state help describe the complex interstices that my clients operate in and the opportunities they have for reclaiming their power.

Community capacity starts with an assessment of community assets. Community capacity approaches to development represent a shift away from an historically deficit-based approach that encourages top-down planning solutions for "problem places" with "problem populations" who are seen to have no agency (Birch 2006). The asset-based approach to development recognizes the survival strengths that communities develop to endure and overcome oppression and disenfranchisement.

The concept of "revitalization" implies that a community used to be vital, had its vitality stripped from it, and community members are seeking to reclaim that vitality. Capacity-building, on the other hand, recognizes collective memories of community norms and practices that precede the status of disinvestment, disenfranchisement, and marginalization (Isaac & Stoltzfus 2012).

Kretzmann & McKnight (1993) identify three kinds of assets that help define capacity in a community:

- *Accessible assets* are located within a community and owned or controlled by that community. An example would be a community bank like South Shore in Chicago, or a depositor-owned credit union.
- *Partially accessible assets* are community-located but not community-controlled, such as a national bank with branches in a community.
- *Inaccessible assets* are those that community members do not have access to, such as banks that refuse to locate branches or make loans in poor communities (a violation of federal law, but nonetheless still prevalent).

Building on this classification, I posit a fourth kind of asset, that of "imperial assets."

- *Imperial assets* constrain the ability to actualize local capacity. These are assets that are used directly against communities by those who seek to manipulate and oppress them. Predatory lending enterprises would be an example of imperial assets.

Community-based organizations build upon accessible assets, leverage inaccessible assets, and push back against imperial assets by exercising two kinds of capacity:

1 *Diagnostic capacity enables collective analysis and understanding*. Diagnostic capacity in community-based organizations is generated through collaborative community engagement and utilizes and enhances local expertise. Diagnostic capacity can be used to identify organizational, economic, social, and political capacity available to community members for developing resources and responding to challenges.

2 *Adaptive capacity* (Sussman 2003) *enables community-based organizations to convene a collective response to internal and external political, economic, and social conditions.* Adaptive capacity is attuned to external conditions, constraints, and opportunities. It enables existing and new social networks. Adaptive capacity is enabled through inquisitive and innovative thinking. Perhaps most importantly, it is sovereign. It is controlled and driven by community goals, needs, and resources.

Community resiliency

Social learning theory proposes that iterative and collective deliberation can prepare community members to respond nimbly to both internal and external challenges to livelihood (defined here as the complex sets of interpersonal, material, and political resources that enable community well-being). The ability to act quickly and effectively when confronted with imperial assets is central to community resilience.

It is useful to be reminded of what community resiliency is *not*, when considered in the context of social learning theory. Community resiliency is *not* a measure of innate individual talent or skill; it is *not* a means of transferring responsibility for well-being from government agencies to individuals or communities; and it is *not* an opportunity to blame the victims for their own structural and instrumental oppression. Community resiliency from a social learning perspective refers to community members' capacity to identify threats and challenges; to help each other react to and recover from threats and challenges; and to collaboratively generate social, political, and physical solutions that can mitigate the causes of those threats and challenges in the future. Thus, planning for community resiliency requires openness to conversations about the structural inequalities that reduce the resiliency of some communities (in my practice, mostly poor communities of color) disproportionately, through no fault of their own.

Friedmann's (1987) conceptions of experiential knowledge and of social learning as a deliberative problem-solving process describe what can happen when inclusive communities build on their own power and assets to act in their own self-interest. Community resiliency is, in this sense, collaborative agency to enact positive social change, which Friedmann emphasizes in *Empowerment* (1992) as the generation of political power out of social power. This connection of political and social power is made by utilizing resources available in "life space" to capture material resources that are withheld from the poor in economic space. Thus, as Lopez and Stack (2001) note, traditional conceptions of social capital as politically neutral, and of the power relations between communities and mediating institutions as fixed, are challenged by Friedmann's conception of empowerment. This view of empowerment presupposes the dismantling of institutional hierarchies that govern relationships between governments, community development institutions, and poor communities.

Three examples of capacity, resiliency and transformation

Three cases help illuminate the relationship between capacity building, community resiliency, and social justice transformation. Enlace Comunitario (Enlace), The American Friends Service Committee of New Mexico (AFSC-NM), and the Sawmill Community Land Trust (SCLT) all demonstrate how principles of social learning can increase organizational and community capacity and advance social justice agendas. Of course, as is appropriate to the social learning tradition, in no way do I claim ownership over the research, outcomes, or analysis presented here. The insights shared here come from collaborative learning within these communities that I was honored to participate in.

Enlace Comunitario

Enlace Comunitario (Enlace) is a nationally known and well-regarded organization in New Mexico that works in domestic violence and healthy relationship intervention and prevention. It bases its work with survivors of intimate partner violence (IPV) on survivor-driven strategies in order to change norms about violence and to promote social justice. Its focus is in the immigrant community in Bernalillo County.

In 2009, Enlace received funding from the Robert Wood Johnson Foundation's "Strengthening What Works" program to evaluate its Promotora program, wherein Latina immigrant women who have received Enlace's intervention services become Violence Prevention Promotoras. These programs are grounded in the process of survivors developing capacity to advocate and lead within their communities through education and service programs, and through survivors' participation in networks and coalitions, to bring about institutional and policy changes. The survivors work in turn to transform structural conditions and create new social norms. The goal of the Promotora program is to co-create an immigrant community free from domestic violence.

Enlace has been a learning organization since its inception in 2000. Its staff are practiced in deliberation, debrief, collective analysis, and program reformulation to improve their programs and activities. Enlace staff took advantage of the Strengthening What Works funding to evaluate their prevention program in a more systematic way. I served as a Project Capacity Consultant for that effort. The idea was to build Enlace's evaluation capacity so that it could improve its already reflective program planning process, and to increase its ability to share lessons learned from their work to create practice-based evidence (Ortsman et al. 2012). The evaluation was participatory—staff took the lead in framing, designing, and implementing the evaluation, while Promotoras helped develop and administer instruments and review findings for collective analysis of outcomes.

One of the key findings of this evaluation was that social capital is an important protective factor against domestic violence. Evaluators defined social capital as networks of mutual support and trust developed among Enlace clients, among the Promotoras, and within the larger immigrant community.[1] As such, the networks built through the Promotora program increase the agency of immigrants and highlight Friedmann's critique of economic space as governed by commodity exchange that ignores the importance of social and territorial relationships.

The evaluation confirmed Enlace's *a priori* assertion that IPV should be addressed as a social rather than an individual problem, and that the social problem must confront policies and practices that enable domestic violence in immigrant communities by politically disempowering those communities (imperial assets). The findings also affirmed Enlace's commitment to working with domestic violence survivors as Promotoras, whose experiential knowledge and analysis were central to the success of the prevention program, and whose participation in the program increased the Promotoras' own ability to enhance their community's resilience.

Enlace also identified strong community partnerships as key to successful outreach and community education, but learned that those partnerships need to be consistent with Enlace's social justice mission lest they lose sight of their primary goals and objectives. They also determined that the professional development and stipends associated with the program not only increased the human capital of Promotoras, but also promoted the sustainability of the program by freeing them to participate collectively in the political movement.

In addition to building on their collective social analysis of IPV prevention in immigrant communities, Enlace staff, Promotoras, organizational partners, and community allies increased their ability to refine goals and objectives in light of collaboratively collected data and to locate new initiatives in this refined analysis. They identified a gap in their strategy of policy and norms transformation. By focusing only on women survivors of domestic violence, they had failed to utilize the solidarity and social capital of male allies. As a result of the evaluation, they initiated a "Male Allies" project.

Sawmill Community Land Trust

The Sawmill Community Land Trust (SCLT) was founded in 1996 to preserve a 27-acre brownfield site in Albuquerque for affordable housing. The Sawmill community is located in a community adjacent to the gentrifying neighborhood of Old Town in Albuquerque, and residents were beginning to feel the pressure of climbing property taxes and insistent developers looking to buy in the community. The SCLT is a non-profit membership organization that seeks to "develop vibrant, prosperous neighborhoods through the creation and stewardship of permanently affordable housing and sustainable economic opportunities" (SCLT, n.d.). The keystone of SCLT's mission is the empowerment of underserved, disinvested communities through civic engagement, education, and advocacy.

The SCLT community consists of its leaseholders, renters, the community members surrounding their developments, and allies throughout the region who support the land trust model. The end consumers of the SCLT (people in the land trust communities who are housing insecure) are also central participants in the organization's governance, policy-making, and activities, the backbone of their sophisticated social learning process. I have been a member of the SCLT board for eight years, and currently am the board Vice President.

A key capacity concern in the SCLT is building a community-accountable and community-driven organization that can fulfil its land trust obligation to sustain the community economically and maintain the affordability of its housing for 99 years. It does this by leveraging federal, state, and city funding into the community and "capturing" that funding into the land trust. It helps fulfil its stewardship responsibilities by building local community decision-making capacity to navigate the complex financial and political shoals of the primary and secondary housing markets. Stewardship is also promoted through collaborative land use decisions that prioritize community meaning and collective well-being over individual wealth creation.

Resiliency and sustained social transformation are ensured by the land trust's ability to protect community members from displacement from gentrification. Stewardship ensures that there are policies and regulations to protect: land from market speculation; rents and housing prices from instability; and community character and values from eroding. This housing security affords economic and social stability against the imperial assets that confront them in the form of gentrifying development.

American Friends Service Committee of New Mexico

In 2009, the AFSC-NM began a project "Community-Based Food Security for Albuquerque Public Schools and the South Valley." This three-year USDA-funded initiative intended to enhance social, ecological and economic vitality of the South Valley of Albuquerque by increasing the number and capacity of South Valley farmers; increasing the number of economically and ecologically sustainable South Valley farm enterprises; and, most importantly, by affirming and enhancing social networks and solidarity among South Valley community-based organizations involved in agricultural development. The AFSC implemented the project in partnership with three community-based organizations in the South Valley: Emerging Communities E-mc (n.d.); La Plazita Institute (n.d.); and Valle Encantado (n.d.).[2] These organizations are dedicated to community-driven social, environmental, and economic development. Emerging Communities celebrates Native American agricultural traditions as central to invigorating their livelihoods and protecting against cultural erosion. La Plazita Institute uses farmer training as a means of healing from trauma by working the land and countering the employment difficulties of their constituents, many of whom have had confrontations with the justice system. Valle Encantado draws on extended family relationships rooted in Hispano traditions of mutual support to envision an alternative to the industrial agriculture model.

Although their strategies and tactics vary, all seek to reclaim forms of livelihood that are place-based and culturally resonant, and some of them serve as examples of Friedmann's (1992) analysis of the articulation of life space as a means of countering the dominance of economic (wholly commodified) space. Along with AFSC's faith-based mission to challenge dehumanizing economic structures, all of these organizations challenge the pervasive perception that economic space is ubiquitous and permanent. All engage life space (the collectively derived and historical norms, networks, and mutual responsibilities) as a place of resistance to economic space.

The project's approach was summarized in six goals: 1) To increase economic development and food security in the South Valley and Albuquerque Public Schools; 2) To increase the entrepreneurial capacity, technical skills, and farmer-to-farmer information sharing of community-based farmers; 3) To increase infrastructure for sustainable community-based farms (cold frames, wells, etc.); 4) To support the development of a South Valley farmers' distribution network/co-op/self-governance body; 5) To develop replicable farmer-to-farmer training models that focus on sustainable economic and agricultural practices; and 6) To increase non-financial resources (their definition of social capital) available to organizational partners through participation in the project.

My role on that project was external evaluator, and my task was to document the expectations, outcomes, and sustainability prospects of the project through a participatory and empowerment evaluation project over three years (Isaac 2012). The project was able to increase access to healthy food through consumption of self-grown produce, increase in WIC (women, infants, and children) sales at farmers markets, and, later, through the La Cosecha CSA, subsidize weekly food bags to low-income people in the South Valley.

The project challenged the industrial food system (governed primarily by the neoliberal metrics of economic space) by increasing the number of small to medium farm enterprises, redistributing capital more fairly within the community, and increasing the number of living-wage jobs. The project utilizes the abundant social resources in the South Valley to leverage limited financial capital. A particularly important example of reclaiming food sovereignty and cultural foodways outside of "economic space" can be seen in the land agreements between farmers and South Valley residents who have yards that were not being fully utilized. These agreements were confirmed by Memoranda of Understanding but usually involved no land rent fees. There were some challenges, but the practice has increased alternative economic exchange through barter (in this case use of the land in exchange for a share of the produce) and represents a wonderful example of the articulation of economic space and life space.

During the three-year project, the partner organizations and new farmers formed the AgriCultura Network (n.d.), a collaborative approach to competing with industrial food distributors in the institutional food market. AgriCultura aggregates the produce from its member farms to sell to Albuquerque Public Schools, restaurants, and grocery stores. The La Cosecha CSA is also part of that aggregation strategy, with the added goal of increasing access to local healthy produce to members of the farmers' own disinvested community.

Community deliberations: diagnostic capacity, adaptive capacity, and transformative capacity

In each of these examples, a group of thoughtful and committed community activists convened *themselves* to understand the causes and characteristics of a shared community problem (diagnostic capacity); to develop a strategic solution to that shared problem (adaptive capacity); and to utilize tools generated by themselves, and in consultation with other community-based planning actors, to restore control over their present and future lives (transformative capacity).

In Enlace, violence is conceived as a social problem that can only be transformed though informed and strategic collective action based in the analysis of the experiential knowledge of survivors and the recognition and nurturing of social capital. The Enlace model also recognizes that the anti-immigrant political climate undermines social capital and requires progressive advocacy to transform that climate. Because of the dangerous political climate and the threats to the safety of IPV victims, the stakes of this deliberative planning process are quite high. Enlace thus works diligently to ensure that all participants in their social learning process are constantly building their diagnostic and analytical capacity to generate rigorous and effective strategies for social change. Indeed, shared learning and intentional cross-training among participants has helped Enlace become an effective advocate for social transformation and social justice in the Albuquerque immigrant community.

In the SCLT, collective stewardship protects individuals from the stacked deck of the housing market, where wealth protects wealth, and which no amount of individual financial literacy can protect against on its own. The SCLT has engaged in 20 years of community capacity building, including cross training, experiential sharing, and practice in community-driven design that has enabled residents, staff, and partners of the SCLT to become sophisticated design critics and social analysts. This social learning is ongoing, and long-standing residents play an important role in helping new residents a) recognize the skills and assets they actually have, but have rarely acknowledged; and b) build new skills and assets through the SCLT deliberative process.

The AgriCultura Network and the AFSC Farmer Training Program affirm that the historical oppressions that resulted in loss of food sovereignty and the rise of the industrial food system require a collective strategy to reclaim food sovereignty. The movement rejects the neoliberal principles that rely on individual commitments to make better nutrition choices, but rather models alternative development, rooted in a process of acknowledging, nurturing, and utilizing social networks and relationships with the goal of restoring community livelihood through historically grounded "solidarity economies" (Miller n.d.).

All of these initiatives involve collaborative problem solving through social learning, and self-determination through asset based development. All have a strategic orientation (focused on action, grounded in collective analysis), and take a long view, recognizing the structural forces (imperial assets) that continue to undermine community capacity and enable injustice.

Though some planners still refer to community building as a professional process, whereby community members are relegated to the happy recipients of designs, plans, and policies that are intended to improve their quality of life, and provide the amenities available to them (like safety from violence, sustenance, and housing), I am encouraged by substantive trends, exemplified by the cases presented here, that are reclaiming resiliency as local, redistributive, co-creation among members of robust communities.

All of these initiatives involve community members engaging in skillful power analysis, enabling them to address their immediate practical needs and interests while working towards resolving the strategic interests and needs that created those problems in the first place (Molyneaux 2001). It is particularly heartening to see how principles of social learning inform (though often implicitly) these struggles for positive social transformation. These struggles are never easy or smooth, nor is the process of social learning. I remain optimistic, however, that the social movements engendered in these cases advance the reclamation of livelihood, meaning, and life space for their participants.

Note

1 The traditional approach to social capital, initiated by Robert Putnam (2000), focuses on the *lack* of social capital in "modern" life—that modern life is almost uniformly conceived as middle and upper class, suburban, and, until Putnam's most recent work, White. In Putnam's vision, we need social policy, planning practice, and design tools to create social capital anew. Susan Saegert and others (2001) presents an expanded view of social capital focusing on long-standing historical, cultural, and social practices drawn upon by disinvested or otherwise stressed communities in the absence of access to market resources. In this view, which I use in this essay, social capital is not lost in these communities. Rather, it represents a vital and critical resource that must be protected and supported by policy and community practice.

2 American Friends Service Committee–New Mexico; AgriCultura Network. Available from: <https://www.afsc.org/program/new-mexico-agri-cultura-network> [3 December 2015].

References

AgriCultura Network. Available from: <http://agri-cultura.org/> [3 December 2015].

Birch, E 2006, "Hopeful signs: U.S. urban revitalization in the 21st century". Paper presented at the *Land Policies for Urban Development Conference*, Lincoln Institute of Land Policy, Cambridge, M.A., September.

Emerging Communities E-mc, State registration. Available from: <https://www.statelog.com/emerging-communities-e-mc-albuquerque-nm> [3 December 2015].

Fetterman, DM 1996, "Empowerment evaluation: an introduction to theory and practice" in *Empowerment Evaluation: Knowledge and Tools for Self-assessment and Accountability*, eds DM Fetterman, SJ Kaftarian & A Wandersman, Sage, Newbury Park, C.A., pp. 3–46.

Friedmann, J 1987, *Planning in the Public Domain: From Knowledge to Action*, Princeton University Press, Princeton, N.J.

Friedmann, J 1992, *Empowerment: The Politics of Alternative Development*, Blackwell, Cambridge, M.A.

Healey, P 2011, "Foreword" in *Insurgencies: Essays in Planning Theory*, ed. J Friedmann, Routledge, Abingdon, UK.

Isaac, C 2012, *Community-based Food Security for Albuquerque Public Schools and the South Valley: Final Evaluation Report*, American Friends Service Committee–New Mexico, December.

Isaac, C & Stoltzfus, A 2012, *Implications of National and International Capacity Building Approaches for NMMS Reflective Community Practices*, New Mexico Main Street, Santa Fe, N.M.

Kretzmann, JP & McKnight, JL 1993, "Mapping community capacity", *Center for Urban Affairs and Policy Research*, Northwestern University.

La Plazita Institute. Available from: <http://laplazitainstitute.org/> [3 December 2015].

Lopez, L & Stack, C 2001, "Social capital and the culture of power: lessons from the field" in *Social Capital and Poor Communities*, eds S Saegert, MR Warren & JP Thompson, Russell Sage, New York, pp. 31–59.

Miller, E n.d., "'Other economies are possible!': Building a solidarity economy", *Grassroots Economic Organizing*. Available from: <http://www.geo.coop/node/35> [3 December 2015].

Molyneaux, M 2001, *Women's Movements in International Perspective: Latin America and Beyond*, Institute of Latin American Studies, London.

Ortsman, S, Lopez Salazar, A, Perez Ortega, V, Benoit Isaac, C 2012, "Enlace Comunitario: Strengthening what works: a case study', Enlace Comunitario, Albuquerque.

Putnam, R 2000, *Bowling Alone: The Collapse and Revival of American Community*, Simon & Schuster, New York.

Saegert, S, Warren, MR & Thompson, JP (eds) 2001, *Social Capital and Poor Communities*, Russell Sage, New York.

Sawmill Community Land Trust. Available from: <http://www.sawmillclt.org/> [3 December 2015].

Sussman, C 2003, "Making change: how to build adaptive capacity", *Nonprofit Quarterly*. Available from: <https://nonprofitquarterly.org/2003/12/21/making-change-how-to-build-adaptive-capacity/> [3 December 2015].

Valle Encantado. Available from: <https://www.facebook.com/Valle-Encantado-138502686210271/> [3 December 2015].

20 The "radical" practice of teaching, learning, and doing in the informal settlement of Langrug, South Africa

Tanja Winkler

Introduction

Planners continue to bemoan the presumed gap between theory and practice. This gap is typically framed by practitioners as a *knowledge transfer* problem, because theoretical knowledge is assumed to be devoid of practical transferability. By contrast, many scholars maintain that theory and practice necessitate *distinct kinds of knowledges* that are shaped by equally distinct ontological and epistemological standpoints. Yet, as Friedmann (1987) reminds us, planning is an interventionist activity that operates at the interface of knowledge and action. Planning theories and practices therefore neither stand in opposition to each other, nor do they substitute each other. Rather, theories and practices complement one another, since, as planners, we need to simultaneously draw on technical (*techne*), theoretical (*episteme*), practical, and ethical knowledge (collectively, *phronesis*) if we hope to "set something new into the world" (Friedmann 2014, p.2). Friedmann's idea of *setting something new into the world*—which is inspired by Arendt's work—thus necessitates "some form of action that, however small, will help pave the way into the future" (ibid.). In other words, "planning actions need to be oriented towards the future" (ibid.).

This action and future-oriented conceptualization of planning entails at least five important operations (Friedmann 2014): (1) a *strategy* about how to proceed, (2) an *ethical judgement* by which the action itself can be justified, (3) taking *responsibility* for the *consequences* of planning actions, (4) *politics* to guide planning actions, and (5) a process that allows for ongoing feedback through *social learning*. I will return to each operation during later discussions of our studio-based project in Langrug. For now, I briefly focus on Friedmann's social learning epistemology, as this "way of knowing" shaped the overall design and delivery of the Langrug project.

Longstanding critiques of the limitations of knowledge production through "scientific," unitary, and universal methods alone, spurred Friedmann (1973, 1978) to initiate a theory of "mutual learning" that involves the production of knowledge amongst diverse actors who come together to consider a common undertaking. Various refinements of this theory ultimately led

Friedmann (1987, 2011, 2014) to posit "social learning" as an epistemology for planning. Explicitly stated, social learning is grounded in the idea of the coproduction of knowledge. Knowing *how* to do something—and knowing *what* to do—thus emerges through continuous and respectful dialogues and engaged social practices amongst all participants of a social learning endeavor (Friedmann 1979). These kinds of assertions then suggest that the gap between theory and practice might be understood as a *knowledge production* problem (as opposed to a transferability problem or a concern for separating different kinds of knowledges), since different actors do not hold, in their individual capacity, a monopoly over knowledge production. Rather, "learning takes place in the company of others" (Saltmarsh et al. 2009, p.7), because knowledge production is inherently a transactional, open ended, and social activity that takes place in a situated context.

For Argyris and Schön (1996), Dewey (1938), and other action-oriented scholars, knowledge must be actionable if it is to be useful. However, Friedmann (1979, 1987) cautions against restricting "useful" knowledge to a narrow understanding of control and instrumentalism, as narrow foci tend to lead to shortsighted outcomes that negate possibilities for transformative actions. At the same time, Friedmann (2011) acknowledges that when planning with diverse actors who hold different standpoints, conflicts may arise. In response, Friedmann (2011) speaks of working *with* and *through* conflicts not by ignoring them but, instead, by placing conflicts and power at the center of an inquiry. Strategies that aim to ignore or oppress conflicts amongst actors equally suppress freedoms of inquiry. An approach to planning that is purposefully geared towards accommodating task-oriented conflicts—while simultaneously working *with* and *through* interpersonal conflicts—might enable more effective forms of learning and doing than consensus-dependent approaches (Fainstein 2010; Flyvbjerg 2001; Friedmann 2011).

While social learning can take place in different contexts through various approaches, my interpretation of Friedmann's epistemology for planning takes shape through a method of "engaged scholarship" (Boyer 1996) that concerns both the discursive and the material nature of planning. Engaged scholarships allow for the coproduction of knowledge by explicitly desisting from establishing narrow strategies that converge on a "correct" answer. Instead, such scholarships involve multiple perspectives on how to tackle an identified problem. Furthermore, engaged scholarships—or community–university engagements—challenge traditional approaches to teaching and learning. They expose students to real-world complexities by allowing them to explore "a world they will actually work in" (Connell 2009, p.225). community–university engagements also expose students to a range of skills that cannot be acquired through academic study alone. And by valuing multiple knowledge claims, I hope to inspire students to become empathic and reflective practitioners who are capable of examining their own professional values when learning *with* community partners. Thus, for those of us who facilitate community–university engagements through our studio-based or other courses, we do so because we hope to transform our teaching and learning endeavors through collaborative praxes that challenge hierarchical modes of knowledge production.

In this chapter, I present a story of our engagements with community leaders and residents from *Langrug*—an informal settlement located within the municipal boundaries of Stellenbosch, South Africa. Here, in Langrug, we were able to leverage participants' distinct competencies because we adopted an approach to social leaning that included all five of Friedmann's (2014) operations.

Our story of social learning

> The South African experience is a useful reminder that the way the city works matters for the poor. This is a country where planning is a key instrument of redistribution. Planning is the embodied product of politics and power. It is also the institutional home for ensuring that the future city will address the needs of all residents. Planning thus needs to embrace a critical role in the fight against poverty.
>
> (Parnell 2013, p.116)

Despite planning's potential role to address longstanding fights against poverty, South African cities are places "where socioeconomic and spatial inequalities are extreme" (Watson 2013, p.168), because current planning interventions "bypass, and even hinder, the lives of poor urban residents" (Parnell 2013, p.117). Regardless then of the state's repeated promises to enhance affordable housing implementations and public service delivery targets in cities across South Africa, state-led interventions are failing to meet the needs of economically stressed residents. By means of an example of this failing, the seemingly progressive—but excessively complex—Upgrading of Informal Settlements Programme (UISP) has delivered scant results since its promulgation in 2004 and amendments in 2009 via the National Housing Code (Huchzermeyer 2011).

Introduced as a response to some of the limitations of earlier post-apartheid housing programs, the UISP is crafted to accommodate various tenure options, including communal land ownerships. It is also crafted to enable incremental and *in situ* housing developments through diverse state subsidy mechanisms, and to incur minimal disruptions to residents' established social networks and livelihood strategies during all four phases of the legislated settlement "upgrading" process (RSA 2004, 2009). However, due to the complexities of informal settlement "upgrading," as well as the inflexible procedures adopted by the state to implement the program, no municipality has managed to fulfill all four requisite phases of the UISP (Huchzermeyer 2011).

Our Langrug story emerges in response to failed state interventions for *in situ* informal settlement "upgrading." However, in order to gain political support for a resident-led planning initiative, we soon learned that we have to work *with*, and not against, the legislated UISP framework. Located on a state-owned parcel of land within the jurisdiction of the Municipality of Stellenbosch, the informal settlement of Langrug is home to 4,088 residents who live in 1,874 makeshift housing structures (or "shacks," as referred to by residents) within an area of approximately 13 hectares. In other words, the population density of Langrug is 317 people per hectare, while the dwelling unit density is 145 dwelling units per hectare. This information is relevant because the municipality's initial planning response was to reduce the density of Langrug to 13 dwelling units per hectare by implementing a layout plan that could only accommodate 172 households. In this initial plan no consideration was given to the remaining 1,702 households. Unsurprisingly, residents mobilized against the local state's de-densification proposal, and sought, instead, assistance from an established Cape Town-based NGO—the Community Organization Resource Centre (CORC)—to accommodate all 4,088 residents via an alternative plan for Langrug. And since CORC had already established a working relationship with faculty and students in the Planning Programme at the University of Cape Town, CORC, community leaders and residents invited us to participate in a resident-led settlement "upgrading" initiative through one of our studio-based courses.

By the time we got involved in this collaborative project CORC had established a rapport with community leaders and residents. Together, they completed self-surveys and self-enumerations of the informal settlement in order to accurately map the location, size, and layout of each existing shack. They also convinced the municipality—after extensive negotiations—to adopt an alternative planning approach that could accommodate all the residents of Langrug, and that could, ultimately, lead to their security of tenure. Extensive negotiations over a two-year period culminated not only in the acceptance of a re-visioning of Langrug, but also in the inclusion of planning officials in the collaborative project. This inclusion paved the way for political support of the project. Planning is, above all else, a political practice (Abers & Keck 2013; Fainstein 2010; Flyvbjerg 2001; Friedmann 2011). Both CORC and planning officials were also able to assist us—as the university partner—with some of the challenges often discussed in the community–university engagement literature, namely: time to build trust with community partners, transparency, accountability, and sustaining engagements with community partners beyond a university timetabled project.

The first meeting with community leaders, residents, officials, and CORC representatives took place six months prior to the involvement of students in the project. At this meeting I cautioned that the students who would be involved in the project were yet-to-be-trained planners with no prior experience of developing implementable proposals. In light of this caution, we identified appropriate learning and knowledge-sharing tasks that students could engage with. At the same meeting, different tasks and responsibilities were assigned to community leaders, residents, officials, and CORC representatives. By assigning different tasks and responsibilities to different participants of the project we were able to successfully address the concern about failing to meet all of the community partner's expectations.

In sum: the Langrug project was deemed to be a success by leaders, residents, officials, local politicians, CORC, and students, as we all learned how to generate new forms of context-specific knowledge that involved more than a mere conceptual understanding of planning. In so doing, we bridged the presumed gap between theory and practice. We also learned how to facilitate opportunities for social learning, reciprocity, power sharing, empowerment, and socio-spatial justice. The collective formulation of research findings and proposals empowered residents and students alike to make informed planning decisions that led to the fulfillment of Phases 1, 2, and 3 of the UISP.[1] All three phases were approved by the Municipality of Stellenbosch six months after completing the studio project. Residents are now awaiting approval for Phase 4 from the National tier of government. Phase 4 of the UISP includes securing state subsidies for the construction of permanent and formal houses. Still, much of the success of the Langrug project is attributed to an approach that encompassed Friedmann's (2014) five indispensable operations. Let me explain by briefly turning to each of these operations.

A strategy about how to proceed

The Langrug project was explicitly conceptualized as a social learning engagement. As such, our strategy embraced the idea of a true sharing of the processes and outcomes of our collaborative efforts, so that our 16-week studio project would avoid becoming a mere teaching tool for students alone. Community partners—as well as planning officials and CORC representatives—were involved during each stage of the process: from identifying the issues under study to collaborating on desired outcomes; from data collection and analyses to the development of planning proposals. Essentially, the studio project was designed to expose students to the values of learning and working *with*, as opposed to *for*, community partners, as such values are promoted in the planning literature on social learning and transformation (Abers & Keck 2013; Beard 2003; Friedmann 2011).

Furthermore, our strategy was grounded in the problems that were identified by residents, rather than the problems that we identified as the university partner. These problems included accommodating all residents within the allotted 13 hectares of land and securing their tenure to remain on the land without the fear of eviction. This grounding allowed us to begin the project with an awareness that solutions to identified problems might reveal unforetold consequences and inevitable risks. These included the risk of additional payments that residents would have to meet as a consequence of settlement "upgrading," or the risk of failing to accommodate a dwelling unit density of 145 units per hectare at costs that were affordable to low-income residents. We also began our project with an awareness that community–university engagements seldom provide immediate benefits for all participants of a collaborative initiative (Pettigrew 2001). In other words, as the university partner, we could not guarantee that our engagements would, automatically, lead to residents' security of tenure or to the construction of formal houses. A strategy about how to proceed thus necessitated ongoing reassessments of all participants' responsibilities so that viable actions could be identified during, and after, the research process, and so that a coproduction of knowledge could take place (Beard 2003; Boyer 1996; Saltmarsh et al. 2009). Residents possessed insightful knowledge of their informal neighborhood, as well as astute understandings of local politics. Above all else, a strategy about how to proceed necessitated respectful engagements that could accommodate diverse standpoints, even when these resulted in conflicts. Through a process of respectful and ongoing dialogue, we were able to work *with* and *through* disagreements. Respect for diversity also informed our adopted ethical approach during our engagements.

Adopting ethical judgements to justify our planning actions

Knowing to what end (namely, *phronesis*) is as important in planning as other forms of knowledge, since this type of "knowing" informs our ethical judgements in situated contexts (Flyvbjerg 2001). In Langrug, our "ends" were geared towards accommodating all households within a bounded parcel of land, while, simultaneously, securing residents' tenure rights. To these ends, we took values of equity and socio-spatial justice seriously. And, as previously stated, we also valued diversity. These values became the means by which we justified our planning actions.

However, since values are constructed through subjective understandings and interpretations, we also engaged with meta ethical questions that included, What, precisely, is the nature and meaning of "equity" and "socio-spatial justice" in the Langrug context? And, what are residents', officials', CORC members', and students' diverse and subjective interpretations of ethical values such as "equity" and "socio-spatial justice"? By exploring these types of questions we were able to gain insights into participants' subjective values, which, in turn, shaped their different understandings of how to address some of the planning issues we were grappling with (cf. Winkler & Duminy 2014; Friedmann 1978). Explorations of participants' subjectivities took place during weekly design sessions and meetings where we facilitated creative techniques—including role-playing, music-making, drawing, and model building techniques—that allowed participants to express themselves through various modes other than language-bound activities alone. Most participants were first-language Xhosa speakers and found it difficult to express themselves only through verbal forms of communication. The value of deploying meaningful and mindful communication techniques is emphasized in Friedmann's (1979) *The Good Society*. In this book, Friedmann also emphasizes the role of civil society for transformative planning actions. Arguably, CORC, community leaders, and residents embraced the idea of *planning for social transformation* through their unwavering commitment to fighting for a more equitable and just layout plan. And in so doing, civil society took responsibility for the consequences of their actions.

Taking responsibility for the consequences of our planning actions

All participant groupings took responsibility for the different tasks that were assigned to them at the start of the project. And, collectively, we took responsibility for the overall consequences of our planning actions. Some of these actions led to implementable outcomes, such as, for example, the construction of a community center, the implementation of additional basic municipal engineering services (including communal toilets and taps), and the establishment of savings associations amongst residents for the purpose of contributing to settlement "upgrading" costs. Other actions led to heated disagreements. These included, for example, disagreements on the amount of monetary contributions made by each household to sustain the established savings associations, as well as disagreements concerning the future role of local politicians and ward councilors in the longer-term "upgrading" process. Nevertheless, knowing how to work *within* the existing political structure, and *with* politically powerful groups, proved to be invaluable to the success of the project.

Politics to guide planning actions

"Planning is an intensely political practice" (Friedmann 2014, p.12). Accordingly, students and residents learned not only how to deploy relevant technical and theoretical knowledge for the purpose of undertaking a planning project, they also learned that "without the strong support from politically powerful groups, no plan is ever likely to succeed" (ibid.). Through the deliberate involvement of planning officials in the project, we were able to mobilize political support for the project. Political support, in turn, resulted in securing residents' legal rights to remain in Langrug. Political support also resulted in the implementation of short-term interventions including "re-blocking" initiatives. The idea of "re-blocking" the location of shacks—which was developed by residents—is explained in the next section.

Adopting an approach that allows for ongoing feedback through social learning

Identifying different tenure options, while aiming to accommodate all residents within the 13-hectare site, necessitated not only a rigorous scrutiny of the relevant legislation, but also an exploration of different layout plans than the mono-functional and detached housing layouts that epitomize state-led developments in South Africa. With the assistance of planning officials, creative solutions to securing residents' tenure of the land were identified. This *de facto* political support from the local state spurred residents to develop their own layout plans for Langrug. They adapted students' initial concepts by building physical models (from discarded cartons) of their proposed layouts. These were presented to us during a day-long design workshop that was followed by weekly design sessions that took place not only in Langrug, but also in our studio at the university. Collectively, residents and students reworked proposals in teams of six "planners" per group (comprising four residents and two students). Each team's different iterations were either rejected or further refined by all participants of the project at the end of each week when we came together as a larger group. Team proposals also included "re-blocking" initiatives that entailed strategies for dismantling existing shacks and re-siting them, so that reconstructed shacks created perimeter-block layouts that were clustered around communal, but semi-public, courtyards, while sites adjacent to the more active thoroughfares were earmarked for mixed-use and multi-storey developments. Proposals thus included a mix of land uses and housing typologies that allow for incremental constructions over a longer period of time, in addition to a sustainable density of 145 dwelling units per hectare.

Through repeated design sessions team members came to know, trust, and respect each other. This is not to suggest that there were no disagreements. Rather, by establishing professional relationships based on trust and respect we were able to engender a process of power sharing and a "willingness to act" despite disagreements (Friedmann 1973, p.247). Three weeks prior to the conclusion of our studio project, community leaders, residents, and students presented selected proposals to the mayoral committee of the Municipality of Stellenbosch. The remaining two weeks were devoted to additional refinements of selected proposals so that these would reflect the suggestions made by the committee. And six months after completing the studio project, the Premier of the Provincial Government visited Langrug, where the final proposals were on display and where she vowed to support the project. This deal-clenching political support from the highest-ranked politician in the province resulted in the official approval of Phases 1, 2, and 3 of the UISP for the "upgrading" of Langrug.[2] In essence, what is being described here is the adopted approach that allowed for ongoing feedback through social learning.

Before concluding, it is worth mentioning that our engagements also included day-long workshops on planning law and housing legislation in South Africa. Langrug residents received certificates of attendance from the university for participating in these workshops. Of greater significance, Langrug residents are now facilitating similar workshops in other informal settlements across South Africa.

Conclusion

There are, of course, limitations to engaged scholarships, and I have spent much time reflecting on these limitations (cf. Bassa et al. 2015; Winkler 2013; Winkler, forthcoming, for a more critical assessment of community–

university engagements). But the Langrug story is an aspirational story. It is a story of hope because it engendered a "radical" approach to teaching, learning, and doing in a situated context. And in this context with its specific history, our project was "radical" in the sense that it was initiated and led by residents. It was also "radical" in the sense that all participants of the project embraced an epistemology of social learning. Accordingly, we sought an approach to planning that would enable the coproduction of knowledge. This, however, necessitated working with the legislation and the state, which, in itself, was a "radical" departure for us, as economically stressed residents in South Africa have become accustomed to more insurgent forms of action in response to failed state interventions. Collectively, we hoped to *set something new into the world*. And we did so, however modestly, by adopting a context-specific *strategy* about how to proceed. We also embraced *ethical values* that included a respect for diversity while embodying concerns for greater equity and socio-spatial justice. Furthermore, we hoped to *set something new into the world* by taking *responsibility* for the *consequences* of our actions and by working with municipal officials who, in turn, were able to guide our actions through the existing *political* structures. We were therefore able to leverage participants' distinct competencies by working *with* and *through* conflicts in a constructive manner. Above all else, our Langrug story represents an example of residents' pivotal role in planning for social transformation. We thus learned how to plan *with* "a self-actualized community who demonstrably took a lead in decisions that would shape the future of Langrug" (Petzer, student reflections, cited in Bassa et al. 2015, p.424).

Notes

1 *Phase 1* of the UISP (the "application phase") necessitates municipalities to apply to the Provincial Government for UISP funding. *Phase 2* entails the "project initiation phase" that includes undertaking socio-economic and demographic studies, conducting geological and environmental impact assessments of the area in question, and installing interim basic municipal engineering services. *Phase 3*—the "project implementation phase"—necessitates the submission to a municipality of a final business plan for settlement "upgrading," the formulation of land occupational rights, initiating the planning process by crafting implementable layout plans, and constructing social amenities and communal facilities. Finally, *Phase 4* (namely, the "housing consolidation phase") concerns property ownership registrations, the construction of formal houses, the construction of additional social amenities, and the implementation of engineering infrastructure and services.

2 Approval for Phase 4 of the UISP is, unfortunately, caught up in political wrangling between the Democratic Alliance (DA) led provincial government and the African National Congress (ANC) led national government.

References

Abers, R & Keck, M 2013, *Practical Authority: Agency and Institutional Change in Brazilian Water Politics*, Oxford University Press, Oxford, New York.

Argyris, C & Schön, D 1996, *Organization Learning II: Theory, Method and Practice*, Addison-Wesley, Reading, M.A.

Bassa, F, Petzer, B & Winkler, T 2015, "At the coalface, Take 2: lessons from students' critical reflections" in *Interface: Planning Theory & Practice*, ed. L Porter, 16(3): 409–434.

Beard, V 2003, "Learning radical planning: the power of collective action", *Planning Theory*, 2(1): 13–35.

Boyer, E 1996, "The scholarship of engagement", *Journal of Public Service and Outreach*, 1(1): 11–20.

Connell, R 2009, "Good teachers on dangerous ground: towards a new view of teacher quality and professionalism", *Critical Studies in Education*, 50(3): 213–229.

Dewey, J 1938, *Logic: The Theory of Inquiry*, Holt, New York.

Fainstein, S 2010, *The Just City*, Cornell University Press, Ithaca, N.Y.

Flyvbjerg, B 2001, *Making Social Science Matter*, Cambridge University Press, Cambridge, M.A.

Friedmann, J 1973, *Retracking America: A Theory of Transactive Planning*, Anchor Press, New York.

Friedmann, J 1978, "The epistemology of social practice", *Theory and Society*, 6(1): 75–92.

Friedmann, J 1979, *The Good Society*, MIT Press, Cambridge, M.A.

Friedmann, J 1987, *Planning in the Public Domain: From Knowledge to Action*, Princeton University Press, Princeton, N.J.

Friedmann, J 2011, *Insurgencies: Essays in Planning Theory*, Routledge, London and New York.

Friedmann, J 2014, "Towards an intellectual autobiography". Unpublished essay. Available from: <http://www.scarp.ubc.ca/sites/scarp.ubc.ca/files/users/%5Buser%5D/profile/Towards%20an%20Intellectual%20Autobiography.doc> [5 August 2016].

Huchzermeyer, M 2011, *Cities with Slums: From Informal Settlement Eradication to a Right to the City in Africa*, University of Cape Town Press, Cape Town.

Parnell, S 2013, "Inclusionary approaches to urban planning lessons in poverty reduction from South Africa" in *State of the Urban Poor Report, 2013: Inclusive Urban Planning*, ed. O Mathur, Oxford University Press, India, pp. 116–133.

Pettigrew, A 2001, "Management research after modernism", *British Journal of Management*, 12 (Special Issue): S61–S70.

Republic of South Africa (RSA) 2004, "National housing programmes: upgrading of informal settlements", *Chapter 13 of the National Housing Code*, Government Gazette, Pretoria.

Republic of South Africa (RSA) 2009, "Upgrading informal settlements. Incremental interventions", *The National Housing Code*, Vol. 4, Part 3. Government Gazette, Pretoria.

Saltmarsh, J, Hartley, M & Clayton, P 2009, *Democratic Engagement White Paper*, New England Resource Center for Higher Education (NERCHE), Boston.

Watson, V 2013, "Planning and the 'stubborn realities' of global south-east cities: some emerging ideas", *Planning Theory*, 12(1): 81–100.

Winkler, T 2013, "At the coalface: community–university engagements and planning education", *Journal of Planning Education and Research*, 33(2): 215–227.

Winkler, T (forthcoming), "At the coalface, *Take 3*: re-imagining community–university engagements from *here*" in *Companion to Planning in the Global South*, eds V Watson, G Bhan & S Srinvas, Routledge, London and New York.

Winkler, T & Duminy, J 2014, "Planning to change the world? Questioning the normative ethics of planning theories", *Planning Theory*. DOI: 10.1177/1473095214551113.

21 Fire, ownership, citizenship and community

Jacquelyn Chase

In this essay I look for elements of John Friedmann's alternative development in an unlikely space: the exurban foothills of northern California. Not only are the foothills a long way from central Brazil, where I did my graduate work in the late 1980s; they are part of a larger cultural region known for anti-state, property rights activism, which seems antithetical to John's alternative development triad of life space, household and community. How can John's framework for alternative development in the third world keep me asking the right questions in a context that seems (a) so alien to the international context where I started and (b) antagonistic to planning?

In Brazil, my focus on household labor and housing strategies drew on parts of John's empowerment model of development, and I produced details about de-peasantization where corporate agriculture (namely, soybeans) was taking hold in central Brazil in the 1980s. I could not claim that the people were practising alternative development, but indeed it was their lack of mobilization in the face of displacement that intrigued me (Chase 1999). After displacement from farms and ranches, households' labor market strategies required a home front in town, and many of them were swept into "friendly" relations with wealthy farmers and powerful local organizations such as the farmer cooperative, the Lions Club and municipal social services. Cement, vacant lots, food donations and even sterilization operations were traded for votes. The urban periphery sprawled as the new inhabitants maintained their ties to the countryside as workers. The urban citizenship of the poor took shape in this tangled web of interdependence with the countryside.

My interest in the ambiguous spaces between city and country has endured. People's lives and the actual physical interface between city and countryside in unincorporated areas and small towns call for a less dualistic approach to life space. My current research in northern California looks at people's desire to maintain a working landscape in foothill areas that have been zoned residential (Chase 2015). My county planning commission work requires that I ask questions and make decisions about land-use conflicts in these spaces.

The portability of development

John ends his book *Empowerment* from 1992 with an epilogue that poses "some questions for rich countries" (Friedmann 1992, p.167). He invites the reader to see the relevance of third-world alternative development to the wealthier global north. He notes that the third world is here—in impoverished urban communities inhabited by immigrants and "excluded minorities." The urban poor in rich countries are just as marginalized from mainstream planning as are the poor of the *favelas* and *barrios* of Latin America. But the poor "here" are actually at a disadvantage because they are more likely to be criminalized in a law and order culture that believes that everyone can be rich. Despite being reviled, inner-city neighborhoods offer hope to Friedmann that an alternative development based on empowerment is emerging here. He speaks of church- and community-based solidarity in Harlem and in Asian-American enclaves. Friedmann's practical suggestions for planners include educating state agencies on empowerment models of development; welcoming social mobilization and social learning; and sharing control of planning with "third sector" actors such as volunteer organizations, churches and non-profits. His tone is cautiously hopeful.

The years since that publication have made John's questions about poverty here even more urgent in the United States. This country is proof that affluence does not guarantee human flourishing. Gun culture, fear of the other, racially motivated killings and anti-state mentalities actively promote and sustain inequality. Welfare reform and gentrification have squeezed the poor out of communities. The global drug economy preys on hopelessness and consumerism of youth.

As John notes, the culture of individualism permeates debates on human rights and poverty in the United States. By the time he wrote that epilogue we were a decade into the neoliberal turn which manifested itself in real cutbacks to government funding and planning, tax reforms that hindered all manner of public investment, and an anti-government sentiment championed by politicians, corporations and ordinary people. What are development planners to think of this?

The kind of place in the United States that I will talk about (exurban foothills of the American west) is where anti-planning rhetoric has most boiled over. A host of new environmental regulations by federal agencies in the early 1970s enraged communities of forest owners and workers in California, Oregon and Washington who felt these restrictions were destroying their livelihoods. The property rights movement was epitomized by "Wise Use" mobilization against plans by the federal government to limit mining and grazing on public lands (Mason 2008). Similar disputes came to a head over the listing in 1990 of the Northern Spotted Owl as an endangered species by the national Fish and Wildlife Service, a move that stopped logging of old-growth forests in the Pacific Northwest (Proctor 1996). The occupation of Malheur National Wildlife Refuge in eastern Oregon in early 2016 by an anti-government militia shows that conflict over public regulation of land use in rural areas is unresolved. The populist claims made by two generations of militant ranchers involved in the Oregon standoff are ironic in light of their own economic privilege and their disregard for the Paiutes' preexisting claims to the same public lands (Glionna 2016).

Sometimes behind the outrageous claims and extremism are real impoverished rural communities, however. Many people lost their livelihoods after the collapse of logging, ranching and mining in much of the rural west. Former extractive communities have been overwhelmed by affluent newcomers, gentrification of the countryside and an environmental sustainability rhetoric that has denigrated the resource jobs that were slipping away (White 1996; Walker 2003). As Richard White writes,

> Most environmentalists disdain and distrust those who most obviously work in nature. Environmentalists have come to associate work—particularly heavy bodily labor, blue-collar work—with environmental degradation. This is true whether the work is in the woods, on the sea, in a refinery, in a chemical plant, in a pulp mill, or in a farmer's field or a rancher's pasture. Environmentalists usually imagine that when people who make things finish their day's work, nature is the poorer for it. Nature seems safest when shielded from human labor.
>
> (p.172)

As environmentalism got stronger and more pervasive there was no deeply rooted tradition in rural development to defend depressed rural communities in the United States. The rural poor hasn't made headlines since Appalachia was in the spotlight between the Depression and the early 1960s. Friedmann hoped the Tennessee Valley Authority would be a vital regional learning institution focused on "the betterment of life in a backward region" (1973, p.5). But by the time he arrived at the TVA in 1952 it was a "tired bureaucracy fighting for its existence, more concerned with saving its budget from a hostile administration in Washington than with innovative action" (Friedmann 1973, p.5). Like many development thinkers of the time, he turned elsewhere. Friedmann's alternative development thinking in books like *Empowerment* (1992), *Life Space and Economic Space* (1988), and his edited volume with Rangan, *In Defense of Livelihood* (1993) was inspired by third-world examples of resistance and survival in rural spaces, not with rural America in mind.

Rural America has not invited the kinds of sympathetic reflections on alternative development that urban communities have. Rural people who have stood their ground against such forces in the United States have been characterized as dangerous oddballs. The whiteness and rudeness of mobilized rural America leaves most progressive academics at best uninterested in its plight, or at worst hostile to it. In response to this silence, a "first world political ecology" has asked why people struggling to rebuild a livelihood in depressed rural areas in this country are not worthy of the attention given to marginalized peasants and forest peoples of the third world (White 1996; McCarthy 2002). A small ethnographic literature on the troubled rural communities of the American west conveys sensitivities to people's real life stories (Brown 1995; Hurley & Walker 2004; Walker 2003). What hope is there for distressed rural spaces in the United States? Can we see past the anti-state rhetoric to alternative futures?

Agropolitan America?

Exurbia is the backdrop against which new models of rural development are emerging, as Pezzoli et al. (2004) show in their "manifesto for a progressive ruralism."

The authors note the contradiction that a region abundant in natural capital is persistently poor, an idea reminiscent of the "development of underdevelopment" of the third world. Rural areas provide valuable ecosystem services and raw materials to outside interests. By calling these places "exurbia," planners and academics inadvertently concede their exploitation by cities. Hobby farms, vineyards, tourist ventures and second homes continue to drain resources such as water and they fail the area's promise as a space for sustainable *food* production. The authors advocate returning to a simple designation of "rural" and to an economic focus on sustainable agriculture.

One hears echoes of Friedmann's agropolitan development in this proposal. Agropolitan development—envisioned mostly for Asia—proposed the creation of rural districts as representative territorial units for rural regions. Rural districts would not be completely autonomous, as John was quick to note, but independent enough to secure management of the environment in the interest of rural people. The agropolitan model would empower rural communities to represent their own interests in planning and policy-making. Today I find myself intrigued by its possibilities for working landscapes in exurban California. I do not mean literally that people should propose agropolitan districts (this would undoubtedly be rejected by locals) but I think the agropolitan ideal can reorient planning to support small-scale land use and the persistence of socially diverse rural communities and it can move people beyond despair of what has been lost. Rural persistence (viability), social mobilization and environmental quality are key to Friedmann's idea of agropolitan development (1988, p.211) and they appear in the "progressive ruralism" of Pezzoli et al. (2004). They can even be found, I will argue, in communities that would probably self-identify as property-oriented and conservative.

Friedmann argued that empowerment in rural communities hinges on control over natural resources (Friedmann 1988, p.211). In the California foothills, fire is a key dimension of the rural environment that mobilizes and defines communities. In what follows, I will look at three cases in one foothill community which illustrate how fire links community, territory, private property and the environment. One is the community-based fire safe councils that are key to negotiating private property rights and planning for fire. The second is the case of how, after a major fire, a group of activists advocated for an exception to the county building code. This exception would benefit low-income fire victims by permitting self-built homes using recovered wood. The third case looks at how community members forced a change in the zoning code to allow for the storage of large machinery on residential properties, thus ensuring the ability to perform land care and road work to prepare the community for fire.

Fire, property and community

Fire mocks the fantasy of living in rural isolation and of managing the land independently of neighbors and the state (Nelson & Dueker 1990; Sturtevant & Jakes 2008). A neighbor's overgrown forest is a hazard to others. An eroded private road means a fire truck might not risk going up it. The reality of the ecosystem as heedless of property boundaries is obvious to people living in fire-prone areas. Although it is still a distant goal to create a large-scale fire safe *landscape* out of a tapestry of hundreds of parcels, organizations such as the fire safe council promote this goal to property owners. The fire safe council also funnels government resources to public commons such as shaded fuel breaks on public roads, and the maintenance of public parks to shelter-in-place.

In the 1970s, the federal government began shifting responsibilities to states for firefighting as this became more expensive (Pyne 1982). Ironically, after the 1980s, as fires became more costly, funds for fighting them dried up. Neo-liberal reforms shrank the tax base at state and local levels and bled federal resources once used for public lands management. Neo-liberalism also implied the privatization and distribution of fire services to private companies, non-profit organizations and volunteer organizations such as fire safe councils. Community fire safe councils were mandated into existence by the State of California after the Oakland Hills fires as fire agencies turned toward prevention and shifted responsibility for fire safety onto communities and households (Carle 2008).

Today in California, disputes between neighbors about creating fire safe landscapes are prevented, mediated and managed by a web of community fire safe councils. These organizations help protect the life space of communities. They tread lightly on people's property rights, but help create wide acceptance of the foothills as a shared fire-prone ecosystem that requires collaboration in order to be lived in. Fire safe councils act as liaisons between property owners, communities, planners and government agencies. Part of the reorientation toward volunteerism means that community organizations like fire safe councils must compete for federal and state money. These resources are rewarded to communities that can find government resources for projects.

Despite being fledged by the state and in tune with its bureaucracy, community fire safe councils are unique in that their boundaries are difficult to draw on a map. This makes them unlike most districts and zones that require clear boundaries. The council that I'm most familiar with has this "fuzzy" territory. There are no maps that delineate an area for which the council is responsible. The council will assist other communities to develop their own councils or they will offer services to communities that do not have councils of their own. Fire safe councils reproduce spontaneously and generously, filling in gaps where people want their own councils by teaching others how to create and sustain a council.

Fire safe councils are a kind of shock absorber between private owners and the state. In areas where suspicions about government overreach are common, fire safe councils work to maintain an appearance of autonomy from the state. One service the council in my study area has offered is "door yard visits" to assess properties for fire preparedness. Council members visit a property only when they have been invited by the owner. The council members reiterate verbally and on paper that the visit is a friendly neighborly service, and in no way connected to state firefighting agencies. The state agencies, for their part, can visit properties and fine their owners, but the council wants to foster a sense of voluntary cooperation rather than to threaten with fines. The council also communicates the state requirements for defensible space (setbacks around dwellings, for example) in brochures, videos, calendars and workshops to the public without any threat of code enforcement. During larger projects involving many properties, it contacts land owners for permission to trespass and to remove vegetation. The fire safety councils in northern California thus provide a sense of collective land-based management for a self-defined territorial community.

The council's efforts are mostly aligned with prevention. The next example in this section looks at how another group focused on recovery after a wildland fire destroyed 200 homes in the community in 2008. The "do-it-yourself" nature of the low-income community was made apparent in the fire's aftermath when many people learned they could not rebuild their "off the radar" homes. Because many of these homes had not been built to code, they were not able to hold insurance; but only people with insurance could afford to rebuild given the high price of materials, labor and permitting. If permitted, the cost of rebuilding could be brought down significantly by using wood that had been burned in the fire. In response to this challenge, a group of residents worked with the county to create an ordinance to allow "limited-density self-built" rural housing that would allow for recycled materials and other waivers to make self-built housing affordable. The activists who enabled the legislation explicitly referenced the communitarian nature of their endeavor. They noted the importance of this detour around the rules to secure a life space for impoverished households and for the community.

Planning for flexibility

In another example of mobilization in the same community, owners advocated for zoning to support a working rural landscape. During the last county general plan update, the community fought to allow the storage of heavy machinery and the placement of outbuildings such as sheds and composting facilities on undeveloped parcels of land. The right to have these things on the land was not framed in private property terms by owners. The main justification for these uses was to prepare for fire on a scale that protected the wider community (Chase 2015). People argued that the benefit of having this equipment in the community overshadowed problems with noise, exhaust and unsightliness that might cause tensions with neighbors. These were seen as concerns that might be more typical in the closer quarters of cities. The initial restrictions in the general plan was evidence that planners and consultants were out of touch with the rural nature and community practices of the community.

The politics of engagement with the bureaucracy are central to John's various renditions of alternative development. The process that led to the zoning changes in this case study included a strong community reaction to an earlier proposed rezone that had been presented to them in "finished" form (a slick document of hundreds of pages, prepared by consultants). There were, fortunately, people in the community who were not intimidated by its polish. They interrupted a process that had been churning for at least two years and redirected it to reflect their vision of the community. Planners went on bus rides to learn more about the community. Coordinated and persistent, people redirected zoning midstream. Of course, as Valverde (2012) shows, such involvement in planning favors those with social and political capital, including a sharp eye, an understanding of planning, time to navigate a bureaucratic process, and the legitimacy of property ownership. These assets are often seized by groups to secure advantages; but to the delight of county planners, the group did in fact seem to speak for the larger community. The people were so effective in bringing the rezone back to the community that their quotes appear as epigraphs to the county's general plan as evidence of public participation and mutual learning.

These cases of community mobilization underscore the fact that property ownership in fire-prone landscapes is mediated by a commitment to community. People who make blunt private property claims ignore that property rights are encumbered with obligations (Rose 1994; Blomley 2005). In a hazardous landscape these obligations and the community work that they require are inherent to living in a fire-prone area. Fire preparation, fighting and recovery are all a kind of "communal work" and part of the "whole economy" that supports the community's life space (Friedmann 1992).

The story of fire conveys a vision of a collaborative working landscape to planners and other officials. The three episodes show how in the context of fire prevention and recovery local property owners also engaged in social learning with land-use planners. Contradictory assumptions about the use of property by owners and officials (planners, insurance officials, fire agencies) were debated. Residents questioned why planners might see rural land care as a nuisance and they forced open the possibility of planning for a hybrid rural/urban life space. These achievements may not qualify as "alternative development," but without the notions of household, community, life space and social learning, it is hard to imagine even detecting these small fissures in property rights hegemony.

Friedmann always meant alternative development to be about democracy. As he turned away from the technocratic model of planning, and drew on his experiences in Brazil, Venezuela and Chile in his early career, he placed more hope in grassroots democracy. Purcell, borrowing from Lefebvre, says that democracy is a spatial project, connected to people's everyday lives and to the real spaces they inhabit (2013, p.43). Purcell's definition of these spaces is strikingly similar to Friedmann's life space: the arenas of organized plural democracy in spaces of life include home, environment and bureaucracy. Rezoning is a political process that takes place in the community itself (Polson 2015; Valverde 2012). I recognize elements of John's bottom-up planning in recent micro-level analyses of planning tools such as zoning, which is more flexible and variable than most people assume (Valverde 2011, 2012).

To close, I want to return to my earlier reflection on how my work in Brazil continues to orient my teaching, research and community work in rural northern California. Many of us do not have the luxury to be exclusively focused on international research. Teaching loads and shrinking resources in our universities, but also service-learning and genuine curiosity about new topics, move our research to the local stage. With the usual anticipation I have shared some of my local research with John over the years. I also share my research in Brazil with my friends in this community, and I expose my expri- ence in California to colleagues and students in Brazil. I do not see the agendas as estranged. Truly, "our fates are intertwined" (Friedmann 1992, p.167).

References

Blomley, N 2005, "The borrowed view: privacy, propriety, and the entanglements of property", *Law and Social Inquiry*, 30(4): 617–661.

Brown, BA 1995, *In Timber Country: Working People's Stories of Environmental Conflict and Urban Flight*, Temple University Press, Philadelphia.

Carle, D 2008, *Introduction to Fire in California, Calif Nat Hist Guides* 95, University of California, Berkeley, Los Angeles, London.

Chase, J 1999, "Exodus revisited: the politics and experience of rural loss in central Brazil", *Sociologia Ruralis*, 39(2): 65–85.

Chase, J 2015, "Bending the rules in the foothills—County general planning in exurban northern California", *Society and Natural Resources*, 28(8): 857–872.

Friedmann, J 1973, *Retracking America: A Theory of Transactive Planning*, Anchor Press, New York.

Friedmann, J 1988, *Life Space and Economic Space: Essays in Third World Planning*, Transaction Publishers, New Brunswick, N.J.

Friedmann, J 1992, *Empowerment: The Politics of Alternative Development*, Blackwell, Cambridge, M.A.

Friedmann, J & Rangan, H (eds) 1993, *In Defense of Livelihood: Comparative Studies on Environmental Action*, Kumarian, West Hartford.

Glionna, JM 2016, "How the Oregon militia standoff became a battle with a Native American tribe", *The Guardian* 6 January. Available from: <http://www.theguardian.com/us-news/2016/jan/06/oregon-militia-malheur-wildlife-refuge-paiute-indian-tribe-sacred-land> [15 January 2016].

Hurley, P & Walker, P 2004, "Whose vision? Conspiracy theory and land–use planning in Nevada County, California", *Environment and Planning*, 36(9): 1529–1547.

Mason, RJ 2008, *Collaborative Land Use Management: The Quieter Revolution in Place-based Planning*, Island Press, Washington, D.C.

McCarthy, J 2002, "First world political ecology: lessons from the Wise Use movement", *Environment and Planning A*, 34: 1281–1302.

Nelson, AC & Dueker, K 1990, "The exurbanization of America and its planning policy implications", *Journal of Planning Education and Research*, 9(2): 91–100.

Pezzoli, K, Williams, K & Kriletich, S 2004, "A manifesto for progressive ruralism in an urbanizing world", *Progressive Planning*, 186: 16–19.

Polson, M 2015, "From outlaw to citizen: police power, property, and the territorial politics of medical marijuana in California's exurbs", *Territory, Politics, Governance*, 3(4). DOI: 10.1080/21622671.2015.1073613.

Proctor, J 1996, "Whose nature? The contested moral terrain of ancient forests" in *Uncommon Ground: Rethinking the Human Place in Nature*, ed. W Cronon, Norton and Company, New York, pp. 269–297.

Purcell, MH 2013, *The Deep Down Delight of Democracy*, John Wiley and Sons, Chichester.

Pyne, SJ 1982, *Fire in America: A Cultural History of Wildland and Rural Fire*, University of Washington, Seattle and London.

Rose, CM 1994, *Property and Persuasion: Essays on the History, Theory, and Rhetoric of Ownership. New Perspectives on Law, Culture, and Society*, Westview, Boulder, San Francisco and Oxford.

Sturtevant, V & Jakes, P 2008, "Collaborative planning to reduce risk" in *Wildfire Risk: Human Perceptions and Management Implications*, eds W Martin, C Riash & B Kent, Resources for the Future, Washington, D.C., pp. 44–63.

Valverde, M 2011, "Seeing like a city: the dialectic of modern and premodern ways of seeing in urban governance", *Law and Society Review*, 45(2): 277–312.

Valverde, M 2012, *Everyday Law on the Street: City Governance in an Age of Diversity*, University of Chicago, Chicago.

Walker, P 2003, "Reconsidering 'regional' political ecologies: toward a political ecology of the rural American West", *Progress in Human Geography*, 27(1): 7–24.

White, R 1996, "Are you an environmentalist or do you work for a living?" in *Uncommon Ground: Rethinking the Human Place in Nature*, ed. W Cronon, Norton and Company, New York, pp. 171–185.

22 Meeting the Other

A personal account of my struggle with John Friedmann to enact the radical practice of dialogic inquiry and love in the new millennium

Aftab Erfan

In 1979, just a couple of years before I was born, John Friedmann published what is quite possibly the most exquisite and at once the least well-known of his 20-some books, *The Good Society*. Organized around the central question of "How should we live collectively with one another" (p.3), and concerned with establishing a moral foundation for planning, *The Good Society* is an expression of Friedmann's utopia.

The book is written in an uncommon format, which Friedmann hoped would "accommodate the largest number of possible meanings, dramatically expanding the spectrum of communicable thought" (1979, p.xvi). It consists of a series of self-contained segments of varying lengths, interspersed with poems, aphorisms, philosophical paragraphs and other "delights" that are intended to "illustrate, contradict, confirm, and illuminate the paragraphs in their immediate vicinity, adding depth and concrete imagery to the more abstract portions of the text" (ibid.).

This short chapter is written as a partial imitation (the highest form of flattery) of *The Good Society*, applying and extending some of the concepts of that book in light of social planning's challenges in the 21st century. I write this chapter as a practitioner of dialogue, as a person who has attempted to be in dialogue with John for the past eight years, and who has come to love John in the process. Much like *The Good Society*, this chapter has "no interest in persuading you, the reader" of any specific argument, but would instead "like you to think from the trampoline of each paragraph into a pattern of your own" (ibid., p.xvii).

What is the utopian vision offered by *The Good Society*?

The defining relationship of the good society is dialogue: a form of genuine speech and deep listening with the power to transform those who practice it. Thus, utopia is found not in the success of regional economic development initiatives or in the construction of global mega-cities, but in the relational space of small groups of people—either inside or outside the institutional framework of the state.

Dialogue as the ultimate answer when we have so many structural problems to deal with? Sounds naïve.

Perhaps, except when we understand the seriousness with which dialogue is defined and the standards to which it is held in this formulation. Friedmann became convinced of the possibility of dialogue as a moral foundation for planning when he read Martin Buber (1937), a Viennese Jewish philosopher for whom dialogue had a quasi-religious meaning. In *The Good Society*, dialogue is characterized as radical practice and its necessary conditions, including appropriate scale, are described in detail and in such a spirited way that they make Jürgen Habermas' communicative action requirements (1981) sound rigid and feeble in comparison.

The basic gesture of dialogue, of our mutual acceptance, implies:

- my readiness to disclose myself to you;
- your readiness to receive my disclosure;
- my readiness to receive your own disclosures of yourself;
- our readiness, in dialogue between us, to hold ourselves prepared for change within (John Friedmann, *The Good Society*, 1979, p.107).

The vision of a society that lives a life of dialogue is a vision of a society where every person is met, accepted, affirmed, confirmed, loved and continually transformed.

What's love got to do with it?

We might say that love has *everything* to do with it, in so far as love is viewed, not as blind, but rather as the capacity to see another for whom they truly are. In dialogue, love becomes possible, and love in turn births humanity. Thus, "being human rises in dialogue" (p.103), Friedmann suggests.

> There are three levels at which dialogue can occur: the first is unconditional acceptance of the other person as someone different from myself; the second is a loving inclination toward the partner in dialogue; the third is a caring for and loyal commitment to the partner. Successive levels of loving relationship, they demand a growing attention to and involvement with each other's lives.
>
> (John Friedmann, *The Good Society*, 1979, p.111)

Friedmann's core quest for human flourishing has typically been described in connection to the material foundations of well-being (housing, healthcare, work, social provisions)—but is there a more unambiguous experience of human flourishing than the experience of love?

> Love is absolutely vital for a human life. For love alone can awaken what is divine within you. In love, you grow and come home to your self.
>
> (John O'Donohue, *Anam Cara*, 1998, p.39)

Are you telling me that John Friedmann is really an advocate for a loving inclination in dialogue? What does that look like? Does he know how to do loving dialogue himself?

Well, let me come to that story, eventually…

The planning field has largely shied away from discussing the subject of love. Perhaps we see ourselves as too much of a public field for such a seemingly private matter to be of interest. Or perhaps we are so proudly secular and grounded in concrete reality that such lofty concepts are irrelevant to us. The notable exception is a special issue of *Planning Theory and Practice* in 2012 that was devoted entirely to the subject of love (where, for full disclosure, I made a contribution as a co-author with Leonie Sandercock, my PhD supervisor and John's wife).

To speak about love in planning is becoming less taboo. But in the pages of *The Good Society* the discussion of love is largely hidden. I am surprised John does not write more about love because I know of his intellectual preoccupation with Hannah Arendt (the woman who wrote a dissertation on love in the life of Saint Augustine) and his poetic fascination with Pablo Neruda (whose volume of love sonnets John has translated from Spanish to English). As I read *The Good Society*, I often get the strange feeling that I am reading about love, or I am about to read about love, but don't quite. The word love is only mentioned a couple of times, and those instances have already been cited in this paper.

Then there is the front cover image (Figure 22.1).

The choice of the painting is as unconventional for a planning text as the content of the book in itself. The naked beauty of the two bodies, along with the fauna and flora that surround them, stand in contrast to the conservative geometric arrangements on the cover of Friedmann's *Planning in the Public Domain* and just about any other planning text published, ever.

What does this painting have to do with the good society? The final lines of the book offer one explanation:

Figure 22.1 Adam and Eve by German renaissance painter Lucas Cranach the Elder (1526)
Cover reprinted courtesy of The MIT Press

> Adam and Eve rebelled against their God; they were estranged from God. Cast out into the world, they recovered themselves, they recovered their freedom. Alone and together.
>
> Without choice there is no freedom; without necessity there is no choice. From the realm of necessity there is no "leap" into the realm of freedom. We have to overcome necessity.
>
> The Garden was God's garden. But earth is our home. And "home is where one starts from," said T.S. Eliot.
>
> To travel to what is farthest, we must go by the path that is nearest.
>
> We must transcend the Good Society.
>
> (John Friedmann, *The Good Society*, 1979, pp.180, 181)

Another, more literal way we may understand this image is as a portrait of a dialogue between the original man and the original woman, at a decisive moment for humanity, to say the least!

Was there a loving inclination in this dialogue? It would be hard to know, since the Bible makes no direct reference to love between Adam and Eve (despite the obvious "bone of my bone, and flesh of my flesh" reference, which can be taken literally or amorously). What we see in this image is the seductively posed Eve in the middle of the act of temptation, offering the fruit of knowledge to Adam. Perhaps the most interesting aspect of the image is Adam's response. He eventually takes the apple; we know he does. But at the moment depicted by the artist, there is an unmistakable look of bewilderment on Adam's face. He is, literally, scratching his head. Should he take the fruit of knowledge from his beloved? Is this action correct or is it only attractive because it is forbidden? Is she to be believed, or is she to be resisted? Do they agree or are they in conflict? What is the transformation in the relationship to each other and to the world as they know it, that is about to be unleashed?

The image of Adam and Eve is a provocative image to have chosen for this book cover. Is it possible that in some subtle way this image is the hidden subtext of the good society, illuminating the difficulties of dialogue, illustrating some of the "forbidden thoughts" (ibid., p.128) listed towards the end of the book? Does it say something about the confusion that comes into play in the relational space that is otherwise idealized by the book? Does it perhaps betray the author's own bewilderment about how to be in dialogue, and more specifically how to be in loving dialogue?

Now for another story, less significant in mythological proportions than Adam and Eve's (except perhaps to those of us directly involved): the story of how I came into loving dialogue with John Friedmann—or rather, the story of how I sometimes, momentarily, come into loving dialogue with John Friedmann.

I met John in my first semester as a PhD student. He had long ago "retired" but was teaching a couple of our required courses, and he was married to the chair of our PhD program, who was also my supervisor. Like the rest of my classmates, I began my years as a PhD student by disliking John. He had a special way of making each of us feel horrible about ourselves and crushing the delicate seedlings we were so tentatively holding as ideas for our PhD research projects. At least that's how we experienced him. He spoke authoritatively and often critically about our work, even though he knew very little about some of our areas of research. He would not let go of some stupid thing we had said in the first class that seemed to be forever defining us in his eyes. His questioning of our work either felt incredibly nitpicky (focused on some seemingly minor aspect of the work, such as a definition of some peripheral concept), or so fundamental (asking us to take a stance on the nature of reality or defend an entire area of planning that encompassed our work) that we didn't know what to do with it. In retrospect the questions were not unfair, but at the time they completely disoriented each one of us. And because he was such a confident questioner and we were such lousy responders, we often felt humiliated. Sometimes we cried after class.

At some point during the second semester I decided that this way of relating to John was not acceptable for me. By this time most of my classmates had decided to put up with him while they had to, knowing that his opinion did not much matter once the class was over. I figured this was not going to work for me because he was married to my supervisor! It would be much more strategic if I could have a functional relationship with him. But, more importantly, I thought it would be very sad to go on disliking him, to *not* find a way of meeting him, because both of us were clearly interested in dialogue. Could we find a way to be in dialogue for our own flourishing and in service of the other? Could we find a way to understand each other? I decided I had to become John Friedmann's friend.

One of the first things I tried was asking John for direction while writing a paper on the democratization of planning for his class. He welcomed the invitation and handed me a stack of books from his shelf: Robert Dahl, Sheldon Wolin, Chantal Mouffe, as well as some of "the original texts," including Jean-Jacques Rousseau's *The Social Contract* (1762) and Aristotle's *Politics* (4th century BC) (1920).

I was quite annoyed by the idea of reading "the originals" as they felt so far removed from the realities of modern day planning I was concerned about. Reading Aristotle in particular was painful because I found it impossible to overlook the sexist and racist lines of thinking that run throughout *Politics.* I felt like I was contaminated by every line I read. I also happened to be reading Aristotle on a beach in Cape Town, South Africa while I was studying with my main community of practice—a global pragmatic bunch of group-facilitators who took every opportunity to make fun of me for what I was reading, because "what kind of a snobby intellectual still reads Greek philosophers?!" Despite my resentment I read every word of *Politics,* because reading Aristotle felt like a test: this was the mountain I had to climb and the dragon I had to slay for John to take me seriously.

I may never know if it was meant as a test, but things did change somewhat after I read Aristotle and was able to discuss it with John. He liked my paper on democratization of planning enough to recommend I prepare it for publication (still on my to-do list). I talked to my therapist about him around the same time, and began to look at my perceptions of the aspects of John's engagement that bothered me—and how they reminded me of my own bothersome habits: being too harsh, being too direct and having the ability to use my intellectual powers to put others down and feel superior. The exploration into myself was painful but also productive.

Around then John and I started going out for lunch once every couple of months—now a seven-year tradition—despite the conversation being occasionally challenging or flat, pregnant with a possibility that we fall back into speaking past each other. Mostly by accident, and occasionally through discovering how to ask the right questions, we have each learned aspects of each others' stories and identities that we find relatable. If nothing else we enjoy our joined exploration of Vancouver's various ethnic restaurants, together enacting the life of cultural nomads that we each are.

Some of our most delightful encounters have been the occasions when we have celebrated our joint birthdays together with close friends. Perhaps it has been the home environment, or the glasses of wine, or the reading of poetry that has eased us unto loving dialogue with each other. Or perhaps, to John's point in *The Good Society*, the size of the groups has been just right at around eight people.

The image in Figure 22.2 is of a card John gave me on the night of my 33rd and his 88th birthday. This is an image of a different kind of dialogue between a man and woman, compared to what we glanced at in Figure 22.1. The figures in this photograph are taking delight in having been discovered in their oddity and accepted by another person. They appear in symmetry to each other, indicating equality, their faces lit up with surprise and laughter. We get a glimpse into what might be going on in their minds via the C.S. Lewis quote that accompanies the photograph: "Friendship is born at the moment when one person says to another, 'What, you too? I thought I was the only one.'"

Let me get this straight: Is this really a chapter about how you got to know John Friedmann? Is this purely a personal account? Or do you have a point?

My intention here has been to give an illustration of a process of intentional, attempted dialogue between two people as a basis for pointing out some learnings that might be useful to other people. I have two points about the challenge and opportunity of loving dialogues in modern times that I would like to make next, but it felt important that the points be grounded in something real. Of course, there is a part of me that's also anxiously thinking, "What am I doing with this chapter? Is it too bizarre? Should I just delete it now?"

“

Friendship is born at the moment
when one person says to another,

‘What, you too? I thought I was the only one.’

C.S. Lewis (1898–1963)

Figure 22.2 Untitled photograph by Franz Kraft
© Borealis Press, Blue Hill ME, USA

Why the anxiety?

The anxiety comes from the knowledge that the chapter will be the black sheep of the book. If it is even accepted into the book, it will be different from most other contributions, which will be written in proper academic form worthy of John and his legacy. The anxiety comes from the fact that what I have to say, or how I choose to express it, does not fit the hegemony of academia and it will be rejected. But this very fear, incidentally, is what I want to make a point about, because whether or not we feel like we "fit" has a lot to do with whether we can get into dialogue with one another.

Point 1: Dialogue across differences in power

Perhaps the biggest barrier to good dialogue is the lack of a sense of equality within relationships. It is almost always the case that planning conversations bring a diverse group of people together and seat them around an uneven table, where some have more power than others. Asymmetries are also unavoidable in marriages, friendships and professional relationships. Friedmann describes the challenge and the hope to overcome it as such:

> [A] condition [of dialogue] is the absence of a dominant/dependent relationship between the partners in dialogue. If dialogue is to flourish, we must learn how to set aside and transcend the social roles in which we have become engaged.
>
> Social inequalities are legion... Children are dependent on adults, gender and ethnic differences are often translated into differences in status power, teachers browbeat their students, bosses intimidate and control their workers.
>
> If the power derived from the juxtaposition of these roles in their respective institutional settings is not bracketed, if it is not in some way overcome, I cannot trust you; and in the yawning gap between power, submission, and revolt, dialogue ceases. The world is reduced to a Hobbesian struggle.
>
> But experience tells us that dialogue with children is often easier than with adults, that women and men are able to meet each other on a place of equality and mutual respect, that teachers can appear to their students as human beings who are also vulnerable, that bosses as well as workers are endowed like other humans and can reveal themselves to each other in these terms.
>
> (John Friedmann, *The Good Society*, 1979, p.105)

I agree completely with Friedmann that dialogue despite power differences is possible, and that it requires transcending the grip of social stratification. My story told above is a story of a person with less social power taking the initiative over a period of time for dialogue with someone with more social power. As a dialogue leader and group facilitator, I often find myself in a position of helping people transcend their power differences in one way or another. Here are a few things that I believe help in this process:

- Those with more social power who want to be in dialogue with others need to realize that they are doing so from an advantaged position. A large body of work on recognizing and naming privilege has brought attention to this issue, but even more simply my example above illustrates the point: as a person who goes against the grain of hegemony in many ways, I sometimes hold back on disclosing myself for fear of not being well received. Of course the fear is partially self-imposed, but it is also largely based in an awareness of the histories of marginalization and my own lived experiences of it. Those who are aware of their privilege tend to be more present to and more patient with others like me, as trust building happens in early stages of dialogue. These socially powerful and psychologically aware people make a large contribution to the possibility of loving, transforming dialogue.
- Those with less social power who want to be in dialogue with others need to realize that their perceptions of reality around privilege and power may also be skewed. We all tend to be far more aware of the areas where we lack privilege and blind to the areas where we do have privilege. As a result, we may be exaggerating and accentuating our own powerlessness by our over-identification with it. This is true for those who appear to have a lot of social power as well. I was astounded when I first realized that John experienced himself as an "outsider," linking it to his family history as a Jew, immigrant and perpetual traveller ("Towards an intellectual autobiography," 2014 p.1). In my mind you couldn't be any more part of the "inner circle" of the world than John, but that was not his experience of himself. Those participants in dialogue, whether outwardly among the more or the less powerful, who are able to loosen the grip of the stereotypes on others and tune in to the actual experience of the person, remembering that the internal experience may not match the apparent external reality, are very helpful in building the conditions conducive to dialogue.
- For both the socially (more) powerful and the socially (more) powerless among us, it is also very useful to have a broad view of what power actually is. We often think of power as dominance, and we think of privilege as being connected to race, gender, age, etc. But there are other qualities of power available. In *Kinds of Power* (1995) James Hillman names 20 kinds of power and thus provides a useful tool for reframing power, assisting us in moving away from a single definition and exercising more power. Hillman's kinds of power include office, prestige, exhibitionism, ambition, control, reputation, influence, resistance, leadership, concentration, authority, persuasion, charisma, rising, decision, fearsomeness, tyranny, veto, purism and subtlety. When we understand power more

broadly, we are less likely to be manipulated by it in others and we are less likely to manipulate ourselves into feeling powerless. This in turn helps create better conditions for relating lovingly to others in dialogue.

Point 2: Dialogue despite conflict

The other commonly confronted difficulty in having loving dialogues is the fact that we disagree with each other. In conflict we find ourselves isolated and disconnecting from those to whom we are meant to be listening and with whom we are meant to disclose our own thoughts. From a broader perspective, conflicts are literally killing us off on the planet today.

It took me many years to understand in my bones that John's fierce expressions of disagreement with what I had to say did not mean that he disrespected me or that dialogue between us had ceased. It dawned on me when, in one of my reflection papers for one of his classes, I went on a bit of a rant about academic culture, complaining about the way in which scholars like to make their point by harshly criticizing the arguments of others, exaggerating the differences between ideas in piercing language. John responded by scribbling one line at the bottom on my paper: "For some of us, the play of ideas is itself stimulating and fun." It had never occurred to me before that *that* was what John loved to do, and that to some degree *that* was what he was doing with us in class! It was only then that I realized for our debates to be "fun," I could play confident and cutting, instead of trying to be nice and accommodating! Our dialogues became much more enjoyable after that.

> Dialogue includes the possibility and indeed the likelihood of conflict. Outside the domain of dialogue, such conflict is destructive: we seek a victory over the other. But within a relation of dialogue, conflict—insofar as it leads to discoveries and transformations of the self—will only strengthen the relation.... To accept one another, as we are, in our otherness, does not mean that we refrain from disagreement and conflict. But in dialogue conflict presumes the continued acceptance of the other in our common project of becoming human.
>
> (John Friedmann, *The Good Society*, 1979, p.103)

Through my professional practice the past few years, I have come to believe that it is actually a lack of comfort with conflict that is the enemy to loving orientation to dialogue. Those who are able to fight early and fight often are much more likely to be able to sustain loving relationships over a long period of time.

The trouble is that conflict can in fact be scary because so much of our world is constructed (by media, schooling, the state, etc.) to appear as black and white, where we are told that "if you're not with us, you are against us." Western ways of conceptualizing conflict do in fact make it scary because of their polarizing tendencies. Eastern ways of conceptualizing are perhaps more useful, as this helpful quoted passage I found in a footnote of John's autobiographical paper (2014) so aptly describes:

> Aristotle declared, contraries "cannot act upon each other," "do not change into each other," and "are mutually destructive." In logical terms, they are mutually exclusive. In contrast, the entire Chinese tradition insists that contraries both oppose each other and 'contain each other mutually': within *yin* there is *yang*, just as within *yang* there is *yin*; or, as one might say, as the *yang* penetrates the density of the *yin*, the *yin* opens up the dispersion of the *yang*. Both constantly proceed from the same primordial unity and reciprocally give rise to each other's actualization.
>
> (Francois Jullien, *A Treatise on Efficacy*, 1995, p.250)

To tie up my two final points in a *yin/yang* relationship, let me put it this way: If we want to be in loving dialogue we need to attend to two seemingly contradictory but in fact complementary impulses within us. The first is the impulse to disagree with each other and in the disagreement to carve out a piece of identity for ourselves, in which we can take pride and feel empowered. The second is the impulse to find our points of similarity, to search for our common humanity and to equalize power, even to become vulnerable. Loving dialogue is possible when these two impulses are well nurtured within us *and* exist in a healthy mutual and reciprocal relationship to one another. Or, in the words of John Friedmann in *The Good Society*:

> Insofar as I disagree with you, I affirm you in your difference from me; but insofar as I agree with you, I confirm you in the humanity we share. Together and apart: we are bound to each other in this double relation.
>
> (1979, p.109)

References

Aristotle, Jowett, B & Carless Davis, HW 1920, *Aristotle's Politics*, Clarendon Press, Oxford.

Buber, M 1937, *I and Thou*, T&T Clark, Edinburgh.

Friedmann, J 1979, *The Good Society*, MIT Press, Cambridge, M.A.

Friedmann, J 2014, "Towards an intellectual autobiography". Unpublished essay available from: <http://www.scarp.ubc.ca/sites/scarp.ubc.ca/files/users/%5Buser%5D/profile/Towards%20an%20Intellectual%20Autobiography.doc> [20 November 2015].

Habermas, J 1981, *The Theory of Communication Action*, translated by Thomas A. McCarthy, Beacon Press, Boston, M.A., 1984.

Hillman, J 1995, *Kinds of Power: A Guide to its Intelligent Uses*, Currency Doubleday, New York.

Jullien, F 1995, *A Treatise on Efficacy: Between Western and Chinese Thinking*, University of Hawai'i Press, Honolulu, 2004.
O'Donohue, J 1998, *Anam Cara: A Book of Celtic Wisdom*, HarperCollins, New York.
Rousseau, JJ 1762, *The Social Contract & Discourses*, EP Dutton & Co., New York, 1913.

Part 5
Chinese urbanism

Mee Kam Ng

Friedmann is a keen advocate of 'thinking without frontiers' (2011) and this can be witnessed by his passionate devotion to China studies in the 21st century, after he officially retired from UCLA. His *China's Urban Transition* (2005) is one of the most comprehensive introductory texts on China's multi-dimensional urbanization processes. Friedmann's bold excursion to literature related to China's urbanization drama helps deepen our understanding of the nuanced relationships between knowledge and action. In *China's Urban Transition*, not only does he challenge himself to study, synthesize and interpret urbanization in a different culture, but by doing so, he also challenges scholars who study Chinese urbanism through particular disciplinary angles.

As Cheek argues in the first paper of this section, Friedmann's 'radical' approach towards transdisciplinary knowledge generation does not always make him popular among experts in different knowledge domains but it nevertheless guides his positive actions in the face of barriers. To Cheek, Friedmann is pioneering a co-production culture of China scholarship. Not surprisingly Friedmann's multi-faceted synthesis of China's urbanization processes is also guarded with a certain degree of scepticism by the practising Chinese planners. After all, urban planning is seen as a 'scientific endeavour' in the authoritative political regime.

If Friedmann and Cheek's understanding of China is more a theoretical and intellectual exploration, Kunzmann's encounter of urban planning practice in China is primarily action oriented, heavily constrained by the language and cultural barrier. As Chinese planning practice is designed and master land use plan oriented, strategic planning is seldom practised especially in second-tier cities. Nevertheless, the 'thinking without frontier' spirit is clearly exhibited – introducing the concept of 'knowledge society' to the city, conducting discursive interviews with different stakeholders through incomplete translation and attempting to decode various encounters through multiple cultural lenses, in order to move from knowledge to action.

The two last papers are written by two Chinese female scholars. If Friedmann has succeeded in bridging urban and China studies, Zhong and Ng further enrich this transdisciplinary endeavour by revisiting Friedmann's key planning concepts with reference to Chinese development practices, cultures and values. Sheng Zhong compares and contrasts Shanghai's industrial restructuring and creative city-making with Friedmann's social learning planning paradigm. While social learning in the Western tradition is more about knowledge production, social learning in China as a kind of 'survival-based pragmatism' means that learners, largely elites, may not start out to be conscious knowledge seekers. And China's social learning experiments also prove that social learning is possible even in hierarchical and non-democratic situations.

Ng considers the qualities of Chinese culture in relation to Friedmann's radical planning paradigm, aiming to transform power relationships to achieve collective self-reliance in a good society. She argues that insurgent citizenship and radical planning are somehow alien concepts in Chinese Confucian culture. Not only does the Chinese culture emphasize human relationships, the Confucian ideal believes that the 'Way' – the origin of values from heaven – can help cultivate people's heart to nurture benevolence and righteousness. The route to the good society is not through transforming power relationships but to first perfect oneself, nourish a happy family, govern a country and then to promote world peace. The ultimate goal of launching insurgent activities and radical planning practices is for people to return to the cultivation of their hearts, to devote selflessly to the well-being of others, a key quality of John Friedmann's advocacy of planning for human flourishing.

References

Friedmann, J 2005, China's urban transition, University of Minnesota Press, Minneapolis.

Friedmann, J 2011, Insurgencies: essays in planning theory, Routledge, London.

23 Ignoring the ramparts

John Friedmann's dialogue with Chinese urbanism and Chinese studies

Timothy Cheek

Writing in 2007, Zou Deci, former director of the China Academy of Urban Planning and Design, declared that *Zhongguode chengshi bianqian* offers "a profound analysis of the politics, economics, culture, environment and governance of China's cities," one that is "worth our while to learn from." Such is the preface to the Chinese edition of John Friedmann's *China's Urban Transition*.[1] It has served as a point of departure for John's dialogue with his Chinese counterparts in and around the Academy over the past decade. It is also the product of some five years of reading and dialogue at the University of British Columbia where John cheerfully engaged the China Studies community as part of turning his professional gaze on China. I joined UBC's Centre for Chinese Research in 2002 and soon met this most congenial of revolutionaries.

I have come to understand both sides of John's dialogue – with Chinese urban planners and with China studies scholars at UBC – as part of his long-term commitment to radical social practice. Mostly, I was amazed at his quiet confidence as he plunged into an extended reading program of recent scholarship on China's urban and rural issues, supplemented with long conversations with several China specialists at UBC and regular participation in our many public talks and seminars. In particular, John has been a mainstay of our intensive China Studies reading group in which we dissected each other's papers in preparation for publication. That John's engagement was something unusual, and indeed a version of the radical social practice he had been advocating since at least his 1979 book, *The Good Society*, only dawned on me slowly. I am a cheerful and interdisciplinary soul, so John's field-crossing from urban planning to modern Sinology struck me as simply interesting. Not so, I came to discover, for some of my colleagues. I have been disappointed by such a guild mentality, but John mounted the disciplinary ramparts as if he were stepping onto the dance floor, with grace and a bit of a flair.

In time I came to read *The Good Society*, in which John lays out what he means by radical practice. As those familiar with his work know, this is always social practice, taking place in small groups and in dialogue in task-specific settings. The goal is to make life better, particularly social life, but it is personal and face-to-face, not hierarchical or directive. Indeed, John insists "All dialogue is open ended and allows for transformation of the self and other in a process of transactive learning" (Friedmann 1979, pp.39–40). Anyone can join in, the conversation is tied to activity, joining thinking and doing, and these groups can link with others informally when it makes sense to those involved. This is the *doing* of the Good Society, in which process is the goal, or at least the best shot at the goal we can pull off at the time. I don't think John has ever said the words 'radical practice' in all our work together, but it has underwritten a decade of shared exploits.

John not only came to the Centre for Chinese Research to deepen his reading on China, he joined the community. When I arrived he was already working with Michael Leaf in our School of Community and Regional Planning on questions of periurban development in China and Southeast Asia. They invited me to join the examination of an MA thesis on urban issues in China and thus I met this astonishing intellectual who brought to mind Pablo Casals (not least because John was still playing his cello then). After the exam we all went up the hill for Chinese noodles and a friendship was born. I discovered in John a mentor for engaged scholarship, love of poetry, and community building. A deeply cultured man, a Viennese intellectual – poet, scholar, musician, and playful trouble-maker for the literal, pedantic, tone-deaf, and self-satisfied – John embraces difference and, luckily for me, has a weakness for Australians.

China's Urban Transition is but one of John's efforts to do a bit of radical practice as well as to extend his knowledge of place making in another part of the world. As readers of the book immediately discover, John sets out to challenge his urban studies colleagues with a strongly historical approach and focus on endogenous factors in China's urban transition in explicit contention – or dialogue – with the general focus on the present and global factors (Friedmann 2007). *China's Urban Transition* is a call to urban planners to take Chinese experience over time as well as over space seriously. At the same time, John's approach and these fruits of his wide-ranging reading of countless specialised studies by China historians, political scientists, geographers, urban planners, sociologists, anthropologists, and humanists of various stripes (how many urban planning texts cite the *I Ching*?) has been a signal contribution and challenge for China studies scholars. John's interdisciplinary application of space, demography, rural and urban sociology, the anthropology of identity, and politics of urban administration plugs Chinese experience into cross-cultural and comparative conversations that break out of the 'China centred' scholarship in which my generation was trained and which still characterizes much Sinological work. For both professional communities this book offers a call to interdisciplinarity – a reminder that we need the analytical focus of disciplines but no one or two intellectual tools is sufficient to get the job done. John ends this book with the hope that Chinese planners can build sustainable development by "'steering the middle passage' between anarchy and stasis" (Friedmann 2007, p.129.) Likewise, he reminds us to seek a balance between local knowledge and comparative insight.

John consistently joined in the activities I arranged at the Centre for Chinese Research, always encouraging and with practical suggestions. When I set out to start a project on 'rethinking Chinese thinking' with legal scholars and political theorists in 2004 John moved smoothly between fields with a sharp but jargon-free understanding of each approach. When I revived the effort in 2011 in a conference on 'Chinese values and universal norms' John was in the middle again. Meanwhile, John brought incisive criticism and fresh perspectives to our papers in the China Studies reading group and in 2005 he brought together the first of our Chinese Urbanism roundtables (this one on identity over time), bringing in students and faculty from history, geography, art history, political science, and urban planning. In all of these activities he was looking for what we could learn from each other and then what we could do, practically, now. This is when I reached for *The Good Society*.

In 2006, when I returned from a stint in Beijing appalled by the air pollution, I discovered the nature of John's 'participation' in the Centre. He became our *agent provocateur* or 'outside agitator.' He encouraged me to set up an interdisciplinary research group: China Environmental Science and Sustainability (CESS). It has long been my wish to bring natural scientists and China studies scholars together to make sense of China's environmental crisis. However, the *habitus* of departments and disciplinary incentives that reward intra-disciplinary publication militate against such collaborations partially by habit and partially by guild mentality. If John has explicit enemies it would be these. Yet his response has not been to complain; it has been to act. He simply started planning our first meeting and a grant application. What has evolved is an ongoing conversation, sometimes quite active, sometimes sidelined by other tasks, but over the years we have built a community of scholars of nature and society to address specific issues in China's environment.[2] We have a long way to go before we can achieve the combination of intellectual synergy and community connection between UBC researchers and communities in China that we seek, but the conversation has begun.

John's approach to China is refreshing but it still faces some challenges both at home and abroad. In *China's Urban Transition* he is explicitly using China as the 'other' with which to challenge the social planning world in Euro-America. It is a useful challenge and his emphasis on endogenous factors in China's current urbanization is a useful corrective to overly abstract models of urbanization that essentially draw from Western experience or assumptions about the universality of globalization. But this comes at a cost. Intellectually, using China to critique ourselves is good for reflexivity but less good for providing a critical analysis of activities in China. John's work has not really engaged the social planning world of state socialism in China as fully as he has engaged the modernist presumptions of the Western planning. China's planners are probably more secure in their technocratic elitism than planners in Western universities or multilateral agencies. This

Chinese high modernism in which 'science' still reigns supreme is buttressed by an anxious and repressive government that will brook no criticism it has not itself vetted beforehand. Thus, John's model of community deliberation and self-determination faces severe challenges from both the scientism and the authoritarianism of actually existing socialism in Xi Jinping's China.

Likewise, John's radical presence in our China community has not always gotten results. For example, partially in response to his own dismay at the planning community in China, John tried to get a number of Sinologists and scholars working on technical aspects of environmental pollution to join forces with scholars and communities in Wuhan in central China for an 'on the ground' planning project to see if we could work together on some research and some solutions for water pollution in that major city on the Yangtze river. Despite some initial overtures, in the end we (including myself) dropped the ball. We were unwilling to let go of our current projects or were unable to see how this proposed collaboration could contribute to or develop our work. This is the challenge of institutionalization, and it remains one that my unit, the Institute for Asian Research, struggles with right now as we have developed a new Asia-focused Masters in public policy. For me, this training programme should incorporate the challenges that John and his like-minded colleagues and students have put forward, but for others of my colleagues what is needed is more models, more mathematical rigour, and bigger data sets. At times I find myself wanting to re-read Mao's *On Protracted War*.

John's approach will continue to irritate the positivists in our community. Surprisingly, it is also a burr in the side of area specialists. I became so used to working with John on trying new things at the Centre for Chinese Research that it was a shock to me to discover the resistance of some of my Sinological colleagues. As the Centre set out a few years ago to revise its mandate and to shape the graduate training at the Institute of Asian Research I invited John as a very active member of the Centre to join in the conversation. In short order (but in polite Canadian fashion) I was taken aside and informed that this was a conversation for specialists and your friend John is not one, after all he doesn't speak or read Chinese – how could he guide us on a China policy curriculum? I am happy to say that this was not the attitude of all my China studies colleagues, but it represented an important part of our institutional culture. On the one hand, those not trained in the finer points of our sub-specialty are not welcome to the table or are lightly dismissed, and on the other hand we abandon responsibility for what happens in any other field, deferring to the wisdom of the specialists of that domain. This is foolishness in so many ways that it does not bear much explanation. Having worked for years against the divides of disciplinary dominion I was appalled to find it amongst area studies scholars – ourselves generally interdisciplinary in approach and subject to the jibes of disciplinarians (Szanton 2004; Wesley-Smith & Goss 2010).

John made a spirited case for bridging Sinological studies with policy issues – something since applied with great success at other universities from the Australian National University's Centre on China in the World to University of Nottingham's China Policy Institute.[3] But John's suggestions fell on deaf ears. This, I have come to see, is that other part of *The Good Society*: the struggle. For John's work it has largely been against the coercive aspects of the world of social planning, and I have inherited from him the same struggle in my patch. I am happy to report that the dialogue John has so encouraged is now taking off at UBC and, meanwhile, I have taken the struggle to my own face-to-face community in a project to use collaborative translation pairs of Anglophone and Sinophone scholars to work on active translation between Chinese and English and so work towards a practical version of co-production of knowledge about China.[4] This includes much of the messiness, misunderstandings, and time-consuming conversations that support what John so encouragingly labels 'dialogue.' But it is worth it. We are training a new generation of collaborative scholars (and with better translation skills as a bonus). They are making a new style of China scholarship built on co-production of knowledge. Much of the skill set and inspiration for this effort comes from reading and working with John – from the inclination to listen first to the willingness to let the interaction change us but also including 'to get something done.'

The conversation with Chinese urban planners likewise is not without its struggles. The translation of John's book, *China's Urban Transition*, reflects this. It is published *neibu* – internal circulation: a residual category of classified documents and publications carried over from the Mao period. *Neibu* books are not available to the general public, at least in spirit, and are not available through normal book shops. In Mao's time these classified materials were things deemed too politically sensitive for ordinary people, the political laity. Only high cadres and professors and others in the priesthood of socialism could deal with any 'dangerous ideas' in such books – whether on local conditions or coming from bourgeois countries. Today, the *neibu* classification is used to circumvent over-zealous censors but comes at the price of diminished circulation. The upside of this prophylactic publishing is that this translation appears to be free from the deletions and changes invariably required of translations published in open (*gongkai*) circulation. Thus, John's book may have a limited audience (ironically among the cadres of the social planning world in China), but at least his voice comes through pretty accurately. Of course, the preface by Zou Deci and the translator's introduction both contain the ideological equivalent of the Surgeon General's Warning: ingesting these products can be dangerous to your (ideological) health (literally "because he is a foreign scholar he cannot avoid some mistakes; readers should take note").

Constrained distribution and ideological caution are not the only challenges facing John's efforts at dialogue with his Chinese colleagues. In his recent visits to Shenzhen he has lamented the continued dominance of the mega-planning approach at the expense of place making. The self-confident modernism John struggled against in Latin America in earlier decadesis alive and well in post-socialist China. Yet, as other papers in this volume attest, that conversation and that struggle to build communities of participatory planning continue in China and with Chinese colleagues.

John has been cheerfully relentless in his search for communities of dialogue – or potential dialogue. As with my community at UBC, this has entailed some struggle. Yet, I have never seen John raise his voice in anger as he tweaked academic pretensions or crossed sacred disciplinary or area boundaries. I have come to see that in addition to learning more about China and offering an urban studies lens for China specialists, John's goal has been to enact the Good Society he had written about in the 1970s. He never mentioned the term to me but I can find the explanation for his actions in that book. The goal of radical social practice, as John wrote there, is not some destination – an improved China curriculum at my university or a unity of mind with Chinese planners – rather, it is the doing, the process, the effort at community and dialogue, and even the struggle. These are the clothing we weave and wear each day that marks us as pilgrims of the Good Society.

Meanwhile, John is translating Rilke.

Notes

1 The book in Chinese: 约翰 弗里德曼《中国的城市变迁》(北京: 中国城市规划设计研究院, 内部资料 2008), 邹德慈《序》。.
2 China Environmental Science & Sustainability Research Group, Centre for Chinese Research, Institute of Asian Research, University of British Columbia. See the Centre's webpage for details: http://ccr.ubc.ca/.
3 The Australian Centre on China in the World (CIW), http://ciw.anu.edu.au/ and The University of Nottingham China Policy Institute Blog http://blogs.nottingham.ac.uk/chinapolicyinstitute/.
4 This is the "Reading and Writing the Chinese Dream" collaborative translation project I run with Professors Joshua Fogel (York University, Toronto) and David Ownby (University of Montreal). See "Reading and Writing the Chinese Dream: introducing a project" at *Thinking China* in *The China Story* website: http://www.thechinastory.org/cot/reading-and-writing-the-chinese-dream-introducing-a-project/ or https://youtu.be/kVn_gcjX6dM.

References

Friedmann, J 1979, *The Good Society*, MIT Press, Cambridge, M.A.
Friedmann, J 2007, *China's Urban Transition*, University of Minnesota Press, Minneapolis. [Chinese translation: Yuehan Feilideman (2008), *Zhongguode chengshi bianqian*. Zhongguo chengshi guihua sheji yanjiuyan, neibu ziliao, Beijing].
Szanton, DL (ed.) 2004, *The Politics of Knowledge: Area Studies and the Disciplines*, University of California Press, Berkeley.
Wesley-Smith, T & Goss, J (eds) 2010, *Remaking Area Studies: Teaching and Learning across Asia and the Pacific*, University of Hawai'i Press, Honolulu.

24 Challenges of strategic planning in another planning culture

Learning from working in a Chinese city

Klaus R. Kunzmann

Introduction

In recent decades China has become an incredibly rich laboratory for urban development and planning. While Chinese planners, whether educated at home, in the USA, the UK, Germany or at other planning schools in Europe, struggle to cope with the immense challenges of rapid urbanization in a complex socio-economic and politico-administrative context, crowds of Western planners, planning consultants and planning scholars rush into the country to share and transfer their theoretical, analytical, methodological, technical or managerial knowledge and competence with local planners in cities and city regions, with planning educators in universities or with bureaucrats in central government institutions. The speed of urban development and change, the strong political leadership, a top-down planning culture, the repercussions of a capitalist market economy under socialist command and control, the dominance of developers and the changing values of citizens and migrants all influence, guide and control their work (see Campanella 2008; Hu & Chen 2015; Wu 2015). John Friedmann (2005) was among the first Western scholars to address the challenges of urbanization in a more theoretical and comprehensive dimension.

In this brief essay I reflect on the challenges a foreign planner faces when working in a Chinese city. Since the 1970s I have frequently worked in other countries and in quite diverse planning cultures. Hence, I have been confronted with the challenges and limitations of transferring planning theory and practice from one planning culture to another. Moreover, from teaching master's degree courses at Chinese universities since 2000, I have learnt much from communicating with Chinese planning educators and students. In his now classic book, *Planning in the Public Domain* (1987), John Friedmann reflected on the many difficulties in moving from knowledge to action. The paradigmatic subtitle *From Knowledge to Action* was what I had in mind when invited to advise the local urban planning institute in a Chinese city, one of the many multi-million second tier cities in the country. Hoping that I could learn more about urban planning in China by being involved in practical strategic development projects, I accepted this invitation. 'Places matter' has always been my guiding principle, as I prefer to learn from places rather than from books, and from working in other planning cultures (Kunzmann 2016). In his well-known essay on emerging planning cultures, and based on Chinese research, John Friedmann briefly sketched the multiple challenges of planning where physical planning and land development as well as socio-economic and environmental planning in China are hardly ever co-ordinated (2005; 2011, pp.170–4).

A Chinese city like many others

The city in China where I work occasionally is located in the northeast (Figure 24.1). Compared with cities in the south, the subject city (population 2010: 3.53 million in the city proper, and 7.677 million within the wider functional urban city region) is not economically thriving, although it is the location of China's high-speed railway industry and one of the more important locations of automotive industries in the country.

The two large state-owned and managed railway and automotive corporations dominate the local economy. In modern China the image of this city is dire. Qualified young people leave the place. They head to more attractive, dynamic cities with entertainment in the South. Local enterprises complain that qualified labour has become a scarce resource and that the city does not attract qualified labour anymore from other regions in the country. The intricate and contradictory history of the city makes it difficult for a foreigner, who is parachuted into the city from another cultural environment, to get a

Figure 24.1 Building the Chinese city
Source: Klaus R. Kunzmann

feeling for the place, to understand the 'path dependency' of urban development processes and the conservative local values. Without language skills to explore written documents and to communicate with local people who really know the city, any insight into the local soul and spirit is almost impossible. Experience from involvement in planning in other cultures and superficial visual impressions when moving around the city remain the only window to learn about this politically and culturally less important second-tier city. Hence, I have debated whether it would have been better not to have accepted the invitation and become engaged in such a venture. I will explain my motives later in this brief essay.

From land use master planning to strategic planning

The institute that invited me is an advisory public institute established by the local government to do practical design and research work on urban development. It offers advisory services to the city and urban governments in the province, serves as a counterpart for foreign consultants who are asked by the city or by the provincial or the central government to advise on development planning projects and is treated as a think-tank to provide information and data for local planning and decision-making processes. The projects the institute usually carries out are traditional design projects for town expansion and urban renewal in the province. Strategic urban development has not been a subject that the institute has worked on before. From around 250 staff working in the institute, located in an industrial quarter outside the inner city, half are planners who have been trained at schools of architecture, civil engineering and geography in China. Some senior staff received training overseas. Most staff cannot communicate in English and have to rely on interpreters to communicate with me. Besides the language barrier, perceptions of the role of urban planning in the wider urban development context also differ.

Originally, my assignment at the institute was rather open and was not linked to a particular project. When asked what kind of project I would like to work on, I suggested developing a strategy to guide the future urban development of the city based on knowledge development, not as a city marketing project, but as a pilot exercise in strategic urban development planning. The idea was accepted and I travelled to China frequently to work on the ambitious project. The challenges I faced were enormous: how to start such a project; how to develop a vague conceptual idea into knowledge; and how to move from knowledge to action in an environment characterized by a different planning culture that was focused on physical planning and urban design.

The strategic concept in my mind was that of a 'knowledge city', a city where future local economic, social and cultural development is based on the advancement of knowledge (Kunzmann 2004, 2008). Admittedly the knowledge city concept is rather fuzzy. It is not what John Friedmann had in mind when presenting his thoughts on *Planning in the Public Domain*. It is rather a kind of a plug-in concept for guiding city development in times of globalization and rapid technological change. The knowledge city strategy combines pro-active physical development with economic, social and cultural economic development. It addresses local structural change and aims to lay sustainable and resilient foundations for an innovative, future-oriented and competitive local economy; it promotes local research and education, higher education and professional education; it supports such strategies and policies by the creation of open cultural milieus and related infrastructure. It is a comprehensive policy with a strong economic dimension, which, however, can only succeed in cities where creating and sustaining a high degree of liveability is high on the political agenda. In a way the knowledge city paradigm is a perfect catalyst strategy to move towards the good city that John Friedmann (1979) has promoted.

The questions were how to prepare for and how to commence this ambitious journey? Here the narrative of my experience and my difficulties in working in another planning practice begin.

The brief project summary I had written for the director of the institute prepared the ground. It describes the project as follows:

> In times of globalization and strong urban competition, knowledge has become an important dimension of urban economic development. With the rise of information and communication technologies, the knowledge society has evolved as the logical succession of the industrial society. Today the knowledge of citizens and the labour force, its public institutions and corporations, its private firms and enterprises, as well as the knowledge of its universities and research is the most important capital of cities. Knowledge is a resource as well as local capital. It attracts investment and qualified labour; it profiles the city in political arenas and in international media. In the information society era, knowledge has become an equally important resource for economic development as mineral resources were in times of industrialization. To retain an entrepreneurial labour force and to attract investors and innovative entrepreneurs, a city has to provide a high quality of life, affordable housing and attractive shopping precincts, a broad spectrum of cultural and leisure facilities, as well as clean air and good public transportation.

In conversations with the director of the planning institute I stressed that the proposed project would be an internal learning and coaching project, to prepare staff for times when urban design projects are no longer high on the political agenda and do not support the economic base of the institute. Learning not by attending training courses initiated by government agencies or local universities, not by sitting in classrooms or reading books, but by experiencing the challenges of carrying out such a project, and from communication with people, players and stakeholders over the course of the process.

Obviously such an ambitious explorative project cannot be carried out without the close cooperation of competent staff members who are curious to explore the challenging theme beyond the routine urban design work, who wish to learn strategic urban planning by doing such a project, who know the city and its political, economic and social conditions, and who speak at least some English in order to communicate. Here the challenges started. Only one junior staff member, trained in sociology, with limited ability to communicate in English, was temporarily freed from other duties to support me in carrying out the work. Her professional experience was to collect, compile and portray urban data. Alarm bells should have rung to warn me not to commit to the project but my Chinese partner and collaborator told me to be patient. In my naivety I thought I could at least throw some tiny utopian stones into the local discourse and planning practice and leave some footprints in the city. I am conscious that such hopes rather reflected my own self-interest. Like John Friedmann (2005, p.xi), I feel that China is a remarkably rich learning environment for urban planners in times of globalization. And I wanted to learn from getting involved.

How to learn about a city

How can one get to know a city? Books of course would be the first option but there are no publications on the city in English, French or German. The official government websites and Wikipedia give only a scant overview. If one does not read Chinese, one cannot read the local newspaper and reports and has to rely on observation and communication with people who live in the city. To learn about the city I suggested beginning with a series of intensive interviews with key local, public and private stakeholders. Apart from learning about the city, the rationale of these interviews was to start establishing a communication platform, which could serve in the future as a horizontal network of communication for local knowledge actors. On other occasions I had learned that communication processes in China are always vertical and top-down, never horizontal. The stakeholders I had suggested to interview were, among others, the Office of the Mayor, the local Planning and Reform Commission, the local Planning Bureau, the International Bureau of the city, a local social welfare institution, a local elite university, a vocational training centre, a local science park, the management of the railway corporation, the FAW automobile factory, the local movie industry, a local newspaper, local entrepreneurs and representatives of the business community. For each interview I had prepared a set of questions targeted to the respective stakeholder. I requested that these be translated into Chinese and sent out ahead of the interview together with a description of the aims and proposed outcomes of the project. Examples of questions are:

- What are the challenges of urban and economic development in the city? Which obstacles (regulations, finances, etc.) make it difficult for the city to compete with cities in Northeast China? What are the weaker points of the city in comparison to competitive cities in Northeast China?

- Who are the strong stakeholders in the city? Who is driving, who is slowing down innovative economic development in the city? How do you see the role of your institution in promoting and developing knowledge development in the city?
- Which activities will you or could you initiate to raise the knowledge profile of the city?
- How do you see the future of innovation in the city? Can the city improve its position as a centre of innovative knowledge in China?
- How do you see the future of the city? What are your plans and strategies, and your priorities for innovative (economic and social and cultural) development in the city?
- Which cities in China and which cities outside China do you consider would be appropriate models for the city?
- Which role does the quality of life in the city play for citizens and labour, for staff and students?

This intensive interview approach is routine in my country but is quite unusual in the working culture of the institute. I had to explain that the purpose of such interviews was not to collect data and factual information, a task I wanted to leave to the local staff at a later stage. I had argued that I would rather like to hear views and opinions about present and future urban challenges in the city, learn about local plans and strategies in the eyes of the interview partners and explore their expectations from the project. Later I realized that the staff of the institute had not translated some of the more qualitative questions. When carrying out the interviews together with a staff member and my bilingual Chinese partner I included these. During the interviews, which turned out to be surprisingly informal, more questions came up.

Ten of these interviews have been undertaken at the time of writing this account. With one exception, the director of the International Bureau, who had been working in Italy for a while, all interview partners were hesitant to communicate in English. Hence I had to rely fully on the translation and communication skills of my Chinese partner. All interviews took place in the respective institution and were always attended by a group of four to six representatives of the institution. They were less formal than anticipated and took an average of three hours, much longer than expected. All interview partners agreed that the interviews be recorded.

For me the outcome was extremely enlightening. What did I learn? First the interviews confirmed much of what I had experienced on earlier occasions, what I had learnt from conversations with Chinese academic planners, from reading selected articles and books on Chinese urban development and planning and from screening more or less regularly the *China Daily*, the politically cleansed newspaper on China for expatriates and foreign visitors. The interviews verified the prevalent top-down culture in planning and decision-making in the country. Urban development is driven by top-down policies. When asking about local policies and strategies, reference was always made to central or at least provincial government policies. Though it soon became apparent that government policies on innovation and economic development related to knowledge development and their implications for local implementation, these were not discussed with other stakeholders at the city level, nor in a broader context. Strategic alliances were not openly initiated. Local platforms of communication have not been established. The city is an archipelago of gated spheres of influence, like gated communities, self-centred with few linking corridors and bridges. Challenges at the local level were openly expressed, such as the low attractiveness of the city for qualified labour, the relative lack of quality of life, the absence of entertainment opportunities and cultural and lifestyle milieus and the presence of traffic congestion problems. The expectations, however, were rather fuzzy. As a rule, Beijing and Shanghai served as reference cities. Benchmarking with more thriving second-tier cities in China was not indicated. The strong inward looking spirit of the local society and the lack of a more international orientation were openly articulated.

During most interviews one dimension of local development never remained unspoken: the importance of land as a means of income for local development. Land is more important in China than people. The availability of land, access to land and the use of land are key determinants guiding city development and management. Any other strategic perspective is subordinated to the whole land issue. Not surprisingly, local knowledge development remained an abstract concept, not linked to urban development.

The interviews gave me a valuable insight into the spirit and values of stakeholders in the city, who are part of the local knowledge development environment. To further deepen my understanding of the city and its knowledge development potential, more interviews will be carried out in the future. Thereafter it is planned to describe and map the knowledge potential of the city, identifying strengths and weaknesses of the local knowledge base, undertake some international and national benchmarking (Manchester, Bilbao, Hannover, Shenyang, Suzhou, Guangzhou), conceptualize cornerstones of a knowledge development strategy for the city and discuss all findings with the stakeholders in the city who were previously interviewed.

How to cope with another planning culture

In Friedmann's essay 'The many cultures of planning', he characterized immersing in another planning culture as 'a surprising, and even painful process, something like jumping into an ice cold stream on a hot day' (2011, p.205). This is exactly what I felt when working in the city. My curiosity of working in other countries and learning from other planning cultures drove me to open the window to planning in other countries. Doing real work in planning practice – not as a short-term advisor of an international development institution or a bank, or as a consultant hired by the government – is quite a challenge.

Three things I have learnt so far: identifying, selecting and compiling information for strategic urban development is a challenge, communication is another one, and doing this in a different planning culture adds an additional burden.

Information: Chinese are obsessed with quantitative data. Qualitative data are considered to be personal opinions. Selecting the right locally relevant information and data has been a permanent challenge. Strategic urban and regional development is based on both quantitative data and qualitative information. Consequently, finding both quantitative and qualitative data for assessing urban knowledge development in a city is an expedition into unknown territory. Information from books, documents and technical reports requires language skills and knowledge about accessibility to local information sources, and time, of course, to explore where information can be retrieved and to read the articles, books, documents and reports. The institute had a small library that subscribed to selected Chinese and a few international journals, though most books and journals focused very much on architecture and urban design. This left me to search and retrieve relevant information on the Internet. Experience in China (and not only there) shows that such information searches are not quite satisfactory. They are a mix of lucky hits, technical and system constraints and cul-de-sacs. For language reasons, reading a quality local newspaper to get a vague impression of the issues was not possible and there were no quality journals available in the city. Moreover, I realized that even colleagues at the institute did not read local newspapers as they were considered to be without any relevance to their work. Finally, the iPhone, which everyone uses incessantly, almost 24 hours a day, is a means of personal communication and orientation rather than a means of accessing significant information relevant to a planning project.

Communication: Reflecting on communication in China is more than just referring to language. The culture of communication is different. My observation is what educators who work with Chinese students frequently report. Brought up in another tradition and social context, questions are rarely asked, even by colleagues in a project team. This makes any communication difficult, as it is a one-way street to knowledge. I experienced two things. For whatever reasons, I rarely got any substantive factual input to the project mentioning conditions and developments which may be essential for the project, and which could even require changing the approach. I could never check whether my deliberations and points were understood or not, or deliberately changed. And if changes in memos or conceptual papers were made in Chinese, I could not check them. Time constraints were always attributed to work pressure. I rarely received open and frank feedback in response to suggestions or memos I had written.

Planning culture: John Friedmann defines planning culture as 'the ways, both formal and informal, that spatial planning in a given multi-national region country or city is conceived, institutionalized and enacted' (Friedmann 2005; 2011, p.168). During a long professional and academic life in Europe, aiming to bridge theory and visionary ambitions with reality and practice, I had been continually confronted with different planning cultures in international comparative research projects (Kunzmann 1995; 2015). The planning culture in China is still very much dominated by producing physical land use master plans to meet the requirements of cities to buy land, develop infrastructure and sell it to developers. Such plans are often implemented within astoundingly brief time periods. As a rule, linking transport infrastructure and functional land-use development is still the main occupation of planners and engineers.

Spatial planning in China is not yet established as a wider, more comprehensive and more strategic approach to urban development, though there are pathways to change ahead. Recently, however, a new term called urban-rural planning, coined by the government, is rising on the planning horizon. This new term has been introduced to expand the land-use planning tradition by widening its scope and spatial dimension. The conservation of the urban heritage has received political support. The developer-led demolition of inner-city residential areas is slowly being reconsidered. Urban regeneration involving residents finds academic interest in planning schools and beyond. The first pilot schemes are under implementation as are the first cautious efforts of community development projects. Nevertheless, strategic urban development and spatial planning (Albrechts 2004; Healey 2006) are still very much uncharted territories.

Towards urban transition

To conclude this very personal voyage into Chinese planning practice I come back to John Friedmann's encounter with China's urban transition, a book written in the beginning of the 21st century, which so far has not been published openly in China. In his foreword John Friedmann expressed his motive for writing the book as follows:

> What is happening in China today is...of world-historical importance. Over the past century China has emerged as a major economic power in Asia. It is now a relatively stable polity undergoing rapid and sustained economic growth, one of the world's largest industrial producers. Within a decade or two, it will also have scientific and technical abilities to rival those of the most advanced nations.
>
> (Friedmann 2005, p.xi)

When it comes to urban, social and ecological development, China is still behind, though there are signs that it will catch up as well, maybe not the way some Western countries, like Sweden, Germany or Switzerland are practising, but following a Chinese path that is deeply rooted in its Confucian tradition. Democracy in China will start from below, not from above. In 2015, the reality of planning in China is still far away from the utopian horizon John Friedmann, a planning visionary, is sketching in his writings on China, though there is hope for change, a hope that community action supported by new virtual media will evolve, where courageous people will grasp an opportunity to establish a platform of communication and dialogue and where owners of small shops will develop survival strategies to defend their spaces against developers and government. With a new generation of planning educators who see the limitations of urban design education, planning with a more social dimension, planning with communities and people and not for people will evolve.

My audacious journey to move from knowledge to action in another country with a different planning culture, in a city facing relative economic stagnation, requires patience. There are opportunities to move ahead as the conditions for planning in China are slowly changing.

References

Albrechts, L 2004, 'Strategic (spatial) planning re-examined', *Environment and Planning B, Planning and Design*, 31: 743–758.

Campanella, TJ 2008, *The Concrete Dragon. China's Urban Revolution and What it Means for the World*, Princeton Architectural Press, New York.

Friedmann, J 1979, *The Good Society*, MIT Press, Cambridge, M.A.

Friedmann, J 1987, *Planning in the Public Domain: From Knowledge to Action*, Princeton University Press, Princeton, N.J.

Friedmann, J 2005, *China's Urban Transition*, University of Minnesota Press, Minneapolis.

Friedmann, J 2011, *Insurgencies: Essays in Planning Theory*, Routledge, London.

Healey, P 2006, 'Relational complexity and the imaginative power of strategic spatial planning', *European Planning Studies*, 14(4): 525–546.

Hu, B & Chen, C 2015, 'Chinese urbanisation under globalisation and the social implications', *Asia & the Pacific Policy Studies*, 2(1): 34–43.

Kunzmann, KR 1995, 'Planungskulturen und Planerausbildung in Europa', *disP*, 123: 49–57.

Kunzmann, KR 2004, 'Wissensstädte: Neue Aufgaben für die Stadtpolitik' in *Stadtregion und Wissen: Analysen und Plädoyers für eine wissensbasierte Stadtpolitik*, ed. U Matthiesen Hg., VS Verlag für Sozialwissenschaften, Wiesbaden, pp. 15–28.

Kunzmann, KR 2008, 'Afterword', in *Knowledge-based Urban Development Planning and Applications in the Information Era*, eds T Yigitcanlar, K Velibeyoglu & S Baum, Information Science Reference, Hershey/New York, pp. 296–300.

Kunzmann, KR 2015, 'Urbanization in China: learning from Europe? A European perspective', *International Journal of Urban Sciences*, 19(2): 119–135.

Kunzmann, KR 2016, 'Places matter' in *The Evolution of Planning Thought*, ed. B Haselsberger, Routledge, London (forthcoming).

Wu, F 2015, *Planning for Growth: Urban and Regional Planning in China*, Routledge, London.

25 Social learning in creative Shanghai

Sheng Zhong

Introduction

Planning in the Public Domain: From Knowledge to Action by Friedmann (1987) was the first planning theory book that I read as a PhD student at the University of British Columbia. The book was unlikely to have been written with China's urbanization in mind; however, I found it to be of great relevance to China's contemporary urban changes, a main theme of my scholastic enquiry as well as a research interest of the book's author.

Friedmann argues that planning theorizing involves three main tasks: examining the philosophical origin of planning, adapting planning practice to local contexts and transferring knowledge from other fields into planning (Friedmann 2008). For *Planning in the Public Domain* (Friedmann 1987), the main theoretical concerns lie in the philosophical homes and the reconstruction of the planning profession. Friedmann identifies four traditions of planning, namely social reform, policy analysis, social learning and social mobilization, and he traces their roots to a wide range of western philosophical foundations. Different from traditions of social reform and policy analysis, social learning is action-based, process-oriented and empowered by empirical knowledge. Compared with social mobilization, another action-based planning tradition, social learning is incremental and conservative. Friedmann thinks that the intellectual root of social learning is John Dewey's philosophy of pragmatism. The author also links this tradition to the writings of Mao Zedong, the founder of the People's Republic, and implies that Mao's theorizing was influenced by Dewey, possibly in an indirect way. This is suggestive of the nexus between the social learning theory and the Chinese sociopolitical practice.

Theorization of pragmatism is said to originate in the West; however, pragmatic philosophy is by no means the monopoly of the western world. Shih (1995) argues that pragmatism is actually deeply ingrained in the Chinese culture and hence has shaped the country's sociopolitical changes. Perhaps this cultural root explains the great significance of the social learning tradition in shaping the Chinese urban trajectory. That being said, the term "pragmatism" has a more complex connotation in the Chinese context.

Dewey's thinking revolves around a theory of knowledge production, and it is understood as a conscious, methodological and well-orchestrated process. All other western social learning literature cited by Friedmann, be it by the Organization Development School or Mumford, follows a similar thread. Mao's writing also takes this perspective. But beyond the application in formal intellectual enquiries, the China study literature also notes the exercise of pragmatism in the quotidian life of the common people. Lu (1999), in his writing about the pre-1949 Shanghai, depicts life narratives of the petty urbanites as "incorporating whatever was appealing and available to make life better (or in some cases to make life possible)" (Lu 1999, p.295). A similar understanding can be derived from Bergère's (1989) depiction of Shanghai's bourgeoisie around the same historic period. Likewise, Shih suggests that pragmatism in China means "flexibility in people's behavior in order to suit the context" (1995, p.3). Here, the meaning of "pragmatism" stresses the survival philosophy of societal members or entities when they are confronted with harsh, hostile and constrained environments.

In contrast to the rationalistic "pragmatism" embodied in the process of knowledge acquisition and application, "pragmatism" as a way of life is exercised in a less conscious and structured way. It is more related to personal and individualistic choices than collective social projects. As the essay will demonstrate in the following sections, this survival-based pragmatism shapes a local version of social learning that in some way departs from the models covered by Friedmann in his seminal book.

The rest of the paper includes three sections. The first section provides a brief narrative of Shanghai's economic restructuring over the past two decades. The second section analyzes Shanghai's trajectory by employing social learning as a theoretical framework and highlights a few unique aspects of Shanghai's experience with this approach. The last section explores the relevance of social learning theory to the broad urban transformations in contemporary China.

Industrial restructuring and creative city-making in Shanghai

As the birth place of China's industrialization, Shanghai established itself as the country's top manufacturing center in the early 20th century and continued to be so till the 1980s. Entering the 1990s, the city's industrial glory gradually became compromised by a combination of obsolescence and policy factors. In order to project the city onto the global stage, Shanghai Municipal Government (SMG) implemented a series of industrial restructuring measures. In the subsequent decade, more than 1,000 industrial firms, mostly state-owned enterprises (SOEs), were either closed down or relocated to the suburbs under government decrees (Shanghai Economic Commission & Shanghai Communist Party History Research Office 2002, p.96). The social cost of restructuring was particularly heavy. By the end of 1998, 1.24 million workers had been laid off from Shanghai's local industrial enterprises (Jiang 2002, pp.68–69).

Many of the inner city industrial areas became urban wastelands and an eyesore for the ambitious and modernization-conscious SMG. The municipal government as well as the old SOE managers who stayed on to manage the remaining industrial assets were desperate to regenerate the affected sites. This was not only because the desolate landscape tarnished the prosperous image of a globalizing city, but also the life and death of a regiment of laid-off workers determined the political stability of the city and possibly the country, given Shanghai's position in the national economic and urban system. The emergence of an arts and cultural production hub in M50, an old abandoned textile factory area on Suzhou Creek, provided an unexpected solution for the municipality and SOE managers.

The transformation of M50 was closely linked to the changes in China's arts world. Before the 1980s, the production of art was expected to cater largely to the political needs of the state. This ideological control became a push factor for some artists to break away from their state employers after the government launched the opening-up and reform policies. In the 1990s, market-based arts institutions such as foreign private galleries began to appear in Shanghai and commercial arts production increasingly became commonplace. At the same time, there was a dramatic rise in prices for contemporary Chinese art in the international marketplace. These acted as strong pull factors for artists to embrace freelancing and independence. However, the conservative state officials' distaste for the new form of "experimental art" pushed the newly independent artists and their enclaves to the margins of society. These changes created a demand for spaces that were suitable for cultural production while remaining safe from state interference. The disused industrial spaces, which were cheap, abundant and often neglected by the state, were a perfect match for such purposes.

Toward the turn of the century, M50 management was desperate to lease out its space to anyone who could afford the rents because the SMG required it to provide monthly subsistence payments, though meager in amount, to over 1,000 laid-off workers. As it happened, M50 became a mix of "chaotic" warehouses and a myriad of small-scale, low-end manufacturing firms in apparel making, printing, food processing and so on. In 2002 and 2003, two groups of artists evicted from two warehouses on Suzhou Creek and West Huaihai Road respectively set up their new studios in M50. At that time, the use of factory space for art production was unheard of by the M50 management and it was not in favor of leasing the spaces to artists for two reasons. First, the site was still defined as "industrial" according to the official land-use maps and hence arts production was in principle an "illegal" use. Second, the types of arts produced, some of which were incomprehensible to the M50 managers while others bore political undertones, were frowned upon by the municipal officials. Allowing such content production in spaces owned by a state-owned company implied ideological contradictions and hence political risks for the property managers. Despite these concerns, the M50 management opened the door to the cultural workers simply because there were not enough "legal" renters from the manufacturing sector to keep the company financially afloat.

The attitude of SMG at that time was quite ambiguous. It kept an eye on the arts production and various types of cultural activities hosted at M50 that might cause trouble to the regime and supported property development that threatened to destroy the fledgling arts enclave at M50. On the other hand, it tacitly allowed the illegal use of industrial spaces for arts production. The SMG's "tolerant" attitude was due to the constraints it faced: if the spaces were kept vacant, the SOE would not generate sufficient revenue to pay the laid-off workers and contain their discontent within manageable levels. In other words, for SMG, the political risk of not allowing arts production at M50 was actually higher than otherwise. Under such circumstances, SMG saw arts production as a makeshift strategy to help Shanghai tide over the restructuring difficulties and, once the situation improved, it could be terminated.

The temporary strategy soon turned out to be an enduring one. The novel use of old spaces with the benefit of retaining the industrial heritage quickly caught the attention of media personnel, urban preservationists, some culture-conscious officials and many others. Agglomerative effects quickly set in. Within a few years M50 rose to a highly desirable place for cultural freelancers and various sorts of creative firms. This change not only put the desolate spaces into productive use again, but also generated at least three other benefits: the removal of low-end manufacturing firms and the "chaotic" image of M50, higher profit for the restructuring SOE and the symbolic transformation of the site into a "cool" tourist hotspot with great potential for city branding. From both the perspective of M50 management and SMG, none of these auspicious outcomes had been anticipated (Zhong 2009).

The accidental relocation of an arts community and the transformation of M50 into an art district made SMG realize that arts, culture and creativity could serve modernization purposes. From that point onwards, more conscious learning and policy-making started to set in. M50's trajectory, which originally was based on a marriage of convenience between cultural production and property development, became abstracted into a model to be promoted by policy-makers. In 2005, the SMG instituted a "creative industry cluster" (CIC) policy that selectively awarded regeneration sites with official CIC titles. At the same time, district governments provided various sorts of preferential treatment to those awarded sites.

Among the official CIC sites, Red Town was a prominent case. It was not an outright replication of M50 although the prototypical model was based on the latter. Unlike M50, the Red Town project was undertaken through public–private partnership (PPP), a new concept that had not yet been tested in China's urban regeneration experiments. The social learning embodied in the Red Town project involved both an application of previously acquired knowledge from M50 and conscious experiment with imported new ideas.

The Red Town site was once a state-owned steel mill (Shanghai No. Ten Steelworks or STS) built at the peak of China's socialist industrialization. The production was relocated to the suburbs in 1997 and came to a complete halt in 2005. In 2004, the SMG decided to build the Shanghai Sculpture Space (SSS) as part of the image lifting strategy before the 2010 Shanghai Expo. Red Town was chosen for this project due to its favorable location and the availability of a huge on-site industrial workshop that was deemed suitable for sculpture display. A partnership between SMG, STS and a private developer called Shanghai Red Town Cultural Development Co. Ltd (RTC) was formed to implement the project.

SMG first rezoned the Red Town site from industrial use to mixed uses of cultural and other public facilities, eliminating the policy contradiction that plagued other sites. It signed a 20-year lease for the big workshop with STS and paid the rent out of the public purse. In addition, it also provided an initial cash subsidy to RTC to jumpstart the SSS. As the developer and operator for Red Town, RTC would be responsible for rehabilitating the workshop into sculpture exhibition spaces and operating the SSS as well as hosting regular cultural events required by SMG. In exchange, the company received use-rights for another part of the STS site at a very low price for commercial development (Zhong 2013).

The physical transformation of Red Town was quite dramatic. After design and rehabilitation, the site's old image association with the socialist proletariat was soon replaced by post-modern cultural hipness and social distinction (Wang 2009). The physical and symbolic transformation brought about by the public-funded SSS spilled over to the commercial part of the project, which was quickly taken up by upscale cultural tenants. The site also became a popular tourist attraction thanks to the arts and cultural events taking place there.

The Red Town project was a big success in the eyes of the three partners. For STS, the project was not only life-saving, but also generated a sizable profit margin. For SMG, the project was a city marketing triumph and a testament to the usefulness of the CIC model and the new PPP-based regeneration strategy. For RTC, the project experience revealed that the city's undervalued industrial property was indeed a gold mine that could be further exploited. A similar project involving the RTC, Baoshan District Government and a reformed state-owned industrial group called "Bund 1919" soon followed on a plot of land even larger than the STS (Zhong 2013).

In the second half of the 2000s, many other sites followed suit in the hope of regenerating former industrial premises. Over 70 such sites were awarded the official CIC title within one-and-a-half years of the program's launch. The CIC title was used by site managers to market and promote their property to potential tenants in the cultural or creative sector. However, most projects did not achieve the same level of physical and economic transformation experienced by Red Town. By 2010, the majority of CIC sites were experiencing high vacancy rates and a significant number of their tenants were not actually in the targeted cultural creative businesses. Despite a few successes, the CIC regeneration model was far from a panacea for the city.

City officials realized that the economic structure of the city had not been transformed fundamentally to generate such a big demand for CIC spaces. Under such circumstances, awarding of official titles for CIC sites would not lead the city quickly into a creative future. In addition, the replication of the same place-making strategies led to the loss of edginess and novelty of urban spaces that further attested to the limit of the model. Faced with these hard truths, SMG temporarily suspended the CIC program. When the awarding was restored some years later, new regulations effectively increased the threshold of obtaining a CIC title which dampened to some extent the entrepreneurial thrust of the governments, SOEs and property developers in adopting the model. Despite this adjustment in CIC policies, Shanghai's practice was considered as pioneering and attracted the attention of policy-makers and development interests from other Chinese cities to adopt and test the model in their own contexts.

Social learning and Shanghai's urban restructuring

Shanghai's experience with urban restructuring and regeneration suggests that social learning underpins the city's spatial transformations. The M50 site provided an important learning experience for the local state officials and the restructuring SOEs' management. For them, the unexpected "happy ending" of M50 offered a positive solution to the convoluted issue of industrial restructuring and site regeneration. The Red Town project reinforced this view and was extended to involve property developers in a PPP to facilitate a planned change. The learning outcome for the local state was the CIC model and relevant regeneration policies which were widely circulated through the media. In addition, the management of numerous old industrial sites also engaged in direct learning by visiting the highly publicized M50 and Red Town sites and exchanging information with their managers. M50 and Red Town managers also frequently appeared in the media and various other public forums to disseminate their knowledge and in so doing also reaped the benefit of additional exposure and marketing of their properties. For property investors, the escalating rents of rehabilitated spaces at exemplary CIC sites taught them to abandon the increasingly saturated traditional market and instead to embrace the city's under-valued industrial spaces.

The Shanghai case demonstrates that social learning can take place in a multitude of situations. First, both successful and failure scenarios offered important insights to learners (Friedmann 1987, p.189). Faced with hard facts, the SMG was open-minded enough to tacitly acknowledge the initial pitfalls of the CIC practice and quickly adjust the norms and policies for subsequent testing. It thus closed the first learning loop while starting a new one in the "double-loop" learning process (ibid., p.185). Second, actors learned from both local and non-local experiences. The idea of industrial heritage conservation, the PPP in urban regeneration and the concept of cultural creative industries all traveled to Shanghai from foreign lands. In this modernization-conscious city, these new ideas were quickly accepted, hybridized and grafted onto the local institutions so that unconventional solutions to post-socialist restructuring could be explored. In this process, the meaning of foreign concepts was modified to suit the local experimental contexts. The local definition of "creative industries" that underpinned Shanghai's CIC policy was a case in point. Third, learning took place far beyond the city boundary. Situated at the forefront of China's urbanization, Shanghai has historically been perceived as an experimenter of new ideas and an innovator for new practices. Indeed, Shanghai's government-backed CIC model drew interests from across the country and had generated a much deeper impact on China's urban built environment than the early social learners could imagine.

Friedmann's social learning thesis provides a valuable theoretical base for examining urban transitions in China. However, as his theorizing was largely based on western experiences, it does not account for a number of nuances in Shanghai's practice. At least three questions about social learning require further articulation.

The first question is whether social learning has to be a conscious effort of learners. Friedmann's conceptualization of social learning revolves around a methodological knowledge acquisition process. In the Shanghai example, particularly its early experience, however, learning took place largely as an outcome of coping with tough situations rather than as a well-conceived and meticulously executed social experiment, although in the later years, things had changed fundamentally. The start of M50 as a prominent art district was "accidental" and the admission of arts studios into M50 by the management was due to a lack of alternatives rather than a perceived rationality behind pursuing an arts strategy. This echoes the pragmatic everyday philosophy exercised by the Chinese people when they are confronted with unfavorable realities (Lu 1999; Bergère 1989). In a survival situation, social learning may take place unconsciously in a style that is less goal-oriented and systematic than what normally would happen in a formal knowledge acquisition scenario. But at the same time, it can also allow whatever is possible (including out-of-the-box "illegal" practices) to emerge and be tested.

Looking longitudinally, the Shanghai case also demonstrates a transition of the social learning model from an unconscious and survival-based type to a deliberate and planned one. And in this process, actors, particularly the local government officials, not only learned how to solve the regeneration problems, but also became more proficient in social learning, a skill or capacity that must be learned and acquired in practice.

The second question about social learning concerns the actors involved in the process. Friedmann (1987) mentions that learners can be organizational leaders (Organizational Development Theory), experts (Dewey and Dunn), local inhabitants (Mumford) and the peasant masses (Mao). The Shanghai case indicates that social learners were largely the elites of the city, including government officials, SOE managers and property developers. Community members, including the laid-off workers and those living near the regeneration sites, were never part of the learning community. For social learners, empirical knowledge could enable them to uncover the opportunities embedded in the restructuring crisis and hence benefit from such knowledge. This was clearly true for property investors and SOE managers. For the state, its power was embodied in setting the learning agenda to serve the purpose of regime stability. As argued by Lin (2002), state involvement in China's urban transformations is not just motivated by entrepreneurialism, but also driven by bottom-line political concerns. It is clear that social learning in Shanghai largely took place in the domain of economic development and physical makeover, while searching for a more participative and inclusive model never attracted policy attention. Therefore, social learning under such a context serves as a mechanism of reinforcing the existing power structure and enlarging social inequalities.

The third question about social learning is what institutional features are conducive to learning. Friedmann suggests that democratic, non-hierarchical and open political systems are better suited for this purpose. Imbued with *Haipai* culture that celebrates openness, liberal attitude, risk-taking and innovation (Lu 1999; Gamble 2003), Shanghai does have a favorable institutional foundation for engaging in social learning compared with other Chinese cities. However, the Shanghai case also suggests that learning could take place in a non-democratic and hierarchical situation, despite the uneven distribution of learning opportunities. Here I argue that the flexibility of the Chinese institutional system is a key for actors to undertake social learning in an authoritarian context. Flexibility means that rules can be bent by social actors in particular circumstances, that stray behaviors can be tolerated to a certain extent by the authority, and that temporary policies contradicting existing rules can be passed to allow the testing of a novel idea. However, China's political reality also implies that flexibility and tolerance only exist in domains such as economic development and physical regeneration.

Social learning and China's urban transformation

Much existing China study literature explains the country's drastic urban transformations by referring to concepts of property rights and rent gaps (Zhu 2002; Tian 2008), pro-growth coalitions and urban regimes (Yang & Chang 2007; Zhang 2002), urban entrepreneurialism (Duckett 1998; Zheng 2011) and marketization and post-socialism (Wu 1997; Wu & Yeh 2007). Rarely has social learning theory entered the radar of China study researchers. Here I suggest that social learning theory is a useful tool for analyzing contemporary Chinese cities because of its alignment with the Chinese cultural and institutional features, the difficulty of managing unprecedented changes in the country and the latest policy reorientation toward renewing older urban areas.

As Friedmann (1987) points out, social learning is conservative as social agents adopting this tradition do not attempt to transform the system; rather, they adapt their behaviors to suit the institutional environment or tinker with the old system in an incremental manner. This conservatism fits two social realities in China: the traditional distaste for "chaos" (*luan*) inherited from Confucian philosophy and the state's monopolistic control of political power.

Contemporary China is unique in the sense that the pace, scale, degree and extent of urban changes are unprecedented. Social actors in China are confronted with constantly emerging new situations, overwhelming details of local specificities and the pressure to give quick responses; therefore, synoptic analysis before action is often not a possibility. The attractiveness of the social learning paradigm is that actions do not have to be taken before a full or even good understanding of emerging issues is gained. Rather, social actors acquire and accumulate knowledge from practice within context and over time, and this gives social learners the wisdom and capacities to address their extremely complex local situations in a gradualist and manageable manner.

Today China is moving toward a "new urbanization" trajectory. The country's New Urbanization Plan (2014–2020) calls for a reorientation of development from periurban greenfield zones to existing built-up areas. While in the past, planners could easily treat greenfield sites as blank slates and accomplish their work in their offices, this becomes virtually impossible in old urban areas where land rights are better institutionalized and incumbent land users are much more powerful than their periurban counterparts. This means future planning tasks will be more political and communicative in nature and the knowledge required to regenerate cities will be open-ended and contextual. This "practical turn" in planning suggests a larger and more diverse learning community that includes all stakeholders in urban regeneration. In this sense, a convergence of China's social learning model toward Friedmann's theoretical articulation can be discerned.

References

Bergère, MC 1989, *The Golden Age of the Chinese Bourgeoisie 1911–1937*, Cambridge University Press, Cambridge, UK and New York.

Duckett, J 1998, *The Entrepreneurial State in China: Real Estate and Commerce Development in the Reform Era Tianjin*, Routledge, London.

Friedmann, J 1987, *Planning in the Public Domain: From Knowledge to Action*, Princeton University Press, Princeton, N.J.

Friedmann, J 2008, "The use of planning theory: a bibliographic essay", *Journal of Planning Education and Research*, 28(2): 247–257.

Gamble, J 2003, *Shanghai in Transition: Changing Perspectives and Social Contours of a Chinese Metropolis*, Routledge Curzon, London and New York.

Jiang, Y 2002, *Tansuo yu Shijian: Shanghai Gongye Gaige yu Fazhan Shijian* [Exploration and trajectory: Shanghai's industrial reform and development], Shanghai People's Press, Shanghai (in Chinese).

Lin, GCS 2002, "The growth and structural change of Chinese cities: a contextual and geographic analysis", *Cities*, 19(5): 299–316.

Lu, H 1999, "Becoming urban: mendicancy and vagrants in modern Shanghai", *Journal of Social History*, 33(1): 7–36.

New National Urbanization Plan (2014–2020) 2014. Available at: <http://www.gov.cn/zhengce/2014-03/16/content_2640075.htm> (in Chinese) [20 September 2016].

Shanghai Economic Commission & Shanghai Communist Party History Research Office 2002, *Shanghai Gongye Jiegou Tiaozheng* [Industrial restructuring of Shanghai], Shanghai People's Press, Shanghai (in Chinese).

Shih, CY 1995, *State and Society in China's Political Economy: The Cultural Dynamics of Socialist Reform*, Lynne Rienner Publishers, Inc., Boulder, C.O.

Tian, L 2008, "The chengzhongcun land market in China: Boon or bane? – A perspective of property rights", *International Journal of Urban and Regional Research*, 32(2): 282–304.

Wang, J 2009, "'Art in capital': shaping distinctiveness in culture-led urban regeneration project in Red Town, Shanghai", *Cities*, 26: 318–330.

Wu, F 1997, "Urban restructuring in China's emerging market economy: towards a framework of analysis", *International Journal of Urban and Regional Research*, 21(4): 640–663.

Wu, F & Yeh, AGO 2007, *Urban Development in Post-reform China: State, Market and Space*, Routledge, Abingdon and New York.

Yang, YR & Chang, C 2007, "An urban regeneration regime in China: a case study of urban redevelopment in Shanghai's Taipingqiao Area", *Urban Studies*, 44(9): 1809–1826.

Zhang, T 2002, "Urban development and a socialist pro-growth coalition in Shanghai", *Urban Affairs Review*, 37(4): 475–499.

Zheng, J 2011, "'Creative industry clusters' and the 'entrepreneurial city' of Shanghai", *Urban Studies*. DOI: 10.1177/0042098011399593 [20 Feb 2014].

Zhong, S 2009, "From fabrics to fine arts: urban restructuring and the formation of an art district in Shanghai", *Critical Planning*, 16: 118–137.

Zhong, S 2013, "The neoliberal turn: 'culture-led' urban regeneration in Shanghai" in *The Routledge Companion to Urban Regeneration*, eds ME Leary & J McCarthy, Routledge, London and New York, pp. 495–504.

Zhu, J 2002, "Urban development under ambiguous property rights: a case of China's transition economy", *International Journal of Urban and Regional Research*, 26(1): 41–57.

26 From the Xinhai Revolution to the Umbrella Movement

Insurgent citizenship, radical planning and Chinese culture in the Hong Kong SAR

Mee Kam Ng

Introduction: my first encounter with the concept of 'radical planning'

When I was a PhD student at UCLA in the late 1980s, an assignment was to critique the Radical Planning paradigm in John Friedmann's book *Planning in the Public Domain: From Knowledge to Action*. To Friedmann, an alternative mode of planning is needed to resolve the ineffectiveness of planning as societal guidance, related to the then unfolding crisis of industrial capitalism in the West. His idea of radical planning is to change 'existing relations of power, whether exercised by the state or global corporations' (Friedmann 2011, p.61). Radical planning is to engender 'social transformation' through the mediation of transformative theory and radical practice (2011, p.11). The ultimate aim of radical planning is 'the structural transformation of industrial capitalism toward the self-production of life, the recovery of political community and the achievement of collective self-reliance in the context of common global concerns' (2011, p.81). Although I no longer have a copy of my assignment, based on the notes I penned in the book I think I raised the following questions on Friedmann's thesis: Is industrial capitalism in crisis? Is mainstream planning (state-led societal guidance) in crisis? How to reconcile public interest with human nature especially when not everyone is kind-hearted and selfless? In the course of restructuring the household as an economy and a political community, how can we differentiate love from control, care from domination? If politics is brought to the household as a daily agenda – how will our lives be affected? Shouldn't our home be a place of refuge from harsh reality? What if some people simply do not want to be involved in politics? How can we know that people living with 'the self-production of life' will lead a happier life? Is capitalism so bad that it has to be discontinued? Could it be perfected?

In retrospect, my responses reflected very much my cultural roots as a Chinese influenced on a daily basis by unspoken Confucian values as well as my upbringing in a colonial capitalist city praised by many as a model of a free market economy. This probably explains why, while I was fascinated by the goal of radical planning to have a 'new orientation of livelihood: of practical, self-managing, self-renewing societies, in which people care first for each other, in a living world' (Williams 1983, p.267 cited in Friedmann 1987, p.342), I had doubts about 'how to get there'.

In what follows, I first discuss why insurgent citizenship and radical planning are rather alien concepts in the Chinese Confucian culture. I then argue that this deep-rooted culture, among others, helps explain why even with the 1911 Xinhai Revolution that ended the dynastic rule in China and the very many social movements in Hong Kong including the most recent 2014 'Umbrella Movement',[1] the discourse seldom touches on the need to transform fundamental social relationships. Nevertheless, traditional Confucian culture carries a vision of the 'Grand Union' or the 'Great Harmony' that is surprisingly similar to the vision of radical planning – the building of a good society for human flourishing. However, it seems that Chinese intellectuals take a more intricate pathway towards this ideal. My essay concludes by advocating radical planning the Chinese way.

Insurgent citizenship, radical planning and Chinese culture

Radical planning and insurgent urbanism to counteract crisis-ridden capitalism

Friedmann's insight of modelling planning as 'the relationship between knowledge and action' took place in the late 1960s (2011, p.134). Seeing the failure of the state in satisfying 'the legitimate needs of the people' and identifying the 'free, oligopolistic markets' as the culprits, Friedmann calls for the 're-centering of political power and civil society, mobilizing from below the countervailing actions of citizens, and recovering the energies for a political community that will transform both the state and corporate economy from within' (1987, pp.312–4). This transformative theory would inform radical practices to redistribute resources to empower citizens, such as reclaiming streets for people and for the development of solidarity or moral economy (Friedmann 2011).

One form of radical practice is what Holston calls 'insurgent urbanism', a spatial manifestation of 'insurgent citizenship' (Holston 1995, p.48 cited in Friedmann 2011, p.121). Insurgent citizenship, Holston argues, 'works against the modernist absorption of citizenship' in state-building, asserting the heterogeneous presence of multiple (and sometimes conflicting) actors with different 'kinds of practices and narratives about belonging to and participating in society', challenging 'fundamental social relations' (1995, p.48). It is a struggle over what it means to be a citizen (1995, p.47). Similarly, Leonie Sandercock (1998 cited in Friedmann 2011, p.221) suggests that 'insurgencies can result from "a thousand tiny empowerments" rather than from revolutionary adventures'. To Friedmann, radical planning helps create spaces for 'insurgent citizenship' to exert the exigency to recognise pluralistic definitions of citizenship to highlight the inadequacies of 'those formal spaces that often exclude their needs and priorities' (Miraftab & Wills 2005, p.201).

According to Friedmann, radical planners should critically analyse the existing reality ('what is so wrong and offensive that it justifies actions to restructure the system?'), mobilise communities to rectify the situation, assist in formulating appropriate strategies of struggle, refining the technical details of transformative solutions, 'facilitating social learning with engaged radical practice', mediating between the mobilised community and the state, helping to boost community participation, 'enhancing the group's course of action through new understandings and becoming personally involved in transformative practice' (1987, pp.303–7; 2011, p.76). Sandercock (1998, pp.158–9) stresses the importance of popular education, social learning through 'talk, dialogue, persuasion and negotiation' and a strong sense of community in building cities that meet the needs of pluralistic citizens.

Reflecting on the questions that I raised at UCLA

I have to confess that it took me quite some time to understand the practice of radical planning. And it was only when I seriously revisited my cultural roots as a Chinese and my life experiences in a colonial market economy that I started to appreciate why I raised all those questions as a response to Friedmann's radical planning paradigm.

A case in point is about whether capitalism is in crisis. In the late 1980s, the once closed and centrally planned economy of China's transition to a socialist market economy was in many aspects modelled on the capitalist practices of Hong Kong, including the leasing of land use rights to raise revenue for infrastructure development. Instead of seeing capitalism in crisis, many Chinese would have, at the time, perceived the capitalist economy and market institutions as the saving grace of a then politically and economically demoralised nation. As a citizen of Hong Kong and a British colonial subject at that time, I did not consider capitalism to be in crisis – at least not in East Asia.

There is, however, a deeper cultural dimension to my reaction to Friedmann's radical planning paradigm – I found it rather difficult to comprehend the oppositional relationships between the state and the people. The Chinese socio-political order is very often considered as the extension of the familial model. There is the belief that a good society once existed in the past and in a good society there should be union of human beings and everything in nature, nourished by the same 'energy of life' (*qi*, 氣) (Nathan 1993, p.926; Yu 1987, p.22). It is a culture that highlights the importance of human relationships: 'affection between father and son; righteous conduct between ruler and subject; distinction between husband and wife; proper order between the old and the young; and trust between friends', and within the family 'the father is righteous and protective; the mother is loving and caring; the elder brother is fraternal; the younger brother is respectful; and the son is filial' (Wang 1991, p.172). However, it is 'duties' rather than citizen 'rights' that are emphasised in these relationships. In fact, there is no equivalent word for 'rights' in classical Chinese (1991, p.167). Two particular duties are highlighted: loyalty to the ruler and filial piety to one's parents (1991, p.169). In return, 'subjects had the *right* to expect their ruler to perform their duty and be benevolent, enlightened, righteous and to observe the proper rites' (1991, p.170, my emphasis). In other words, 'the ruler's *right* to loyalty depended on his fulfilling his own duties of being filial to his parents and kindly towards his people' (1991, p.171, my emphasis).

In theory, the quest for harmonious human–nature and interpersonal relationships should inspire the Chinese to be less materialistic and calculating, and more intuitive and sentimental, whether at home or in society (Liang 2015, and p.211). This perhaps explains why I was overwhelmed by the need to 'liberate' households as a political community in radical planning (Friedmann 1987). The Confucian ideal has an alternative route to save a fallen world.

Appeal to the 'Way' for better or worse

In Chinese culture, the gap between theory and practice, ideal and reality or 'the transcendental and real worlds is not that distinguishable' because it is believed that through spiritual cultivation and self-discipline, a moral force – the 'Way' (*dao*, 道) – the origin of values from heaven, can directly shine on people's everyday lives (Yu 1987, pp.6–10). Indeed, Chinese culture sees each person as an end, that is, every person has intrinsic moral value, 'all are saints in the street' (Yu 1987, p.36) and considers 'humanity the most valuable in heaven and earth' (Yu 2007, p.306). The culture sees the person as an integrated whole with opposing qualities such as rationality, emotion, will and lust extending outward to integrate with everything in nature and reaching inward to accomplish human relationships (Yu 1987, p.37). Hence, the most important thing is to encourage everyone to cultivate his/her heart to harmonise with the social and cosmic order in order to reach a higher moral ground (1987, pp.38–9). Hence, the Chinese culture emphasises 'internal transcendence' and the importance of 'benevolence' (morality and emotion cultivated in a person) rather than 'justice' (1987, p.28).

While there is no concept of radical planning in Chinese culture, traditionally, a Chinese intellectual is expected to use the 'Way' to save, manage and change the world (Yu 2007). He should debate about truths and practise speaking truth to power as a natural calling (2007, p.184). In fact, historically, the remonstration system had been institutionalised for intellectuals to exercise their 'objection or dissent' functions in the state apparatus. And at the same time, a Chinese intellectual should use the 'Way' to critique a wayward world. When a functioning system was threatened, 'the intellectual fought loyally on its behalf' (Wang 1991, p.294). 'If the system was corrupt and degenerated, he criticised it boldly and worked hard to remedy it. If the system rejected him, he would play his role outside, by various forms of protest' (1991, p.294). Or he would go to the community and educate the moral development of the common people, encouraging them 'to act virtuously in the spirit of harmony, righteousness, benevolence and deference' (Chan 2014, p.11). Hence, the Chinese 'Way' is not to mobilise people to fight for their rights. Rather, it is to appeal to the cultivation of their hearts to nurture benevolence and righteousness. And to the Confucian scholar, 'if the Way is destined not to prevail, there is nothing human can do' (2014, p.14). Although 'heaven' does sanction 'rebellions' against failed rulers to take back the heavenly mandate from a sinful regime (Gregor 1981; Wang 1991), it is seen as a God-sent mission rather than citizens' right to revolution.

In other words, the route to a good society is through 'moral cultivation by regulating unhealthy desires and refining feelings and attitudes' as well as regulating society by 'the basic principles of human relationships and roles' to help achieve a harmonious and ethical society, which is the goal of Confucian governance (Chan 2014, p.2). And it is the duty of the governing party to guarantee the livelihood of the people. 'Without that assurance how could they [the people] "cultivate propriety and righteousness"?' (Mencius, para.22 cited in Gregor 1981, p.58). And 'the fulfilment of man's moral obligation to himself could only be accomplished in a network of mutual obligation with those with whom he shared love, affection, respect and benevolence' (1981, p.64).

When the 'Grand Way' or the 'Great Harmony' was pursued, human virtues flourished, individuals of talent, virtue and ability ruled, trusting and caring social relationships grew, public and common spirit thrived, people 'did not treat only their own parents as parents, nor treat only their own sons as sons' (Chan 2014, pp.2, 6). The ruling entity would 'distribute sufficient land for each household to maintain a decent living standard; educate them about the five basic social relationships; consult their opinions in important matters; impose light taxes; prevent market monopoly and ensure the sustainability of common-pool resources' (2014, pp.10–11). This public-spirit-centred vision of a good society is surprisingly similar to the projected outcome of radical planning.

These deep-seated cultural values probably help explain why the 'rights' discourse has yet to be rooted in the Chinese community of Hong Kong even though insurgent activities have been an important trait of the former British colony. Rather than exerting their rights to be recognised as pluralistic citizens, insurgent activities in the Chinese culture serve to remind the government or the state of their duty to be benevolent, enlightened and righteous.

From the Xinhai Revolution to the Umbrella Movement: a hundred years of insurgent activities

The liberal British colonial government and the then emerging Chinese economic interests in Hong Kong had been instrumental in instigating the Xinhai

Revolution that eventually overthrew the corrupt and high-handed Qing Dynasty in 1911 and established the Republic of China (Fok 2011). Dr Sun Yat-sen had studied in Hong Kong since he was 17 years old and had been thoroughly impressed by the neat and tidy cityscape, high sanitary standards and low corruption practices under the British colonial rule. In a speech at the University of Hong Kong in 1923, Sun admitted that his revolutionary thoughts originated from reflecting on the order and efficiency of the administration in Hong Kong. And the Xinhai Revolution was sustained by the continuous and generous support of Chinese businessmen in the colony (ibid.). However, Sun's revolutionary thoughts were solidly rooted in Confucianism. To Sun, individuals are a constituent part of 'an organic and historic whole', thrusting into 'a community having a history, a tradition and a configuration of problems' within which they work out their destiny (Gregor 1981, p.63). Sun contended that '[i]f we want to recover our national spirit, we must reawaken our long-possessed moral values found in the *Great Learning*..."study the world to gain knowledge, with sincerity and a pure heart, perfect oneself, nourish a happy family, govern a country to promote world peace"' (Sun 2011, p.247, my translation). In other words, the overthrowing of the Qing Dynasty did not negate the need to cultivate one's heart to become virtuous as the first step towards the good society.

Colonial Hong Kong had been 'punctuated by a long list of socio-political movements, communal mobilization, economic sanctions, collective class actions...and patriotic resistance' such as workers' strike-boycott against the British in the Second Opium War (1856–60), the 1884 anti-French riots, anti-Japanese boycotts during the 1894–95 Sino-Japanese War, 1894 social unrest over sanitary measures imposed to control the bubonic plague, the 1904–5 boycott protesting against America's exclusion of Chinese immigrants, the 1911 Xinhai Revolution, the 1912–13 Tramway Boycott for the right to use mainland coins, the anti-imperialist demonstrations in the 1919 May Fourth Movement, the 1922 Seamen's Strike for a wage hike and the 16-month (June 1925 to October 1926) Guangzhou-Hong Kong general strike-boycott, and patriotic campaigns to aid China's War of Resistance against Japan (1937–41) (Chan 2004, pp.xix–xxi).

According to Lam (2004, p.59), Cheung and Louie (1991, p.10), Lau and Wan (1997, p.6) and Wan and Wong (2005, p.6), from 1949 to 2002, a total of 8,223 social conflicts took place in Hong Kong, an average of 155 conflicts per year. Most of these conflicts were of short duration and involved primarily the local state, though since 1989 an increasing number of protests were directed towards the distant Central Government. According to police figures, from 2005 to 2014, 49,508 public meetings and processions took place in the city. In other words, there were around 13.6 public events or processions per day in the last 10 years. Lam (2004, p.229) argues that there has been a paradoxical co-existence of political activism and a culture of de-politicisation such as stressing the importance of stability and prosperity, labelling social activists as troublemakers and a tendency for political actors to suppress their political behaviour in a culture highly sensitive to politics. In addition to these factors, I would like to suggest that the deep-rooted unspoken Confucian culture may also account for the high level of social activism on one hand and relative political stability and peace on the other. The 79-day Umbrella Movement (a version of the 'occupy' movement in Hong Kong) is a case in point.

While the Movement was no doubt an urban insurgent event, its aim was not to exert pluralistic citizenship nor to challenge 'fundamental social relations' (Holston 1995). The trio (two professors and one pastor) who initiated the Occupy Central with Love and Peace (OCLP) had acted like typical Chinese intellectuals in the Movement. In their *Manifesto on OCLP*, they stated that the campaign aimed 'to strive for the election of the Chief Executive by universal and equal suffrage in 2017'. The initiators hoped that through society-wide dialogue and deliberation, a legitimate democratic proposal on the election of the Chief Executive would be formulated for the consideration of the Central Government. And if the Central Government ignored the proposal and suggested an undemocratic election method, civil disobedience acts would follow. Unfortunately, on 31 August 2014, the Standing Committee of the National People's Congress in China announced a framework whereby the Chief Executive candidacy would require over 50 per cent endorsement of a 1,200-member Nominating Committee believed to be basically biased towards corporate and mainland interests. After a week of a campaign of class boycott, students stormed the Civic Square in the Central Government Offices on 26 September and then the trio announced the start of OCLP in the small hours of 28 September 2014.

The use of tear gas by the police to disperse the protestors aroused public anger, leading to spontaneous crowds occupying major thoroughfares in Central (Admiralty), Mongkok and Causeway Bay. The Movement lasted 79 days and then the originally peaceful movement turned into bloody conflicts among the pro- and anti-OCLP camps. After the police applied escalated force on the protestors, the trio decided to turn themselves in to the police on 3 December 2014. Failing to persuade the Central Government to grant universal and equal suffrage to Hong Kongers, they called for a redirection of the movement towards the community, promoting democratic education and developing a social charter to reclaim spaces for the people. Although the Umbrella Movement did not materialise into anything concrete, those who had participated in one way or another in the OCLP were touched by all the unusual scenes in economics- and efficiency-first Hong Kong: the colourful tents in 'Admiralty Village'; the plurality and variety of all kinds of art forms; a mobile democracy school; make-shift library and study spaces; hearty chats among strangers; sharing of resources, knowledge and thoughts; co-management of space, wastes and materials donated by others; reciprocity and mutual care… Without knowing it, those who had occupied the major thoroughfares of the city had had a taste of the 'Grand Way' or the 'Great Harmony'! The author witnessed the tear gas moments and many cried for the loss of their city to a heartless Government. Although the protestors were fighting for universal and equal suffrage the final goal was to make Hong Kong a better place. The last sentence in the Open Letter that the trio wrote before they turned themselves in to the police was: 'Grief over my Hong Kong! God bless my city!' (see footnote 3). Like many Chinese intellectuals in history, the trio were willing to sacrifice their privileged position and comfort and face possible persecution for the city. The moral force they conveyed was one of the most important factors that drew so many people to the streets to fight for the future of Hong Kong.

Radical planning and insurgent citizenship the Chinese 'Way'?

The Chinese route to the good society does not focus on transforming power relationships. Rather, it starts with the 'Way', self-cultivation of the heart so that we can unify with nature and with one another, to recognise humanity as the most valuable quality in heaven and Earth. Through internal transcendence, we become benevolent and righteous, having the strength and will to devote selflessly to the well-being of others. For Chinese radical planners, the 'Way' is to remonstrate with those in power and to educate the common folks not only about tactics and strategies of socio-economic transformation, but also about the importance of identifying necessary actions that will bring about human flourishing and virtuous relationships. Chinese radical planners, in the grand tradition of Chinese intellectuals, always appeal to people's self-cultivation of their hearts to appreciate their moral duties to realise the rights of others as the route to the 'Great Harmony'. This does not mean that they will shy away from insurgent activities. On the contrary, insurgent activities may be seen as heaven-sanctioned actions to challenge or oust a sinful regime. Yet the purpose is to return to the foundation of a good society – to allow people to return to the cultivation of their hearts to be virtuous and righteous. This may not sound particularly radical but this is consistent with the ideal spirit that so often characterises John Friedmann's thoughts. As he argues, a good life is 'rather about the quality of human relationships' (1998, p.20).

Notes

1 The 'Umbrella Movement' was a social resistance movement to protest against the undemocratic decision framework made by the Standing Committee of the National People's Congress (SCNPC) on the election of Hong Kong's Chief Executive on 31 August 2014. According to the Basic Law, the mini-constitution of Hong Kong, a nomination committee should nominate democratically Chief Executive candidates who will then be elected by universal suffrage. However, the SCNPC determines that a 'broadly representative nominating committee' will 'democratically' nominate two to three candidates for the office of the Chief Executive (each requires support from more than half of the members) before they can be selected by universal suffrage. It was called the 'Umbrella Movement' because people used the umbrellas to protect themselves from pepper spray and tear gas applied by the police.

References

Chan, J 2014, *Confucian Perfectionism: A Political Philosophy for Modern Times*, Princeton University Press, The Princeton China Series, Princeton, N.J.

Chan, MK 2004, 'Foreword' in *Understanding the Political Culture of Hong Kong: The Paradox of Activism and Depoliticization*, ed. WM Lam, M.E. Sharpe, Armonk, New York.

Cheung, PL & Louie, KS 1991, *Social Conflicts in Hong Kong, 1975–1986: Trends and Implications*, Hong Kong Institute of Asia Pacific Studies, The Chinese University of Hong Kong, Hong Kong.

Fok, KC 2011, *Xinhai Revolution in the Records of Hong Kong and Macau*, Commercial Press, Hong Kong (in Chinese).

Friedmann, J 1987, *Planning in the Public Domain: From Knowledge to Action*, Princeton University Press, Princeton, N.J.

Friedmann, J 1998, 'The new political economy of planning: the rise of civil society' in *Cities for Citizens: Planning and the Rise of Civil Society in a Global Age*, eds M Douglass & J Friedmann, John Wiley & Sons, Chichester, pp. 19–35.

Friedmann, J 2011, *Insurgencies: Essays in Planning Theory*, Routledge, London.

Gregor, AJ 1981, 'Confucianism and the political thought of Sun Yat-Sen', *Philosophy East and West*, 31(1): 55–70.

Holston, J 1995, 'Spaces of insurgent citizenship' in *Making the Invisible Visible: New Historiographies for Planning, Planning Theory*, ed. L Sandercock, Franco Angeli, Milan, pp. 37–56.

Hong Kong Police Force, Public Order Event Statistics, n.d. Available from: <http://www.police.gov.hk/ppp_en/09_statistics/poes.html> [2 December 2015].

Lam, WM 2004, *Understanding the Political Culture of Hong Kong: The Paradox of Activism and Depoliticization*, M.E. Sharpe, Armonk, New York.

Lau, SK & Wan, PS 1997, *Social Conflicts in Hong Kong, 1987–1995*, Hong Kong Institute of Asia Pacific Studies, The Chinese University of Hong Kong, Hong Kong.

Liang, SM 2015, *East and West Culture and their Philosophy*, People's Press, Shanghai (in Chinese).

Manifesto on Occupy Central with Love and Peace, n.d. Available from: <http://oclp.hk/index.php?route=occupy/book_detail&book_id=11> [6 August 2016].

Miraftab, F & Wills, S 2005, 'Insurgency and spaces of active citizenship: the story of Western Cape anti-eviction campaign in South Africa', *Journal of Planning Education and Research*, 25: 200–217.

Nathan, AJ 1993, 'Is Chinese culture distinctive? – A review article', *The Journal of Asian Studies*, 52(4): 923–936.

Occupy Central Trio's Letter to the Hong Kong People, 2014. Available from: <http://oclp.hk/index.php?route=occupy/eng_detail&eng_id=61> [20 September 2016].

Sandercock, L 1998, *Towards Cosmopolis: Planning for Multicultural Cities*, John Wiley, New York.

Sun, YS 2011, *Complete Collection of Sun Yat-sen Volume 9*, Academy of Social Science, Beijing (in Chinese).

The Works of Mencius, in the Four Books, n.d., trans. J Legge, Culture Book, Taipei.

Wan, PS & Wong, T 2005, *Social Conflicts in Hong Kong, 1996–2002*, Hong Kong Institute of Asian Pacific Studies, The Chinese University of Hong Kong, Hong Kong.

Wang, GW 1991, *The Chineseness of China*, Oxford University Press, Hong Kong.
Williams, R 1983, *Year 2000*, Pantheon, New York.
Yu, YS 1987, *A Modern Interpretation of Chinese Traditional Thoughts*, Joint Economics Press, Taipei (in Chinese).
Yu, YS 2007, *Intellectuals and Chinese Cultural Values*, Time Newspaper Press, Taipei (in Chinese).

Postscript

John Friedmann

I am deeply honored by the many essays appearing in this volume. I have always been surprised how the written words we send out into the world are received by potential readers. Often, of course, there is no response at all. At other times, perhaps years later, the author may receive an e-mail from a former student about how this or that word of hers had moved him and changed his life. And always, of course, the author rejoices when by chance she discovers her name attached to a footnote in an academic journal or reads the occasional faint praise in a review by an esteemed colleague. Rarely, however, do we see how our work has actually borne fruit by contributing to the research of our colleagues, thus generating a whole new body of work. This has been my fortune a couple of times throughout my long life, most recently with my essays on the world city hypothesis in the 1980s and now again, with the rich variety of reflections on my work between the covers of this book.

Thank you all!

In this brief response I hope to accomplish two things. In the first part, I will briefly recount part of my history as it relates to planning and so establish my positionality within our field. In the longer second part, I will respond to some of the essays published here and how they address urgent issues for our profession under the following headings: social values; communicative action planning; the variety of planning cultures; civil society, territory, and self-empowerment; re/engaging the state; and regionalism. I leave this response without conclusion, because our collective work will never be done, and the present moment is but a marker in the flow of time.

I

In 1955, I was one of the first students in the United States to receive the doctor of philosophy degree in planning. Mel Branch, who taught us basic elements of physical planning, had received his PhD from the Graduate School of Design at Harvard, but my degree from the University of Chicago was an interdisciplinary degree in the social sciences. The Program for Education and Research in Planning had been founded in 1946 by Rexford Guy

Tugwell, the former Governor of Puerto Rico who, a few years later, was succeeded as head of the program by Harvey S. Perloff, who was the supervisor of my dissertation and would become a good friend.

A social science-based planning was something unheard of at the time and called for reflection on the question of what is planning. We had little to go on in our search for an answer. Clearly, planning would have to be something more than an abiding concern with land use or urban design. To explore a foundation for a social science-based planning, Tugwell had urged Edward Banfield, a new faculty member still working on his doctorate in political science, to convene what turned out to be the first-ever seminar on planning theory, where we debated authors such as Karl Mannheim, Herbert Simon, and Friedrich Hayek. A decade later, Perloff was to publish his own response to the question of what is planning, in an influential text entitled *Education for Planning: City, State, and Regional* (Perloff 1957). In this early post-war period, the Chicago experiment would serve as a model for the rapidly expanding academic field of planning throughout the country.

I have continued to wrestle with the concept of "planning" throughout my life—transactive, knowledge/action, insurgencies—but it was like chasing a will-o'-wisp: no sooner did I think I had it nailed, than other versions appeared, and there were never even the beginnings of a consensus about the nature of our field and its corresponding theories. And so the planning academy accepted the inevitable by embracing radical uncertainty about its own identity. Planning schools would be professional schools that for the most part adopted the Perloff model of the planner as a generalist with a specialty tacked on rather than constituting an academic discipline like any other, with a body of theory and widely accepted foundational works. Instead, the quality of planning education would be guaranteed by an accrediting body that enforced minimum curricular standards. And that is where matters have been left.

But inevitably, planning as a field of studies and practice continued to evolve. A significant change occurred in the mid-1970s as the neoliberal revolution swept over the land and led to planners' new role as advocates of marginalized populations in the nation's large cities, working closely with communities and local citizens. Henceforward, social justice concerns would predominate. Two decades later, environmentalism would be incorporated into the curriculum along with the new language of sustainability and resilience. Today, planning education reflects the general concerns of citizens in our increasingly multi-cultural cities, and practice has become less state-centered, as many of our graduates choose to define their careers by working for community-based organizations and other not-for-profit organizations.

Planning has also evolved institutionally, as associations of planning schools started to appear on all the continents. The first World Congress of Planning Schools was held in Shanghai in 2001, with the fourth congress scheduled to meet in Rio de Janeiro later this year. Both planning practice and education thus appear to be thriving even though we continue to disagree on a theoretically grounded answer to the question of "what is planning?"

Vive la différence!

I have written of my own intellectual journey elsewhere, and will not repeat it here (Friedmann forthcoming). Let me simply say that I have spent much of my professional career as a regional development planner overseas. I began in Latin America (Brazil, Venezuela, Chile), spent two years with the US Operations Mission in South Korea, collaborated for several years with the United Nations Centre for Regional Development in Nagoya, Japan, and made occasional visits to Nigeria, Mozambique, and South Africa. All of these experiences have left their mark. The last 15 years, as an honorary professor in the School of Community and Regional Planning at the University of British Columbia, I have worked intensively on questions of urbanization in the People's Republic of China and as an Honorary Foreign Advisor to the China Academy of Urban Planning and Design.

II

In this second part of my brief "response," I will focus on what I perceive to be some urgent issues which we confront as innovative and progressive planners and that are touched upon in many of the contributions to this volume.

Social values. In an increasingly materialistic world, progressive planners need to search for and articulate social values that will guide their interventions. As I perceive our profession today, especially in North America, planners are increasingly freed from bureaucratic constraints and can become actors in their own right: to choose where and when to intervene as consultants, as members of community organizations, as participants in non-governmental organizations, or as senior planners in municipal and state/provincial governments. Planners can also choose to become political actors. It is not surprising therefore that three of the writings frequently cited in the chapters of this volume are *The Good Society* (1979), *Empowerment: The Politics of Alternative Development* (1992), and "The Good City" (2000), all three of which were attempts to set out some general principles for a radical or progressive planning beyond social justice and environmental stewardship. Some of the authors in these pages have not only cited these works but have critically engaged with them, among them Libby Porter, Mike Douglass, Aftab Erfan, and Tanja Winkler.

Perhaps I should say a few words here about my own value orientation, and how I came to it. With the advent of neo-liberalism by the mid-1970s, we were all being challenged to define our personal position vis-à-vis the new free enterprise economics that claimed unconstrained market calculation as the only valid framework for thinking about human life. I strained to find a language that could not be readily reduced to the all-embracing logic of the market. And so I happened upon the key value expression I called *human flourishing*; the basic building block of human society as the *household* rather than the individual; the *production of life and livelihood* rather than consumption; *interpersonal dialogue* rather than abstract communication; equal status for *use value* relative to exchange value; and *dis/empowerment* as an appropriate language to talk about poverty. Carefully defined, these terms have helped me to argue for new solutions to social problems which, for the most part, are caused by the economic logic globally invoked by private corporations and the state. All told, they are terms, as Libby Porter argues, that are invested with hope. But in the end, I remain skeptical and question whether they are sufficient to chart a course towards another future than the one on which we are embarked.

Communicative action planning. All planning practice takes place in both space and time. Traditionally, planners have taken the long view, but with increasing complexity, the general speed-up of events in "liquid" times (Bauman 2007) and the radical uncertainty about the future under the linked-up system of global capital have forced us to shorten the distance between knowledge and action. As early as 1993, I tried to articulate this in a short article on what I called a non-Euclidean mode of planning (Friedmann 1993). Planning should become more present-oriented, I argued, while moving in a general direction towards a more distant, desirable future. The article caused a bit of a stir among academic planners, though practitioners tended to respond with a shrug: "So what else is new?" In time, and with various other contributions along similar lines, non-Euclidean planning became more widely known in the academic literature as communicative action planning.

Innovative planning thus combines what most people would perceive as a contradiction: on the one hand, emphasizing action with a relatively short-term time horizon in the present; on the other hand, utopian thinking about a distant future that may never be reached. This contradiction can be bridged, I thought (and still think), through a process of *social learning* that would lead planners through a sequence of tight feedback loops to act on the basis of actually observed phenomena and eventually lead them to reconsider strategies, their understanding of the current situation, and ultimately the very vision that had initially inspired their action. Such a "crossing [of] the river by feeling the stones," a saying attributed to Deng Xiaoping on the opening of China in the 1980s, might be called pragmatic, but it is more accurately called social learning.[1]

Long-term vision is thus an essential attribute of communicative action planning. Diane Davis acknowledges this in her contribution, but poses a series of questions about what she calls "constructing planning practice" around utopian thought. She wonders how utopian thinking might be reconciled with participatory planning in small-scale, modest, and more pragmatic undertakings. In her chapter, she gives a brief account of a difficult utopian exercise at MIT called "The Just Jerusalem Competition," which searched internationally for ideas to "improve conditions in that quintessential world city." But rather than trying to answer her questions directly, I would point the reader to the case studies contributed by Keith Pezzoli and Tanja Winkler. Pezzoli describes a planning process for transforming a 20,000-square-foot site in East San Diego into a Neighborhood Food Network and as a learning hub for food production throughout the region. It is a small site with grand ambitions. Similarly, Tanja Winkler's community, a shanty town of more than 4,000 residents on the boundaries of the municipality of Stellenbosch, South Africa, is situated on a mere 13 hectares of land. The approach involved a partnership between the University of Cape Town and the residents of the Langrug community. Tanja describes one unanticipated outcome of this difficult, drawn-out process with these words:

> It is worth mentioning that our engagements also included day-long workshops on planning law and housing legislation in South Africa. Langrug residents received certificates of attendance from the University for participating in these workshops. Of greater significance, Langrug residents are now facilitating similar workshops in other informal settlements across South Africa.

These two examples show that even small projects can have outcomes that reach far beyond the site of initial effort and in the process pose novel challenges.

The variety of planning cultures. The question of how planning is actually performed through the medium of existing institutions and in ways that are culturally congenial is increasingly highlighted as different forms of planning are coming to be practiced globally. The European Union brought this question of difference to the fore and led to a recognition that planning in, say, Poland is done in ways that are quite distinctive compared to, for instance, planning in the Netherlands. Or to cite another example, participatory planning is far more common in Canada and the United States than in Russia or Japan, where organized civil society is relatively weak. These differences, obvious as they are, can lead to miscommunication across national boundaries. This is beautifully illustrated in Klaus Kunzmann's chapter where he describes his bewilderment and frustration in trying to break through the language and cultural barriers in an effort to assist the local planners of an unnamed second-tier city in northeastern China.[2] In different ways, two other contributions on China, respectively by Sheng Zhong and Mee Kam Ng, gently teach us about some aspects specific to Chinese planning culture. Here is Sheng writing about social learning in Shanghai's planning community:

> Contemporary China is unique in the sense that the pace, scale, degree and extent of urban changes are unprecedented. Social actors in China are confronted with constantly emerging new situations, overwhelming details of local specificities and the pressure to give quick responses; therefore, synoptic analysis before action is often not a possibility. The attractiveness of the social learning paradigm is that actions do not have to be taken before a full or even good understanding of emerging issues is gained.

And Mee Kam lays out a Confucian paradigm for what may one day become a culturally and institutionally specific Chinese version of planning theory:

> For Chinese radical planners, the 'Way' is to remonstrate with those in power and to educate the common folks not only about tactics and strategies of socio-economic transformation, but also about the importance of identifying necessary actions that will bring about human flourishing and virtuous relationships. Chinese radical planners, in the grand tradition of Chinese intellectuals, always appeal to people's self-cultivation of their hearts to appreciate their moral duties to realise the rights of others as the route to the 'Great Harmony'.

Direct confrontation of authority is frowned upon in China.

Civil society, territory, collective self-empowerment. Since the 1980s, I've thought about the possibilities of a "radical" form of planning, by which I mean a planning with and for small, autonomous, self-governing communities in constant tension with an all-encompassing state. Inspired by what I would later call the anarchist tradition of planning, I had initially looked at examples in Peru and Chile of self-constructed informal settlements located on the margins of their respective capital cities, Lima and Santiago (Friedmann 1988). A decade earlier, Mike Douglass and I had invented what we called "agropolitan development" in the high density rural parts of Asia (Friedmann & Douglass 1978).[3] It turned out to be a contested notion, however, because rural industrialization, meant to underpin an alternative development such as this, was still relatively unknown. It would experience explosive growth in China during the 1980s and 1990s and was occasionally referred to as a form of *in situ* urbanization, or the creation of a city-in-the-field.

Several ideas were brought together here: territory, the distinction between life space and economic space, the "whole economy" of use and exchange values, and the self-production of life and livelihood, all rather abstract notions, which I drew upon to construct my utopian community. I was thus happy in these pages to read the contributions of Jacquelyn Chase and Michael Hibbard where some of these concepts are firmly grounded. I will focus on Hibbard's account of 160 years of history of several Indigenous communities in Oregon and Alaska and their ongoing struggles for tribal sovereignty (autonomy) and the progressive evolution of a hybrid, mixed economy of traditional self-subsistence and the market in an effort at achieving another modernity.

Two things strike me about these communities' engagement with transformative planning. First, the long history of these struggles, which are still ongoing, though considerable progress has been made in recent years. More importantly, far from being stand-alone struggles, they are part of an emancipatory movement that straddles three continents: the many hill tribes of Southeast Asia, Aboriginal Australia and New Zealand, and the Indigenous peoples of the Americas (Scott 2009; Porter 2010; Walker et al. 2013). The stories told by Hibbard are but the tip of the iceberg.

Re/engaging the state. I begin here with a lengthy quotation from a recent book by Robert Beauregard (2015, p.173).

> Planning can best be realized if the state is strong and democratic and local governments are given legal and financial support, develop the capacity to mediate private and public investments, and have equal status in intergovernmental relations. My dual concern is the relative silence in planning theory and practice regarding the importance of a welfare-oriented state and an overreliance on civil society among progressive planning theorists. No matter how much popular support planners have, it will be of little value if the state—at all levels—fails to maintain a substantial planning policy and to address structural injustices. The state has to be a countervailing force to and a defender of collective compassion for less advantaged people and places.

I am in complete accord with this statement. But where in the real world can such states be found? In America, the welfare state was largely dismantled in the 1980s and replaced by the present warfare state. In the EU, the welfare-oriented state continues at half-mast, but financial insolvency in the Mediterranean countries and former Soviet countries to the East has greatly reduced the role of the national state. There is more hope in Canadian provinces where a civil society has indeed been very active and, with the newly elected Liberal government of Justin Trudeau, social and environmental justice are again on the political agenda. Then, too, there is the chaotic situation in much of Latin America and Africa, not to mention the war-torn Middle East. The lack of an active civil society in the well-ordered states of East Asia—China, South Korea, and Japan—where planning is for the most part a function of central governments, means there is little hope that a locally based planning will ever take off, and the question of "engaging the state" remains moot. The same could be said of the Russian Confederation.

A more refined analysis might lead to some modification of these assertions. What is clear, however, is that several of the contributors to this volume are implicitly critical of what I have here called community action planning, among them Bish Sanyal, Robin Bloch, Chung-Tong Wu, and Sheng Zhong.[4] Planning, as they see it, means planning by the state. As for myself, I have never been explicitly anti-state, though I have occasionally championed "anarchistic" forms of planning (see above). But I do believe that in democratic societies, progressive, innovative planning requires strong actions on part of a civil society constantly pushing the state "from below."

Regionalism. The regional scale of planning has fascinated me throughout my professional life. After my Master's degree, I worked for the Tennessee Valley Authority (TVA) for a couple of years, and it was river basin development which was my first encounter with a planning region. My PhD dissertation in 1955, based on this experience, documented that economic growth was centered on urban areas and became the basis for my core/periphery thesis the following decade. By the mid-1970s, I made yet another shift, in response to what I perceived to be an opportunity for the development of high-density rural areas in Asia for an agropolitan development, which I mentioned earlier. Debates on this concept continued for several years, but in another turn in the early 1980s, this time taking a global view, I proposed the world city hypothesis, which stirred a good deal of interest and culminated in an international conference convened by two geographers, Paul Knox and Peter Taylor, in 1993. The turn of the millennium was marked by an international benchmark conference, this one convened by Allen J. Scott on global city regions (Scott 2001). The idea that cities could no longer be defined by their municipal boundaries alone but required a broader, regional perspective had taken root. The rapidly growing city regions, especially in Asia, which extended over densely populated rural areas, gave impulse to so-called periurban studies (Friedmann 2011). My restless regional imagination did not stop there, however, and continued to explore yet another dimension of the urban: the immense pluricentered urban regions that were emerging in the Yangtze Delta and elsewhere in Asia, and to which I have referred by various names, including "urban super-organism." As yet no publications have resulted from this research, but together with André Sorensen of the University of Toronto, we are planning to hold a workshop on the governance of these gigantic urban assemblies.

I have gone on at some length about regionalism, because my contributions to these debates serve to stress that as a scalar concept, regions can embody many different forms. Several contributions to this volume have picked up on different facets of my work on regionalism, including Bish Sanyal who develops a cultural critique of territory, Chung-Tong Wu who has done work on border regions in China, Michael Leaf who is concerned with the appropriate language for periurban phenomena, Roger Keil who writes about the variety of suburban formations, and Saskia Sassen, herself a major scholar of global cities, who has picked up a reference to an early working paper of mine on the "post-urban" which eventually morphed into "urban super-organism."[5]

I have come now to full stop. But our joint planning enterprise will continue, as we grapple with the many issues you have posed in these pages and those, as yet unknown, that will challenge us as the 21st century unfolds. Planning has been a vocation for me in Max Weber's sense (Weber 1946). I hope that for you and many others it will turn out to be the same.

Notes

1 For a similar shift to social learning in the business world, see Senge (2006).
2 For many other examples, see Healey and Upton (2010).
3 Agropolitan districts were conceived of as self-governing rural areas of between 50 to 150 thousand people centered on towns or small cities.
4 For a powerful indictment of state planning, see Scott (1998).
5 For a longer account of this evolution of regional concepts in relation to ongoing developments in the global economy, see Friedmann 2013.

References

Bauman, Z 2007, *Liquid Times: Living in an Age of Uncertainty*, Polity Press, Cambridge, UK.

Beauregard, RA 2015, *Planning Matter: Acting with Things*, The University Press of Chicago, Chicago.

Friedmann, J 1979, *The Good Society*, MIT Press, Cambridge, M.A.

Friedmann, J 1988, "The barrio economy and collective self-empowerment in Latin America" in *Life Space and Economic Space: Essays in Third World Planning*, ed. J Friedmann, Transaction Publishers, Brunswick, N.J., pp. 108–145.

Friedmann, J 1992, *Empowerment: The Politics of Alternative Development*, Blackwell, Cambridge, M.A.

Friedmann, J 1993, "Towards a non-Euclidean mode of planning," *Journal of the American Planning Association*, 59(4): 482–485.

Friedmann, J 2000, "The Good City: in defense of utopian thinking", *International Journal of Urban and Regional Research*, 24(2): 460–472.

Friedmann, J (ed.) 2011, *Pacific Affairs*. Special issue on "Becoming urban: periurban dynamics in Vietnam and China", 84(3): 425–434.

Friedmann, J 2013, "Planning for sustainable regional development" in *RDD: Regional Development Dialogue*, 34(2): 1–10. (*RDD* is a publication of the United Nations Centre for Regional Development in Nagoya.)

Friedmann, J forthcoming, "Planning as a vocation: the journey so far" in *Encounters in Planning Thought: Sixteen Autobiographical Essays by 16 Key Thinkers in Planning*, ed. B Haselsberger, Routledge, London.

Friedmann, J & Douglass, M 1978, "Agropolitan development: towards a new strategy for regional development in Asia" in *Growth Pole Strategy and Regional Development Policy: Asian Experiences and Alternative Approaches*, eds F-C Lo & K Salih, published for the United Nations Centre for Regional Development, Pergamon Press, Oxford and New York, pp. 163–192.

Healey, P & Upton, R (eds) 2010, *Crossing Borders: International Exchanges and Planning Practices*, Routledge, New York.

Perloff, HS 1957, *Education for Planning: City, State, and Regional*, published for Resources for the Future, Inc., The Johns Hopkins Press, Baltimore.

Porter, L 2010, *Unlearning the Colonial Cultures of Planning*, Ashgate, Burlington, V.T.

Scott, AJ 2001, *Global City Regions: Trends, Theory, Policy*, Oxford University Press, New York.

Scott, JC 1998, *Seeing like a State: How Certain Schemes to Improve the Human Condition Have Failed*, Yale University Press, New Haven.

Scott, JC 2009, *The Art of Not Being Governed: An Anarchist History of Upland Southeast Asia*, Yale University Press, New Haven.

Senge, PM 2006, *The Fifth Discipline: The Art and Practice of the Learning Organization*, Doubleday, New York.

Walker, R, Jojola, T & Natcher, D (eds) 2013, *Reclaiming Indigenous Planning*, McGill and Queen's University Presses, Montreal & Kingston.

Weber, M 1946, "Politics as a vocation" in *From Max Weber*, eds HH Gerth & CW Mills, Free Press, New York, pp. 77–128.

Index

Page numbers in italics refer to figures. Page numbers in bold refer to tables.

Taylor & Francis eBooks

Helping you to choose the right eBooks for your Library

Add Routledge titles to your library's digital collection today. Taylor and Francis ebooks contains over 50,000 titles in the Humanities, Social Sciences, Behavioural Sciences, Built Environment and Law.

Choose from a range of subject packages or create your own!

Benefits for you

» Free MARC records
» COUNTER-compliant usage statistics
» Flexible purchase and pricing options
» All titles DRM-free.

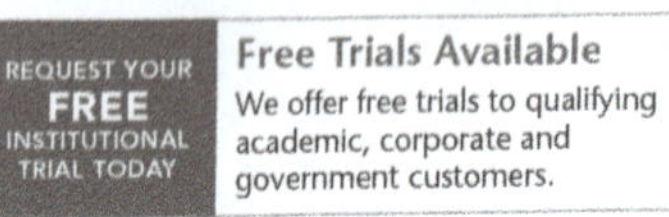

Free Trials Available
We offer free trials to qualifying academic, corporate and government customers.

Benefits for your user

» Off-site, anytime access via Athens or referring URL
» Print or copy pages or chapters
» Full content search
» Bookmark, highlight and annotate text
» Access to thousands of pages of quality research at the click of a button.

eCollections – Choose from over 30 subject eCollections, including:

Archaeology
Architecture
Asian Studies
Business & Management
Classical Studies
Construction
Creative & Media Arts
Criminology & Criminal Justice
Economics
Education
Energy
Engineering
English Language & Linguistics
Environment & Sustainability
Geography
Health Studies
History
Language Learning
Law
Literature
Media & Communication
Middle East Studies
Music
Philosophy
Planning
Politics
Psychology & Mental Health
Religion
Security
Social Work
Sociology
Sport
Theatre & Performance
Tourism, Hospitality & Events

For more information, pricing enquiries or to order a free trial, please contact your local sales team:
www.tandfebooks.com/page/sales

Routledge
Taylor & Francis Group
The home of Routledge books
www.tandfebooks.com